From Fascism to Libertarian Communism

Georges Valois (far left) with the writers of the *Nouvel Age littéraire,* including Henry Poulaille (third from right), during the heyday of the Librairie Valois. Photograph courtesy of M. Henry Poulaille.

From Fascism to Libertarian Communism

Georges Valois against the Third Republic

Allen Douglas

UNIVERSITY OF CALIFORNIA PRESS
Berkeley · Los Angeles · Oxford

University of California Press
Berkeley and Los Angeles

University of California Press, Ltd.
Oxford, England

©1992 by
The Regents of the University of California

Library of Congress Cataloging-in-Publication Data

Douglas, Allen.
    From fascism to libertarian communism : Georges Valois against the
Third Republic / Allen Douglas.
        p.   cm.
    Includes bibliographical references and index.
    ISBN 0-520-07678-8 (alk. paper)
    1. Valois, Georges, 1878–1945.   2. France—Politics and
government—20th century.   3. Right and left (Political science).
4. Politicians—France—Biography.   I. Title.
DC373.V3D68   1992
944.081'092—dc20
[B]   92-15114
                                                                  CIP

Printed in the United States of America

9 8 7 6 5 4 3 2 1

The paper used in this publication meets the minimum
requirements of American National Standard for Information
Sciences—Permanence of Paper for Printed Library Materials,
ANSI Z39.48-1984. ⊖

To Fedwa, for inspiration and for faith

Contents

Acknowledgments

To write a biography is to link two lives through words—that of the subject with that of the author. Love of learning was a gift to me from my parents, whose nurturing of it (and me) continued long past the social norm. Their supplements to my graduate fellowships were crucial. Without their support, I would be neither where nor who I am.

My undergraduate advisor at Cornell University, Professor Edward W. Fox, introduced me to the joys and puzzles of Third Republic France, for which I shall be forever grateful. At UCLA, my *maître* (the English term "mentor" would diminish the relationship), Professor Eugen Weber, guided the doctoral dissertation that later became the first half of this book. His advice and example have been invaluable.

Researching Georges Valois has brought with it the privilege of living and working in France. I am grateful for a Fulbright grant that sponsored my early research on this topic and for the support of the Franco-American Commission in Paris. At the Commission, Mme. Geneviève Acker's combination of knowledge and graciousness has been a godsend for visiting scholars. A summer grant from the National Endowment for the Humanities also permitted a trip to Parisian and regional archives.

Personnel at the research institutions where I worked in France—the Bibliothèque nationale, the Archives nationales, the Archives de la Préfecture de police de Paris, the Archives municipales de Paris, the Archives départmentales de Seine-et-Marne, the Mairie of the fourteenth arrondissement in Paris, the Bibliothèque de documentation internationale contemporaine at Nanterre, the Musée social—have been uniformly cheerful

ix

and efficient, on occasion going out of their way to help a foreign scholar. (I was also lucky enough to have avoided most of the slow-down strikes.) It is largely for this reason that entering these buildings (which sometimes meant walking through some extraordinary architecture) never failed to brighten my spirits.

Numerous Frenchmen have helped in the various stages of the confection of this book. Dr. Fred Kupfermann was encouraging and provided me with a copy of his doctoral dissertation. Professor Philippe Ariès did me the honor of inviting me into his home to talk to me about his uncle, Nel Ariès, and his and his family's close contacts with the Action française. Louis Lanoizelée, for years *doyen* of the booksellers of the Quais, shared his memories of Valois and helped me to locate materials. Henry Poulaille and Hélène Patou also shared memories, and in Poulaille's case, his personal papers and correspondence with Valois. M. le Commissaire divisionnaire Jean Druesne took time out from his busy schedule to talk to me about the manners and customs of the French political police.

This book would certainly not have been the same without the gracious assistance of Philippe Gressent-Valois and Roger Maria. Roger Maria provided invaluable information on Valois's last years and copies of otherwise unavailable material. Philippe Gressent-Valois spoke freely about his father and granted permission to examine what remained of Georges Valois's personal papers. These papers were recovered thanks to the *lycée* professor Etienne Jaillet who found them, returned them to M. Gressent-Valois, and organized them. M. Jaillais, who has just died tragically, shared his find (and so much else) with an openness that gives credit to the idea of the republic of scholars.

Numerous are the Frenchmen who aided my stays in their country, and my appreciation of its culture, through their hospitality and the honor of their friendship. My only regret in listing them is the fear of inadvertently omitting one: Georges Bahgory, Francis Bokhara, Jacqueline Cohen, Philippe Cardinal, Françoise and Annie Delaveau, Jean-François Fourcade, Rosalyne Gaude, Jérôme Lentin, Danièle Verlinde.

I am also grateful to American friends and colleagues who have encouraged me over the years: David Bodenhammer, David Gordon and David Gordon (both of them), Robert Hellmann, Patrick Hutton, Paul Mazgaj, Michael Miller, James Piscatori, Jaroslav Stetkevych, and Suzanne Pinckney Stetkevych. The University of Southern Mississippi and the University of Texas at Austin aided my research in numerous ways during the years I served on their faculties.

It has been my good fortune to work with the knowledgeable and help-ful people at the University of California Press. Lynne Withey, assistant director at the Press, has been my guardian angel. My copy editor, Peter Dreyer, through his painstaking and skillful readings, has certainly im-proved the manuscript and saved it from numerous imperfections, as have my three well-informed and searching readers. It goes without saying that any errors that remain should be laid at my door, not theirs. Finally, I would like to thank Holly Bailey for her very useful advice and welcome encouragement.

To mention my debt to my wife, Fedwa Malti-Douglas, is to save the best (and most important) for last. My companion in the many years that saw the development, first of this research topic, and then of the book it-self, she has aided me (and it) in ways that I would be at a loss to enu-merate. From emotional support to practical assistance and intellectual and scholarly advice, there is no aspect of this book (or my life) that she has not touched. Her love, and the example of her own scholarly success, have been invaluable sources of inspiration.

Introduction

Over forty years after the end of World War II, fascism continues to fascinate and frighten us. Scholars are still debating its nature, its controversial relations to socialism and other major currents of European civilization, and its puzzling ability to attract sophisticated and discerning individuals. In no country are these issues more dramatically posed, or more continually debated, than in France. There, the representatives of fascism, partly because they never exercised real authority, maintained their greatest revolutionary purity. There, also, they included some of the nation's most brilliant figures. Perhaps as a result, the history of French fascism and its close relations with the well-established current of French radical right-wing thought and action have continued to occupy scholars on both sides of the Atlantic.

At the center of French fascism stands an enigma with which all students of the phenomenon have sought to grapple: Alfred Georges Gressent, better known as Georges Valois. It was he who came from the radical right to found France's first fascist party in 1925. But it was also Georges Valois who, before World War I, sought to link revolutionary leftists with radical rightists in a dynamic new coalition. Most paradoxically, alone among the leaders of European fascism, Valois voluntarily abandoned both fascism and the right to pursue a second career as one of the most original theoreticians and political organizers of the French left. His saga is unique: from reaction and fascism to what he himself called "libertarian communism."

If the word *fascist* has remained an insult among all respectable Frenchmen (as it has in the United States), the radical rightist currents of which fascism formed a part are showing new life and vigor in the homeland of the Rights of Man. Beyond the spectacular political rise of Jean-Marie Le Pen and his Front national, lie a welter of other movements from the hyperintellectualism of GRECE and the "Nouvelle droite" to the racist brutality of politicized skinhead gangs. For France's revolutionary rightists, at least for those who read and think, Valois remains a potent reference and his surprising career an important political lesson.[1]

•   •   •

Few lives seem to invite the historian and biographer more than that of Valois. This paradoxical individual was one of the most colorful, versatile, and often influential men of twentieth-century France. He has always occupied an important place in historical accounts of French fascism, of the French radical right, and of the corporative and syndicalist movements. And yet he has never received a major biography.[2]

Certainly, Valois did everything he could to prepare for the eventuality. He wrote two sets of memoirs and made sure that all his ideas and experiences were preserved for posterity, which he was well-positioned to do as an important book publisher and journalist. In addition, his political activities earned him the attention of the French police, whose archives are now open.

Probably the biggest obstacle to tracing Valois's life has been his career. His political odyssey was virtually unique in Third Republic France. The trip from left, even radical left, to right was a common one, both for politicians like Alexandre Millerand and Aristide Briand, who evolved from the radical left to the respectable center and right, and for "revolutionaries" like Jacques Doriot, who traveled from communism to fascism. Valois, however, began his political life as an anarchist and anarchosyndicalist. As a young man, before World War I, he converted to Catholicism, monarchism, and social reaction. And then, after years of service to French royalism, he broke with the monarchist Action française to found the Faisceau, France's first openly fascist movement and the most powerful right-wing league in the mid 1920s. Within three years, however, Valois was on his way back left, and he spent the 1930s as a nonconformist French leftist working with virtually every major political group on the left. A resister during the Occupation, he died opposing fascism in Bergen-Belsen in February 1945.

Such a career defies normal historiographical categories. It is not simply that historians often specialize in either the right or the left. More to the point, the questions that guide historical research are often different. The problem that dominates the historiography of the European radical right (if not the right in general) is usually its relation to fascism. The rise of fascism, World War II, and the Nazi genocide have been such dramatic and morally anomalous events in the history of Western culture that historians have naturally sought to understand related movements in terms of them, whether as precursors, as parallels, or simply as tarred by similarity or collaboration. It is from this perspective, that of the European radical right, that Valois has been most often studied.[3] Since historians (despite the endeavors of the Annales school) still usually reason developmentally, there has been a tendency to understand figures who go from left to right in terms of their rightist destinations (the recent works of Zeev Sternhell and Philippe Burrin are good examples).[4] What was it in their original positions, in their political circumstances, that explained their evolution? But Valois ended on the left. Should his leftism define his rightist period? This is, of course, as he wanted to see it, and as his family would have us understand him. Yet Valois was a genuine radical rightist, and one of the most important, in terms of both political influence and of doctrine, in modern France. Clearly any explanation of his personality, his ideas, or his political activities must take his entire life as its basis. (None of the existing studies of Valois really does so.) By the same token, Valois's career is the ideal vantage point from which to study the relations and differences between the French radical right and left.

Valois's political and ideological evolution is clearly the central challenge of his biography. It even mystified contemporaries, many of whom attributed it to opportunism, corruption, or worse. A careful examination of Valois's career absolves him, however, of both charges. By the same token, his ideas were not a consistent blend of left and right. As a rightist, he was a true rightist, authoritarian, frequently reactionary, and often anti-Semitic. As a leftist, he was genuinely universalist, progressive, and egalitarian.

Is there unity in such a life? Most of those who have looked at both parts of Valois's career have seen it in terms of Georges Sorel and Sorelianism.[5] Not only did Sorel himself flirt with both rightists and leftists (though he never shifted basic political allegiances like Valois), but Valois all his life confessed himself a Sorelian. And yet, as I shall show, Valois was much less a Sorelian than he appeared, and even less than he claimed, to be. One of the reasons for his frequent evocations of Sorel was that the latter was one of the few masters he could comfortably claim on both sides of the political spectrum. Valois was heavily influenced by Sorel, but he was influenced at least as much by others, such as the proletarian writer Lucien Jean, the reactionary biologist René Quinton, and, for many years, the monarchist doctrinaire Charles Maurras. Besides, Valois's fundamental conceptions, his attitude to problems of society and politics were essentially different from those of the author of *Reflections on Violence*.

Throughout his entire career (and this distinguishes him sharply from Sorel),[6] Valois was a utopian modernizer, consistently opposed to the conservatism of Third Republic society. The term *utopian* has had many meanings, including both unrealistic optimism and the perfection of a new society. But what perhaps most distinguished many of the utopian socialists, and also Valois, was an essentially rational, implicitly optimistic and instrumental, view of the new society: it must be created and function according to a set of predetermined principles. These may or may not be sufficient, but they are absolutely essential. Hence the utopian believes in the importance of knowledge as much as, if not more than, power. He will not trust solutions to evolution. By the same token, he need not tie his revolutionary goals to the triumph of any one class or group. Potentially, any of a number of groups could introduce his social model. Finally the utopian approach to social problems implies a mechanistic or hydraulic view of society and human nature. Valois spoke of the revolutionary as an engineer who had to direct the torrents of human history (or human passions, according to context) into the right constructive channels.[7] It was these characteristics of the utopian tradition that were consistently present in Valois's thought. Other elements, which themselves varied among the utopian socialists, like concern with communal structures, total human liberation, or the need for a new religion, were also frequently, but only intermittently, present in Valois's formulations.

Such utopianism well defines the most fundamental, and hence consistent, level of Valois's thought and action. He abandoned the left as a young man, as he put it, because its members could not answer the question: once the revolution was accomplished how would the factories be run? Given his view of human nature, the workshop without masters would not function. Both on the right and after his return to the left, Valois developed and defended his social models. In later years, he was able to harmonize this utopianism with an evolutionary view of society by suggesting that the revolution might be greatly delayed if the proper techniques were not found.

Attention to social organization also marked Valois's more specifically political conceptions. Real power, for him, always lay with the economy, not with the political institutions of the Third Republic. This was the basis of his antiparliamentarianism. Revolutionary activity thus also meant, not so much the seizure of power, as the creation within the old society of the social and economic structures (whether corporatist, syndicalist, or co-operative) of the new. Indeed, for Valois, the two processes were one and the same. He always scorned those who thought that they could control the state while leaving the economy in the hands of their enemies. Besides, only the right combat formations would create the right social results.

With this mechanistic view of social engineering went a concern for practical detail even in contemporary affairs. It never sufficed for Valois to declare that the workers were exploited, or to show the reality of human misery. He insisted on explaining the precise mechanisms by which the plutocrats (or the trusts; or, during his Maurrasian period, the *quatre états*) defrauded Frenchmen, among other things in order to bring these activities to an end. At times, Valois's utopianism led him to plans or anticipations of future mechanisms that bordered on fantasy. Finally, this distinctive utopian cast of mind helped explain his continual search for new political formulations.

But utopianism never meant for Valois (as it had, for example, for Charles Fourier) an apotheosis of agricultural society, a retreat from modern industry. On the contrary, Valois was a consistent radical modernizer. His utopian systems were designed to create, not just harmony, but aggressive technical progress, the latter being essential to the former. This was as true of Valois's rightist as of his leftist periods, though the social implications of technical progress in the two cases were different. As a reactionary with Maurras, for example, he simply denied that technical progress need change eternal social realities; as a radical leftist in the 1930s, he made technological change the basis for a communist society. He stands thus with that group of French modernizers who, since Saint-Simon, have sought to coax or force more dynamism out of the relatively conservative French bourgeoisie.[8] Indeed, Valois always opposed the social and economic conservatism, the *douceur de vie* qualities of Third Republic society, with its sluggish population growth, its large agricultural sector, and its preservation of medium-sized and small family enterprises. He dreamed of a modern France of great roads and bridges, served by powerful machines and abundant energy. This, as much as anything else, cast him into opposition to the dominant groups in the France of the Third Republic.

Yet Valois blended his modernizing critique with hostility to the social system in France, largely blaming the latter for his country's lack of dynamism. His tendency to see the battles of plutocratic factions behind the day-to-day realities of French politics supported a deep suspicion of the rich and powerful. Valois's consistent view of French politics evokes Anatole France's description of Pengouinia:

> The Pengouin democracy did not govern itself; it obeyed a financial oligarchy that created public opinion through the newspapers and held in its hands the deputies, the ministers, and the president. It sovereignly disposed of the finances of the Republic and directed the foreign policy of the country.[9]

Social resentments that nourished his modernizing critique obstructed alliances with his country's modernizing business leaders. It is this that created the constant relationship of approach and withdrawal that characterized Valois's dealings with modernizing French businessmen and technocrats, from his royalist campaigns of the early 1920s through the desperate struggles of World War II.

A utopian mind-set, attention to detail, social and economic organizing: for Valois these were simply realism. Thus he never, even temporarily, separated his practical and political activities from his thought. Thought nourished and was instructed by action. Even his most mundane commercial activities were intimately tied into his social organizing and thus his politics. Hence one cannot really understand any single sphere of his activity outside the total context of his life and thought. And Valois's activities were manifold: publishing, syndicalist and corporative organizing, journalism, monetary and economic theory and organizing, political activity, and, of course, theory. At the same time, Valois's notoriously shifting ideological odyssey demands the careful analysis of each aspect of his life in its own temporal frame.

Hence the plan that has been followed in this book. The chapters each deal with a major period in Valois's political, personal, and ideological evolution. Chapter 1 chronicles his childhood and youth, through his adolescent anarchism, the rebellion against it, and his earliest right-wing formulations. Chapters 2 and 3 explore Valois in the Action française, both before the war, when he was the leader of the royalist campaign to obtain working-class support, and in the early 1920s, when he created his own economic theories and led coalitions of businessmen in a series of monetary and political battles. Chapters 4, 5, and 6 recount the Faisceau adventure, Valois's most ambitious and influential attempt to seize power and remake French society, during the monetary and parliamentary crises of the mid 1920s. Valois's return to the left after the Faisceau forms the subject of the rest of the volume, with chapter 7 recounting his period of respectability when he collaborated closely with all three left-wing parties.

Chapter 8 covers the middle 1930s and Valois's activities as part of the left-wing opposition to the Popular Front. During this period, he also completed his new, highly original, leftist blueprint for the revolution and the new society. The last three chapters chronicle Valois's attempts to head off, and then to deal with, World War II. Chapter 9 explains his attempt to overthrow fascism without war, chapter 10 his activities during the *drôle de guerre*, and chapter 11 his resistance, final philosophical formulations, and heroic death.

Though Valois had an extraordinary number of individual successes and achievements to his credit, his saga, like that of most radicals, was one of ultimate failure, in that he never succeeded in overthrowing the Third Republic or creating his new society. By the same token, his life helps us to understand the defense mechanisms of Third Republic society, its essentially conservative social and political dynamics. Valois's career exemplified the divisions reigning among the Third Republic's often individually distinguished, but collectively disunited, critics. On the right, Valois was consistently unable to forge an alliance between the Republic's rightist and its leftist opponents. Fundamentally, each group was more satisfied with the existing state of affairs than willing to work with its opponents across the political divide. In later years, Valois was equally unsuccessful in stimulating the revolutionary ardor of his leftist comrades. His attempts, however, provide us with an unusual view of the underbelly of Third Republic politics, just as his unusual intellectual saga has left us with some of the most original, and often still instructive, political and social ideas to come out of twentieth-century Europe.

ONE

Childhood and Youth

A rebel with a taste for order, a loner with a gift for leading others, Georges Valois combined a burning sense of injustice with a profound distrust of demagoguery. His identification with a disadvantaged social group never resulted in either a true class consciousness or class-based ideology. Valois's consistent opposition to the political and social structure of his society was expressed through a striking ambivalence between left and right, optimism and pessimism. The origins of these traits are clearly marked in the turbulent and contradictory conditions of his youth and early childhood.

THE EARLIEST YEARS

Jouarre is a small town in the department of Seine-et-Marne, about twenty kilometers east of Meaux in the Brie, the gently rolling district linking the Paris basin and Champagne. In that town on November 25, 1875, Valois's parents were married in a civil ceremony. Edmond Alfred Gressent hailed from Neuville Ferrières in upper Normandy; his bride, Berthe Joséphine Evrard, was from Paris. Her father was in the café business in Paris, and his *rentier* widow had come back to her home in Jouarre for the marriage of her daughter. The young couple (Edmond was twenty-nine, Berthe eighteen) settled in Paris in the fourteenth arrondissement. He was a butcher; she worked as a seamstress.[1]

Three years later, on October 7, 1878, Berthe gave birth to Alfred Georges Gressent, later to be known as Georges Valois. Officially, the boy was "presented . . . as the son of Edmond Alfred Gressent." But according to Valois's younger son, Philippe, M. Gressent was not the father. Edmond was fair, as befit his Norman ancestry, but the little Alfred Georges was suspiciously dark, almost African in appearance. Valois had a relatively dark complexion and wavy hair for a Frenchman, but nothing out of the ordinary for a Mediterranean. Philippe insists, however, that when he grew up, people in his neighborhood asked his mother why she had married a black.[2] The story must have been handed down from Valois himself, who carried the question with him all his life. Besides, the next two acts in the family drama only served to confirm Valois's mother's bad reputation.

When Valois was three, his father died. In his memoirs, Valois explained that the cause was a work accident and that his father's convalescence drained the family finances. Such crises were familiar in working-class circles, but this one was particularly hard on the young Alfred Georges. By his own account, he was frequently cold and hungry. According to Philippe, he was virtually abandoned by his mother, left to fend for himself in the corridors of the building and on the street. When Valois was five, his family stepped in and sent him to live with his grandmother in Jouarre, in an environment he described as "a garden full of flowers and light."[3]

In his memoirs, Valois says not a word about what became of his mother, an odd omission in a book otherwise dripping with filial piety. Mme. Gressent survived into the 1930s. As soon as he was old enough, her son took over her support, and he visited her regularly as long as she lived. But Valois never let his family come along, and his children did not even know that this grandmother existed until she died. Thus did Valois balance his strict sense of duty with his shame at what he considered his mother's moral failings.[4]

This severe early childhood crisis contributed to the formation of several permanent character traits, notably an inflexible moral posture. On sexual matters, this went beyond conventional proprieties to border on prudery. For Valois, sexual irregularity, even the widespread practice of keeping mistresses, was the beginning of personal and political corruption. And, despite his associations, early and late in life, with anarchism, he stayed clear of anything resembling an apology for free love.[5] Valois's insistence, despite his own obvious dedication to work, on the basic laziness of human beings, his claim that people only did what they were forced to do, must have been nourished by his judgment of his mother. His sense of the fragility of civilization, his belief that decadence and chaos were as likely as progress and order also surely reflected his experience.

If Valois was ashamed of his mother, he remained proud of his grandparents, often taking his family to the grave of his grandfather. The fu-
nerary monument stands out in the little municipal cemetery of Jouarre.
Among crosses and ex votos rises an antique column, proud in its pagan
symbolism: "Here rests a free thinker who lived for the Republic and not
by it, Frédéric Eugène Marteau." The column was defiant: Jouarre was located in a part of the Brie called the "Terre sainte" for its reactionary,
Catholic sentiments.

Born in 1822, Marteau was a skilled metalworker who had proclaimed
the Republic in his foundry in 1848. Widowed once, he married Valois's
grandmother (her second nuptials as well). He maintained his interest in
politics, serving for a time as assistant to the mayor of Jouarre. In his six-
ties, he raised his new grandson in the civic idealism and stern political
morality that had characterized the rising republican movement in France.
If his epitaph separated him from the corrupt politicians who exploited his
ideals, it also testified to his unshaken faith.[6]

Georges's grandmother abstained from political activity, but she was a
conservative Catholic, and the coexistence of his grandparents' ideologies
provided the young Gressent with a duality of political reference. While
his grandfather fed him the republican interpretation of recent French history, his grandmother presented the views of the Republic's conservative
and reactionary opponents. When, in his twenties, Valois made his great
shift from left to right, he characterized it as the renaissance of his grandmother's influence. Though he never made the claim, Valois's return to
the left in 1927 can be associated with that of his grandfather.[7]

Valois's grandparents maintained a stable, ordered environment, combining an underlying emotional warmth and strong discipline. His grandmother believed that work was God's will. After school there was home-
work; when that was finished, there were always weeds to pull. This
atmosphere is best illustrated by an incident that made a strong impression on Valois. One holiday, an aunt laid a box of toys before the delighted
child, but his grandmother insisted that they be replaced by one small
trumpet: since Georges had no family fortune, he should not get the
wrong ideas about life. Despite the aunt's pleading, the old woman had her
way, and the toys were returned. Georges's pleasures were those of a
beautiful day in the Brie, an intimate chat with a grandparent, or a visit
with relatives. He was happy in this highly disciplined atmosphere, and a
powerful sense of constraint and warm, maternal love were fused in the
image of his grandmother.[8]

Georges's grandfather represented a classic type of social promotion.
The son of a peasant, Eugène Marteau had raised himself from skilled

worker to *rentier*, one who lived from the product of his investments. He retained the worker's respect for labor and machines and the artisan's dedication to a job well done. Attached to the house was a workshop, where Georges spent many happy hours admiring and aiding his grandfather at work. Valois's class background thus mixed proletarian with petit bourgeois features, and all his life he took intense pleasure in working with his hands.[9]

His grandfather's workshop was not the only exposure Georges had to technology. Marteau and his grandson spent a month in Paris visiting the centennial exposition of 1889. They passed entire days at the Galerie des machines, where Georges's grandfather excitedly showed him the latest technical developments. As he put it, "the Galerie des machines, progress, and the Republic were henceforth rigorously associated in my mind." The association would dominate his later years. The high value placed on manual labor by both grandparents rooted firmly in Valois's consciousness a type of socialism characterized by a sentiment of the dignity of labor and the idea that work was the only proper occupation for an individual.[10]

ADOLESCENCE: THE CONFLICT DEVELOPS

If Valois's childhood was one of external order willingly accepted, his adolescence was one of conflict: between Georges's desire to stay in school and the pressures to get a job. His response was a combination of evasion, largely through travel, and rebellion in the form of anarchism.

Valois was precocious; at five, he could already read. In school, he won first place and prizes. At twelve, he completed the *école primaire*, the basic school for children of the people, and his family urged him to choose a trade. But he wanted to devote his life to science. His family objected: without an independent income, that was impossible. Valois's first response was to postpone the problem by staying in school on any pretext. For a year he followed a special course of studies; then he convinced his family to let him enter a vocational school, the Ecole professionelle Diderot in Paris. Not that he wanted to spend his life with machines, but at least this permitted him to slake his thirst for mathematics, physics, and chemistry. He won a scholarship for a three-year program, but was expelled for participation in a student demonstration over the quality of the food. Thus ended Valois's formal education. Years later, while working in Paris, he followed courses in Latin, Greek, and mathematics. He read avidly whenever he could, but for the rest of his life his education was his own and his formation that of an autodidact.[11]

Such educational differences were powerful class markers in Third Republic France; and nothing better stimulated Valois's social resentments. He disdained those bourgeois whose comfortable status permitted them to continue their studies. Throughout his career, Valois almost always opposed bourgeois intellectuals of the French left, of whom Jean Jaurès, Edouard Herriot, and Léon Blum were most typical.[12]

After the Ecole Diderot, Valois held three jobs. He was discharged from the first after getting into a political argument with his boss, laid off from the second, and fired from the third, with a chemical manufacturer, when he was caught performing experiments in the laboratory. His employer, who had discovered Valois's anarchist leanings, was afraid he was making bombs, a reasonable fear at the time. Valois tried to continue his studies, reading late into the night. As he put it, a seventeen-year-old encounters one enemy in this situation: sleep.[13]

EVASION AND TRAVEL

Unhappy with his work in Paris, unwilling to give up his dream of a life devoted to science, Valois turned to an evasion from his problem: travel. Between 1895 and 1904, he saw Singapore, Indochina, Switzerland, and Russia. Shortly before his seventeenth birthday ("and some devil pushing me"), Valois signed on as assistant to a French merchant in Singapore. Valois drank in the exoticism of this busy port while selling watches and cotton. He had been hired with the intention that he would eventually succeed his boss, and he could have made a career of it. Instead, after a year, he grew homesick and, on the suggestion of a French planter, went for a cure in French Indochina. In Saigon, Valois found his desire to return to his homeland strengthened and, abandoning a colonial career, he returned to Paris and another series of jobs.[14]

A few years later, in December 1901, still unsure about his future, and wishing to "find himself," Valois again decided to leave, this time for Geneva. There, a professor suggested that he take a position as tutor in Russia. In March 1902, Valois left for Russia, where he was entrusted with the education of Alexander Vatatzi, a youth about eight years his junior. Alexander's father was governor of the province of Kaunas in Lithuania and resided in the city of Suvalkai. Valois lived happily amidst this aristocratic family, forming strong ties to both son and parents. He was impressed with the vastness of the Russian steppe. Its seemingly endless nature, where no object stood between the eye and the horizon, contributed, Valois thought, to the Russian tendency to alternate between torpor and sudden, often irrational, activity.[15]

Valois's travels gave him a global sense of politics. For him, French politics were always the reflection of international, when not extranational, rivalries. He naturally conceived of economic and social conflicts in geopolitical terms. Valois met the world through trade and travel, not through literature and history. His general impression was that international commerce, even civilization itself, resulted from organization imposed on chaos and backed up by force. The world outside Europe was a mass of surging peoples held in check by ever-watchful governments.[16]

Not least significant was Valois's discovery of that elusive quality called national character, and with it his own national consciousness. He did not appreciate being called a "bloody Frenchman"[17] in the Indies or receiving a still more colorful epithet in Dortmund. Crossing Germany, Valois found the locals brutal, crude, and sentimental, but with a good police force. He considered the Russians lovable (unlike the Germans) but also quite unlike the French. He was not sure, however, how much these differences were caused by the racial mixture of Asiatic and European and how much by Russian topography.[18]

Valois received his greatest shock from his contact with eastern European Jewry. Suvalkai was in the Jewish pale of settlement, and Valois gave lessons to local Jewish families. Arriving in Russia with Dreyfusard ideas, he expected Russian Jews to be assimilated like French ones. He was stunned to discover a ghetto community with its own language, customs, and national ferment. Valois was also struck by the prevalence of anti-Semitism in eastern Europe. His conclusion at the time was that the Jews were a nation within a nation, destined to come into bloody conflict with the Russians.[19]

These youthful travels, when added to Valois's later trips outside Europe, indicate a considerable wanderlust. His yearning for new places was certainly related to the emphasis, crucial to his thought in the first half of the 1920s, on the contrast between rooted and migratory nations. A consistent tendency of Valois's mind was to project the contrast between order and chaos onto space, and thus to link order, discipline, constraint, and physical rootedness, on the one hand, and chaos, indiscipline, unbridled egotism, and migration on the other. If this image of rootedness was a cliché on the French right, made famous by Les Déracinés of Maurice Barrès, Valois transformed it from a partly social to a completely geographical concept. For him, social mobility itself was never a danger.[20]

REBELLION AND ANARCHISM

Valois was raised in official republicanism. From his adolescence to 1904, he gave his allegiance to anarchism. If travel was an evasion from the conflict between study and work, he himself recognized that his anarchism was a rebellion against it. Here was a young man, obliged to work while others, socially more fortunate but neither as talented nor as dedicated, lackadaisically pursued their studies. Valois was not one of those brilliant children of the people, like Charles Péguy, who were singled out for scholarship support. Was he less promising? Or less lucky? In either case, he blamed society, and called the bourgeois democrats' dedication to science hypocrisy. There is truth in Paul Desjardins's remark that Valois "simply charged against the obstacles to his own development." Of course, Valois was not the first young man to generalize his discontents in this manner. The years between his stays in Singapore and Russia, from 1897 to 1901, marked Valois's greatest involvement with the anarchist movement.[21]

Valois first fell in with the group around the journal *L'Art social*, attracted by its commitment to anarchism and the social application of art and literature. At *L'Art social*, Valois met influential syndicalists like Paul Delesalle and Fernand Pelloutier, founder of the Bourse du Travail movement. Pelloutier may have contributed to some of Valois's most enduring ideas, like his preference for economic organizing over political solutions. Valois also made the acquaintance of the anarchist and former philosophy teacher Charles Albert Daudet, known as Charles-Albert. In 1921, when Valois and Charles-Albert were on opposite political sides, he called him "a man of perfect courtesy, cultivated and with a sure artistic taste."[22] It was also probably Charles-Albert who introduced Valois into the circles of the *Temps nouveaux*, a newspaper run by Jean Grave and perhaps the most important doctrinal organ of French anarchism.[23]

For a year, Valois was a disciple of Augustin Hamon, who considered himself a scientific anarchist. At the time of the Popular Front, Hamon published a widely read exposé of France's business and financial oligarchies. Besides occasionally contributing to the *Temps nouveaux*, Hamon edited his own journal, *L'Humanité nouvelle*, to which Valois contributed book reviews on political and social-scientific topics.[24]

The effects of Valois's years with the anarchists were far-reaching but imprecise. Their importance lay less with his adoption of largely anarchist positions in the 1930s than with their contribution to permanent elements in his thought. He always considered the state, if not in opposition, at least in clear contrast to society and its productive apparatus. Though Valois reversed his judgment of the necessity of the state during his career, he never changed his understanding of its nature. Like the anarchists, he believed the role of the state would not be changed by handing it over to the political right or left. No matter what his alliances at any given time, Valois was willing to work with those on the other side of the political center; what mattered most was their attitude to the state and production. Valois shared with the anarchists, and kept to the end of his days, a profound aversion to parliamentary socialism. This was what he meant when he thanked heaven "for having kept me away from the world of socialism."[25]

One should not overestimate the ideological purity of the milieu in which Valois spent these years. His associates and reading were as often revolutionary socialist and anarcho-syndicalist as anarchist, a difference not as great before 1905 as it would be later. During both his right and left periods, Valois emphasized the leftism and anarchism of his early political activities in Paris, in the former case to show how far he had come, in the latter to establish his leftist bona fides. Broadly speaking, this was correct. But the gulf between radical right and radical left was not as pronounced as it would be later. In particular, linking the two extremes was a current of protest that Patrick Hutton has labeled "populist," which attacked the rich and the Opportunist Republic with arguments deriving as much from nostalgic defenses of the little man and notions of foreign or vagabond capital (when not anti-Semitism) as from faith in the proletariat or more "scientific" analyses of capital and wages. Though Valois mentioned none of them in his memoirs, populists like Auguste Chirac wrote frequently in L'Humanité nouvelle, and even Hamon was open to anti-Semitic arguments. If Valois's concept of the state owed much to anarchism, his notions of French politics always had much in common with those of the populists.[26]

Valois also met two men whose impact would last long after he had left anarchism behind: Georges Sorel and Lucien Dieudonné, called Lucien Jean. Sorel, an engineer turned social philosopher, was entering his most syndicalist socialist phase when Valois met him in 1898 during the older man's Thursday visits to L'Humanité nouvelle. Sorel's erudition and pitilessly scientific analyses made a powerful impression, and Valois also sympathized with his castigation of parliamentary socialism and bourgeois democracy. Moreover, as Claude Polin observes, "Sorel had a horror of the University," which obviously would not have displeased Valois either. Years later, when once again on the left, Valois uncharacteristically blamed the syndicalist for having led him away from democracy. Sorel was probably responsible for raising the prestige of revolutionary syndicalism in Valois's mind, but it is difficult to gauge the extent of Sorel's influence on him at this early stage, because after a period of separation, he was also in touch with the prophet of violence later.[27]

Through *L'Art social*, Valois met Lucien Jean, who was eight years his senior and an exceptional, even charismatic person. Descriptions of Jean verge on the hagiographic: "There are words that sound wrong in front of him. He is a veritable saint," one friend wrote. In Valois's words: "He was simple, he was good, he was just." As a sickly youngster, Lucien Dieudonné had been operated on several times. He was left with one leg shorter than the other and always remained in precarious health. After entering the Collège Turgot, he was obliged at the age of sixteen to take employment as a draftsman at the Préfecture de la Seine when his father died. A few years later, married with two children, he took a second job at night. To avoid problems at the Préfecture, Dieudonné used the pseudonym Lucien Jean. Between his employment and his poor health, Jean had little time for his principal joy, writing. When he died in 1908, at the age of thirty-eight, all he left behind was a collection of short stories.[28]

In Lucien Jean's case, as in his own, Valois concluded that a faulty social organization had prevented him from fulfilling his promise. (Jean himself was more modest.)[29] A frequent companion of both Valois and the more prolific "proletarian" writer Charles-Louis Philippe, Jean was a devoted syndicalist and a fervent Dreyfusard. Opposed to violence, he believed militants should set examples of work, dignity, and morality. Lucien Jean remained in Valois's eyes the model of disinterested syndicalist activity, of simple down-to-earth realism, and of the true worker's dedication to the job well done. He was the perfect proletarian writer and the victim of a society that was certainly not open to all talent. For Valois, it was always figures like Jean, caught in the precarious spaces between working-class and petit bourgeois status, not proletarians ground down by misery, who served as the archetypal victims of social injustice.[30]

THE PERSONAL TRANSFORMATION

Valois's anarchism was swallowed up in the personal transformation that was his bridge from adolescence to adulthood. Military service was the first experience that caused him to revise some of his ideas. Between his trips to Singapore and Russia, Valois was drafted as part of the class of 1898. He entered the military with the standard anarchist assumptions: that army life was degrading, that officers were narrow-minded and noncoms brutal. He was delightfully surprised. None of the alleged evils of

military life bothered him. With his relatively spartan upbringing, he did
not find the physical conditions of service difficult. As for the noncommis-
sioned officers, if they were a bit brutal, it was not hard to stay out of
trouble; and Valois found that discipline left a man possessing self-control
with complete mental freedom. Valois even found the army fun. The
highly structured and disciplined environment was congenial. He also enjoyed feeling part of a large, directed machine and was so enthusiastic during maneuvers that he strained his health. After six months he was hos-
pitalized and discharged.[31]

Following his return from Russia in August 1903, Valois found work
with the publishing house of Armand Colin, whose scholarly books had
excited his admiration as a child. Valois impressed its director, Max
Leclerc, and rose to the position of general secretary. Valois later declared
that it was at Colin that he discovered his vocation for the book industry.
There also he began syndical organizing, helping, with Pierre Monatte, to
found the first *syndicat* of publishing employees.[32]

The years at Armand Colin saw Valois's personal and ideological transformation. This change was so extreme and so total, absorbing all aspects
of his life, that it was a personal crisis. The transformation itself seems to
have taken place during parts of 1904 and 1905. But it brought to a head,
and resolved, for a considerable period of time at least, conflicting impulses and influences from Valois's childhood and adolescence. These included his home environment, the conflict between work and study, his
military experience and the lessons of his travel and political activities. In
1904, Valois was twenty-six. With this crisis he said a belated goodbye to
his adolescence and began his adult life. It would be a mistake always to
take Valois at his shifting word concerning his personal metamorphosis.
In particular, his political shift cannot be treated, as he later wished, as the
result of erroneous deductions, of a purely intellectual error.[33] It formed
part of a larger process converting a free-thinking, anarcho-syndicalist
without ties to job or family into a married, Catholic, authoritarian
antidemocrat.

While still in Russia, Valois married Marguerite Schouler, a young
woman of Protestant Alsatian and Swiss origin. In 1903, she bore him a
son, Bernard (a daughter, Marie, followed in 1907, and a second son, Philippe, in 1910). With a wife and child to support, Valois had to get a steady
job, which he did at Colin. Accepting his responsibilities as husband and
father meant the resolution of the conflict between work and study, and it
was not without regret that Valois set aside his youthful ambitions. Yet he
gloried in the fact that his family ties gave a new direction to his intellec-

tual investigations. For him, the family was a system of constraints obliging the father to work, and often opposing fundamental human drives.
Once accepted, it became a deeply cherished institution, canalizing otherwise anarchic passions.[34]

While at Colin, Valois reexamined his intellectual baggage. abandoning
most of his political views and replacing them with the ideas of his first
book, *L'Homme qui vient: Philosophie de l'autorité* (The Coming Man:
Philosophy of Authority), published in 1906. This first fully formulated
set of social and economic doctrines served as the basis for all his later
thought and action. This sweeping shift was not without antecedents. As
an anarchist, Valois read Paul Bourget and Maurice Barrès, and, while he
was in Russia, Taine and more Barrès. Valois greatly admired the latter's
Leurs figures, whose views of the relationship between financiers and the
French parliament matched his own. Taine, and especially his *Histoire de
la littérature anglaise*, also had a formative influence. Besides a generally
reactionary stance, Valois seems to have taken from Taine a reductionist,
often organicist, positivism and a tendency to treat societies as though
they were biological entities.[35]

Valois's disenchantment with the left, like Sorel's, was partly owing to
the outcome of the Dreyfus Affair. Like most anarchists, Valois, after initial indifference, joined the Dreyfusards. He became disillusioned with
large sections of the French left when the principal result of the affair
seemed to be the entry of a number of former revolutionaries into the government and of a new clique of republican politicians into power. This disenchantment deepened during Valois's involvement in the unionization of
the book industry. To Valois, it seemed that most of the syndicalists were
less interested in organizing the world of labor than in escaping it. He con-
nected this to the contempt for work he felt was general among socialist
intellectuals. Finally, he claimed to have discovered that Colin's competitor Fayard had had one of its employees start the *syndicat* in the hope of
creating an incident between Colin and its workers that might be exploited
to persuade the syndicalized schoolteachers to shun the reactionary Colin
and order their texts from Fayard instead. As Valois's first "discovery" of
the manipulation of workers' movements for capitalist goals, this served
as a paradigm for later explanations of how political and social movements
were diverted to the service of politicians and financiers.[36]

More important for Valois was the question he posed to the other
members of the *syndicat:* after the revolution, how would the factories be
run?[37] The question remained fundamental, and Valois always insisted
that his social formulations were based on its proper solution. Even as a

young man, he rejected the answer that, after the revolution, new psychological conditions for production would be created. Based on the impressions he had formed of the motivations of his co-workers, he believed that workshops without masters would not work. Once Valois had adopted a pessimistic (or fixed) view of human nature, the standard syndicalist, socialist, or anarchist hopes for a postrevolutionary society evaporated. Whatever sympathy Valois felt for the left's critique of modern society, he could no longer accept its historical goals. Disenchantment with one aspect of revolutionary thought led him to a reexamination of all his political assumptions and, with their abandonment, to a steady movement rightward.

THE NEW DOCTRINAL SYNTHESIS

Valois's personal transformation resulted in a set of original, and, for him, fundamental ideological formulations, expressed in *L'Homme qui vient*. His new synthesis was built around a scientific law and a historical myth. The law he entitled the law of least effort, and he considered it a basis for all his subsequent thought.[38] According to Valois, all humans spontaneously seek the least possible effort, the least possible muscular and mental strain. Though he gave no proof of this law, he seems to have derived it from two considerations: that human energy, like all energy, follows the path of least resistance; and that humans avoid pain, and any prolonged effort creates fatigue and eventually pain. This meant that a hungry man would perform only the effort necessary to satisfy his simplest needs. Additional effort to obtain a higher level of consumption or satisfy future needs was out of the question. Of course, this conclusion does not follow logically from Valois's law. He merely suggested the rationalizations that would be used to block effort for future consumption: there was no point in setting aside for the morrow; food would surely rot or be stolen. This doctrine of invincible human laziness was really the unexamined premise of Valois's social thought.[39]

The historical myth pictured man in a state of nature where life was not only nasty, brutish and short, but indolent. Men, following the law of least effort, once they had filled their bellies, simply lay down and did nothing. Among this mass, one man, stronger or more ambitious than the rest, decided to impose his will upon the others, to force them to produce for him. For this he invented the whip. It was the constraint of the man with the whip that forced men to rise above animality and enter the path to civilization. Later in the same work, Valois proposed an alternate picture. The first men were cannibals, man being a tasty and easy prey. Only later did some learn that it was more efficient to make a conquered enemy work. In either case, Valois considered the resulting flagellocracy the model for all societies.[40]

For Valois, however, the man with the whip, the master, the aristocrat, was just as susceptible to the law of least effort as those he dominated. The master is obliged to perform his functions of domination and organization by the threat of competition from other masters, by the demands of the slaves, who want an ever-greater return for their work, and by the threat of being supplanted by some slave who feels he could be a better master. These last two forms of pressure work because the slaves realize that the master, by creating work, has increased their well-being. The somewhat naïve anthropology covered a mythification of capitalism.[41]

Thus, work and material progress are generated only by the constraint of man upon man, and the social organization that best promoted this constraint became for Valois the fundamental question in political economy. Valois recognized, further, that if this constraint was eternal, its forms were not. In the state of nature, brute force and slavery were necessary to oblige men to work. Once the earth was fully occupied, Valois explained, hunger forced men to submit themselves to a master who would provide sustenance. The new master was the entrepreneur, the capitalist who obliged men to contribute their labor under his direction in the interests of greater production. Such conceptions dictated social and economic conclusions. Since without his constraint workers would only produce the bare minimum, surplus value belonged rightfully to the master, though it would be enlightened of him to distribute part of it to his workers. In a particularly harsh passage, Valois explained that it was altogether fair for salaries to tend toward subsistence levels; workers received compensation through participation in the rise of the general level of civilization. The master/capitalist had a right to a larger remuneration as a return for his larger risks, and he had a right to leave his fortune to his son as an incentive to its creation.[42]

More originally, Valois claimed that the egalitarian distribution of the surplus would be a loss for all. A large mass of wealth in a few hands could not be consumed by these few who would be obliged to invest it, increasing capitalization. If this surplus were distributed, workers would waste their share "on good wines, on big juicy steaks, on beautiful women clothed in finery and on fancy entertainments." Nothing would be set aside for the future and civilization would crumble. Too many toys were no more healthy for the people than for the young Alfred Georges.

Socialism was as absurd from the point of view of production as it was unjustified by moral or philosophical considerations. Though machines
might eliminate much manual labor, their supervision demanded an
equivalent mental strain. Socialism was the dream of those too weak to
engage in the struggle for life. There were no natural rights to work, sustenance, or happiness, only those of struggle and the strong.[43]

Not surprisingly, Valois considered war a necessity, and not a terribly
evil one. It was nature's way of choosing the nation fittest to carry on
technical and economic progress, success going to the hardest-working and
best-disciplined country. Even the contest was beneficial, since it forced
nations to work as hard as possible so as to create the greatest possible surplus for armaments. Though war against a neighbor to steal his goods
may have been the first "least effort" solution, international rivalry
constrained all nations to the steady improvement of their productive
apparatus.[44]

The best government would be that of the person with the greatest interest in the continued prosperity of the nation—a hereditary monarch
(anyone else being tempted to prefer his particular interest to the general
good). The monarch, too, needed to be prodded into doing his job, and this
would be the function of an assembly representing the different material
interests of the nation. Political democracy would leave the state prey to
special interests. In the competition for public office, politicians would
outbid each other in the favors they offered to their constituents. Rival
parties were not groupings of like-minded people but competing factions,
each with its own clientele. In a clear parody of Third Republic history,
Valois explained that democracy would first be instituted by the powerful
(read: Orleanists and other business groups) who wished to manipulate
the state. Soon, however, by dint of the repetition of the doctrine of popular sovereignty, the people would desire to control the state themselves.
They would elect a new class of men, "hungry dogs" (read: Radicals),
whose livelihood came from politics and who would in turn soon be
bought off by the rich. Thus the rich, although ostensibly chased from
power, would continue to control the state, now fully corrupted.[45]

Valois wrote L'Homme qui vient in 1905 and 1906, in what he described
as intellectual isolation.[46] Nevertheless, his earliest critics tried to determine his sources. The unanimous first choice was Nietzsche. As Valois
recognized, the attribution was not always disinterested, since the use of a
pagan German by a Catholic Frenchman could prove embarrassing.[47] Indeed, L'Homme qui vient, with its tough rhetoric and its adulation of the

strong man, exudes a Nietzschean flavor. Valois frequently mentioned having read Nietzsche, and later in life was happy to quote him positively. Yet, Valois insisted that Nietzsche's role in his intellectual evolution had been largely destructive, Nietzsche having, along with Sorel, helped liberate him from the democratic illusion. The only positive idea that Valois admitted to having taken from Nietzsche was that humanitarianism was a stratagem invented by the weak to disarm the strong; in fact, this is the only clearly Nietzschean idea in *L'Homme qui vient*.[48] Valois's man with the whip was not a superman, but the initiator in a system of constraints that bound him as it did his servants.

Valois acknowledged a debt to Paul Bourget, though the brutal struggles of *L'Homme qui vient* are far from the conservatism of the author of *L'Etape*. Valois agreed with Bourget that science, properly applied to human affairs, supported conservative and authoritarian politics.[49] The influence of Taine may have been less conscious. But Taine had defined the two most powerful motors of human transformation as "nature and constraint." Further, his "law of mutual dependencies" may have suggested Valois's law of mutual constraint.[50]

Because of Valois's twenty-year involvement with Charles Maurras and their subsequent bitter conflict, the question of Maurrasian influence on *L'Homme qui vient* is delicate. Valois's arguments in defense of hereditary monarchy and against democracy were commonplaces of the propaganda of Maurras's Action française. On the other hand, certain earlier chapters of the book agree neither with royalist politics nor with Maurrasian views of French history. Legitimacy, Valois wrote, was the intellectual product of aristocrats who, corrupted by the pleasures of their station, or no longer suited by their training to a changing society, wished to mask their weakness. The slaves, the reservoir of national energy, are not duped. It is then that they make "French Revolutions." Their desire for new leaders is reflected in their slogan: careers open to talent. The revolution is followed by a bitter contest for power, culminating in the triumph of the strongest and most worthy leader. Valois ended his chapter with a tribute to Napoleon reminiscent of Maurice Barrès's famous scene from *Les Déracinés:* "Be thou praised, sole and true master, true leader, true king, O thou Napoleon."[51]

In the following chapter, however, Valois explains that a caesar is not a true king, any more than someone who helps you kill your father and wishes to take his place can be your father. This chapter, however, was added to the already-completed text just before printing, on Maurras's recommendation, one supposes. Maurras's influence on Valois's intellectual transformation was apparently nil, and it was only after Valois joined the Action française that he was heavily affected by the royalist thinker.[52]

The man to whom Valois gave most credit was a natural scientist. Valois's arguments had a Darwinist flavor, and some of his ideas were common among right-wing French Social Darwinists. Yet he never used Darwinian vocabulary. For Valois in 1905, as for many French leftists, Darwinism represented a belief in evolution and thus in progress—a doctrine used by anticlericalists and democrats.[53]

The natural scientist Valois felt posterity would recognize as greater than Darwin was René Quinton. Quinton created this minor stir by the publication in 1904 of *L'Eau de mer, milieu organique*. Valois may have learned of Quinton through his own reading, through an article in the *Revue de métaphysique et de morale*, or through the writings of Paul Bourget.[54] In any case, what Bourget seized upon in Quinton was really quite different from what captured Valois's imagination, and both drew conclusions hardly explicit in the biologist's original work.

Quinton sought to prove that, life having arisen in the sea, seawater has remained the vital environment of animal cells. Multicellular animals, and especially the vertebrates, were live aquariums (Quinton's image) whose bodily organization was geared toward the maintenance of their cells in an environment as close as possible to seawater. Quinton hoped future researches would establish a general law of original constancy: cellular animal life, originating in given physical and chemical conditions, tends toward their maintenance in the face of changing global conditions. Among its aspects would be a law of thermal constancy, stating that animals tended to maintain the relatively high original ocean temperature in the face of the constant cooling of the globe. The original response of the animal kingdom to the cooling of the globe had been to accept the resulting decrease in cellular efficiency. Only with the vertebrates were animal cells maintained in their original environment and correspondingly greater efficiency.[55]

For Bourget, Quinton had shown the harmony of tradition (constancy) and progress (evolution). Valois agreed, but for him the "light" came with Quinton's discovery that life struggled to keep up with a progressively cooling globe. It was absurd to speak of a better future; optimum conditions had been reached in the past and a constant effort was needed to maintain them. Life called forth species in its effort to survive, and man was the vessel of election. Men could improve their protection against cold through work and economic development, not needing to thicken their biological skins, only their technological ones. Nature traced man's duty: work so that life could survive on an increasingly hostile planet.[56] If, for Valois, work was socially the product of the mutual constraint of man by man, on the level of the species, it was the result of a cosmic constraint by nature. In the early 1930s, Valois sharply criticized some of Quinton's own later exercises in biological sociology, but he took from Quinton the explanation of the biological imperative for work and technical progress he would carry to his grave.[57]

When Valois began *L'Homme qui vient* in 1905, he was a freethinker. By the time he had finished, he had converted to Catholicism. Fatherhood made Valois suddenly aware of his own mortality. His intellectual development led him to a search for faith. One day, as he tells it, while walking in the Luxembourg gardens thinking about the mystery of maternal love, he suddenly found himself enveloped in a maternal warmth that at once gave him hope and confidence. Recognizing the source of his inspiration, he recited: "I salute you, Mary." The feminine nature of the revelation was hardly coincidental. Shortly afterward, Valois received instruction in the Catholic faith, learning his catechism in his late twenties.[58]

In all three aspects of Valois's personal transformation—daily life, political and social theory, and religion—the same phenomenon appeared: the total, even joyous, acceptance of an environment of order, discipline, and constraint. And yet this acceptance was not free of ambivalence or masochism. We can almost hear Valois's voice behind the words he put in the mouths of his mythical slaves: "Strike us, master, if you love us, and do not abandon us, so that we shall not become wandering dogs again and so that we shall not return to the laziness of animals. Strike us so that we shall remain men."[59] Constraint and chaos were personal issues for Valois. It is not hard to see in this dichotomy of lazy animal and man that between Valois's own early abandonment and his later affectionate control by his grandmother. The vehemence of his new convictions covered the doubts he had had to overcome. Years later, some of these would come back to the surface.

NEW ALLIES

Valois was certainly not the only young man discovering the virtues of Catholicism, authority, and physical vigor in 1905. His transformation fit the wave of youthful conversions noted by observers from Martin du Gard to Romain Rolland. Some of the same causes were clearly in play, especially on the social and intellectual planes.[60] Yet, Valois's subjective

feeling was one of solitude: he had made the crossing alone, and only discovered friends on the other side. He even claimed that his first impression, after emerging from his self-imposed isolation, was surprise at the
progress of left-wing doctrines.[61]

Valois's first step was to get his new book published. Receiving a cool
response in republican circles, Valois submitted his manuscript to Paul
Bourget. The latter, delighted to find a new, forceful adherent to monar-
chist politics, suggested he offer his book to Maurras. Shortly afterward,
Valois met Maurras himself, and in 1906 the recently founded Nouvelle
Librairie nationale published *L'Homme qui vient*.[62]

Once Valois familiarized himself with the Action française, he found
much that was congenial. Unlike the pious and aloof aristocrats he had
learned to despise in childhood, the Action française was a collection of ardent young men, many of them former republicans like himself. Led by a
dynamic political thinker and a polemicist of genius, they, also like Valois,
favored the monarchy for reasons that had more to do with political
philosophy than tradition. Valois met the Pretender, Louis d'Orléans, at
Ostend. The duc d'Orléans impressed him favorably, and Valois added a
sentimental assent to his rational conclusions. By then he had clearly decided that, as Bourget had put it, his place was with the Action française.[63]

These changes received their seal through a change in name. *L'Homme
qui vient* was the first work published under the name Georges Valois.
Gressent chose the name Valois because, still working for the republican
Armand Colin, he did not want his political opinions known.[64] Though he
never legally changed his name, Gressent kept the pen name long after he
left Colin, when his political opinions were a secret to no one. He also kept
the monarchical-sounding "Valois" after his return to the left in 1927 and
encouraged his children to use it for themselves. Clearly he liked the
name. It represented the man he had become. Besides, had he ever really
been a Gressent?

TWO

Valois in the Action Française, I

Ideological Reaction and
Flirtation with Labor

From 1906 to 1925, Valois was an exemplary Action française militant. After his break with Maurras and his return to the left in 1927, Valois sought to characterize this embarrassing involvement as an aberration, the result of the accidents of French politics.[1] While such an argument could be made for those who flirted with the Action française, like Georges Sorel, it will not do for Valois. He was a major leader, writer, and organizer for the royalists; for almost twenty years he shouted: "Vive le Roi!" Valois was not far from the truth when he claimed that all that was social in the Action française was his work,[2] and his influence upon its social and economic doctrines was immense. Valois's membership in the Ligue d'Action française influenced his alliances, just as his thought was greatly affected by contact with this most self-consciously intellectual of French political movements.

VALOIS, THE ROYALISTS, AND THE COURTSHIP OF LABOR

The Action française had started as a small nationalist club in the last years of the nineteenth century. Its first journal appeared in 1899. The daily paper, which became the mainstay of the movement's influence, emerged in 1908, two years after Valois's adherence. Few of the Action française's early members were traditional royalists, and the Ligue was far from enjoying the predominance in monarchist circles it was later to obtain. When Valois joined, the Ligue was a small, determined group struggling for recognition.[3] His contribution was part of that struggle.

The ambiguous position of the Action française with regard to traditional royalism had its reflections in the social and economic sphere. Would the Ligue continue the proper traditions of the conservative bourgeoisie, or would it, in a world of increasingly visible industrial discontents, formulate its own program? More than anyone else, Valois personified the second choice.

As the Action française gained stature, Valois's position within the organization more than kept pace. He joined in 1906 as one of the young men the nationalist and Catholic revival was sweeping in. By World War I, however, the police were touting him as a possible new member of the *comités directeurs*.[4] Valois's rise to dominance over economic and social policy implied conflicts with others with a claim to Action française labor practices—conflicts that played themselves out across the Action française's attempts at recruiting workers, socialists, and syndicalists. Though Valois's success in recruitment was meager, that over his rivals was total.

At first, Valois was concerned that the neoroyalists might be working with Pierre Biétry's *Syndicats jaunes*, a group of antimasonic and antisocialist unions, with the reputation of being strikebreakers, that personified for him a reactionary, patronizing attitude to workers. Valois was assured that nothing was farther from the truth, although the Action française had, in fact, maintained close relations with Biétry for years. Toward the end of 1908, however, it broke publicly with him, when Maurras apparently decided to seek an alliance with organized labor.[5]

The workers whom the Action française approached were syndicalist, hostile to parliamentary socialism, and indifferent to the fate of the bourgeois republic. Action française doctrine considered the syndicalism of French workers to be a healthy rejection of Jacobin individualism, but it also recognized that these workers' revolutionary goals derived from Jacobin traditions.[6] Maurras probably never departed from a belief in corporatism as the solution to all economic and social ills. The creation of royalist corporations would take time; and nothing in Maurras's strategy implied that mass support was essential. The Action française's flirtation with the Confédération générale du travail was largely tactical—the CGT's neutrality might be necessary for the success of a royalist coup. In the Dreyfus Affair, organized labor had come to the defense of the revisionists. If nothing else, syndicalist connections might help pressure potential contributors who feared strikes.[7]

This change in Action française tactics was also related to a meeting between Maurras and Firmin Bacconier in the early summer of 1908. Bacconier was the leader of an independent royalist group, L'Accord social, which was corporatist, antimasonic, and anti-Malthusian. Rather than helping Bacconier, the meeting strengthened Maurras's interest in working-class propaganda. Maurras took on Emile Para, a royalist syndicalist who had been working with Bacconier, as a contributor to his new daily. In addition, the distribution of the Action française was altered, fewer copies being sent to rich quartiers and more to working-class neighborhoods like Belleville. This new line gave Valois his big chance.[8]

From the time of his conversion, Valois had tried to attract former colleagues. In L'Homme qui vient, he called anarchists strong men whose only error was to believe that they could do without society. The revolutionary socialists were also strong men, but the application of their theories would bring society to an end.[9] Self-praise combined with an opening to anarchist and syndicalist circles.

Valois kicked off his campaign with the publication in 1907 of "La Révolution sociale ou le roi" in the Revue de l'Action française. The two important movements of the age, he said, were "the Action française and the Confédération générale du travail." In 1908, this study was separately published and distributed in the Bourses du travail. That April, Valois began an "Enquête sur la monarchie et la classe ouvrière" in the inaugural issue of the Revue critique des idées et des livres. Valois published a copy of a letter sent, along with a copy of La Révolution sociale ou le roi, to leading syndicalists or intellectuals who confined themselves to purely syndicalist philosophy, a definition excluding those who, like Jaurès, could be counted on to defend the Republic. In respectful imitation of Maurras's Enquête sur la monarchie, Valois hoped to gain a wider audience for his views, while opening contacts with leading syndicalists. The copy sent to Alexandre Aulagnier, secretary of the Union des syndicats de la Seine, included a short handwritten note asking to meet. (Valois was not alone in courting Aulagnier; the Bonapartists also made advances.)[10]

Valois directed his correspondents to three issues: Does the Republic aid the working class and the progress of syndicalism? If not, what solution do you recommend, the revolution and anarchy or the monarchy? Should not the workers ally themselves with the monarchy against their exploiters? The responses were published, with discussions by Valois, in the Revue critique from May 1908 to May 1909, and as a book, La Monarchie et la classe ouvrière.[11] Thirteen people answered Valois, including Georges Sorel; the anarchists Jean Grave and Eugène Deniau-Morat;

several syndicalists, including Emile Guillaumin and Emile Janvion; and one royalist syndicalist, Darguenat.

As Valois probably expected, only Darguenat concluded in favor of the monarchy. Valois was probably most hopeful of a sympathetic response from his old master. Instead, Sorel sidestepped the issue, noting that whatever the potential virtues of the monarchy, the workers would have nothing to do with it since it was associated in their minds with the suppression of the Paris Commune in 1871. The anarchists, Grave and Deniau-Morat, answered that all governments were bad, Grave adding that what was worst about the Republic was what it took over from monarchy and empire. The other correspondents, though willing to accept, in varying degrees, Valois's critique of the Republic, were not interested in his panacea. In an almost fatherly tone, Guillaumin pointed out that it was easy to project all the virtues on a future government. The monarchy was as pure under the Republic as the latter had been under the Empire, a point echoed by Deniau-Morat.[12]

Valois reserved his most flattering introduction for Janvion, a friend of Lucien Jean's, and since 1899 the leader of an antimasonic, anti-Semitic campaign in syndicalist circles. Janvion had known Valois as an anarchist. Combative by nature, and with a reputation for prowess in street-fighting, Janvion was quite at home in an attack on the Republic, but even he refused to follow Valois onto the terrain of the monarchy, observing that a king without politicians would be a monarch without a clientele and would not last twenty-four hours.[13]

As a maneuver toward the CGT, the Enquête was a failure, but Valois assembled enough testimony to convince his reactionary allies that the workers were not overly attached to the present Republic. Any consideration of the monarchy among syndicalists was an advance. One of Valois's correspondents admitted that when he first received his letter, he took it to be a hoax. He could understand aristocrats wanting to bring back the king, but workers? By the time he had finished reading Valois's brochure and several of the responses in the Revue critique, however, he had at least learned to take Valois seriously.[14]

The letter instituting the Enquête was signed "Un syndiqué, Georges Valois." There was some truth in this qualification. After joining the Action française, Valois continued at Armand Colin. The first syndicat of publishing employees having died from internal dissension, Valois helped found a new one in 1907. With his encouragement, it joined the CGT, and Valois and a friend, Joseph Boissier, became delegates to the Union des syndicats. Valois made no headway among the revolutionaries at the Bourses du travail and, faced with the hostility of the publishers, the venture was short-lived, convincing Valois that nothing could be accomplished within existing labor organizations. Valois's political activities also caused problems. Still at Colin, he had not let his employers into the secret of his pen name. This proved particularly embarrassing when he was called upon to help edit books written against himself.[15] Without another source of income, Valois stayed on at Colin while casting about for a solution.

Valois's *Enquête* did rope in one authentic syndicalist, Emile Janvion, who decided to work with the royalists, apparently to get support for his newspaper, the *Terre libre*, which appeared in fall 1909. Janvion helped to organize workers' meetings with Léon Daudet and Mahon, the leader of the Amicale royaliste. It was rumored that Janvion was receiving Action française money through Valois, and it is likely that the latter tried to use Janvion as a contact with the syndicalist movement, with Marius Riquier, a royalist who worked for both the *Action française* and the *Terre libre*, as go-between.[16]

Valois had competition for the position of syndical expert, chiefly from Emile Para. In 1908, with Valois and several others, Para founded the Union des syndicats royalistes. He also wanted to launch a newspaper, *La Commune*, with himself as editor-in-chief. The paper was to have begun in October 1908, but, owing to disputes within the Union, the project was abandoned and the Union dissolved. Para resented Valois's activities and sought to force him and Janvion out. Valois, in turn, boasted that Para's signature would disappear from the *Action française*. It was Valois who triumphed.[17]

Despite his verbal attention to labor, Valois spent less time with workers than with intellectuals, the most prized of whom was Georges Sorel. Leader of the "new school" of socialism, Sorel was associated with the *Mouvement socialiste* and violently opposed to parliamentary socialism or any other form of collaboration with the bourgeois Republic. After celebrating the virtues of direct action in *Réflexions sur la violence*, Sorel went on, in *Les Illusions du progrès*, to an impassioned critique of the Republic's democratic ideals. His contempt for democracy and celebration of the heroic virtues offered promising convergences with integral nationalism. The royalists had not needed Valois to become aware of the potential usefulness of the "new school," but with his revolutionary past and personal acquaintance with Sorel, he seemed the logical person to effect an alliance between the two groups.[18]

Undeterred by Sorel's response to his *Enquête*, Valois continued his courtship, using the *Revue critique* as an intellectual meeting place for the royalists and "new school" writers like Sorel and his disciple Edouard

Berth. In 1910, Valois proposed that he and Sorel found a review, the *Cité française*, along with Berth and Pierre Gilbert, a royalist and frequent contributor to the *Revue critique* who made a speciality of literary anti-Semitism. The project was killed when Sorel insisted on adding the revolutionary syndicalist Jean Variot to the editorial committee. This would have given him three votes to the monarchists' two, and Valois refused. Though Sorel remained in contact with the nationalist movement and the Action française, he had no further dealings with Valois.[19] Sorel could tell that his young admirer was interested in proselytism, not discussion.

POLITICAL AND SOCIAL FORMULATIONS

Valois's role in the Action française directed his thought to three areas: French history since the Revolution; the Third Republic and labor; and the role of the working class in the restored monarchy. Valois was always eager to acknowledge an intellectual debt to Sorel, a position echoed by modern scholars. But in Valois's writings between 1907 and 1914, the influence of Maurras is equally important. The point is more than academic. In later years, after his break with the royalists, Valois liked to argue that he had always been a Sorelian, that Maurras's influence had been slight. This position supports the notion that Valois held views that, expressed openly in his fascist period, were just below the surface of his royalism. Neither proposition is correct. Before the war, Valois was both royalist and reactionary.

Valois recognized that behind the syndicalists' revolutionary eschatology was an interpretation of French history. As the bourgeoisie had replaced the aristocracy in the nineteenth century, the proletariat would replace them in the twentieth. Valois denied that the revolutions of 1789, 1830, 1848, or 1870 marked the ascension of the bourgeoisie. One sector of the bourgeoisie had helped to engineer the revolution of 1830, but even then, they did not hold power. The solution of the mystery lay in the Maurrasian doctrine of the *quatre états confédérés*. These four groups, Protestants, Jews, freemasons, and resident aliens, acting for themselves and as agents of foreign powers, had provoked the revolutions to disorganize French society. For Valois, the *quatre états* were more than a topos, they were a historical reality that explained the history of France and the workings of the Third Republic: "Under this brilliant light, everything becomes clear."[20]

The Third Republic, especially since the Dreyfus Affair, saw the triumph of the *quatre états*, who used their power to dispossess Frenchmen through raids on French savings (like the Panama affair), the exploitation of French workers or their replacement by foreigners, and the manipulation of the workers' movement. As Valois explained it, popular socialism had begun as a revolt against those whom the workers took to be the rich, but who were actually the bourgeoisie of the *quatre états*. The socialist movement, however, was taken over by the politicians, of whom Jaurès, servant of the Jews, was the best example. For the *quatre états* who financed it, parliamentary socialism diverted popular resentment, while frightening the French bourgeoisie into political concessions or even a partial expropriation of French wealth. The syndicalist movement was a healthy reaction against the individualism of 1789. By banding together in the defense of their professional interests, the workers spontaneously recreated those republics (really corporations) that were the social and economic skeleton of the old regime. If under the monarchy the *syndicats* would protect the interests of the working class, under the Republic their action was "always" diverted into the service of the *quatre états*.[21]

The syndicalist movement was infected with a belief in the *révolution sociale*, the result of the application by the workers of the doctrines of progress and moral evolution, which were well on their way to becoming the official religion. Valois also tried to show, in two different scenarios, that any serious attempt at a socialist revolution would lead to a wholesale transfer of property from French into Jewish hands. More important, under the Republic, through the enrollment of militants in masonic lodges, propaganda, and outright corruption, freemasons and Jews controlled enough leaders to steer the syndicalist movement. In the Dreyfus Affair, originally indifferent anarchists and syndicalists were led into a movement that resulted in a great increase in Jewish power and clear advantages for France's foreign enemies.[22]

Valois agreed with Sorel that democracy was the political system least conducive to an independent workers' movement. He disagreed about the efficacy of violence. Under the Republic, Valois insisted, an independent working-class movement was not possible. Only the monarchy could protect syndical independence. For the role of the working class under the monarchy, Valois developed an original model. A strongly organized and class-conscious syndicalist movement would pressure the bourgeoisie for higher wages. The bourgeois, thus blocked from exploiting the workers and prevented by the monarchical constitution from exploiting the state, would have to seek an increase in profits through technical progress. Pressure from the workers would thus maintain the bourgeois in their proper role of organizers of production and distribution. Though this theory of mutual constraint can be found in embryo in *L'Homme qui vient*, Valois did not hesitate to give credit for it to Sorel; and it was probably Sorel's *Réflexions sur la violence* that crystallized the model in his mind. Sorel had stated that the proletariat would, through its forceful opposition, stir the bourgeoisie to life and restore to it the heroic and military virtues it had once possessed. Thus both bourgeoisie and proletariat would be saved from decadence.[23]

Despite superficial similarities, Valois's concept was different. Valois spoke of the proletariat and monarchy as "ramparts" enclosing the bourgeoisie, which for maximum efficiency should not be set up between classes but separately within each branch of industry. Localizing the mutual constraint within separate industries was corporatism. The system, though kept in constant tension, was static. Social structures would force conflicting interests into harmony. With Sorel, however, proletarian violence would stimulate the bourgeoisie into returning to the aggressive posture that made Marxist predictions of revolutionary conflict possible. Where Valois's mutual constraint was static (and utopian), Sorel's class struggle was dynamic. To invoke Valois's terminology of 1924, he, like Maurras, supported the theology of "Being"; Sorel was wedded to "Becoming."[24] When Valois put his thought into a historical mode, it was Manichaean and Maurrasian. The forces attacking France, the *quatre états* and their plutocratic allies, represented "Gold." The forces for national defense and regeneration, the monarchy and the syndicalist movement, represented "Blood," a symbolism from Maurras's *L'Avenir de l'intelligence*, described by Valois as "the finest book of the century."[25]

The role Valois assigned to the *quatre états* was associated with a large dose of anti-Semitism. In his prewar writings, the Jews received more attention than any other *état*, even the freemasons, who by their position in republican and socialist politics might have warranted more discussion. The Jews dominated the three other groups, making the alliance possible. Valois even divided the bourgeoisie into three parts: the Jewish, the clerical, and the Judaized.[26]

In the Dreyfus Affair, Valois felt he had been manipulated in the Jewish interest; in Russia, he had discovered that Jews could be nationalist (i.e., Zionist) as well. These suspicions of the Jews were undoubtedly strengthened in the Action française, where anti-Semitism was widespread and where Léon Daudet consistently tried to use anti-Semitism as bait for workers. As a Catholic, Valois could not accept the Maurrasian contention that the Church benefited from being purged of its originally Jewish nature. But neither did he echo the religious and almost obscurantist anti-

Semitism of the marquis de la Tour du Pin. With the Jews, as with others, Valois always knew the difference between polemic and insult. Though he might defend someone else's right to use the expression *sale petit juif*, he never used it himself.[27] Valois avoided the inflammatory language of Edouard Drumont and even the slightly less vicious but more colorful vocabulary of Daudet. The moderation in tone was typical of Valois's rhetoric generally; it may have helped him to drop anti-Semitism entirely in the 1920s and work closely with many Jews in the 1930s.

For Valois, the Jews were a nation cut loose from their soil and unable to fix themselves again in any territory. Over the centuries, they had become incapable of tilling the soil, obliging them to live among and at the expense of other nations. While Jews used the powers of Gold to dissolve their host nations, they used the forces of Blood to maintain unity among themselves. Since a society based on traditional corporations would be closed to them, the Jews favored one atomized by democracy. Echoing the Maurice Barrès of the Dreyfus Affair, Valois explained that the Jews sought to destroy that concrete and territorial French patriotism that would exclude them and to replace it with the ideal patriotism of the public school textbooks, one close to their own, which would facilitate their acceptance. Jewish successes were not owing to any special talents but to audacity and the absence of moral scruples. Jewish businessmen paid their workers well, even too well, Valois claimed, and made up their losses from the brothels and cabarets where the workers spent their earnings. The Jews also corrupted national morals through degenerate literature. One of the functions of the nobility, according to Valois, should be to preserve national morals by refusing to receive Jews in their salons.[28]

Besides being an anti-Semite, Valois was also a profoundly religious Catholic. In 1913 he published *Le Père: Philosophie de la famille*. In this apotheosis of the family, the last traces of Nietzschean rhetoric are gone. The style is homiletic and moralizing, saved from the ridiculous only by its evident sincerity. Though not theological, the book is religious in spirit, and biblical references abound. Valois described *Le Père* as a book of ancient truths retold in modern form. The essential argument is that when regulated by the right institutions, human passions are good and give men the strength to face life. Only when left to develop anarchically do they become vices. The most important regulatory institution is the family. Not coincidentally, the first vice discussed was nomadism, the desire to roam the earth's surface in quest of new experiences, and Valois illustrated this longing with references to tropical isles and endless steppes. For him, the foremost value of property was that, along with the family, it fixed man geographically and broke the spirit of nomadism.[29]

Though a work on morals, Le Père concerned itself to a large extent with public life, treating social organization from the standpoint of the individual or the family. The conclusions were familiar, but the style of argument had changed. In a typical case, the Father, Valois's hero/protagonist, decides that society is not just and that he will rebel, since everyone should be his own master. When he commands his sons to aid him, they refuse, answering that they too wish to be their own masters. The Father sees the error of his ways and all returns to order.[30] The clash of forces of Valois's earlier works has been replaced by humility and an understanding of the wisdom of the traditional order, the man with the whip by a loving patriarch.

Valois did develop a justification for the multiplicity of nation-states that, despite affinities with Social Darwinist arguments, seems original. Each nation was an experiment on the part of life. The particularities of one nation's development might lead it into an impasse. Thus, ancient Rome was destroyed by the absence of a hereditary principle, bringing down with it all the nations it controlled. With a variety of states, the solution to one country's problem might be found in another. Or, if the leading nation was in an impasse, another could continue the march of civilization.[31]

THE CERCLE PROUDHON

While Valois was writing Le Père, his glorification of a Christian order, he remained in contact with the Sorelian "new school," converting Sorel's chief disciple, Edouard Berth, to monarchism. The story of this conversion is also that of the Cercle P. J. Proudhon, Valois's most interesting prewar venture.

Berth, who was three years older than Valois, had been raised in a middle-class family. He was preparing for the agrégation, when under the influence of Sorel and the Dreyfus Affair, he abandoned his academic career to devote his life to the service of the proletariat, becoming Sorel's most ardent, and faithful, admirer. Berth followed the intellectual development of his new master. He, too, placed his hopes in a revolutionary syndicalist movement, and his contempt for democracy and exaltation of the heroic virtues were, if anything, less restrained than Sorel's. Berth met Valois through Sorel, who apparently used him as a go-between in negotiations with Valois. Berth developed a deep personal sympathy for

Valois, which survived serious political disagreements and lasted until Berth's death in 1939. In later years, he was quick to defend his friend against those who doubted his good faith.[32]

The idea for the Cercle Proudhon originated with Henri Lagrange, a student and *camelot du roi* (the camelots were newspaper hawkers who acted as the paramilitary arm of the Action française). Condemned for publicly slapping President Armand Fallières, Lagrange was one of those bold young men making a name for the Action française. In March 1911, he suggested to Valois that they found an economic and social study group for nationalists. Valois persuaded Lagrange to open the group to non-nationalists who were antidemocratic and syndicalist.[33] It was also Valois who chose Proudhon as the group's patron: a brilliant stroke. Proudhon was free of paternalistic taint. His plebeian and French origin and his contemptuous treatment at the hands of Marx made him ideal for those who resented German Social Democracy. Proudhon's writings were so superficially unsystematic and contained so many apparent contradictions that he could be used by people who might agree about little else. And unlike Sorel or La Tour du Pin, Proudhon was dead and could not disavow his new disciples. Proudhon's patronage helped attract two men who were not royalists: Berth and the syndicalist schoolteacher Albert Vincent.[34] Within a year both had been won over to the monarchy.

When officially founded in December 1911, the Cercle included Berth and Vincent and the royalists Lagrange, Valois, Gilbert Maire, René de Marans, André Pascalon, and Marius Riquier. Pascalon, whose real name was Becheyras, had formed part of Para's stillborn Union des syndicats royalistes. René de Marans, an admirer of Sorel and a frequent contributor to the *Revue critique*, had come to the Action française from the Catholic social movement, forming a link between traditionalists and the Cercle. All were intellectuals or workers in intellectual professions; each made his living through books, whether as librarian, archivist, writer, teacher, or, in the case of Valois, editorial secretary.[35]

The Cercle's most important creation was the *Cahiers du Cercle Proudhon*, which published articles by members of the Cercle and engaged in polemics with those who took note of its existence. Four *Cahiers* appeared in 1912 and one in 1914. In 1912, printing was set at six hundred copies, two hundred to subscribers and about one hundred more per issue sold on the street in Paris. Though the Cercle had no official leader, and the *Cahiers* no editor-in-chief, Valois was the leading spirit in both.[36] Besides contributing his share of articles, he answered most of the attacks made on the Cercle and probably oversaw the editing of the journal.

The stated goal of the Cercle Proudhon was to study the organization of the French economy and society. More specifically its founders wished to commit the Action française to a prosyndicalist position, to make it impossible for the plutocrats to turn the nationalists against the workers in the name of order. Lagrange and Valois wanted to end the philanthropic approach to social problems among nationalists, blocking any return to a "senile conservatism," while deterring the use of syndicalist troops against the nationalist movement.[37]

While the Cercle had some success with the nationalists, it had little among the workers. Valois himself recognized that Action française support for the three-year law (backed by the Cercle) blocked an alliance with labor. Against the growing nationalist movement, backed up by the fists and canes of the camelots, the workers lined up behind the limitation of military service to two years. Nor was Sorel brought into the Cercle. A testimonial dinner held for him in May 1912 failed to attract the guest of honor.[38]

Valois's greatest success was the conversion of Berth and Vincent. Vincent had come to the Cercle as a republican, admiring Proudhon for his federalism, his rural origin, and his opinions on the family. Like Proudhon, Vincent was moralistic and antifeminist. He turned against democracy because it led to divorce, abortion, and pornography: *la vie facile*. These evils affected the nation. The declining birthrate left France defenseless, while rural to urban migration drained life from the countryside. But Vincent was afraid that allegiance to the king would mean less than total support of the working class. Valois answered that under the monarchy, workers would defend their interests, if need be against the crown itself.[39]

Despite his attacks on intellectuals, Berth was one in every fiber of his being. Thus, he clothed his allegiance to the monarchy in an original and intoxicating set of ideas. Though he showed considerable respect for Maurras, the main props in his new intellectual construction were Proudhon, Nietzsche, Bergson, and Sorel. Between 1912 and 1914, Berth admired most Proudhon's quintessential Frenchness; like Rabelais, Proudhon was a *frondeur gaulois* who blended his rebelliousness with a natural sense of order.[40]

The chief force pushing Berth toward the monarchy was his horror of decadence and adulation of heroism, force, and war. Citing Proudhon and Nietzsche, Berth linked democracy, plutocracy, Jews, and the intellectuals with mediocrity, envy, pacifism, and femininity. Christianity, heroism, war, and masculinity were the creative forces in history. Berth proceeded from the Sorelian glorification of class war to an idealization of international war, transforming Sorel's glorification of violence, which referred to the actions of the workers, into a cult of force. Impressed by the recent Italian campaign against the Turks in North Africa and the subsequent Balkan Wars (1912–13), Berth excitedly announced the revival of a warlike spirit in Europe. France too would have to compete, for Berth had become a nationalist as well. The poor needed the fatherland more than the rich, who could take their money anywhere, and national solidarity represented the same spirit of sacrifice as class solidarity.[41]

The state, now necessary, should be a Maurrasian monarchy, described by Berth as "war personified." There was no conflict between this idea and syndicalist opposition to the state, he insisted. For Berth, the democratic state was abstract, pacific, and bloated, weak where it should be strong (the executive) and present where it should be absent. The monarchy was personal, warlike, and limited, but strong. Replacing the democratic state with the monarchy would remove the state from the realm of production, fulfilling the syndicalist dream of absorbing the political into the economic. Like Vincent, Berth calmed his proletarian conscience by accepting Valois's contention that, as syndicalists, they would resist any royal encroachment on their liberties. Berth's monarchism did not mean acceptance of integral nationalism as a philosophy. One element in a creative tension, Maurras represented the Apollonian ideal and Sorel the Dionysian. Berth cited Nietzsche to the effect that both were essential to a truly forceful classicism.[42] Berth also took the precaution of using a pseudonym in the *Cahiers* and publishing his *Méfaits* with a socialist editor.

Berth's dependence on Nietzsche and Sorel had some paradoxical results. Berth did what Valois had been accused of, using Nietzsche to justify the monarchy. Similarly, it was Berth, much more than Valois, who had created a bridge from Sorel to Maurras. Finally, to the extent that the Cercle Proudhon radiated a prefascist spirit, this was more the work of Berth than of Valois. Berth's dynamic Sorelian, and hence Bergsonian, authoritarianism in many ways prefigured the ideological climate of Mussolini's Fascism. His treatment of the Jews, much more emotional and generalizing than Valois's, was closer to the way anti-Semitism would later be used in German National Socialism. This is particularly ironic, since Berth would be writing apologies for Lenin when Valois was founding France's first fascist party. History does not always run in straight lines.[43]

Valois's activities in the Cercle Proudhon and his increasing visibility irritated many, including the royalist economic old guard. In 1912 its two most influential representatives were the marquis de la Tour du Pin and his disciple Jean Rivain. Founder and proprietor of the *Revue critique des idées et des livres*, Rivain had not, unlike de Marans, followed Valois into the Cercle.[44]

Valois's projects as described in *La Révolution sociale ou le roi* were compatible with La Tour du Pin's ideas. Both opposed solutions based on charity and both wished to see proud, class-conscious workers harmonizing their interests with those of their employers in vertically organized corporations. The main differences were in tone, tactics, and friends. La Tour du Pin saw the reorganization of society as part of the recreation of a Christian social order. Valois left religion aside when discussing social questions, at least at the Cercle. The old guard may also have been disturbed to see him so obviously playing up to revolutionaries like Sorel and Berth. Proudhon's patronage was the last straw. To men like La Tour du Pin who had grown up on the French right in the nineteenth century, Proudhon was anathema. He was the writer who, in addition to saying, "Property is theft," had asserted: "The Church is evil." None of these elements was essential to Valois's conceptions, which, in *Le Père*, had been formulated in a very conservative manner. However, as he was to discover again and again, even rhetorical concessions to the left drew hostility from the right, despite René de Marans's argument that there was no contradiction between the Cercle Proudhon and the teachings of La Tour du Pin.[45]

La Tour du Pin enjoyed great prestige in royalist and Catholic circles. One of the founders of the Catholic social movement, he remained a monarchist when the Catholic Count Albert de Mun rallied to the Republic. By lending his support to the fledgling Action française, the marquis won them a sympathetic hearing in potentially hostile Catholic monarchist circles. Rivain, besides running the *Revue critique*, was a member of the *comités directeurs* of the Action française and, through his wife, had the support of the influential Countess Mme. de Courville. Nevertheless, it was Valois who triumphed. Maurras personally presided over the first meeting of the Cercle in December 1911, and the Action française continued to give the group its enthusiastic support. Rivain resigned from the *comités directeurs* and took the *Revue critique* out of the intellectual orbit of the Action française. La Tour du Pin was promoted to the position of respected, but ignored, figurehead.[46]

Maurras did not choose Valois for doctrinal reasons. In one of their first meetings, Maurras had cited La Tour du Pin in answer to Valois's syndicalist projects. In the almost obsequious dedication Valois wrote for *La Monarchie et la classe ouvrière*, he reported to Maurras that he had, thanks to him, profited from the marquis's teachings. Maurras was willing to risk the hostility of La Tour du Pin and his friends because he considered Valois's work with the left more promising. In the years before 1914, the Action française appeared to be riding the crest of a wave, and the overthrow of the Republic was more pressing than social conservation. Maurras's support for Valois was also personal. Unlike Para, Bacconier, or La Tour du Pin, Valois had no connections with royalism outside the Action française, no divided loyalties.[47] To this, Valois added a clear willingness to flatter *le maître*.

THE NOUVELLE LIBRAIRIE NATIONALE

Jean Rivain's departure from the Action française had other advantages for Valois. In 1912, Rivain left the Nouvelle librairie nationale, and his place was taken temporarily by René de Marans, whose poor health left the direction of the Librairie open. Valois then took over the direction of the Action française publishing house with the backing of a few aristocratic friends. He was thus able, without leaving the book industry, to end his equivocal situation at Armand Colin. Valois explained his political evolution to Max Leclerc, and the two parted on good terms.[48]

Valois ran the Nouvelle Librairie nationale long after he had left the Action française, earning a steady income and a powerful position within the royalist movement. Under his direction, the Librairie was a commercial and artistic success. Authors like Maurras, Daudet, and Bainville sold well, but the financial success of what still remained fundamentally a royalist propaganda outlet testified to his managerial skills.[49]

Valois's two chief assistants were Joseph Boissier and Pierre Lecoeur. A huge, muscular young man, Boissier had come to Paris without resources and taken work as a house-mover. Later he worked with Valois at Armand Colin, and Valois hired him at the Librairie. Royalist and patriotic, Boissier distinguished himself in street battles and waited impatiently for the chance to avenge the French defeat at Sedan. Valois had great affection for Boissier, whom he compared to Hercules: a good-natured giant, proud, brave, loyal, and gifted with inexhaustible energy. He died a hero's death in 1915 during the Artois offensive.[50]

Valois's relationship with Lecoeur was not as happy. Lecoeur was one of the leaders among the *camelots* who battled the nationalists' foes, often arriving at the Librairie with the scars of the previous night's brawls. Apparently jealous of Boissier, Lecoeur stole some volumes and tried to implicate Boissier. Valois discovered the plot and forced him to write a confession. Lecoeur, however, had a powerful patron within the Ligue: Maurice Pujo.[51] In the years to come, they would have ample opportunity for revenge.

The period from 1906 to 1918 was also that of Valois's political apprenticeship, when he acquired the skills of a propagandist and political activist. He presided over or spoke at meetings in the provinces and in Paris, before sympathetic audiences or in workers' quarters like Montrouge, saw meetings ended in an uproar by opponents, and learned to handle hostile audiences determined to shout him down, to answer contradictors with sarcasm or with arguments.[52]

THE GREAT WAR

On August 2, 1914, sharing in the patriotic enthusiasm of that "glorious morning," Valois went off to war. His record was brilliant. Beginning the war as private in a territorial battalion, he rose to the rank of *sous-lieutenant* by May of 1916. Three times cited for bravery in action, he received the Croix de guerre and the Légion d'honneur. Valois's battalion was assigned to the Verdun sector. There, he became the leader of a volunteer *corps franc* engaged in dangerous reconnaissance missions. Valois electrified this small group, creating an atmosphere of close fellowship, which became for him the model for the reconciliation of Frenchmen by the war. He volunteered for the most dangerous missions, and his citations show that he accomplished his tasks with courage, intelligence, and *sang-froid.*[53]

Valois, who had found maneuvers exciting, enjoyed his wartime service even more. The *corps franc* spared him the tedium of the trenches. His service combined the order and constraint of military life with adventure and comradeship. He took an almost sensual pleasure in the rigors of his charge:

> Do you remember, comrades, the night marches, our hearts beating during silent approaches, searching the woods, the branches whipping our faces and tearing our hands, the exaltation, the fear overcome, the excitement of captures; the races in the fog; and the ambushes on summer nights in the fields of wild flowers; and the long waits in the rain; and the exhaustion, and the delicious rest on the straw of the stables.

Addressing a veteran's rally a few years later, Valois said he felt exhilarated when returning to the front after a leave.[54] The war created a climate well adapted to his personality: a life of action in the service of an unquestioned ideal, within a highly structured, ascetic atmosphere. Valois's ambition was satisfied as well, and it was probably during the war that he discovered he had a talent for leading men.

When he was injured in an accident in October 1916, Valois's life was saved by an operation arranged by Léon Daudet. In September 1917, Valois was assigned to interrogate prisoners at Annemasse for a short time and then released from service toward the end of that year.[55]

When Valois discussed the war, he emphasized fellowship and organization, never destruction or death. The ideal that emerges from his account is that of a conscientious soldier, fraternally aiding his comrades, not a Homeric warrior wreaking destruction upon his enemies. Years later, when an antimilitarist, Valois claimed that he had deliberately avoided killing anyone. Given his military functions, this is possible. Besides, he seems never to have been personally attracted by acts of violence. Though he could admire those who engaged in street-fighting, he always avoided it himself.[56]

While still at the front, Valois began a book of reflections on the war. The result, Le Cheval de Troie, was published in 1918. Valois had concluded that, given the double line of trenches, no offensive using conventional materials could break through enemy lines. What was needed was a technique for crossing the trenches while conserving the element of surprise. A war of maneuver could then be engaged and ultimate victory achieved. The soldiers of the Entente were in the same position as the Greeks before Troy. In a passage written in 1915, Valois proposed that the new Trojan horse should be a "mechanical monster" capable of crossing the trenches and, armed with machine guns and poison gas, destroy the enemy defenses. In addition, it should safely transport troops past enemy lines, where, with the aid of following troops, they could fight a war of movement. In the chapter Valois finished in November 1917, he declared that the available tanks, though promising, were not sufficient; most critically, they did not transport troops. When the English used tanks to rupture the German lines on November 20, 1917, however, Valois claimed not only that the solution had been found but that his 1915 predictions had been validated.[57]

Before this date, Valois had been considerably more pessimistic. If his "mechanical monster" might take time to produce, the war was likely to go on for some time. In a passage that the censor evidently found too demoralizing to be printed, Valois noted that with available techniques, it would take several more years at best just to push the Germans back to the border. Like the Greeks before Troy, the French would have to arm themselves with patience. France would have to organize for a long war, straining its productive apparatus and its inventive genius to the utmost.[58] Valois clearly overestimated the endurance of the Central Powers (and of the Entente). Yet he was fully prepared to see French life organized indefinitely around maximum production and minimal consumption. He made a similar prediction during World War II.

But in 1918 the war ended, and Valois returned to his peacetime pursuits as publisher and Action française militant. The war had opened new perspectives and increased his ambition. Before the war, Valois was building his position within the Action française. His ideas, though original, were heavily influenced by Maurras. Though he sought alliances with other groups, especially on the left, he always did so as a royalist. After the war, he became more independent in both spheres.

THREE

Valois in the Action Française, II

Conspiring with Business

After 1918, Valois entered his first major period of accomplishment, becoming the leader of several major organizations and an influential figure in French political and economic life. Though victorious, France inherited severe problems from the war, and politics was dominated by the complex and interrelated issues of inflation, monetary and financial crises, reparations, reconstruction, and international debts. This was a new orientation for debate, which before the war had turned on more easily understood ideological issues. Since Valois had by 1918 become the royalist social and economic expert, the new climate increased his influence. War also changed the position of the Action française, its credit in the eyes of the public having been raised by Léon Daudet's prewar warnings of German infiltration and his role in denouncing traitors. But the wartime practice of working closely with republicans like Georges Mandel and Georges Clemenceau tempted the Action française to use its influence to affect government policy at the expense of its independence.[1]

There were no ambiguities, however, in the war's effects on Valois. Victory convinced him that French decadence was not irreversible. Frenchmen had demonstrated to the world, as he had to himself, that they still possessed that vital energy without which a nation, no matter how well organized, could not achieve greatness. Unlike so many of his contemporaries from all ends of the political spectrum who correctly judged France weakened, Valois endowed his country with his own optimism and energy. Political and social conflicts melted before a common dedication to victory, and Frenchmen were not resistant to authority when properly led.

Valois called this complex of attitudes "the spirit of victory." It remained an important part of his thought for almost ten years.[2]

This spirit suggested that France was ripe for a national and authoritarian revolution. The contrast between the hesitations and ambiguities of the royalist position and Valois's activities, carried out in the name of royalist principles, led to his gradual estrangement from Maurras.

VALOISIAN ECONOMICS

Valois's attempts at economic organizing were based on his own doctrines, set forth in 1919 in *L'Economie nouvelle*. Most of the positive conclusions had been prefigured earlier, but since he considered *L'Economie nouvelle* a scientific discussion of economic theory, Valois felt obliged to refute liberal and Marxist economics.

Valois's critique of liberal economics is more revealing of his economic knowledge than of the weaknesses of laissez-faire theory. For the royalist, the theory of value was the cornerstone of classical economics. According to Valois, the classical economists taught that the value of an object lay in the importance given it by humans or its utility, in turn defined by the individual's judgment of his needs. Hence value was subjective, based on human desires. Confusing the descriptive with the normative, Valois declared that it was impossible to build durable institutions on such quicksand. This theory justified individual private property and made state intervention in the name of the common good impossible. Finally, if desire were the measure of value, it might eventually, in a situation of dearth, give such a high value to unavailable goods that people would resort to violence to obtain them.[3]

This reflected Valois's belief that price theory derived from the theory of value, making liberal economic theory not only immoral and dangerous but unscientific. Its major feature, the law of supply and demand, was powerless to explain economic phenomena and totally false.[4] Prices were determined by the costs of production. Economists had been misled by the coincidence of large sales with low prices and smaller sales with higher prices, which was simply because increased production lowered unit cost and hence price. Moreover, if supply and demand created prices, these might fall below the cost of production, which, he thought, would be inconceivable. Valois did not realize that supply and demand were not final causes but mechanisms, the costs of production, for example, determining the supply curve. He was equally unaware that prices acted on the allocation of factors of production, so that in a competitive market, prices and costs tended toward equilibrium. Valois did argue that, under special circumstances, excess demand might permit a temporary "sur-profit." But this would stimulate increased production and wipe itself out. (That is, of course, the way the liberal economic model works.) Indeed, the whole discussion reflects a total ignorance of equilibrium analysis, all the more glaring since this branch of economics had been developed (and discussed in French) since Sismondi. Nor did Valois regard demand as an independent variable; consumers simply buy more when prices are lower. Valois's ignorance of the concept of elasticity of demand is somewhat less serious, since this was a more recent development in economic theory. Nevertheless, mathematical models for elasticity had been developed by the end of the nineteenth century.[5] Valois's ignorance of micro-economic theory rendered ludicrous his critique of the liberal economists.

In the postwar years, Valois did not remedy this lack. In his 1924 preface to a new edition of L'Economie nouvelle, he changed none of his earlier ideas. Though his moral and political arguments had been strengthened, his economic points had not. If anything, Valois demonstrated the same misunderstanding of the components of the demand curve he had previously shown for supply.[6]

None of Valois's limited formal training had been in economics; and he credited Sorel with having made the dismal science attractive by persuading him that it was an exciting social science that could be dealt with in an essentially literary and deductive manner. There was no need to wade through the boring figures of Paul Leroy-Beaulieu.[7] Even in macroeconomics, where Valois had a better knowledge of both theory and practice, his inability to use mathematical models deprived many of his projects of necessary precision. In no other area was his lack of formal education more of a disadvantage. But Valois nonetheless considered himself, and was considered by his colleagues, an expert in economics. For example, Louis Dimier, one of the best-educated men in the Ligue, noted that Valois suffered from the lack of a good general education, but insisted that he made up for this with his knowledge of economics.

Valois was right when he claimed that there was a general ignorance of economics among the men of the Action française. He himself did have a more modern approach to economic practice than some of his predecessors among the royalists. La Tour du Pin, for example, argued that any taking of interest, as opposed to profit that entailed risk, was usury and should be barred from business practice. Valois did recognize the role of capital in production and the function of interest in its distribution.[8]

It was not enough to dispose of laissez-faire. One also had to tackle the liberals' Marxist opponents. Valois had more familiarity with Marxist ideology, at least in its more popular forms. He recognized that Marxism was both a philosophy of history and a theory of production. Valois countered Marx's historical materialism by denying it and replacing it with a statement of philosophic idealism. Though Valois's other economic and social ideas were brought into accord with this idealism, many of the arguments themselves were potentially ambivalent.[9]

The rejection of economic determinism served a critique of the Marxist interpretation of history. The clashes that had marked nineteenth-century French history were not between classes but between parties competing for political power. In the most important recent conflicts, like the Boulanger and Dreyfus affairs, all classes were represented on each side. Behind these conflicts lay, not economic interests, but different metaphysical systems. The first was the ideology of progress and evolution; the second that of order and existence, represented by Catholicism. Against the idea of progress, Valois noted that the fall of Rome had certainly brought about a drastic and prolonged regression in material conditions.[10]

Valois attacked the concept of a class as a group of people with common interests. Social classes existed, but economic classes were a myth. The former reflected income and living style; they did not concern production. In this realm, there were no horizontal classes possessing common interests opposed to those of other groups in the productive process. All involved in the production of the same goods—workers, technicians, managers, or employers—had the same basic interest, the prosperity of their industry. The fundamental natural conflicts were between industries and regions. Valois did not deny that specific groups within an industry had their own interests. Workers, for example, sought the highest wages while their employers sought to limit these. Such oppositions were reconcilable and less important than common corporate interests.[11]

Valois claimed to have discovered this fact during the war. In the trenches, men spontaneously specialized in trades, some in the manufacture or trading of objects, while others guarded their fellows. Hierarchies mirrored those in society. If it was true that officers and men ate or took their recreation separately, they did their work together. Captains joined their companies, artillery with artillery, infantry with infantry.[12] As he would frequently for the next several years, Valois used the solidarity of an army on campaign as a model for a society at peace.

Since Valois did not accept class competition in the economy, he could not accept the Marxist explanation of the exploitation of labor either. Recognizing that this concept was based on the labor theory of value, he argued that, since other factors, such as capital and command (entrepreneurial authority and direction), were essential for production, and hence components of value, the entrepreneur's surplus was not stolen from the workers. Valois distinguished between the return received for entrepreneurial effort and the return on capital, which he considered much the smaller component of profit in enterprises where the director/owner also supplied the capital. Nevertheless, although he clearly approved of interest, Valois did not specifically defend the return on capital as distinguished from that for managerial labor or entrepreneurial risk. Marx simply condemned entrepreneurs—a group of producers—by refusing to recognize their economic function, Valois asserted. The summit of the Marxist edifice was the classless society, but Valois considered production without constraint an absurdity. This had, however, been said before. The only novelty to Valois's argument was the claim that the economic breakdown in Russia showed the impossibility of a communist organization of production.[13]

Nevertheless, despite his banishment of class conflict from history and the economy, Valois recognized the prevalence of conflict and of what to him were unfair economic practices in French society. These could be explained by frictions generated by the law of least effort, or by the clash of ideologies. Yet Valois also localized the problem in a group of people who acted as the repositories of social evil. Like his Marxist opponents, Valois believed that the day-to-day routines of politics were manipulated by groups that could be scientifically analyzed or politically denounced.[14] Before the war, this role had been filled by the Maurrasian *quatre états confédérés*. Life at the front seems, however, to have dissolved Valois's hostility to Protestants and Jews. After the war, references to Jews in his writing were rare and largely devoid of ideological significance.[15] Now Valois spoke of the plutocrats. Although he was undoubtedly referring to much the same group of people, the change of term represented a move away from the Maurrasian mental universe. Plutocrats were people defined by an economic role, however illegitimate. Also, the flexibility of the term left Valois open to building a wider political base.

But who were the plutocrats? They were those who, on a large scale, abused (morally if not always legally) the freedom of the marketplace created by laissez-faire theory. While carefully avoiding causal connections that might suggest a historical materialism, Valois pointed out that liberal economic theory, rather than expressing the interests of the bourgeoisie, admirably served those of the plutocrats, here referred to elliptically as Jews. This took place largely through financial manipulation. Variations in stock and bond prices, not caused by supply and demand, were provoked by speculators. The plutocrats, like the *quatre états*, were behind all

French political parties, which they controlled through the financing of
newspapers and political campaigns, when not by outright corruption.[16]

For Valois, plutocracy was an international phenomenon, often overlapping with economic imperialism.[17] The plutocrats explained the otherwise inexplicable, like Woodrow Wilson's intervention in favor of the Bol-
sheviks. The nationalization of Russian land seemed the prelude to a
gigantic operation to force Russian peasants to work for German and
American bankers. The plutocrats were behind projects like the attempt to
corner the capital-goods industries in countries whose industrial plants had
been ruined by the war (Germany, the United Kingdom, and the United
States were thus excluded). They became a factor of world-historical significance with the Russian Revolution. A victorious France was confronted with two distinct but cooperating barbarisms, the plutocratic and
the Bolshevik. Valois assimilated both to the eternal barbarian, always
ready to steal the goods of the producers. One pillaged directly, while the
other stole under the cover of financial institutions. Each possessed its
own ideology—liberalism and Marxism respectively; both were wrong
and to be combated.[18]

The defeat of the two barbarisms demanded the replacement of both
systems by Valois's "new economics." This began with the definition of
the science itself. Rejecting the descriptions of Adam Smith and Leroy-
Beaulieu, Valois defined economics as the science of the conditions and
means by which man—that is, the human species—transforms, captures,
exchanges, or accumulates those things, plants, animals, or inanimate objects, usable for the conservation of the individual and of the species.
Though Valois never suggested such paternity, this concept may have
come to him from the Russian (and French) anarchist Kropotkin who
shared Valois's tendency to mix biology and society.[19] In either case, this
definition not only underlies many of Valois's economic propositions but
also reflects the angle from which he viewed social reality. As in 1906, Valois was concerned with the species, not with individuals.

By concerning himself with the usable, Valois actually limited himself
to the beneficial. His theory of value followed directly: an object possessed
value not because it was desired but because of its ability to serve the preservation of the species. In his own words, value was dictated by physiology, not psychology. Seeking to meet objections head on, Valois only exposed the ambiguities of his position. Did not morphine, though harmful,
have a high value for the addict? Valois answered that this value, and any
value attached to a harmful product, was the result of a deviation of the
instinct of self-preservation, caused in this case by the pathological state of

the addict. However, since Valois made no distinction between true and false value, he left open the question of whether value did or merely ought to represent utility. In his own mind, Valois resolved the problem by explaining that it was the role of the politicoeconomic system to maintain the proper concordance between man and nature, to see that people got what was good for them.[20] Insisting that reality accommodate itself to morality, even if this morality had a utilitarian/biological basis, helped Valois criticize aspects of contemporary capitalism and base a moral critique on scientific arguments.

For Valois, economics was also a universal science of human society. There was no production without constraint, and the family was its first institutionalization. From the law of least effort Valois also derived the principle that men will always prefer the theft of others' goods to the labors of production. In addition, since the regions of the earth were of differing economic value, the peoples of some areas would always be tempted to steal the land or goods of more favored peoples. One of the prerequisites of production was, therefore, a military state to protect producers from the barbarian. The state was the protector, not merely of property, but of the entire productive system.[21]

More significantly for the future, Valois added a dynamic element to his system: the law of the intellectualization of effort. Manual labor is tiring. So the law of least effort suggested attempts to reduce the physical strain of production through new tools or techniques. These, however, demanded a higher level of concentration, replacing the physical with an equivalent mental strain. Valois gave this equivalence a Quintonian label: the law of the constancy of human effort. As men continued to seek relief, effort became increasingly intellectualized, and an economic and social system that maximized mutual constraint guaranteed technological progress. Intellectualization marked social evolution as well. The brute force of earlier times was replaced by subtler forms of constraint, in which the assent of intelligence played a part.[22]

Valois did not defend free-market competition. He never considered competition viable, for reasons so obvious to him that he simply assumed them in 1919, only stating them explicitly in 1924. Consumers lacked real market power because of a fundamental lack of information. A disloyal businessman could always ruin a competitor by selling an adulterated product at a lower price. By the time the consumer perceived the fraud, it was too late. Valois's refusal to consider demand as an independent variable also reduced the market power of the consumer. To this Valois added the familiar argument that competition obliged employers to reduce

salaries below a decent minimum. Its net effects were the slow destruction
of French traditions of quality and the social debasement of the workers.[23]

To enjoy the benefits of personal initiative without the destructive effects of free competition demanded a self-regulating system forcing the
free play of interests into certain channels. For Valois, this was his regime
of syndicalist mutual constraint, a systematization of the dynamics he had
proposed in 1907. Employers would be under pressure to lower prices and,
all other ways of achieving this being blocked, would have to do so
through technical improvements, increasing the productivity of the workers and forcing them to better their professional qualifications. The result
would be high salaries, low prices, and a high rate of capitalization. Valois
characterized the system then operative in France as unilateral syndicalism: everyone was organized for sale, but no one for purchase. Workers
put pressure on their employers for higher wages. The employers re
sponded by raising prices, which brought renewed demands for higher
wages. In addition, the weak state was exploited by workers demanding
shorter hours and employers seeking tariffs and special favors.[24] Valois's
models are not, however, by themselves, conclusive. The model of unilateral syndicalism could be corrected by improving the bargaining power of
the employers, but Valois always opposed the creation of a Confédération
générale du patronat. There would then be no reason why the pressure
should come from the workers in one system and from the consumers in
the other. Only the problem of the state would remain.

The advantages Valois expected from his system can be seen in the
way he wished it to operate. He did not want organization by classes
(nonexistent in the economy) but by industries. Despite the syndicalist
vocabulary, the conception was corporative. Classwide organizations
would promote class conflict; organization by industry would promote
cooperation. Implicit in this was the assumption that once Frenchmen in
the same industry met face to face, they would recognize both the reason-
ableness of their differing particular interests and their overriding common ones.[25]

Consultation among labor and management representatives within the
same industry was essential for the formulation and acceptance of new
procedures. Valois expected syndical organization to achieve for whole industries the process of rationalization that Taylorism performed for individual enterprises, to eliminate the anarchic wastefulness of capitalist production of which socialists had long complained. The *syndicat* would
impose standardization, reducing costs, and take over marketing, freeing
managers to concentrate on technical improvements. Finally, technical ad-

vances, once developed, would be imposed on all. No longer would French entrepreneurs be permitted to content themselves with a modest profit and stand in the way of industrial progress. The means of enforcement were simple. The refractory would be denied the benefits of the *syndicat*, an economic death sentence.[26] Valois proposed a solution to a problem that had confronted French social thinkers since Saint-Simon: how to force more dynamism from the conservative French bourgeoisie.

Syndicalization would also permit a new relationship between state and economy. Valois was opposed to direct government intervention. The state was incompetent in the matter, and civil servants administered enterprises in which they had no interest badly. Nevertheless, the state had a responsibility to intervene when the actions of a group of producers threatened public order. This happened, according to Valois, when, for example, a *syndicat* tried to abuse a temporarily favorable market position by sharply raising prices, the only recourse of the buyer being violence. Prices should be set by agreements between *syndicats*. In the case of abuses, however, the government could intervene upon the complaint of the injured *syndicat*. Thus, despite all the self-regulating aspects of his system, Valois still counted on the intervention of a wise government to preserve equilibrium. Already, in *Le Cheval de Troie*, Valois had explained how the government could use the *syndicats* to organize wartime production. That even in peacetime the government might direct the economy into certain channels was not excluded.[27]

To keep conflicts to a minimum, Valois counted on his "spirit of victory": the mood of heroism, unity, self-sacrifice, and discipline that the war had generated among Frenchmen. Victory implies enemies, and Valois's syndical structure was not neutral. In a detailed fantasy, Valois imagined himself as president of the publishing corporation. One of the main topics on the agenda, after the neat disposal of some vestigial social conflicts, was the reconquest of the Russian book market, recently reopened by the retreat of Bolshevism. Capital was scarce because a consortium of international bankers was trying to raise a loan for the last soviet in Tibet. The French government opposed the loan, but it had to fight the international consortium, which was backed by the government of a large, democratic financier-dominated country (the United States). The printers' union provided the solution by refusing to print any notices, circulars, or certificates for the loan. Valois, as president, was sure that the majority of bankers would accept this solution with relief, and that the bank employees themselves would agree not to handle the loan.[28] Such techniques remained typical of the way Valois wanted syndical organizations to impose their will on national and international political forces. In the late 1930s, he would propose similar tactics against Nazi Germany.

None of the essentials of Valois's system was new; they had been succinctly stated in *La Monarchie ou la révolution sociale*. To a sympathetic observer, Louis Dimier, Valois had given up his support for a strong, autonomous workers' movement and substituted more conservative mixed *syndicats*. If there was a misunderstanding, Valois himself was partly to blame, since he had claimed in 1921 that his original conception of the mutual constraint of horizontally organized classes was not truly replaced by constraint within vertical structures until after the war. What had changed was really emphasis. Before the war, Valois had stressed the importance of a strongly organized working class; afterward, compromise within corporations. Before the war, there were more references to Sorel; after it, more to La Tour du Pin. The change in emphasis was related to a dramatic shift in alliances. Up to 1914, Valois had courted syndicalists and workers. He himself characterized his first postwar period by the phrase: "With the barons of industry."[29]

CORPORATIVE ORGANIZING AND THE BOOK INDUSTRY

Valois had not waited for the armistice to get down to work. In May 1918, he formed a committee to create a Confédération nationale de la production (CNP) with a few engineers, industrialists, and bankers, none of them important royalists. In October, Valois proposed the syndical organization of demobilization as the group's first task. The CNP was to work with existing groups and provoke their restructuring along vertical, corporative lines. But, in July 1919, a competing group, the Confédération générale de la production (CGP) was founded by the economic modernizer and organizer Etienne Clémentel (then minister of commerce), Louis Loucheur, and André Tardieu. Though it may have been at least partially a response to Valois's group, the CGP had one major difference. Conceived of as a pendant to the CGT, it represented management and was to sit, along with the workers' federation, in a Conseil économique. The new group nonetheless succeeded in wrecking the CNP, since the major industrialists preferred to work with the association that enjoyed official blessing.[30]

Valois started afresh in March 1920 with the Confédération de l'intelligence et de la production française (CIPF). Unlike its predecessor, this new organization was clearly attached to the royalists. A young engineer of the Ligue, Georges Coquelle, became secretary-general and Valois's principal collaborator, while Action française notables were given honorific posts.[31] As with the CNP, Valois wanted to work directly with existing *syndicats*. When the groups resisted, whether because of liberalism (the employers) or Marxism (the workers), economic and intellectual means of persuasion were to be employed. *Syndicats jaunes*, characterized by Valois as workers' groups existing solely thanks to the financial support of management, were to be avoided. Further emphasizing his separation from the *jaunes*, Valois condemned Pierre Biétry's capital-sharing schemes.[32]

The CGP experience had shown Valois that the government would not sit by while an Action française militant organized the economy. Thus, if the CIPF were not to be swept away like the CNP, it would have to organize at least one industry and develop a practical mechanism for organizing others. Valois solved both problems in his own corporation, the book industry, where he had his first and most lasting success in economic organization.

During the war, Valois had continued to run the Nouvelle Librairie nationale from the front. One of the first publishers to resume operations after the mobilization, the Librairie paid a dividend during the war, as it did every year from 1912 to 1925.[33] When Valois was released from active duty in 1917, he extended his activity to the book industry as a whole.

In Valois's eyes, postwar French publishing was both over- and underorganized. The industry contained a myriad of publishing houses competing in complete chaos and risked takeover by a trust with international plutocratic connections, Hachette. Through its Messageries, Hachette monopolized the distribution of books (and newspapers) in railroad stations and small bookstores. Rumors circulated that Hachette, backed by Standard Oil, was about to corner the manufacture and distribution of French books and newspapers. Though he respected the centralization and rationalization of trusts like Hachette, Valois felt that they eliminated the necessary mutual constraint. Thus Valois wanted to organize the book industry to modernize production and spread French civilization, but also to prevent the dominance of trusts. According to Valois, he began with patriotic motives and made his discoveries about Hachette from 1918 to 1920.[34]

In November 1918, with Theuveny of the Renaissance du livre and Besancenet of Flammarion, Valois founded the Société mutuelle des éditeurs français, of which he became director for 1918 and 1919. Already in 1916, Paul Gillon of Larousse had set up the Société d'exportation des éditions françaises to promote French books abroad. In 1919, Gillon accepted Valois's proposal to merge their organizations into an institution for centralized purchasing, distribution, and marketing. On May 18, 1920, an

assembly of publishers and booksellers founded the Maison du livre
français with a capital of two million francs. Gillon became president,
while Valois took over the actual direction as *administrateur-délégué*, a
post he held, without pay, until 1925.[35]

Now Valois found himself at war with Hachette. Though few of the
publishers shared his ideas about plutocracy, their irritation at Hachette's
market power was one of their principal motives in joining the Maison du
livre. Valois's former boss, Max Leclerc of Armand Colin, became one of
Hachette's most vocal critics. At first, Valois tried to work with his giant
competitor. By 1921, however, he found himself personally involved in a
fight with one of France's most powerful economic institutions. The battle
meant conflict with the Banque de Paris et des Pays-Bas, which had just
underwritten the augmentation of Hachette's capital. More important, it
led to Valois's lifelong, often obsessive, war against the bank's director,
Horace Finaly.[36]

So far, only the publishers and a few booksellers had been organized.
Valois moved toward organizing the whole industry at the Semaine du
livre. The Semaines were a nineteenth-century invention of the Catholic
social movement: conferences called to deal with specific social problems.
Valois adopted the name but modified the concept. The meetings should
be between the representatives of different branches of an industry, and
the Semaine the founding meeting of a corporation.[37]

During the summer of 1920, Valois began planning a Semaine du livre,
aided by Martial Buisson, an advertising director and former camelot du
roi. Help also came from José Germain, then in the process of organizing
a Confédération des travailleurs intellectuels. The printing and paper *syndicats* agreed to attend, and the ministries of commerce and education gave
their blessing. The Semaine, held in November, dealt with creative
thought, raw materials, manufacture, marketing, and so forth, and created
specialized conferences to work on problems like model contracts for authors and the production of paper.[38] With the success of the Semaine, the
CIPF was launched. Semaines were organized in other industries: construction, foreign commerce, advertising. The most important, however,
was not industrial at all: the Semaine de la monnaie.

TO THE SEMAINE DE LA MONNAIE

Like most Frenchmen, Valois had never given monetary problems more
than fleeting attention before World War I. After the war, however, he increasingly saw them as important, and eventually they became a distinc-

tive feature of all his royalist and later fascist campaigns. This was not only because problems with the franc became major public issues between 1922 and 1928 but also because he came to believe that monetary instability was the main way international plutocrats were fleecing French producers.

Valois began in 1919 with a series of articles in the *Action française* on *la vie chère*, the dramatic price rises that followed the end of the financial solidarity of the Allies. Valois first concluded that life was dear because the French had been impoverished by the war. As prices continued to rise, however, he changed his analysis. By the beginning of 1920, Valois recognized that price rises were not caused by increases in the costs of production but by a decline in the value of money, by inflation. The principal cause, he insisted at this time, was what is now called cost-push inflation. Higher salaries (caused by his "unilaterally syndicalized economy"), unmatched by increases in productivity, led to higher prices and a deflated currency. In passing, he mentioned that the Bank of France permitted the process to continue by increasing the amount of paper in circulation.[39]

In July, Valois added the explanation that would dominate all the others: the Bank of France had reduced the value of the franc by printing too much money, money without backing. Money for Valois was not a sign or convention but merchandise (generally gold) whose value was its value as merchandise but whose form had been adopted for ease of exchange. Paper money was a receipt for merchandise pledged or deposited and should be issued only on the receipt of properly endorsed and discounted commercial paper. Advances to the state must be fully covered by the bank's gold reserves. Any other money was false money, which diminished, proportionally, the value of all the paper money in circulation. This fraud was actually worse than the debasing of the coinage for which kings had been stigmatized. In the old system, not only was the alteration more immediately apparent but the value of money in private hands was not affected. Valois was not against increases in the money supply. If production grew, they would be produced automatically by a rise in the value of the commercial paper brought to the bank for discount. This brought Valois close to the quantity theory of money, and he tended to calculate as if it were operative, excluding the consideration of velocity. Nonetheless, when it was a question of cause, Valois stayed away from considerations of quantity, which would have led him to the law of supply and demand. The loss in the value of money was caused directly by its lack of backing. International exchange rates had nothing to do with the balance of payments either. They merely reflected changes in gold value.[40]

Inflation was caused by the state. Such inflation was particularly serious, since it threatened the state, production, and French society as a
whole. Most immediately harmed were the *rentiers*. It was no secret that
inflation meant the partial confiscation of their capital, already badly hit
when Russian, Austro-Hungarian, and Turkish government bonds were
rendered worthless. It was mostly the small *rentiers* who were caught.
The rich, if their money was not in stocks, could transfer to safe foreign
currencies or securities in time. The dispossession of the *rentiers* discouraged saving, and the spirit of saving was one of the pillars of civilization.[41]

More serious for Valois was the damage to production. An unstable
currency made it impossible to establish long-term contracts, particularly
troublesome in publishing, where advances were made on a fairly long-
term basis. But inflation even played havoc with normal business practices. Manufacturers set prices, not based on the cost of the raw materials
consumed, but on their replacement cost, pushing prices up even faster.
As long as everyone maintained the fiction that a franc was a franc, real-
istic accounting of gains and losses was impossible. Manufacturers over-
stocked raw materials, creating an artificial demand for them. Suppliers
then overproduced, and once the storage facilities of the manufacturers
were filled, the boom was followed by a bust. The French were being encouraged to consume and produce for the internal market when their impoverished state required them to save and export. Such economic disturbances had social effects. Besides ruining *rentiers* and businessmen,
inflation misled the workers, who agitated for ever higher wages. Seeing
the ease with which these were accorded, the workers then concluded that
they had been robbed before—and became revolutionary.[42]

To such familiar arguments, Valois added a distinctive and more crucial
one. Inflation provoked a real transfer of value into the hands of foreigners and plutocrats. Foreign debtors could pay their debts at a fraction of
their value (this did not apply to reparations, figured in gold), while
French debts, due in a stable foreign currency, would be paid at true value.
Similarly, a French firm buying goods in a foreign market and paying in
a month would pay full value, whereas a foreigner purchasing in France
would gain at the end of the month.[43]

The rapid deflation that set in around the end of 1920 was almost
equally dangerous. It discouraged investment; and just as inflation created
artificial profits, deflation created artificial bankruptcies when businesses'
paper returns would not cover paper costs. During deflation, it was foreign
creditors who benefited, while foreign merchants could still turn things to
their advantage by stipulating payment in francs, whose value was on the

rise. In effect, Valois could argue both sides of the issue because he saw the franc, cut loose from the gold standard, as susceptible to plutocratic manipulation. Monetary instability formed the occasion for large-scale raids on French production.[44]

For most of these problems, Valois had one solution, the *franc-or*, a money of account. Accounts were to be recorded in *francs-or*, that is, the gold value of the 1914 franc. At the moment of payment, the number of paper francs due would be equal, in gold value, to the amount previously agreed upon in *francs-or*. This could be done for all payments: salaries, loans, deposits, national and international commerce, in effect, indexing all monetary agreements. In Valois's scheme, the indexing was based on the price of gold, rather than on the internal price level. If this system of calculation were used by the government, the *rentiers* would be protected (or the government in the case of deflation). If not, at least Frenchmen could protect themselves in their dealings with one another and with foreigners. This system, which Valois continued to advocate in one form or another for the rest of his life, appealed to him for its honesty and transparency. The *franc-or* would not solve the serious financial problems the French had inherited from the war. But it would protect them from the manipulations of foreigners, financiers, and plutocrats.[45]

At first, Valois's monetary campaigns met with little sympathy. His claim that the franc had lost two-thirds of its prewar value was considered by many to be disloyal—financial defeatism. In some circles, especially those that had lost heavily in the crisis following the deflation of late 1920, inflation was considered good for business. An attempt to convince the leaders of the Maison du livre was met with shocked incomprehension. Valois was beginning to wonder whether he was a lone prophet or simply wrong when an athletic young man, a war hero like himself, came into his office to tell him that his monetary campaigns were fascinating. This man, Jacques Arthuys, was to be his closest collaborator for the next eight, very stormy years. Arthuys was born in Belfort in 1894. An officer's son, he had been educated in Catholic secondary schools and received his law degree at Nancy in 1913. His war record was brilliant: twice wounded, commissioned in 1915, lieutenant in 1916. Transferred to the air force, he commanded fighter and bomber squadrons in France and Italy. He earned four citations and the Legion of Honor. In 1920 Arthuys resigned from the military to found a building materials firm in Roubaix-Tourcoing and, apparently, to engage in public life.[46]

Valois published Arthuys's *Le Problème de la monnaie* in 1921. Though he differed with Valois on a few minor points, Arthuys agreed with him on the major ones. Both gave the same definition of money and attributed rising prices to fiduciary inflation. When explaining this rise, however, Arthuys invoked the supply and demand of money and held that although the primary cause of the decline of the exchange rate might be monetary inflation, the adverse balance of payments also played a role. All this gave his analysis greater sophistication than Valois's.

Nevertheless, their conclusions were identical. Arthuys condemned inflation as dishonest, unjust, bad for business, and dangerous for society. He was as keenly aware as Valois of the problems posed by a rapid deflation and in his conclusion was searching for some way of putting a stable currency into circulation alongside the legal one. Valois's *franc-or* was the ideal solution. Though not a royalist, Arthuys shared Valois's skepticism about the ability of the republican government, already in his view the author of so many calamities, to solve France's problems.[47]

Other allies were forthcoming, including Eugène Peschier, a consultant in foreign commerce, and Valois persuaded the Semaine du livre to demand the *franc-or* and call for a Semaine de la monnaie.[48] This project demanded the cooperation of business interests outside the book industry. Valois made these contacts, very largely thanks to Eugène Mathon, one of France's more powerful economic magnates. Born in Roubaix in 1860 into a commercial family, Mathon had founded his own textile firm by 1880. Even before the war, he organized a number of economic groups for the textile industry and the Roubaix-Tourcoing area. During the war, Mathon stayed in occupied Roubaix, where he spied for the allies and recorded claims against the Germans. After the war, his importance increased with the foundation in 1920 of the Consortium de l'industrie textile de Roubaix-Tourcoing, and, in 1922, of the Comité central de la laine, including over six hundred woolen manufacturers and merchants. Like Valois, Mathon saw the corporation as a coordinating and modernizing force. A standardized salary policy, for example, was designed both to protect the workers and force out inefficient producers. Mathon ran his enterprises in the authoritarian Catholic paternalistic traditions of the department of the Nord. La Tour du Pin and the conservative social theorist Frédéric Le Play were his masters in social theory, and he was a resolute opponent of the young Catholic labor movement. His lifelong concern with social and economic organization was as much the result of his sense of Christian duty as the defense of his interests or the fear of communism.[49]

Shortly after the armistice, Mathon met Valois and was impressed by the young man and his syndico-corporatist projects. Though he may have sincerely accepted Valois's concept of organized workers putting pressure on their employers, Mathon, with his aristocratic temperament and suspicions of unionism, obviously never meant to question the absolute right of patronal authority. Mathon threw his support to the recently founded periodical the *Journée industrielle* on condition that it promoted *L'Economie nouvelle*, and he helped circulate Valois's book among his colleagues in the Nord. Mathon saw himself as Valois's daring, production-oriented but nationally minded, industrialist, and for some time Valois did too. Mathon had a particular interest in a stable system of payment; inflation drove up the prices of his imported raw materials. Further, many Nord industrialists employed large numbers of Belgian workers, often paid in combinations of Belgian and French francs. Unstable currencies only increased their problems.[50]

Mathon was as eager to organize as Valois, and he had more connections. In February 1921, at a meeting of the Association nationale d'expansion économique, Mathon, its vice president, proposed a Semaine du commerce extérieur, which was set for June 1921. Most major economic organizations (excluding workers) participated. The government was represented by the minister of commerce, and by Alexandre Millerand, president of the Republic, who gave a talk lauding the Semaines. After such a success, a Semaine de la monnaie became possible, and in late 1921, an organizing committee was formed comprising Valois, Mathon, Arthuys, Peschier, Coquelle, Lucien Romier (editor-in-chief of the *Journée industrielle*), and Georges Bonnet of the Conseil d'état. Bonnet had attracted Valois's notice in 1920 when he called for a system of international payments that would preserve countries like France from losses caused by fluctuating exchange rates.[51]

Valois also won the collaboration of Frédéric François-Marsal, a former minister of finance and director of the Banque de l'Union parisienne. In the politics of French banking, the Banque de l'Union parisienne, with its right-wing and Catholic connections, frequently opposed the Banque de Paris et des Pays-Bas. As finance minister during most of 1920, François-Marsal had made himself unpopular in some circles by stabilizing advances from the Bank of France, which provoked a rapid deflation and an economic crisis. The Semaine de la monnaie allowed him to embarrass his pro-inflation opponents and marked the beginning of a period of cooperation with Valois.[52]

Finally the Bank of France, opposed to further advances, showed its support when Jules Décamps, director of the economic studies department, also joined the organizing committee. After the Semaine, in September, the governor of the Bank of France, Robineau, asked Max Leclerc, who sat on the Conseil d'escompte, how the bank could aid Valois's projects. Valois, who denied having profited personally from such offers, asked the bank to increase the Maison du livre's credit.[53]

With the support of the Bank of France came that of Raphaël-Georges Lévy, senator and member of the Institut de France, who accepted the presidency of the Semaine. The president of the Republic and most of the cabinet also gave their patronage. The Semaine met from June 6th to 11th, 1922, and represented most of France's largest economic groups. Topics included: the mechanism of inflation and its effects on all aspects of the economy, the alternative policies of stabilization—a return to the gold standard or deflation versus conversion to a different parity or devaluation (Arthuys defending the latter), technical palliatives (Valois and the royalist lawyer Marie de Roux defending the *franc-or*), and a criticism of the administration of industries by the state.

François-Marsal summed up the Semaine when he stigmatized fiduciary inflation as the modern way of debasing the coinage. Though some proponents of inflation were present, none dared defend it. The organizations present voted unanimously to oppose any recourse to inflation by the government. Other resolutions asked the state to reduce the fiduciary circulation, give up its industrial monopolies, reduce expenses, and make Germany pay. In addition it was recommended that accounting and contracts in *francs-or* be admitted.[54]

The Semaine de la monnaie was a great personal success for Valois. Though he was only *rapporteur général adjoint*, the theses he had argued for two years were publicly consecrated. It was he who had launched the movement for the Semaines and whose contacts permitted the union of producers' organizations with financial technicians that gave the Semaine its force. It must have been quite an experience for this young man, without advanced education, family fortune, or connections, to take his place as a monetary expert among high-ranking civil servants, ministers, and members of the Institute.

THE ETATS-GENERAUX CAMPAIGN
AND THE MONETARY CRISIS

Such collaboration made it clear that Valois could have a brilliant future if he left politics aside. His projects, however, always had strong political implications. After the war Valois entered the *comités directeurs* of the Action française, though this merely convinced him that no one was doing anything other than getting out a newspaper and spreading a doctrine. But the newspaper was now open to him and he was editor of the Sunday *Action française économique et sociale*.[55]

Valois was convinced that the parliamentary republic was headed for disaster and that the Action française had nothing planned to meet this contingency. In December 1921 he won Maurras's approval for a national campaign. It is unlikely that Maurras took any of Valois's activities too seriously; that the Republic might be overthrown or the monarchy reinstated by an assembly of producers never seemed very likely. But Valois's projects attracted people, and especially money, to the Ligue, giving the royalists entrée into that branch of the French elite where their influence was weakest, big business. Valois considered economic organization the best way to oppose the plutocrats and to wrest the state from their hands. He was now convinced that such organization, on a national scale, was possible. What for Maurras was an interesting sideshow, for Valois was an attempt to seize power.[56]

Valois's project was to call for a new Etats-Généraux. The national representation of economic groups was not a novelty. He had originally wanted to organize something similar through the CIPF. Now he sought to include all the groups from the Semaines. The movement for the Etats-Généraux was launched at a giant meeting at the Salle Wagram in Paris on December 18, 1922. The Comité d'action consisted of Mathon, Max Leclerc, Bernard de Vesins, Paul Robain, Ambroise Rendu, Coquelle, Martin-Mamy, Etienne Bernard-Précy, Auguste Cazeneuve, and Valois.[57]

Robain and de Vesins were leading royalists. Ambroise Rendu, also a royalist, was a deputy from the Haute-Garonne. Like Mathon, Martin-Mamy spent the war in the occupied Nord. From 1923, he served as Mathon's spokesman on the *Télégramme du Nord*, and worked with several of Mathon's corporatist enterprises. Another Mathon client, Bernard-Précy was more talented and more ambitious. Before the war, he had founded the *Journée industrielle*, which, thanks to Mathon's support and the collaboration of Romier made itself a reputation in industrial circles. Auguste Cazeneuve had several points in his favor: he was Arthuys's father-in-law, a personal friend of Valois's, and on the board of the *Journée*. From a manufacturing family, Cazeneuve had founded a machine-tool company and after the war created the Fédération des Syndicats de la construction mécanique, électrique et métallique, uniting forty-four organizations. Finally, Georges Coquelle, who was on the committee when it was founded, did not stay long. Apparently restive under Valois's control, Coquelle sought to build an independent position at the Action française. He was replaced on the committee by Arthuys and forced out of the movement. This would be Valois's last victory within the Action française.[58]

From April 1923 on, the committee had its own organ, the *Cahiers des Etats-Généraux*, which appeared monthly through the beginning of 1925. Theoretically, the *Cahiers* was an independent publication under the patronage, but not engaging the responsibility, of the committee. In fact, the *Cahiers* was a propaganda mouthpiece, its administration in Valois's and Arthuys's hands. The *Cahiers*, addressed to the "elite," had a limited circulation. The first-year goal of 2,000 subscriptions was probably never attained,[59] and the main financial burden was borne by Mathon and his economic groups. From this new platform, Valois could speak not only in greater independence of the royalists but also in the hope of reaching a different audience.

The Comité styled itself a group of Frenchmen whose sole point of agreement was the desire to call the Etats-Généraux. In fact, this implied a great deal else. Though the members of the committee disavowed the word, their major premise was antiparliamentarianism. France's institutions were to blame for her financial crisis. The fundamental vice of the parliament was that it combined sovereignty and representation. As representatives, the deputies sought the greatest advantages for their electors and opposed new taxes. But, since they were sovereign, they could impose the contradictory wishes of their voters. Hence, the tendency to vote expenses without revenues. This problem would be solved by organizing the representation of interests outside the state rather than within it. In Maurrasian terms, the state should be sovereign and independent of the representative organization. The Etats-Généraux would be this independent representative body, without formal constitutional powers, but with tremendous moral authority. Republicans and royalists differed, of course, about the best way to organize the sovereign, but they could agree about the representation of interests before that sovereign.[60]

Like the old Etats-Généraux (this was historically questionable), the new one would reflect interests, not electors or currents of opinion. It would represent not only economic organizations of the type Valois was building but also the regions, which were ignored by the overly centralized state. Finally, the moral and intellectual interests of France, religion, family, and the sciences, would have their voice. This was not to be an economic parliament like those proposed by Henry de Jouvenel or Anatole de Monzie. The constituent groups would be represented by their presidents or delegates elected long before. Valois even claimed that the movement was neither antiparliamentary nor antirepublican, but above and outside partisan politics. It was obvious, however, that the Etats would diminish the power of the parliament. The initial program of the committee asked that, to spare the French further divisions, the 1924 elections be postponed, and the current parliament maintained in office indefinitely.[61] This would not only cheat the left of its hoped-for electoral victory but also reduce the legitimacy of the legislature.

Neither Valois nor Arthuys expected their movement to result in a system of checks and balances. For them, the ship of state was headed for disaster; and their argument was reasonable. The French state was spending over forty billion francs a year (the most conservative figure) and taking in about twenty. The rest was covered by borrowing. Not only was the long-term debt so big that its service threatened to devour the state's income, but the short-term debt was so large that if, as the result of a crisis of confidence, the treasury notes were not almost completely renewed, the treasury would be forced to suspend payment. Reparations would not cover this debt, even if they were paid, which neither Valois nor Arthuys expected. They recognized that large-scale cash payments depended on German prosperity and exports. Payments in kind had been blocked by businessmen who wanted to preserve the profits of reconstruction for themselves. Arthuys felt that the only way to make the Germans pay would have been to seize the maximum material and negotiable securities after the armistice. This sum, though small, was preferable to a huge debt that, Ruhr or no Ruhr, would probably never be paid. Valois and Arthuys did have a solution but neither expected it to be adopted freely by any republican government: a drastic reduction in expenditures through the sale of all state monopolies, the elimination of all subsidies, the firing of huge numbers of civil servants, and a lowering of living standards. Such a program was political suicide. As for a capital levy, Arthuys considered it a spoliation and impossible to realize in practice.[62]

This left the alternatives of inflation, repudiation or bankruptcy, a drastic reorganization, or a combination of all three. The Etats-Généraux should block any recourse to inflation or make it the signal for revolt. Bankruptcy, unless very carefully organized, would destroy the Republic. The Etats-Généraux could then step into the void, and the royalists would have their chance to impose the monarchy. Alternately, a crisis might come from a conflict between parliament and the Etats-Généraux. Valois certainly did not believe the argument he used when he suggested that conflict between the two was impossible since each represented the nation. In fact, he assumed that the Etats-Généraux would give a more honest representation than the parliament, where "cheating" took place. If, by some miracle, the Republic should survive and put its house in order, Valois would at least have his economic reorganization and the defeat of the plutocrats. Thus, the movement for the Etats-Généraux really was what Valois later claimed it to be: a conspiracy against the security of the state.[63]

The campaign got off to a good start. A second meeting held on March 2 brought a crowd estimated by the sponsors at 2,000. Local committees were formed in Bordeaux and in Tarbes in January, at Rennes and Nantes in April, and in Alsace and Algeria in May.[64] In May, François-Marsal's Etats-Généraux des familles de France was given favorable coverage in the *Cahiers*.[65] The 1923 campaign culminated in a Paris meeting on October 18. Six thousand invitations were sent to representatives of professional and local groups. Of the 646 who attended, 78 represented agriculture, 290 the liberal professions, and 277 industry and commerce; half were from Paris, half from the provinces. All the regions of France were present, though the Nord and the Ile de France had by far the largest groups. At the meeting a unanimous show of hands moved a text approving the government's actions but calling for the organic representation of interests in line with the committee's program.[66]

The organizers considered this a success and the campaign seemed to have built a great deal of momentum. In fact, the October 18th meeting was the movement's high-water mark. Already in 1923, Valois had had to overcome a number of problems. The first was the assassination of Marius Plateau in January 1923. Plateau was the secretary of the Ligue, and the Action française had threatened that the death of any of its leaders would provoke reprisals. When no revenge was taken (the camelots did wreck the offices of a hostile newspaper, but to Valois this was insufficient), Valois concluded that the royalists had lost credibility. More serious, Plateau had been in charge of the camelots du roi, who acted as the Action française's tactical arm. He had been a friend of Valois's and had taken an interest in his projects. Plateau's functions were taken over by Valois's greatest enemy within the Ligue, Maurice Pujo.

The two men had taken a dislike to each other from the time Valois joined the Action française. Pujo's resentment increased as Valois moved up in the Ligue. Valois returned from the war covered with honors; Pujo earned neither promotions nor decorations. Pujo's jealousy only increased as Valois, because of his industrial and monetary campaigns, came to be considered one of the four aces of the Action française, along with Maurras, Daudet, and Jacques Bainville. Pujo entrusted the principal organizational tasks, and in particular the camelots, to Pierre Lecoeur, who could then begin his revenge on his former boss. From 1923 dates the campaign within the Action française against Valois.[67]

The next setback came from outside. In early 1922, Valois had created a Comité de liaison des grandes associations representing not only his CIPF but also groups like the CGP and the Comité républicain du commerce et de l'industrie, formerly known as the Comité Mascuraud. Valois used the committee as a lobby on matters on which most businessmen were in agreement, like nonrecognition of the Soviet Union. It was another matter when he tried to get it to back the *franc-or*. By spring 1923, the republicans on the committee had become anxious about Valois's campaigns. Chaumet, president of the Comité républicain, asked the members to declare their allegiance to the constitution. Valois shelved the measure, and when Chaumet resigned in protest, the Comité de liaison was dissolved. Valois took the occasion of the break and of the departure of Georges Coquelle to reorganize the CIPF and change its name to the Union des corporations françaises. The new organization eliminated all elections; section heads were appointed by Valois. As important as the condemnation of the democratic principle was the tightening of Valois's control.[68]

The Etats-Généraux project also received a barrage of criticism from left and center. The most penetrating of Valois's critics was Francis Delaisi, largely because he shared many of Valois's premises. Like Valois, Delaisi was convinced that the Republic was manipulated by financiers and that the only solution lay in widespread syndical organization. But Delaisi was a technical advisor to the CGT and his alliances were with the parliamentary left.[69]

The Semaines continued, with Valois treating them as preparatory meetings for the Etats-Généraux. A Semaine des PTT (postal, telegraph, and telephone services) was called for the beginning of May. Paul Laffont, under secretary of state for the PTT, agreed to attend. A week before Valois's Semaine was to begin, however, a competing Semaine républicaine des PTT was organized by Delaisi and Painlevé. Chaumet's Comité républicain joined Delaisi's Semaine, and Laffont, not wishing to take sides, attended both.

Each side accused the other of playing politics. Painlevé and Delaisi claimed that the Etats-Généraux movement was a reactionary plot. Valois accused Painlevé of organizing an electoral meeting. Delaisi argued that Valois's large associations represented only the leaders of French industry and not the average Frenchmen who made up the bulk of the users of the PTT. Delaisi, for example, included groups like the Fédération nationale des coopératives, the Fédération nationale de la mutualité et la coopération agricole, the Fédération des commerçants et industriels moyens, and the Fédération des maires de France. More significant, Delaisi, unlike Valois, included representatives of the postal workers. Valois countered that the Semaine represented the public's needs; the postal workers would treat with the state afterward. Both sides claimed complete success. Valois took the counterfeiting of the Semaine idea as a tribute. In fact, Delaisi and Painlevé not only copied titles like Semaine and Cahiers de doléances but made similar claims for the near-magical efficacy of the Semaine technique and the importance of the postwar movement for economic organization.[70] The republicans had made a point: Valois's open and loyal representation of interests depended on which interests were represented.

The Etats-Généraux movement came apart in 1924. Other events of that same year, however, convinced Valois that the possibilities for action were even greater. The background was France's continuing financial and monetary crisis. At the Semaine de la monnaie in June 1922, Valois and the Bank of France had helped François-Marsal condemn inflation. During the rest of 1922, Valois opposed any further inflation caused by increased advances from the bank, following his earlier conclusion that the price of the dollar followed the level of advances. By the end of 1922, however, he considered the problem of advances from a new point of view. Since the franc was a paper currency and not exchangeable for gold, its value was not based solely on the amount of gold or merchandise covering the francs in circulation but also on the probability that the state would repay the bank. Continued repayment was necessary to maintain the state's credit. In other words, the constant psychological pressures for a lowering of the exchange rate (which Valois now concluded could provoke inflation) necessitated gradual deflation through the reduction of the level of advances. Valois thus considered the decision taken in the end of 1922 to only repay one billion, instead of the two originally set by François-Marsal, a dangerous inflationary move. In the same line, suggestions in parliament not to pursue repayment also threatened the franc.[71]

The credit of the state was also based on its chances of recovering anything from its principal debtor, Germany. Hence the price of the franc was closely related to the invasion of the Ruhr in January 1923. This firm act did temporarily raise the franc. Yet the general trend was downward throughout 1923 despite the stability of the level of advances. Valois now blamed international finance, especially the determination of political and financial forces in England to force an evacuation of the Ruhr. A French retreat would have the political advantage for the British of reducing

French influence in Europe, and the financial advantage for the speculators of forcing further inflation. A mere announcement by the British government that it did not expect the Ruhr venture to succeed, or that it did not consider French finances sound, lowered the franc. The franc was under attack by a coalition of British and German interests, international finance, and the French left. The renewed activity of the French left, its objections to the Ruhr venture, made it an agent, conscious or not, of the anti-franc campaign. The risk of a Radical-Socialist government, which would increase expenses and reduce taxes, further undermined the state's credit.[72]

Valois did not absolve the government of responsibility. The franc could be defended by resolute action in the Ruhr and unwavering repayment, combined with reduction of expenses and the adoption of gold prices for imports and exports. In addition, Valois called for state action (including executions) against Frenchmen and resident foreigners active in the anti-Ruhr, inflationary campaign. During the franc crisis of late 1923, Valois blamed the minister of finance, Charles de Lasteyrie, who had provoked the current wave of speculation by again failing to continue repayment and, even worse, by playing with the idea of using the amortizement funds for the treasury. De Lasteyrie was driven to this by the deputies who, fearing for their reelection, voted expenses without taxes. The crisis was thus a *crise de régime*. By the end of January, Valois moved his attacks upward to Poincaré, accusing him and de Lasteyrie of keeping the truth, that speculation was not the cause of the fall of the franc, from the public, and of failing to take the necessary steps to keep France from sliding down the slippery path of Germany and Austria.[73]

Attacking Poincaré was unusual for the royalists. On the nationalist right, Poincaré had long been a symbol of patriotism and probity, and this included the Action française. Poincaré's reaction was to grant Valois the personal interview he had requested for some time. Valois proposed that the statesman adopt his dictatorial program, assuring him France would support him. Not surprisingly, Poincaré declined. Considering a crisis imminent, Valois also went to see General Charles Mangin, well known for his right-wing sympathies. Asked whether he would accept executive power if offered by a national assembly, the general said yes, an answer that committed him to little.[74]

Valois's interest was not only in potential dictators but in actual ones as well. In early January he spent a week in Rome with de Vesins, Mathon, and Bernard-Précy. In Paris Valois had met a young fascist, Curzio Suckert, who now introduced him to some of the notables of the new regime.

Valois met Francesco Coppola and Enrico Corradini and found their aggressive Italian nationalism hard to take. He was also received by the Duce himself. Valois readily admitted being conquered by Mussolini's immense charm and prestige. In Italy, Valois found a regime and an ideology in many ways congenial to him. In addition, in January 1924, the Fascist regime was still in its infancy, and it was hard to see which of its promises would not be kept. In Valois's case, this left room for later disappointments. The most attractive thing about Fascism for Valois was its success. Here was a movement that had accomplished the great national antiliberal revolution that the Action française only talked about.[75]

Returning from Italy, Valois threw himself into a violent polemic with de Lasteyrie. From the end of January on, the government was engaged in the time-consuming process of pushing through new tax projects designed to restore confidence in the franc, then at a record low. In February, de Lasteyrie provoked Valois's anger by introducing a bill to outlaw the *franc-or* in any of its forms. For Valois, this was tyranny, since it prohibited honesty in dealings between Frenchmen. He concluded that the government was planning a new inflation and wished to deprive the public of its only means of defense. In fact, despite Valois's assertions to the contrary, there was a risk that a move toward gold reckoning would lead to a further decline in the franc. This law may also have been a means of dampening Valois's activities, which might have looked threatening during this period of crisis. But most important, the generalization of gold reckoning would make it politically impossible for the government to use inflation to reduce the internal debt.[76]

Valois responded with an article ending: "Lasteyrie Démission" and a vigorous and somewhat demagogic campaign. He sought to gather popular support by explaining that during inflation everyone lost except financiers and bankers. The bankers gained because they could buy foreign currencies to prevent the real value of their holdings from declining, while depositors, repaid in nominal value, lost money. The other stratagem Valois imputed to the bankers was more sophisticated. During a period of inflation, businessmen, who found the costs of replacement higher than their returns, were perpetually in need of advances of circulating capital. To obtain these, the businessman started by discounting his merchandise and finished by giving the banker a share in his capital. Eventually the bank controlled the enterprise.[77]

Valois considered a political crisis imminent and tried to organize a coalition around the Etats-Généraux movement. At another large meeting on February 21 in Paris, over eight hundred representatives heard urgent warnings by Valois, Arthuys, Mathon, and Leclerc. One had to go beyond the organization of interests to the reorganization of the state itself. The final resolution called for the prorogation of parliament, an independent government with full powers, and the permanent separation of the credit of the franc from that of the state through an amortizement fund supported by the receipts of a privatized government monopoly. That same day, Valois addressed a group of deputies gathered by Ambroise Rendu. Events seemed to be moving his way. Contrary to Valois's expectations, Poincaré and de Lasteyrie were able, by March, through decree laws, new taxes, a loan from American bankers, and maneuvering on the international exchanges, to restore much of the recently lost value of the franc. Despite Valois's claim to have saved the franc, none of his suggestions were adopted, and the main effect of his campaigns seems to have been that when the government was overturned in the Chamber under ambiguous circumstances on March 26, Poincaré replaced de Lasteyrie with Valois's ally François-Marsal and the prohibition of the *franc-or* was dropped.[78]

Early 1924 also saw a vigorous aggression from Bernard-Précy, who began by trying to weaken Valois's influence within the Etats-Généraux committee, suggesting that Valois was a visionary, incompetent, or socially dangerous. By the end of February, Bernard-Précy resigned, and on the 23d, his *Journée industrielle* published an editorial roundly attacking the *franc-or*, signed by Romier. Later articles treated Valois insultingly. At the same time, rumors were spread, chiefly that as a young man Valois had served in the tsarist political police. Valois claimed to be the target of a coordinated campaign by Pujo and Lecoeur within the Action française, Bernard-Précy, and the Sûreté générale: the whole directed by those financial interests threatened by his campaigns. Bernard-Précy's ambition could explain his behavior, since Valois stood in his way in the fight to represent the interests coalesced around Mathon. Pujo and Lecoeur had ample motivation and surely spread any nasty rumors that came their way. Valois claimed the police had fabricated his "Russian dossier," that they sent menacing letters, and that they had him followed. The letters were probably a bluff organized by Bernard-Précy. Valois's claims to have been followed deserve more serious consideration, since he demonstrated later that he was quite capable of identifying police agents tailing him. Political involvement in such smear campaigns was not outside the mores of the Third Republic. Valois won the war of blackmail. He discovered that Bernard-Précy had been convicted during the war of having stolen money orders destined for soldiers in the trenches. Threatened with publication of this, Bernard-Précy was forced to resign from the *Journée* and retire from public life. The anti-Valois campaign ceased abruptly.[79]

Despite this victory, Valois's Etats-Généraux movement was dead. The government was not going to call a meeting of the Estates, and neither were they going to create themselves. When, in October, the government founded a Conseil économique national, Valois proclaimed this the "first convocation of the Etats-Généraux by the French government," and asserted his paternity.[80] In fact, the advisory body, selected by the Cartel des gauches government, was far from his original plans. The most obvious reason for Valois's failure was that France experienced neither bankruptcy, catastrophic inflation, nor revolution. The Etats-Généraux movement was an attempt to seize power backed by big business. As a group, French businessmen declined to move. The later French fascist Henry Coston has stressed the importance of the Comité des forges in explaining the failure of French industrialists to rally to Valois. Valois's relations with this powerful group were poor, and he regularly found himself in polemics with Robert Pinot, vice president of the Comité. Valois's position on the Comité des forges was carefully nuanced. Though he needed its support, it was opposed to his projects, and he considered it typical of the type of industrial barony he wished to tame. Nevertheless, it would be a mistake to overstress its importance. Jean-Noël Jeanneney has shown that the iron men were considerably less united than they seemed to their critics. Coston's argument seems based on no more than Valois's testimony.[81] The Comité des forges was typical of many economic groups, like the Comité republicain du commerce et de l'industrie, whose accommodation with the regime was sufficiently good that they had no reason to seek its replacement, particularly since that regime was fully prepared to defend itself.

OLD ACCOMPLISHMENTS AND NEW POSSIBILITIES

Valois's efforts had not been wasted. He had built organizations whose cadres would prove useful in the future. In February 1924, he founded the Ligue du franc-or, largely grouping those already on board, chiefly members of the Action française.[82] More important was the Union des corporations françaises. As director, Valois had replaced Coquelle with a worker, Pierre Dumas. Like Valois, Dumas was a former anarchist and revolutionary syndicalist, but his syndical experience was greater: assistant secretary at the CGT and for ten years secretary-general of the Fédération nationale des travailleurs de l'habillement. Dumas had been converted to nationalism by the war and to the Action française by Valois.

Along with Rémi Wasier, a former railroad worker, he was part of that small group inside the Action française whose allegiance was more to Valois than to the Ligue.[83]

By 1924, federations had been organized in a wide variety of industries. In March, a placement office was set up as bait for workers. Among the oldest groups was the Corporation de la mécanique et de l'électricité, founded in 1920 and with several constituent *syndicats* of workers and engineers. The Fédération des transports, founded in 1920, lost many of its adherents in 1922. Revived in May 1924 it began a newspaper, *Le Rail,* which claimed a hundred subscribers. Valois's men also created groups in the insurance industry and banking, jewelry, construction, music, and commerce. Most of these corporations were small. Among the larger were the pharmacists, with about a hundred members, and the Fédération du commerce, with 207.[84]

Valois's biggest problem was the recruitment of workers. He had started on the wrong foot by helping to break a strike in the publishing industry in 1919. Nevertheless, he was able to assure workers' representation at the Semaine du livre. At the later Semaines, however, he ran into the resolute opposition of the industrial representatives. With even Mathon against him, he was forced to give way. Besides, his decision to exclude both revolutionary and yellow unions restricted his choice.[85]

Constantly, in the *Cahiers des Etats-Généraux,* Valois had called for the postponement of the elections. They were held, nevertheless, in May 1924. The Action française, delighted with the reputation Daudet had made for himself in the Chamber, fielded candidates in Paris and its suburbs. Valois bitterly opposed participation in the elections. Not only was antiparliamentarianism one of his firmest principles but he considered that the Action française, by coveting seats, seemed like just one more party vying for its slice of the governmental pie. He also found running for office embarrassing as a member of the Comité national pour la convocation des Etats-Généraux. Nevertheless, he agreed to head the royalist list in the popular fourth district of the Seine. After what he described as a nationalist, veteran-oriented campaign, Valois received 13,270 votes, third on his list, but 4,000 short of election. The results were a disaster for the Action française, all of whose candidates were defeated. Even Daudet was not returned.[86]

The royalists' defeat was part of a general victory of the left that brought the Cartel des gauches to power. Valois rejected the idea that the mass of Frenchmen wanted a government of Radicals or Socialists. They had chosen the least effort and, to spare themselves heavy taxation, sought a strong Radical opposition. Miscalculation had brought the left to power.[87] For over a year, Valois had been saying that a Radical-Socialist government would bring about a monetary crisis, because of the social welfare measures it would propose, and an immediate loss of confidence. Moreover, he and Arthuys knew, as most of the public did not, that a large packet of bonds would be falling due in 1924 and 1925, fruits of the borrowing of Bloc national governments, which the Cartel would have to pay.[88] The financial and monetary crisis Valois and Arthuys had announced since 1921 seemed unavoidable. Valois fully intended to take advantage of it. He would apply the lessons of the Italian experience and of his own campaigns to build a genuine mass movement, one that would succeed where the Action française had failed.

FOUR

The Faisceau, I

The Period of Transition

In May 1924, Valois, now in his late forties, became the leader of his own movement. The group he founded became France's first fascist organization, the Faisceau, in the process breaking with the Action française. The circumstances surrounding this separation and the ill feeling they created dominated the Faisceau's history.[1] The movement, however, preceded the organization. Two preparatory periods ran from May 1924 to February 1925 and from February to November 1925. The Faisceau, fully launched by the end of 1925, reached its height in June of 1926 during the combined monetary and parliamentary crisis. After the formation of the Poincaré government in July 1926, the Faisceau declined; it died in 1927 and was buried in 1928.

IDEOLOGICAL FOUNDATIONS

Formulating a doctrine for the new movement was a principal activity for Valois during 1924 and 1925. Since he now aimed openly at the conquest of the state and sought a coalition beyond the frontiers of royalism, Valois left his role of economic expert to develop a set of independent political doctrines. These doctrines were given their principal expression in *La Révolution nationale* (The National Revolution) and *La Politique de la victoire* (The Politics of Victory), published in 1924 and 1925, respectively, along with Jacques Arthuys's *Les Combattants* (1925).

Valois built his doctrine around two interrelated ideas: a historical geopolitical interpretation and a theory of human society. Valois had long considered war inevitable. Now he gave it a geographic focus. Those who lived in the favored climate of the Mediterranean had constantly to defend themselves against invasion from the north, whose peoples preferred its warmth and comfort to the cold of their forests and steppes. The Mediterranean was the sacred lake of civilization. Its peoples, rooted in the soil, lived under threat of invasions from the nomadic pillaging barbarians of the north. What was true in the fifth century was true in the twentieth, and would remain so as long as oranges did not grow in Pomerania. Valois was reasonably vague about the identity of the barbarians. They could be Germans or Slavs poorly rooted in the soil, or those Asians held in check by the tsarist or British empires. Invasions could be the descent of Bolshevized Central Asian hordes or the Franco-Prussian war. Civilization thus depended on a military state; its frontiers were the work of the warrior, not the producer.[2] This conclusion was related to the second of Valois's foci, the role of the bourgeoisie in the nation.

Valois evoked the work of the Sorelian René Johannet, *L'Eloge du bourgeois,* rejecting its conclusion that the bourgeoisie should control the state. The nature, even the virtues, of the bourgeois rendered them unfit for rule, Valois argued. They are the administrators of the national wealth, their specific virtues being honesty, prudence, and thrift. Honor for the bourgeois means the payment of debts and fidelity to contracts; his view of the world is commercial and juridical. By contrast, the type Valois called the *combattant,* or warrior, understood the importance of a nation's immaterial capital, its reservoirs of morality and courage.[3]

As long as the bourgeois stayed in his proper role, all went well, as during the Ancien régime when Colbert was the model of the bourgeois in the service of state and nation under the *combattant* Louis XIV. When the bourgeoisie tried to rule, as in nineteenth-century France, problems began. If barbarians attacked, the bourgeois reaction was to count the troops on each side, and, if the result looked doubtful, try to buy off the enemy. In contemporary terms, that meant making trade agreements with the Soviet Union in hopes it would stop its subversive propaganda. The *combattant* knows that the number of troops can be multiplied by the immaterial forces of courage and will; while the bourgeois will sell the national patrimony in a fruitless attempt to buy off the barbarian.[4]

For the bourgeois, the state was a commercial enterprise, a giant workshop. Their economists invoked the principle of comparative advantage, wanting nations to specialize in particular branches of production, a dangerous doctrine, since trade disturbances could force nations to go to war to survive. The *combattant*, however, knew that a state was first of all the organ by which a group of families were assured of their continued existence on a given territory. Hence, self-sufficiency, especially in foodstuffs, should be the first goal of national production. Bourgeois rule had equally noxious social effects, Valois argued. Focusing on material benefits created a social system that damaged the working-class family. Often the bourgeois were misled by their own virtues, seeking, for example, to minimize workers' salaries, since they would make better use of the money. The mark of bourgeois rule in the state was parliamentarianism, the extension of the old town councils to the nation. Since the bourgeois had no leisure to run the state, they delegated their power to politicians. Too often, this became corruption when the bourgeois resorted to his natural instinct to buy power, to control with money.[5]

By 1919, however, many bourgeois realized that something was awry. But in the postwar movements for economic organization, they limited themselves to restoring their former corporative organizations. Lacking a sense of the state, they failed to tackle the parliament. Similarly, despite repeated demonstrations that monetary instability robbed them, French businessmen refused the *franc-or*, instinctively understanding that currency was the business of the sovereign, of the *combattant*, and shied away from even a fictional money of account.[6] Thus Valois explained his own failure.

Behind the appearance of bourgeois rule was the reality of plutocratic control. This conclusion was not new. What was new was that Valois considered the Bloc national as much affected as the Cartel des gauches, and that he was willing to name names. The Bloc national was run by the Comité Billiet, dominated by Robert Pinot of the Comité des forges, while the Cartel was manipulated by Horace Finaly of the Banque de Paris et des Pays-Bas.[7]

Finaly, however, received much more attention. In August 1924, Valois began a personal campaign against the director of the Banque de Paris, continued with a tenacity approaching monomania until the latter's fall from power in 1937. To Valois, Finaly was the typical representative of international finance, and the one with the greatest power over the French state. Finaly, a naturalized Hungarian Jew, was the real dictator at the Banque de Paris et des Pays-Bas, one of France's most important commercial banks. According to Valois, he used the bank to try to control French press and publishing through a paper trust. Consistently directing the bank against France, Finaly favored the interests of American capitalism and Standard Oil.[8]

More dangerous for Valois was the fact that Horace Finaly combined economic with political power. He was the organizer and financial backer of the Cartel des gauches, the power behind the scenes in the Herriot government and the ministry of finance. Since 1919, Finaly had promoted inflation and organized a wall of silence around Valois's campaigns. He pushed Lasteyrie first toward inflation and then into an attack on the *franc-or*, only to drop the hapless finance minister and throw his support to the Cartel. Under the Cartel governments, Finaly was preparing further inflation and, to this end, trying to take over the Bank of France. Finaly used inflation to raid French savings and swallow up French industries in accordance with the two techniques Valois had explained before. Speculation on the exchanges was that much more lucrative for a banker who knew when unusual demands on the treasury would provide more inflation. The other technique was the takeover of enterprises through successive participations in their capital. Valois accused Finaly of promoting a catastrophic inflation to seize control of French industry.[9]

Valois saw Finaly as one of the principal personalities uniting international finance with the revolution and the author of all the pro-Soviet campaigns in France, pushing Herriot into passivity before the internal communist menace. As usual, Valois was eager to show the mechanisms of this sinister cooperation. First, the financier could organize a strike against a competitor. Second, rapid fluctuations in the value of money created ideal conditions for social unrest, while the threat of revolution helped lower the value of the franc. Valois would not say which group was duping which. What mattered was their effective alliance under Finaly's direction.[10]

But why Horace Finaly? Why did Valois choose, and retain, this banker as the focus of his campaigns? Was it because the Hungarian Jew made an easy target? Was he the classic scapegoat? Although Finaly's origin was not an insignificant factor, the major causes lay elsewhere. First of all Valois had run across Finaly in his own fight with Hachette. In Valois's first article against Finaly, most of the accusations concerned the book and newspaper industries. Yet in later years Valois claimed that during the early campaigns around the Maison du livre, he had not been aware of Finaly's general importance, which he discovered subsequently, during his monetary campaigns.[11]

The most important reason was that if Valois unquestionably overshot the mark, he was just as unquestionably aiming in the right direction. In a series of special reports prepared for the cabinet of the minister of the interior, Horace Finaly is referred to as the "financial gray eminence" of the Cartel des gauches. Finaly and the Banque de Paris et des Pays-Bas acted as the financial wing of the Herriot government, he had an office at his disposal in the ministry of finances, and he came to Herriot's aid in personal financial matters as well. His leftist politics and financial power were well enough known to have inspired a character in Jean Giraudoux's 1926 novel *Bella*. Valois certainly knew much of this, especially the battle between Finaly and Joseph Caillaux. If Valois did not make the discovery himself he may have been led to it by François-Marsal who, both as director of the Banque de l'Union parisienne and as Millerand's ally, opposed Finaly.[12] Valois was not alone in concluding that the Cartel governments, despite their public protests, were inflating the currency as fast as they could. Keynes made a similar assumption, although he attached a different value judgment to it.[13]

Horace Finaly was a cultivated man with many contacts in literary and political circles. Born in Budapest in 1871, he came to Paris along with his parents in 1880 and was naturalized in 1890. He attended the Lycée Condorcet and became a close friend of Marcel Proust, with whom he kept up a correspondence. Along with Proust, Henri Barbusse, and Léon Blum (who dedicated some poems to him), Finaly contributed to a small literary journal, the *Banquet*. In later years, he discussed mathematics with Paul Painlevé. Following in his father's footsteps, Horace entered the Banque de Paris in 1900, rising to the position of *directeur général* in 1919. In his work with the bank, Finaly helped in the administration and reorganization of a large variety of enterprises. He was among those who facilitated the French establishment of Standard Oil and generally favored Franco-American industrial and financial collaboration. In 1920, Horace Finaly became an officer of the Légion d'honneur. He remained closely involved with French industrial and financial affairs until his resignation from the Banque de Paris in 1937.[14]

Like most people in and around the Action française, Valois overestimated the importance of his own activities, automatically magnifying the role of any opponent. Up to 1918, Valois had lived in the belief that a handful of international financiers operating behind the fictions of republican politics were the real masters of France. This judgment was widely shared on the left as well. These forces, however, were faceless abstractions. When, after the war, Valois discovered one of those who quietly held more power than most politicians, he concluded that this man, Finaly, exercised all the power he had long ago assigned to international finance.[15]

The rule of international finance had been threatened, Valois claimed, by a revolution that took place on August 2, 1914 when, in a wave of patriotic ardor, thousands of Frenchmen became *combattants*. Marked to the depths of his soul, the *combattant* had discovered true nobility, and he retained this special spirit long after the war. Those who had fought were "national" because, coming from all levels of society, they had been united in the fraternity of arms. These men had not fought for liberty or the rights of man but for the France of which they had a special vision. When the *combattant* in the trenches asked himself why he was fighting, he first thought of his family and his home, the two becoming generalized into a vision of the France he was defending, a concrete historical entity he came to love.[16]

With love of France went a new confidence. Every soldier went off to war, Valois asserted, asking himself whether France was finished as a great power, a personal question for each man who measured himself against his German equivalent. After the battle of the Marne, the doubt had passed and the *combattants* became the first of the generations of victory. Preceding them were the generations of defeat, without faith in the future; and this included many nationalists like Poincaré. They were old age and death; the generations of victory were youth and life—a renewal of elites like that of the French Revolution. The élan of the *combattants* had been broken, however, by the counterrevolution of 1919, which returned the old parliamentary groups to power.[17]

But the power of the old generations would not last. Two young movements, communism and fascism, both *combattant* reactions against the rule of money, were in a race for power. Their differences were geographic. Communism, having failed to reorganize the Russian economy, set out to pillage Europe, threatening to turn the hordes of Asia against Western civilization and plunge Europe into a new dark age. The French communist was not a pillaging nomad, but a brave man opposed to the injustices of the current economic system, or a veteran for whom the bourgeois represented an *embusqué*, someone who had gotten himself an exemption or a soft job in the rear. Fascism was the Latin, Mediterranean counterpart to communism; the fascist was the *combattant* of the south. The southern warrior, unlike the northerner, had to live on the land. He created the peace that sheltered civilization. The southern *combattants* were the successors to Rome and arose in all Latin countries.[18]

The form taken by this movement in France would be Valois's "national revolution"—against the generations of defeat, against the liberal state, and against plutocracy. Valois hoped to unite everyone whose interests or sentiments had been wounded by the dominance of the bourgeoisie and the plutocrats: the workers, the *combattants*, the new generations,

and all those who thought nationally. Valois went out of his way to indicate that Jews were welcome. Still thinking in ethnic terms, he hoped
that the Jews' "innate concern for justice" would lead them to his revolution instead of international finance. The national revolution would in-
stall the dictatorship of the *combattant*. *Combattants* had learned that effective action demanded a leader, a *chef*. Royalists and republicans could
create a temporary dictatorship and new economic structures, leaving constitutional problems for later. The new society would direct all classes toward greatness—that is, the determination to avoid least-effort solutions
in the national interest. Greatness for the *combattant* was risking his life
for his country. For the bourgeois, it meant placing morality ahead of personal gain, and for the worker, dedication to the highest standards of
workmanship outside any concern for remuneration.[19]

Valois did add one fresh element to his description. Coal had been the
principal energy source for the nineteenth century. A product appropriate
to an inhuman social system, it condemned miners to a miserable existence and polluted factories and cities. The energy of the twentieth century
would be hydroelectric power—fresh, clean, sparkling. The factories of the
future would be light and airy. For the first time, Valois envisaged technological progress as the basis for an improved social system. Nothing was
farther from the Maurrasian mental universe. This idea, which may have
been planted in Valois years earlier from Kropotkin, would not get its full
development for several years. Valois was still within the French right—
to some extent, within the reactionary right—and took care to devote a
section of *La Révolution nationale* to the praise of the royalist leader.[20]

There was, however, a change in tone. Valois became more demagogic,
using a more fascist vocabulary and imagery. He placed a tremendous emphasis on newness, youth, and force as against the rottenness and decrep-
itude of the old institutions, glorying in his self-appointed role as revolutionary, trying to give the impression of determination, of a readiness to
use force. For him at least, this language was new—a sign of the attraction
of Italian Fascism.[21]

THE FIRST PERIOD OF TRANSITION

These ideas were directed to two major groups: workers, especially communists, and veterans. Valois never used the accepted term for veterans,
anciens combattants, but rather *combattants*, to indicate that their action
would continue.[22] From May 1924 to February 1925, he made his initial
contact with both groups.

Within two weeks of the elections, Valois was explaining his plans at two dinners, the first with friends, the second with allies. The first meal took place on May 22 at the home of one of Valois's more recent conquests, Franz van den Broeck d'Obrenan. Two years Valois's senior, this wealthy heir had been born in France of naturalized Dutch parents. As a businessman in Morocco, he had worked briefly with General Louis Lyautey, the colonial administrator. Van den Broeck was a member of some of the most exclusive Parisian social circles. Formerly a member of the retinue of the duc d'Orléans, he stayed on the margin of the Action française and was a candidate for election on the same list as Valois in 1924. Though Van den Broeck never exercised a political role, he was always ready to make available his car or his house, and he became one of the principal financial backers of the Faisceau.[23]

The other meeting took place on the 29th with Lucien Moreau, Bernard de Vesins, and Charles Maurras. Valois presented a plan to unite all nationalist groups, republican, Bonapartist, or monarchist, the veterans, and a large share of workers, around the national revolution. The Action française would take advantage of the period of transition to engage in a huge propaganda effort, Valois offering to bring out a new edition of the *Enquête sur la monarchie* and print a propaganda brochure by Maurras. Valois believed that, in open competition with Bonapartists and republicans, the Action française would have a good chance of winning through the force of its doctrines. It would be up to the Pretender to play the providential savior. Valois, who was after all an Action française militant, would direct the operation, while Maurras was to be relegated to a sort of intellectual suzerainty—honored, but effectively divorced from control.[24]

Valois thought what he offered the royalists reasonable. The parliamentary Republic would be destroyed and the Ligue would have a fair chance to impose its solution. But this judgment was based on two assumptions: that the royalists themselves could never overthrow the Republic, and that no plans were on foot to find the necessary allies. Neither proposition was unreasonable, but how many radical movements would admit them? Nevertheless, Maurras accepted Valois's plans. He may have been legitimately interested in seeing what might come from Valois's efforts (the agreement was surely interpreted differently by the two parties). The Pretender, who had no special affection for the Action française, readily accepted. The mass of the Action française gave its support to the new policy, readily accepting Valois's scheme of a competition between communist and fascist currents, within the second of which the royalists would triumph.[25]

None of this involved organizational discontinuity. Those interested were asked to join the Ligue du franc-or and the Union des corporations françaises. Calls were still made for the Etats-Généraux and, in November 1924, a Semaine de la propriété commerciale was held. Valois still disposed of the *Cahiers des Etats-Généraux* and his column in the *Action française.*[26] Only gradually were new organizations created to house the new allies.

In charge of recruitment within the nationalist leagues was Hubert Bourgin. As with so many others, Bourgin was led to the nationalist right by his wartime experiences. These were not at the front but in party committee rooms. A graduate of the Ecole normale, *agrégé,* and *docteur ès lettres,* a professor at the Lycée Louis le Grand, and the author of numerous academic works, Bourgin had been a member of the reformist Proudhonian wing of the SFIO, where he collaborated with Lucien Herr and the then-socialist Charles Péguy. During the war, he adapted easily to righteous condemnation of German militarism and ardent patriotism. Bourgin served the Socialist minister Albert Thomas as liaison with the Socialist party and its parliamentary delegation. He was horrified by the defeatism and political maneuverings of the wartime SFIO, becoming increasingly nationalist and antiparliamentarian in reaction.[27]

In 1917, Bourgin helped found the Ligue civique, a patriotic nonpartisan organization designed to raise morale on the home front. In 1922, representing the Ligue on the Comité de liaison des grandes associations, he met Valois. His admiration for the younger man grew with acquaintance, and by 1924 he had joined the Etats-Généraux movement. Shortly after the war, Bourgin had tried, without success, to organize a national socialist party. Now, completely opposed to parliamentary rule, he eagerly joined Valois. In June 1924, Bourgin founded the *Chronique des ligues nationales,* a small publication distributed free to the leagues and over a thousand newspapers and designed to lead the leagues to unified action behind the national revolution. In the fall, Bourgin, who was also secretary-general of the Ligue des patriotes, organized a Conférence des ligues nationales for closer cooperation.[28]

On Armistice Day, November 11, 1924, Valois organized a giant rally for veterans in Paris under the auspices of the Etats-Généraux committee. On Valois's own admission, the response was less than overwhelming. The meeting did introduce Valois's ideas to a new public, among whom he found two important new friends. André d'Humières, a chevalier de la Légion d'honneur, had served, like Arthuys, in aviation. Before the war he had been a planter in the East Indies. D'Humières had little political experience but an aptitude for organization, which Valois appreciated.[29] More important was Serge André. Born in 1890, André was a graduate of the Ecole des hautes études commerciales de Paris. During the war, he had served as an officer in the cavalry and then in the air force, earning the Croix de guerre. Serge was a director of the family firm which specialized in the importation of motor oil, marketed in France under the brand name Spidoleine, and in May 1925 its capital totaled 15 million francs. Between 1919 and 1923, André was codirector of *L'Opinion*, a respected daily paper. Serge André placed his many contacts at Valois's disposal, patiently bearing the commercial problems his political engagement brought him. Unflinchingly loyal, he was, with Van den Broeck, one of those whose financial sacrifices made the movement possible.[30]

Aided by d'Humières and Arthuys, Valois spent the winter recruiting veterans. The originality of his themes spoke to a new public. Valois received letters reflecting a genuine excitement. Readers found that his antibourgeois heroism expressed feelings they had never been able to formulate. These were France's genuine fascists, who up till then had been without a voice. Later, they joined by the thousand, and Valois was borne up by the wave.[31] He was also helped by the red scare that gripped large sections of the French public after the Communist and Socialist demonstrations accompanying the November 1924 Panthéonization of Jaurès. In the winter and spring of 1924–25, the right-wing papers of France, including the *Action française*, terrified their readers with reports of imminent revolution. The red scare frightened Frenchmen into all the antiparliamentary leagues, while giving Valois's own movement a more anticommunist coloring. After having been sufficiently concerned to organize a potential military riposte, Valois decided, by mid 1925, that the red scare had been fabricated.[32]

The anticommunist panic hardly helped Valois's other project, the recruitment of communists and, if possible, an alliance with the Communist party. Taking advantage of a request from the local section of the Action française, Valois addressed a meeting in the communist center of Périgueux on October 12, proposing an alliance, against the plutocrats, for the national revolution. The Communist mayor, Marcel Delagrange, came to the stage to accept. The effect was dramatic. The audience applauded madly.[33]

Of course, the "historic" meeting at Périgueux was not so spontaneous. Marcel Delagrange was a former railroad worker, fired for participation in strikes, who had become secretary-general of the local *syndicat*, municipal councillor, and mayor. As mayor, he met Countess Thibaut de

Chasteigner, a war widow in her late thirties and president of the Périgueux royalists. She and Delagrange spent enough time together to persuade local wags that they were lovers, and Delagrange's behavior certainly reflected her influence.[34]

Valois was excited. The long-sought alliance with the workers seemed within reach. Delagrange and Valois continued their discussions in December in the latter's Paris apartment, each with the authorization of his party. In the political climate of the moment, Valois's actions seemed dangerous to many. A shocked Mathon asked to see the proofs of *La Révolution nationale* before the printing. Inside the Action française, people began to doubt Valois's judgment.[35] By the beginning of 1925, Valois was attracting new allies, but was becoming estranged from some old friends.

THE SECOND PERIOD AND THE
WEEKLY *NOUVEAU SIECLE*

The period from February till the Faisceau's foundation in November 1925 saw the creation of much of the infrastructure of Valois's movement. The most important event, however, was the publication of the weekly *Nouveau Siècle*.

Valois had not planned a weekly. He wanted a daily paper, more popular than the *Action française* and with more information. But Auguste Cazeneuve, entrusted with raising the necessary 20 million francs, gave up by the end of 1924. Even Van den Broeck only raised 200,000.[36] Valois did not want to lose momentum. The financial crisis showed no signs of abating, and he had already engaged a team of journalists. In January 1925, therefore, he opted for a weekly as preparation for the daily. The name *Le Nouveau Siècle* (The New Century) was chosen by Valois to stress the progressive aspect of his movement. Maurras objected. A weekly, unlike a daily, would be a doctrinal organ, competing with the *Action française*, and threatening his authority over dogma. Valois went ahead anyway. The *Nouveau Siècle* appeared on February 26, officially replacing the *Cahiers des Etats-Généraux*. Eighty thousand six-page copies were priced at thirty centimes. Arthuys shared the editing with two veterans of French conservative political journalism, Jacques Roujon and Léopold Marcellin, freeing Arthuys and Valois to concentrate on politics.[37]

The *Nouveau Siècle* was subtitled "Journal de la fraternité nationale veut la politique de la victoire," the last part of which was changed in June to, "pour la politique de la victoire." The first two pages were devoted to articles on the week's events, usually by Jacques Roujon, Léopold Marcellin, or Hubert Bourgin. Arthuys's short "Billet du combattant" appeared on the first or second page. The first page also carried a political cartoon. The organization of the third page was based on an idea of Valois's. Its top half was divided into three parts of two columns each. The two outer sections carried titles and were accompanied by sketches. On the left was "The Horde," illustrated by a hirsute barbarian, sword above his head. On the right was "The Legions," illustrated by a Roman legionary, sword in his scabbard. The two sections carried news and comment about the international communist menace on the one side and various reactions against it on the other. The top of the two center columns was devoted to a short doctrinal statement, comment or polemic by Valois in large boldface type, either written in response to current situations or quoted from *La Révolution nationale*. The visual message of the page was clear: the barbarian left on one side, Valois's rightist fascism on the other.

Most of page 4 was given over to Bourgin's *Chronique des ligues nationales*, which thus became part of the *Nouveau Siècle*, and to a "Chronique des combattants." The fifth page covered economic and social affairs; the sixth leisure and the arts. Despite the relatively forceful writing of Valois and Arthuys, the general tone of the paper was respectably dull. The *Nouveau Siècle*, like most of the French right, was hostile to modern art, modern literature, and short skirts or short hair on young women.

The *Nouveau Siècle* was exploited by the Société française d'informations politiques, économiques et sociales, founded on February 25, 1925, with a capital of fifty thousand francs. The largest subscribers were Van den Broeck, Mathon, Cazeneuve, and Serge André. During the summer the capital was raised to 525,000 francs. The multiple voting series A shares were bought by the original subscribers plus Bertrand de Lur-Saluces, a friend of Valois's and leader of the Bordeaux section of the Action française, and another royalist, Léon de Lapérouse. The most important contributions came from Mathon and Van den Broeck. Valois had more than enough money for his weekly, but not enough for a daily.[38]

It was among veterans, and particularly those who had written about their experiences, that the *Nouveau Siècle* achieved its initial successes. The most prestigious recruit, Philippe Barrès (son of Maurice) joined in March. Born in 1896, Philippe volunteered when the war broke out, serving first in the cavalry, and then, at his request, in the infantry. Cited three times, he was appointed chevalier de la Légion d'honneur. Since the war, Barrès had written for newspapers like the *Echo de Paris* and *Le Fi-*

garo and had authored a book based on his wartime experiences. He had also been an unsuccessful candidate on the Bloc national ticket in 1924.[39]

In his book, Philippe Barrès expressed ideas on the war very close to those of Arthuys and Valois. The latter's contrasting of heroism and the bourgeois spirit enchanted him. He was not a royalist and was drawn to those elements in Valois's program that promised a truly national union, including republicans, workers, and former Dreyfusards. Like his father, Barrès considered the French Revolution as much part of French tradition as the monarchy. He helped Valois move from Charles Maurras to Maurice Barrès. To the prestige of his name, Barrès added a budding reputation of his own and contacts in the Ligue des patriotes and in Lorraine. Philippe became one of Valois's most loyal and perceptive collaborators.[40]

With Barrès, Valois had gathered the leadership of his movement. Adding Van den Broeck, André, and Arthuys gives the cluster of men who made the Faisceau possible. None was ever effectively part of the Action française, most were veterans, and all were tied to Valois by friendship and mutual esteem. Neither political amateurs nor cynical opportunists, they stayed with Valois through the difficult days that lay ahead.

Barrès was important for Valois's next step, the creation of a veterans' organization: Les Légions pour la politique de la victoire, officially founded in April 1925. Arthuys was president but organization was turned over to d'Humières. As propagandist, d'Humières hired Marcel Bucard, a former seminary student and richly decorated war veteran. *Légionnaires* were supposed to be combat veterans of either the Great War or one of the colonial wars that had followed. Frenchmen over twenty who were too young to have fought but who had finished their military service could join as "aspirants." No member of parliament could join, and anyone who ran for an elective office above municipal or general councillor would have to resign. *Légionnaires* were eventually instructed to buy a uniform consisting of a blue suit, blue shirt and tie, a tricolor pin, and a cane. Throughout the coming months Valois, Arthuys, and Bucard held meetings in Paris and the provinces, attracting audiences of up to five hundred.[41]

To reach the general public, Valois depended on the *Nouveau Siècle*, which was not doing brilliantly. He coordinated attempts to increase circulation with aggressive press campaigns. The most important was against Joseph Caillaux. Valois had no particular animosity toward the Radical financier, whom he knew to be an opponent of Finaly. Shortly after Caillaux's installation in the finance ministry's offices on the rue de Rivoli, Valois met with one of his advisors. When, however, on June 27, Caillaux obtained an additional 6 billion francs in advances from the Bank of France (the level had already been raised by Anatole de Monzie), the opportunity was too good to miss. On July 2, a special edition of the *Nouveau Siècle* screamed: "The Franc Assassinated, The Guilty Party: Joseph Caillaux, The Accomplices: The Members of Parliament." Valois's full-page article, however, was a lengthy restatement of his positions on the nature of money and the causes of inflation.[42]

With Caillaux, Valois combined two propaganda themes, the monetary and the *combattant*. Not only was Caillaux, like all finance ministers, stuck with an insoluble financial muddle, but he was still considered a traitor in many quarters. Caillaux took the bait and had Valois prosecuted for attacking the credit of the state. This was exploited in the following issue of the *Nouveau Siècle*, which compared the military and financial records of the two men. A letter of protest was signed not only by Action française members (Valois had it sent to section presidents) but also by many genuinely shocked personalities. Valois increased the printing and had five thousand copies hawked on the streets, especially in front of the Stock Exchange, where the provocation would have maximum effect. Three weeks later, posters urged Parisians to read the *Nouveau Siècle*, prosecuted by Caillaux for telling the truth about money and finances.[43]

Valois claimed that Caillaux had adopted his ideas. Caillaux's "national liberation" loan, with its low rate of interest and payments tied to the exchange rate, did have much in common with the *emprunt-or* Valois recommended. Nevertheless, Caillaux's loan was pegged to the pound sterling, which, though stable, was not tied to gold. It was also reserved for the holders of national defense bonds. Valois decided to address this point. Why should the guarantee against inflation be limited to these Frenchmen? Justice demanded the *salaire-or* for workers.

This was the theme of the July 23 special edition. Under another banner headline, Valois defended the *salaire-or*, and Arthuys contributed a study on the need to compensate the more modest *rentiers*. For salaries (and prices), Valois proposed a quarterly *franc-or* based on the average exchange rate of the previous quarter, smoothing out fluctuations and counteracting the observed delay between changes in the exchange and those in purchasing power. Valois's *franc-or* replaced the sliding salary scale (*échelle mobile*) demanded by the Socialists and Communists and tied to the cost of living. Like all proponents of automatic adjustment systems, he did not trust the managers of a more complex system to calculate it fairly. Besides, a system based on the cost of living would always be behind actual price rises. In August, the *Nouveau Siècle* adopted the quarterly *salaire-or* for its employees, and banners calling for the *salaire-or* were hung in the headquarters of the Union des corporations françaises.[44]

Of the 58,000 copies of the July 23 special number, 24,000 went to Hachette for distribution throughout France, 21,300 to subscribers for free distribution, and 8,000 to street hawkers in Paris. The unsold issues were to be given away after 6:00 P.M. at cafés and railway stations. Results were disappointing, only 1,570 issues sold. Accordingly, the sale was continued on the 24th, and more copies given away to bank employees. The following week unsold numbers were still being handed out at the Bourse du travail. Nor did August bring better results. At the end of the month, Hachette, which could reach those on vacation, sold less than a third of its 3,600 copies. The men of the Action française considered these results derisory and gave the paper little future.[45]

Valois linked the *salaire-or* campaign with a major attempt to organize banking employees. In *L'Economie nouvelle*, he had already shown how he thought syndicalized bank workers could thwart the maneuvers of international finance. Catholic unions were unusually strong in this area, and among many of them royalist influence was considerable. Though the bank and stock exchange corporation was not the largest in the Union des corporations françaises, it contained some of Valois's most active supporters. The president, Maurice Denis, was a banker and former engineer who had been with Valois since the CIPF. During spring 1925, Valois made a new convert in the banking world who immediately became one of his most important collaborators: René de la Porte who wrote under the name Lusignac.[46]

De la Porte came from one of France's most distinguished political families. His great-grandfather had been minister under Louis-Philippe, his grandfather a collaborator of Gambetta's, and his father minister of colonies in three cabinets. Reacting to the unfilled promises of the republicans, de la Porte turned to socialism, serving as Guesdist delegate to several SFIO congresses. During the war, he left the Socialist party, disgusted with it and with democratic politics. After the war, in which he served with distinction, he left France to work in the Far East, but illness forced him to return home. In April, he joined the fascist movement, and by August he was contributing articles to the *Nouveau Siècle* and writing the column on the *franc-or*.[47]

De la Porte was a junior bank officer, and banking workers went out on strike in the end of July. The strike was backed by the CGT, the CGTU, and the Catholic unions, presenting Valois with a difficult situation. His doctrine opposed strikes. He also felt that this strike had been fomented to break Caillaux, whose exchange guarantee loan threatened to save the franc. The strike did look for some time, as the strikers hoped, as if it would hinder the new loan. And Caillaux, who did his best to break the strike, was apparently not getting full support from banking circles. But Valois was well aware of the precarious position of bank employees. In the first of the *Nouveau Siècle*'s "Enquêtes corporatives," in July, an anonymous bank employee explained that with the salaries paid, it was just possible to get by as a bachelor. Besides, Valois could probably see that he was not going to win over workers by opposing the strike. He and de la Porte decided to support it, while criticizing its opportunity. UCF members were advised to maintain solidarity. Valois tried to convince the strikers to demand the *salaire-or*, but supported them when they chose the *échelle mobile*. After the strike was broken in September, Valois and de la Porte tried to turn the disappointment of the workers against Caillaux, who was still in power.[48]

THE BREAK WITH THE ROYALISTS AND WITH MATHON

Like all Parisians who could afford it, Valois went south for August, to Saint-Gaudens in the Pyrenees. Arthuys and Cazeneuve were a few miles away at Montréjeau. Between them they planned the fall campaign. Valois wanted to launch a national fascist movement and make his paper a daily. Marcel Delagrange and Valois made plans for another Périgueux meeting, at which the mayor would try to effect a mass conversion. Valois ill contained his enthusiasm. At a meal he, half jesting, half wishfully, appointed Delagrange governor of Périgord. The remark, repeated by local *ligueurs*, became a plot to take over Périgueux with the help of the Communists and declare an independent state. The story was carefully spread by Valois's enemies within the Ligue.[49]

The Action française was not the only area where Valois ran into unexpected opposition. In late summer 1925, he quarreled with Eugène Mathon. Up to July, things had gone well, and Valois expected Mathon to introduce the *franc-or* into the economy of the Nord, in coordination with his campaign in Paris. The chief cause of friction was Désiré Ley, secretary-general of the Consortium du textile. Ley, a former textile worker, administered Mathon's corporative organizations, which he apparently used as a spy network. His chief function was "the defense of order," that is, strikebreaking. To Valois, he was a Uriah Heep, manipulating Mathon through obsequious flattery. As early as 1921, Valois told Mathon that he considered Ley dangerous and dishonest. During the red scare of

1924–25, at Mathon's request, Valois worked with Ley's home-grown intelligence service, but he soon decided that Ley's information was false when he discovered, among other things, a document with a crude error in Russian.[50]

According to Valois, it was his July denunciation of the manufactured Communist danger that forced Ley to act. By August, Valois's dealings with the Communists and his cooperation with striking bank workers allowed Ley to paint him as a dangerous collaborator. Mathon ordered the staff of the *Nouveau Siècle* to Roubaix. Valois countermanded the order. After a heated exchange of letters, Mathon resigned from the administration of the *Nouveau Siècle*. Mathon and Ley had other means in mind to defend their interests, apparently including the illegal importation of arms and export of capital. With Mathon went Martin-Mamy. Since Max Leclerc also resigned quietly at this time, nothing was left of Valois's Etats-Généraux coalition but Arthuys and the royalists.[51] Soon Valois would be separated from these last as well.

The quarrel with the Action française was related to a new figure in Valois's political life, François Coty. Born François Spoturno, Coty was a Corsican who had built up the well-known perfume company from scratch. Fabulously wealthy, he was elected senator from Corsica in 1923 under conditions of corruption so blatant that the election was invalidated. This did not increase his love for parliament. In 1922, Coty bought the *Figaro* and embarked on a second career as editor. Shortly after the foundation of the weekly *Nouveau Siècle*, Coty sent an agent to offer ten million francs to transform the newspaper into a daily. Valois considered the offer incredible, but on the insistence of the agent went to see Coty with Arthuys. The three agreed that the direction would stay in the same hands and that Coty would withdraw his support if he ceased to approve the newspaper's line. Nevertheless, Coty got very favorable mention in the *Nouveau Siècle*, and, that summer, Valois began plans for daily publication. The sums Coty offered, however, began to shrink, first to six million, then four, and finally, by July, a million and a half. At the time, Valois took Coty for no more than a rich perfumer who wanted to get the smell of money off his hands.

In April, Maurras told Valois he needed 150,000 francs quickly. Valois suggested Coty, and on Maurras's insistence, the two men went to see the perfumer, who agreed immediately. When, in July, Valois told Maurras about the million and a half promised for the *Nouveau Siècle*, Maurras asked that it be shared with the royalist daily. Valois refused.[52] The papers were competing for the same funds.

By the end of August, the royalist leadership was becoming uneasy about Valois. Did he merely want to convert communists to nationalism and incorporate them into his movement, which was reasonable, or was he seeking a tactical alliance with Communist organizations, which seemed the height of folly? Then there was the story about Périgueux. Finally, during the spring and early summer of 1925, Valois had been vigorously attacking Pujo for taking no action against the Communist menace the newspaper kept denouncing. Valois sought a special mandate for action in the heavily Communist Parisian suburbs. Moreau and Maurras wondered what he would have done with the authority.[53]

Valois pursued other projects while in the south in late August and early September 1925. He wanted to buy the *Télégramme de Toulouse*, fuse it with the pro-royalist *Express du Midi* and create a *Nouveau Siècle du Midi*. He had mentioned this to Moreau and Maurras but did not take sufficient pains to clear his rapidly evolving plans with the other directors of the Ligue. To some of them, Valois seemed to be charging across the Midi making commitments, buying newspapers, altering the political foundations of the Action française, out of reach and out of control.[54] Besides, the uses to which Valois put his own organ were sufficiently disquieting. Maurras's reservations about a weekly *Nouveau Siècle* appeared justified in July when Valois set forth the doctrines later printed in *La Politique de la victoire*. These did not always agree with those of the Action française, and Maurras had no control over them.[55]

Along with the Nouvelle Librairie nationale and the UCF, the *Nouveau Siècle* gave Valois considerable leverage to maneuver the royalists. He strengthened his power with a Comité de liaison to coordinate the activities of the *légions*, the *Nouveau Siècle*, the UCF, and the Ligue du franc-or. To Valois, this was action, the formation of coordinating committees to cement tactical alliances. What he did with the *légions* or the *Nouveau Siècle* was, to a certain extent, his own business, but the UCF was part of the Action française.[56]

All this added fuel to the dormant rumor campaign about Valois's youthful activities and police connections. Temporarily quashed by Valois's victory over Etienne Bernard-Précy, it was publicly revived during the election by Valois's old enemy Emile Para. In 1925, these stories were spread by Valois's enemies within the Ligue. Worse, he was now being separated from his friends. Léon Daudet's suspicions were raised by suggestions that either Valois or his eldest son, Bernard, had been involved in the mysterious death of Daudet's son Philippe. Bernard had been a good friend of Philippe's, and the two had apparently shared some adolescent adventures, as well as a growing unease about their fathers' politics. The young Daudet had been involved with anarchists, and Georges Valois had been an anarchist in his youth. Perhaps his son had introduced Philippe to anarchism? Rumors spread that Bernard had accompanied Philippe on his flight from home, and someone testified that Bernard had been with Philippe at the railway station. The allegations were investigated by Pujo and Pierre Lecoeur, who kept Valois, but probably not Daudet, in the dark. Intense personal grief, a conspiratorial view of politics, and the very real ambiguities of the case made an explosive mixture in Daudet's mind. It was not hard to turn his suspicions against Valois. Besides, he was trying to reenter the Chamber, and he found Valois's antiparliamentary campaigns embarrassing.[57]

In the beginning of August, Maurras wrote to Valois objecting to plans by the Nouvelle librairie nationale to reprint some numbers from Charles Péguy's periodical *Cahiers de la quinzaine*. Though Valois had long admired Péguy, Maurras had a powerful aversion to the barely repentant former Dreyfusard and philo-Semite. Valois replied that he intended to be his own boss at the Librairie. Two weeks later, Maurras sent a second letter accusing Valois of enrolling *ligueurs* in the *légions*. Valois denied the charge and counterattacked by attempting to put Maurras on the spot: on his return they would discuss Maurras's plans to restore the monarchy in 1925. Valois, who had been building his movement with what he thought was royalist backing, responded to Maurras's attempts to exercise authority in a highly provocative manner.[58]

Maurras's worries were not assuaged by a rally Valois and Arthuys addressed at Roanne on September 20. Officially a function of the local section of the Ligue, the meeting was conducted as a gathering of the *légions*. There was no royalism in the speeches, the audience sang the Marseillaise, and the speakers draped themselves at every opportunity in the tricolor flag. In front of six hundred people, Valois criticized Maurras's *part du combattant*, a wartime monetary award for combat veterans that Valois had publicly supported in 1918. The *Nouveau Siècle* gave the meeting an enthusiastic write-up, reporting all the nationalist (as opposed to royalist) staging but mentioning neither that the meeting had been called by the Action française nor Valois's criticisms of the royalist leader. Valois and Arthuys returned to Paris convinced that their formula, the broadest possible coalition backed by the organizational infrastructure of the Action française, would carry them to victory.[59]

Staff members of the UCF had asked to see the closely guarded subscription lists. When added to the Comité de liaison, this could mean that

Valois was planning a schism. If not, what was the meaning of his remarks to *ligueurs?* While Valois was almost always correct in public, he did not hesitate to criticize Maurras and the Ligue privately. The Action française was finished, Valois asserted, since it lacked the will to move; the future lay with his movement. When repeated, such remarks did not cast Valois's motives in a flattering light.[60]

Nor did his choice of allies. In his attempt to build a broadly based movement, Valois had developed contacts with many sections of nationalist politics, not excluding the Bonapartists, who were anathema to the royalists. Many (including some police correspondents) believed that his principal financial backer was the antiroyalist duc de Camastra. Pujo's staff fed reports to Maurras and Daudet that the duc and other nonroyalists, like Philippe Barrès, were taking Valois out of royalist politics. Finally, after the assassination of Marius Plateau, and again after that of Ernest Berger in the spring of 1925, Valois called loudly for retaliatory murders and taxed the more cautious royalist leadership with cowardice. When it came to street-fighting, however, he was never among those exchanging blows. One of the first principles learned by those engaged in radical politics was that those members who pushed most vocally for violent and illegal tactics were often working for the police.[61]

Valois also underwent a personal change during the summer of 1925. Bourgin described this as the emergence of a butterfly from a chrysalis; the fully mature Valois had finally appeared. Since his adolescence, Valois had always had an ambivalent reaction to authority. A great respect and desire for it coexisted with a strong will to be independent, even a leader. When Valois joined the Action française in 1906, he placed himself under the authority of a political organization, just as he placed himself under the more theoretical sovereignty of church and prince. After the war, as Valois's corporative ventures prospered, he became used to leading his own groups. By summer 1925, as success seemed assured, as throngs of converts brought the respect of followers and the adulation of fanatics, Valois developed greater confidence and a taste for power. When Maurras tried to impose openly an authority once tacitly accepted, Valois's reaction was his adolescent one of rebellion. The new confidence that spelled leadership for some, was arrogance and dictatorial tendencies to others. His fertile imagination and willingness to take risks could be seen either as breadth of vision matched by daring or as a lack of realism rendered dangerous by an equal lack of caution.[62]

Leading royalists did not know what to make of their ambitious lieutenant. Was he trying to lead the royalists, without their consent, into an antiparliamentary coalition? To Maurras, this was Boulangism or worse. At the end of the line would be wholesale arrests of the leaders, forced prematurely into illegal action. In either case, Valois's groups competed with the Ligue. When Valois reached Paris on September 21, even he could see a crisis brewing. At royalist headquarters, Colonel Georges Larpent, a retired officer, tried to interrogate him about charges he had been enrolling *ligueurs* in the *légions*. Valois cut him off, replying that he would pose the questions in that organization.[63]

A day or two later, he received a letter from Maurras that though friendly in tone, vigorously criticized the political line he had been developing since 1924. Maurras brought out those points where Valois differed from Action française doctrine. No, the royalist insisted, parliamentarianism was neither the creation nor the political expression of the bourgeoisie. The role of the *quatre états*, on the other hand, was considerable. Maurras considered the Republic almost an accident in French history. The attack on the bourgeoisie, which Maurras described as nine-tenths of France, was particularly foolhardy; and he concluded that such political tactics would not be tolerated at the Action française. In the defense he wrote in 1927, Valois claimed that his ideas had not changed, and that Maurras's attack was a pretext. Maurras was right. It was Valois who had moved away from his earlier emphasis on the *quatre états* and was groping toward a more organic historical explanation of the parliamentary Republic, just as it was Valois who had changed tactics with his demagogic attacks on the bourgeoisie.[64]

The letter infuriated Valois, and he called for a meeting to discuss the political orientation of the Ligue. On October 7, Maurras, Daudet, Moreau, and Robert de Boisfleury demanded that Valois give up his plans for the daily. This would have aborted the young fascist movement, and Valois refused. Not only did he believe in the future of his projects but he was beginning to suspect a plot to separate him from his allies and reduce him to powerlessness within the Ligue. When Maurras insisted, he offered his resignation. This took everyone by surprise, and Maurras spent an hour trying to talk him out of it. Valois maintained his decision. Moreau only wanted a resignation from the *comités directeurs* and the *Action française économique et sociale*, but Valois resigned from all his posts except those at the Nouvelle librairie nationale and the Ligue du franc-or.[65]

The separation was made public in the Sunday *Action française*. Valois explained his reasons for coalition and his regret at having to leave the Action française in order not to compromise the royalists by his new alliances. Maurras was equally cordial, praising Valois and regretting that "serious disagreements" about tactics had forced a separation. The royalist leader even expressed the hope that the *adieu* would be an *au revoir,* that Valois and the monarchists would work together again in the future.[66] The smoothness of the separation glossed over the difficulties that had caused it. With time, the competing interests and mutual suspicions would only ripen.

Valois had been a member of the Action française most of his adult life, but less than two years after their separation, he and his former colleagues could only find one point of agreement: he had been an outsider within the organization. Both he and they were wrong. Valois's ideas fitted within the structure of Action française ideology; he was no less antiliberal, antidemocratic, or reactionary than the other *ligueurs,* even if his elitism had a more earthy quality to it. His labor and economic campaigns were one of the royalists' tactical options. If he brought his own special qualities and had his own outside contacts, so did Daudet and Bainville, and it was not until 1923 that these became a problem. Nor was he socially isolated. He had a great deal of affection for Daudet, which was returned. He had been good friends with Marius Plateau and had had an excellent working relationship, backed up by mutual respect, with Lucien Moreau. Louis Dimier had also been a good friend before his own break with the Action française in 1920.[67] Valois did not warm personally to Maurras. They did, however, work together smoothly for a long time, one reason being general tactical agreement. More important, Valois had been under Maurras's intellectual spell for a long time. His public praise was not all politics. It also reflected genuine respect for Maurras's dialectic. Though this intellectual influence began to wane after the war, the respect survived a good deal longer. The closeness of the association made the separation all the more awkward.

Valois's separation from the Ligue was a serious blow. The Roanne formula was now impossible, though he still hoped for some cooperation from the royalists. But the break eased Valois's next step: the foundation of France's first fascist party.[68]

THE BIRTH OF THE FAISCEAU

Valois and Arthuys had chosen Armistice Day, November 11, to launch their new movement. By then, the *Nouveau Siècle* was to have become daily, but Valois's separation from the royalists, added to his break with Mathon, left him suddenly without funds, delaying the paper's transformation. First an October and then the crucial November 11 deadline was abandoned. In the absence of the daily, Valois did what he could. By November 8, posters announced his inaugural meeting to the Parisian public. Over thirty thousand invitations were mailed to potential supporters: leaders of right-wing groups like the Ligue des patriotes and its recently founded youth group, the Jeunesses patriotes; the Fédération nationale catholique; Millerand's Ligue républicaine nationale; and veterans' associations. Reaching the mass of Frenchmen required lists of potential sympathizers. Valois and his staff used professional directories and mailing lists like those of the UCF, the Nouvelle Librairie nationale, and doubtless also the Etats-Généraux movement. Every Parisian *légionnaire* was ordered to attend with uniform and cane.[69]

The response was excellent. Almost four thousand people overflowed the main auditorium into the corridors and a smaller room below.[70] The standards of the twenty Parisian *légions* surrounded the podium. The staging, if modest by later standards, was effective. Grown men, veterans of the Great War, were carried away at the sight. Philippe Barrès spoke first, calling on the audience to recreate the comradeship of the front and rid themselves of the politicians and the generations of defeat. Arthuys followed, spitting out his phrases in an abrupt military style. He was the first to pronounce the word *fascisme*. But it was a French fascism he called for, adapted to local conditions, without clubs or castor oil. The crowd greeted Valois with an ovation. Inspired by his audience, he gave one of the better speeches of his career, a detailed exposition of the Faisceau program, including his economic, social and financial nostrums. Despite the complexity of the subject, he held the audience's attention and drew frequent applause. Valois announced the foundation of the Faisceau and presented a flag to the first battalion of the *légions*. To close the meeting, he led the assembly in the second stanza of the Marseillaise.[71]

After the meeting, over 250 *légionnaires* marched, standards high and flags unfurled, to the Arc de triomphe and the tomb of the unknown soldier. A coat check at the Salle Wagram allowed the blue shirts to display their matching finery in the Paris streets. After a short talk by Valois the *légionnaires* went home. At the same spot, an hour and a half earlier, the Republic had performed its own tribute to the dead.[72]

The weak member of the family was the *Nouveau Siècle*. Only 391 of the 3,000 issues entrusted to professional hawkers were sold; even the fascists were disappointed. But Valois had launched his movement—his goal, the conquest of the state. A few weeks later, he told an old friend who had stayed with the royalists: "If in one year, we haven't done it, I'll throw in the towel." But Valois's success would depend on more than his determination. He would need a broad coalition and a continuous flow of money. More important was a factor beyond his control, the ability of the republican government to handle its financial and monetary crisis.[73]

FIVE

The Faisceau, II

The Drive to Take Power

The year for Valois to prove himself, to lead France's first fascist movement with the declared aim of taking power, was 1926. The background was the financial and political crisis he had long predicted. The government was not the only enemy: Valois was drawn into an often violent battle with the royalists and an undeclared war with the Jeunesses patriotes.

By November 1926, Frenchmen had cause to be concerned. In the first flush of victory, the Cartel des gauches had forced President Alexandre Millerand's resignation in 1924, and the subsequent Herriot government, besides transferring Jaurès's ashes to the Panthéon, withdrew the French ambassador from the Vatican and sought to introduce the laws separating church and state into Alsace-Lorraine, infuriating the right. The undoing of the Cartel was, however, as Valois had predicted, the financial problem. Faced with large short-term debts, Premier Edouard Herriot and his finance minister, Etienne Clémentel, continued to float loans while casting about for a solution. This led to further inflation and pressure on the legal ceiling on advances from the Bank of France. On April 3, 1925, Anatole de Monzie replaced Clémentel. A week later, however, the Herriot–de Monzie government was overthrown when the Senate disapproved its financial projects.

Paul Painlevé formed a new government, with Joseph Caillaux as finance minister. Caillaux's conservative policies were designed to reassure the center, while his past as a victim of Clemenceau brought him the support of the left. None of this stopped the Cartel majority from disintegrating or the financial situation from worsening. A third Painlevé government, formed in October 1926, fell in less than a month. The spectacle of the Cartel unable to achieve a majority so soon after its electoral victory hardly flattered parliamentary institutions. The political and financial floundering contributed greatly to the success of the November 11th Salle Wagram meeting of the Faisceau.

INITIAL SUCCESS

Valois sought to exploit his Wagram success with a mass meeting in Périgueux on the 17th. But meeting again in red Périgueux was now almost a provocation. Marcel Delagrange had been denounced by his party and had lost his post as mayor. The meeting room was pre-packed by the local communists and socialists in a rare show of unity. After the left had had its say, Valois dominated the crowd long enough to make his speech attacking the bankers and plutocrats. Delagrange accepted Valois's criticisms of the plutocrats but insisted that only communism could provide the solution. It is unlikely that Valois won many converts, but he served notice on communists that they were welcome in his movement, and on the French public that he was serious about seeking working-class support.[1]

Back in Paris, the major problem was still the newspaper, and thus money. Eugène Mathon took the occasion of the Wagram meeting to publicize his break with Valois. Valois and his agents had been dropping Mathon's name while trying to raise money from Nord businessmen in the UCF. Désiré Ley cut Valois off from industrial circles in the Nord. François Coty became scarce after November 11: the perfumer was waiting to see how the fascists would do on their own before underwriting their movement. The situation had become critical. On December 4, Valois called a meeting with Franz van den Broeck, Serge André, Jacques Arthuys, and Philippe Barrès. The capital of the weekly *Nouveau Siècle* just covered current expenses. The fascists would need to support their daily, which would run at a loss for at least a year, plus the expenses associated with creating a public for it. Valois also knew that others were ready to take his place. Several established right-wing leagues were trying to found dailies, and new groups were sprouting up to take advantage of the crisis, like Ernest Mercier's Redressement français and Jean Goy's veteran-oriented Front républicain.[2]

But hesitation was not in Valois's vocabulary; and his friends agreed to move forward, mobilizing all their available cash. Valois pledged all his assets and went into debt; Arthuys and Serge André did likewise, to the extent that their participation in family businesses permitted it. A few hours later this decision was communicated to Auguste Cazeneuve, who shared the administration of the *Nouveau Siècle* with André. Cazeneuve was shocked; to move ahead without adequate backing was the height of folly, he insisted; he would liquidate the society. When Valois protested that this was a stab in the back, Cazeneuve resigned, leaving what he considered a pack of madmen behind him. The *Nouveau Siècle* became a daily on December 7, and Valois's gamble seemed to be paying off, as throngs of Frenchmen joined the Faisceau: 115 a day during the first week of December. A month after Wagram, 5,000 new members had joined, a striking figure.[3]

WAR WITH THE ROYALISTS

Valois could smell success. New members and subscribers packed into Faisceau offices to meet the leader. Journalists from Europe and America came for interviews. The next target was the Latin Quarter. The students there had just displayed their nationalist sympathies by rioting when the Cartel government tried to place a political friend in preference to the first choice of the faculty. The fascists' generational themes and call for action were also well geared to the proverbial impatience of youth. A meeting (backed by a special issue of the *Nouveau Siècle*) was called for December 14 to found a university section of the Jeunesses fascistes.[4]

By 8:30, over eight hundred people filled the Salle d'horticulture. A handful of *légionnaires* kept order. No sooner had Hubert Bourgin opened the meeting than a Dr. Guérin interrupted, "Is Valois an honest man?" Ruled out of order, he repeated his question, and Georges Calzant rose to his feet shouting, "Valois is a wretch!" When Bourgin ordered the offending gentlemen removed, the battle began. Action française students, massed in the front rows, quickly captured the podium. The royalists soon got the upper hand, filling the room with stink bombs and camelot songs. Valois was carefully isolated from his supporters. He stood helpless, white and trembling with rage and humiliation. Once the police arrived, the royalists left, their work done. The meeting had been destroyed and Valois publicly chastised. Neutrals in the room were as surprised as Valois. They expressed their dismay that champions of order should be fighting each other.[5] The explosion of the Salle d'horticulture was the culmination of a process that had been developing since Valois's departure from the Action française.

Though he had left the Ligue, Valois remained loyal to the Pretender. Valois notified the duc d'Orléans of his separation from the Action française. The impending crisis in France dictated his new alliances, as a part of which he would no longer publicly confess himself a royalist. The duke gave his approval. Besides satisfying his political conscience, Valois hoped to lay the groundwork for future cooperation with the Pretender behind the back of the Action française.[6]

Severing the umbilical cords connecting Valois to the royalists was complicated. The Union des corporations françaises, successor to the CIPF, was almost entirely Valois's creation. But it was a branch of the Ligue, and a large percentage of its members were royalists. At first, Valois kept his post as president, hoping to maneuver the UCF, and eventually the Ligue, into cooperation. The only result was conflict with royalists in the UCF. Valois resigned on October 28th, followed by Pierre Dumas and René de la Porte. In a last-minute flurry of activity, membership lists were copied and the heads of corporations decided whether to stay or join Valois in the newly founded Faisceau des corporations. In the end, Valois felt that an attempt had been made to have him deposed by the UCF, while the royalists felt that he had tried to carry the UCF out of the Ligue. In its last report on the UCF, the *Nouveau Siècle* pointed out that the royalist organization had abandoned Valois's syndicalo-corporatist schemes. Instead, passing under Firmin Bacconier's control, it turned to a more paternalist corporatism based on insurance and family allowances.[7] Valois had so completely absorbed the labor and socializing options of the Action française that when he left, it snapped back to its social doctrines of 1908, appropriate to the fundamentally conservative role performed by the royalist organization for the rest of the interwar years.

Most royalists, surprised by Valois's departure, considered him ungrateful. A few shared his judgment of the Ligue's inactivity and hoped for common action, but a growing number discovered with perfect hindsight that they had always suspected Valois. Among the leadership, his attempt was not taken too seriously. The *Nouveau Siècle* had never done well, and Valois's backers seemed likely to desert him at the first sign of trouble. Within a month, it was hoped, a chastened Valois would be begging for his old job: hence the policy of courteous reserve.[8]

Valois's early successes took the royalists by surprise. More disturbing, a significant number (though far from the majority) of the new members of the Faisceau came from their own ranks. Few important royalists left, and even some who were expected to follow Valois stayed with the parent group. The fascists had better luck with the rank and file: camelots and *commissaires*, the young and the restless. They came in small numbers but continually, showing the effects of a consistent recruitment drive.

Some were recent converts from the Jeunesses patriotes, young men with a taste for action. Others, however, were well-established royalists, disgusted with the Ligue's inaction. Heading the camelots was Pierre Lecoeur, who seemed to be losing the battle with his former boss. The Ligue responded by placing an interdict on all Faisceau activities. Violators faced expulsion. Camelots were forbidden to attend the Wagram meeting on November 11. "As a measure of discipline and to avoid unpleasant discussions," it was forbidden to read or bring copies of the *Nouveau Siècle* into camelot offices. Such measures excited as much curiosity as obedience.[9]

Meanwhile, royalists and fascists were finding nobler reasons for mutual suspicion. In October, Coty carefully informed Valois and Arthuys of the relations between Charles Maurras and Jacques Bainville on the one hand and the Radical-Socialist politician Anatole de Monzie on the other. Valois and Arthuys were stunned; they believed that de Monzie, Herriot's finance minister, was an agent of Horace Finaly's. To be his friend was almost to commune with the devil. To test this new piece of information, Valois and Arthuys published an article attacking de Monzie. Within days, Maurras asked the two younger men not to start a campaign against the politician, because de Monzie, now minister of justice, had promised to help with the Bajot-Daudet affair (a judicial sequel to the death of Daudet's son, Philippe). Valois agreed, but he was deeply shaken. For people like him, who considered even the camaraderie between opposing deputies a subtle form of treason, this confirmation of Coty's accusations suggested that the royalists might be allies, or tools, of the plutocratic forces he fought.[10]

For his part, Maurras tried to separate Valois from some of his followers. Shortly after the break, Maurras treated Bourgin to a lecture on Valois's virtues, pointing out, as an aside, the dangers that Valois's imagination and the possibility of rash or illegal action could pose for an educator and civil servant. The maneuver backfired. A few weeks later, Bourgin tried to use his credit with the Daudets to halt the growing estrangement. "No," Mme. Daudet answered, evidently convinced of Valois's connection with her son's death, "some things could not be prevented." In October, Serge André asked Maurras whether there could be some form of purely tactical cooperation. Maurras refused and treated André to a discourse on Valois's qualities similar to the one Bourgin had received.[11]

Meanwhile the public postures of the rival newspapers were quite proper. The *Action française*, after announcing the break, ignored Valois's activities, and even the foundation of the Faisceau. A public explanation became essential, however, at the Ligue's annual congress, November 25 to 28. Bernard de Vesins explained that action demanded calm deliberation in the light of a proven doctrine, not a rush to do something in the approaching crisis. Despite references to a "spirit of panic," the general tone was one of regret; Valois had been a good friend. As important as the public statements were the private conversations with provincial *ligueurs*. Valois's ambitions were criticized, and the story was spread that he had taken a large sum of money with him when he left. Valois, in turn, invited select royalists to his study. He chastised the royalist leadership, calling the Action française the "party of the assassinated." When relayed to the opposite parties, these charges further embittered relations. [12]

While the provincial *ligueurs* were still in Paris, the *Action française* published a series of veiled attacks on Valois's positions. The partners in a right-wing coalition were not trustworthy, Maurice Pujo wrote; many were hastily formed groups susceptible to police penetration. Only the unreliable and the impatient had been lost. In a more serious charge, Daudet noted that the encouragement of plots was the last resort of a government in trouble. [13] Daudet reflected a growing sentiment that Valois's fascism was part of a plot to ensnare the Action française. The nationalist coalition would lead to an illegal conspiracy and the arrest of the leadership. As promoter of the campaign, Valois was acting as a police agent. Many leading royalists could not believe that Valois had sold his political soul to the devil, so a second theory circulated to the effect that he was being led by the minister of the interior, playing on his impracticality and ambition. Yet the royalist leadership made no public charges. More serious charges would lay them open to the dual reproach: either Valois really was a sinister character, and the Ligue had been wrong to trust him for so long, or this trust had not been misplaced and he could not be guilty of such heinous crimes. [14]

An open attack on Valois awaited the end of all cooperation, a good public pretext, and assurance that a swift blow would be fatal. All three conditions were filled in the first two weeks of December 1925. One connection, the UCF, had already been severed, though squabbles over Valois's resignation continued until December. The other link was the Nouvelle Librairie nationale, which had been directed by Valois since 1912. In 1921, at Valois's request, and in consideration of the value he had added to the Librairie, the directors of the Action française gave him 200 shares, to which he added 254 purchased from his own funds. With 454 out of 1,000 shares, Valois became the principal shareholder and a member of the board of directors. [15]

Valois's first reaction after his resignation was to give up the Librairie. But Lucien Moreau and the other directors felt that he had a moral right to it, and Valois decided to stay on. The problem of the Librairie's royalist authors remained. Valois offered to cede to Maurras, Daudet, and Bainville, his most important authors, their contracts and unsold books. With a little goodwill, these problems could have been solved. But goodwill was in short supply. In October, M. de Resnes, one of the directors (and president of the board of directors of the Ligue), came to see Valois to discuss the Librairie. To his surprise, Valois asked him to sign over his share of the rights and stock of the company. Shocked, he refused and reported this suspect action to the other royalists.[16]

By November, Moreau decided it was not safe to leave the Librairie in Valois's hands. He decided to provoke the dissolution of the company by asking the directors (all royalists save Valois) to resign from the board. The plan went awry when two directors, besides Valois, refused to go along. One of them, Colonel Milleret, vice president of the Bordeaux section, informed Valois about the maneuver. Infuriated, Valois decided to fight. M. de Resnes was injured in an accident, and could not attend the subsequent meeting. This left the board at six. Robert de Boisfleury would have had the right to break a tie, but he had neglected (and Valois had not reminded him) to renew the formalities as president and was reduced to one ordinary vote. Valois, with the aid of the same two directors, Milleret and the comte de Lur-Saluces, president of the Bordeaux section, had three votes, and the board was deadlocked. The issue then went to a meeting of the shareholders. Valois, adding the votes of his supporters to his own, controlled 621 shares, the majority, and took control of the Nouvelle Librairie nationale. Valois felt that, morally, the firm belonged to him. Most royalists were just as sure it belonged to them. Not only had old friends learned to distrust one another, but Moreau, Maurras, Daudet, and others felt Valois had stolen their publishing house. The "theft" convinced the doubtful of Valois's treachery and justified any counteraction.[17]

For months, rumors had circulated of enormous sums at Valois's disposal. On December 4th, after his dramatic meeting with Valois, Cazeneuve explained the Faisceau's financial plight to Bernard de Vesins. The two men agreed that it was in everyone's interests to end this mad venture. The royalists concluded that a swift blow would topple Valois's movement.[18]

Only a pretext was missing. The royalists had long thought Valois's behavior duplicitous: he was publicly cordial to the Ligue and considered membership in the Faisceau compatible with loyalty to the Pretender, but at the same time, he competed ruthlessly for camelots and held his own in the private slandering match. Some *ligueurs* believed Valois was still working with Maurras.[19] The fascist leader was not above taking advantage of this situation, just as he had not advertised his break with Eugène Mathon to businessmen in the Nord. The royalists seized upon two interviews in Italian newspapers, one in *Il momento* on November 7 and the other in the *Tribuna* on December 8. Valois had criticized the royalists' electoral ventures and general inaction: the Ligue had no future. This was not new, and it was milder than some of the things said before, but it was public. The contrast between these interviews and Valois's published remarks in France was given as the reason behind Dr. Guérin's question, "Is Valois an honest man?" at the Salle d'horticulture meeting on December 14, generalizing a small incident into an attack on the integrity of the aspiring leader.[20]

Breaking up the meeting was a more eloquent argument than any Maurras could develop. Valois and his new followers wanted action. The royalists gave it to them, embarrassing Valois and showing that the royalists were still a force to be reckoned with. After the meeting, a shocked Bourgin got the explanation from Pujo: this meant war. In the newspaper, however, the royalists only mentioned the issue of duplicity and the Italian interviews. Brilliant but unstable, Valois had left the Ligue because he had been denied authority he obviously could not handle.[21]

This was less than they thought. For weeks Valois had been suspected of being an agent of a plan by Painlevé and Abraham Schrameck, minister of the interior, to create a fascist plot and arrest all the nationalist leaders. This information had been leaked to the royalists by contacts in the Sûreté, and they considered it confirmed when another source reported military preparations to crush the plot. The royalists gave the story maximum private circulation, passing it on to those in their own and other *ligues* who thought the punishment out of proportion to the crime.[22]

For public consumption, the newspaper began a campaign of insinuations along the pattern: "We are not prepared to accept the dreadful thought that Valois . . ." The principal suggestion was that he had to be working for the monarchists' republican enemies. Maurras saw Finaly behind Valois; Daudet saw Finaly or Aristide Briand. In the following weeks, Maurras and Daudet grew steadily bolder, calling Valois a traitor (without saying to what) and his departure from the Ligue an attempted schism. Meanwhile, Maurras continued his "investigation" by publishing stories of Valois's dangerous dealings with Communists.[23] This was fine for those who viewed political reality through the pages of the *Action française*, but many other nationalists judged the royalists severely for taking out their private rancors so violently. Even many of the Jeunesses patriotes felt the camelots were too given to brawling.[24]

All was not well inside the Ligue either. Milleret and Bertrand de Lur-Saluces were excluded. In his emotional farewell, Lur-Saluces explained that he accepted the necessity of coalition and a temporary dictatorship to precede the restoration. The count maintained contact with the Ligue through his daughter, who became president for 1926 of the Gironde women royalists. In defecting, Lur-Saluces took with him a number of intransigent Catholic royalists, undoing years of work by the Action française in these circles. Added to Valois's contacts with the Pretender, this threatened to break the Ligue's virtual monopoly of French royalism.[25]

The royalist show of force was also designed to raise morale. The camelots who had been at the meeting rejoiced at their success and became the center of animated conversations in Ligue offices. A minority of camelots, more sympathetic to Valois, disapproved. Over twenty were expelled in the days following the meeting. Several worked for Valois or the Nouvelle Librairie nationale, but others were only guilty of questioning royalist tactics. Mere suspicion of relations with the fascists brought summary expulsion.[26]

Valois was shocked that the Action française, whose force of will he had underestimated, had turned its talent for public disruption against him, and indignant that men he had known for twenty years could question his honesty. After an initial public jab, Valois heeded the advice of his friends by ignoring the royalists. The Nouveau Siècle responded with indignant demands for proof but little discussion of the charges.[27]

Most of Valois's readers did not also read the Action française. Until Maurras or Daudet came up with something really damaging, he could adopt a superior attitude. Though the fight was a welcome excuse to those reluctant to honor financial pledges, the hostility of the royalists brought with it the sympathy of their enemies. Besides the left, with whom cooperation would be difficult for some time, these included many Catholics resentful of bullying by the atheist Maurras. Valois was looking to a new audience: the veterans who, though nationalist, were also staunchly republican.[28] But this put the Faisceau in competition with other nationalist ligues.

THE FAISCEAU, THE ACTION FRANCAISE, AND THE OTHER LIGUES

Though the nationalist ligues greeted Valois's enterprise with public sympathy, his political line put limits on cooperation. The Faisceau was vigorously antiparliamentary: no deputy could become a member. Most of the ligues were run by present or former members of parliament. Some, like the Ligue des patriotes and particularly Millerand's Ligue républicaine nationale, had considerable influence in parliamentary circles. The call for a dictator was also not congenial to groups like the Ligue des droits des réligieux anciens combattants. These differences made Bourgin's job as president of the Conférence des ligues nationales particularly delicate.[29]

There were material frictions as well. Valois competed for funds and members. More serious, his agents recruited from within the *ligues*, most extensively in the Ligue des patriotes, of which Philippe Barrès was a member and Bourgin secretary-general (problems of divided loyalty forced his resignation in 1925). Fascist agents performed similar chores in other organizations, enrolling any *ligueurs* they could and assembling huge lists of right-wing Frenchmen, whom they bombarded with propaganda and requests for funds. Valois's converts were usually the younger, more active and generous members who were tired of speeches and hoped that this new group would finally do something. Such losses were particularly damaging because the republican nationalist leagues lived off a relatively circumscribed public. Not only were their boards of directors interlocking, but many members supported more than one organization.[30]

In an oblique but accurate attack, Maurras wrote that for a maker of fasces, Valois was quite a divider, as Pierre Taittinger could testify.[31] Indeed, he could. The Faisceau carried on an intense, though barely public, competition with Taittinger's Jeunesses patriotes. Taittinger, a deputy, was a leading figure in the Ligue des patriotes and the head of its youth group, the Jeunesses patriotes. Founded in 1924, the Jeunesses had grown, like other *ligues*, in the atmosphere created by the Cartel victory. The shooting of two of their members on the rue Damrémont gave them martyrs and national publicity, and under Taittinger's guidance, they developed their own image and a certain autonomy from the parent organization.[32]

This autonomy created tensions. The Ligue des patriotes, led by General Castelnau, was conservative, far removed from thoughts of illegal action. The youths who followed Taittinger were impatient and antiparliamentary. Taittinger coated his basically anticommunist message with calls for action and denunciations of parliament, wrapped in paramilitary formations and grandiose demonstrations. To the distress of the more conservative leaders of the Ligue des patriotes, he also engaged in a flirtation with fascism. His imitation, however, was purely superficial, and, being backed by some of the Republic's most important economic interests, including the Banque de Paris et des Pays-Bas, he was not about to cooperate seriously with Valois. In fact, Taittinger's aggressive public stance was designed to hold onto the impatient and canalize the fascist current in France.[33]

The Jeunesses, the Faisceau, and the Action française competed for members. Police records show a constant flow of young men between the three groups, determined essentially by the reputation of power and the promise of action. Two groups could thus always unite against the third. During the fall of 1925, holding out the bait of cooperation, Taittinger helped widen the gulf between Valois and the royalists.[34] This fit in with Taittinger's pro-fascist oratory and with another group the Jeunesses were absorbing, the Légion of Antoine Rédier.

Rédier, leader of a veterans' group and editor of the *Revue française*, founded the Légion in August 1924. The program of the new group read like a naïve version of Faisceau propaganda. The Légion was antiparliamentary and wished to replace the present government, though it was not sure with what. Rédier was sure, however, that a leader, a *chef*, was called for, and that the veterans should spearhead the conquest of power. In addition, he was staunchly nationalist, firmly anticommunist and socially reactionary. Active sections were created in provincial centers. A weekly, *Le Rassemblement*, was printed in batches of fifteen to twenty thousand. Rédier had few illusions that his 10,000-member *ligue* could alone redirect the destinies of France. His goal was the one Valois had caressed, to provoke an alliance spanning the right wing from the republican nationalist *ligues* to the royalists. The only taker was the Jeunesses patriotes. The provincial focus of Rédier's group complemented the largely Parisian strength of the Jeunesses. Taittinger was liberally supplied with funds, while Rédier, though he had a personal following, lacked backers. In the spring and summer of 1925, Rédier and the Jeunesses moved toward fusion, with the new organization, Les Jeunesses patriotes–La Légion, featuring Rédier as vice president and de Neufville-Gounelle of the Jeunesses as *délégué-général*. The new alliance threatened to eclipse the infant Faisceau.[35]

But the honeymoon did not last, and Valois's agents were not inactive. Rédier discovered that he did not enjoy working under the "authoritarian" Taittinger. A crisis arose when Taittinger, under pressure from General Castelnau, fired de Neufville, who was considered too "fascist," at the end of November. At the same time, large numbers of young men left the Ligue for the Faisceau. Faced with this hemorrhage, Taittinger made his peace with de Neufville, whose dismissal was blamed for the desertions.

Rédier then began to lead his own current from within the organization in favor of Valois's groups. By December 15th, he left the Jeunesses patriotes, calling on all Légion members to follow him. Privately, he urged them to join the Faisceau. He himself planned to transfer his staff to Faisceau headquarters, but he never did so.[36]

One cause of Rédier's hesitation was probably the battle between the Faisceau and the Action française. The Jeunesses and the other *ligues* now joined the attack on Valois, privately echoing royalist charges that Valois was a divisive figure or perhaps a police agent. By March 1926, Rédier directed those still listening to join the Faisceau. A prolific if undistinguished author, Rédier retired from active politics in return for a Faisceau pledge to support his literary career. It is hard to judge how many of his followers joined the Faisceau. At Nantes, where the Faisceau had no organization, the local group refused to bolt the Jeunesses patriotes. On the other hand, two of Valois's most important local leaders, Guéguen of Rouen and Auguste Lajonchère of Lyon, were Légion men. At the least, the Légion helped the Faisceau establish itself in provincial cities where Valois lacked contacts.[37]

Meanwhile, the Action française intensified its front-page campaign against Valois, groping toward new accusations. The most serious was not new: the police were blackmailing Valois with his "Russian dossier."[38] The second charge was that he had stolen the subscription lists of the *Action française*. As proof, Maurras printed the letters of readers who had received complimentary copies of the *Nouveau Siècle* and whose addresses, they assured him, could not have come from any other source. Valois pointed out, however, that he could, and often did, obtain these addresses from other sources, like the lists of the Nouvelle Librairie nationale, which included those who had ordered any royalist publications. When some UCF addresses, and no doubt those of old subscribers to the *Cahiers des Etats-Généraux*, were added, Valois could reach a significant percentage of *ligueurs*. Not that stealing the lists would have been unusual. Valois accused the royalists of stealing his, and there was evidence that he had taken as many addresses with him as possible when he left the UCF. Nonetheless, every time an Action française *ligueur* received a piece of Faisceau propaganda, his anger was redoubled against the man who had stolen his address.[39]

On January 15th, Valois broke his demi-silence. In a long rambling article he denied the principal royalist charges and publicized his own complaints against the Ligue. From this day till his death, Valois and the Action française were engaged in an often vicious public polemic.[40]

The battle was not merely literary. After the aborted Faisceau universitaire meeting of December 14, Georges Calzant declared that Valois
would never be allowed to address the students, a challenge taken up with
a second Faisceau universitaire meeting on January 29. The fascists had
been able to protect their other recent meetings by means of a large police
force of their own and systematic filtering of the audience. Similar precautions, backed up by a large force of *légionnaires*, were taken for the new
meeting in the Latin Quarter.

That afternoon, however, a group of Action française students and
camelots entered the hall, smashed the chairs and lamps and filled the
room with gas and stink bombs. When the *légionnaires* arrived, the atmosphere was unbreathable. After much scrubbing and aeration, the audience could enter and the meeting began. The fascists gave their
speeches, but Valois and Arthuys had to cut theirs short since, having
been gassed during the war, they found the atmosphere of the room difficult to tolerate. The few disruptive elements who had managed to enter
were easily dispersed. Outside, camelots and students were frightened off
by the stronger fascist guard. Finally, a group of camelots and students
who attempted to demonstrate in front of Valois's house in the Place du
Panthéon were frustrated by a band of *légionnaires* already stationed
there. Valois had faced down the royalists. By the end of January, the Faisceau universitaire had two hundred members. But the royalists had made
their presence felt. Public obstruction of this sort became a fact of life for
Faisceau meetings in Paris and many provincial cities. Battles were provoked in Strasbourg and Mulhouse, and in Lyon Valois was hit with a jar
of mustard. Furious, he had to be calmed by Barrès.[41]

The royalists made their attacks as personal as possible. Daudet turned
his pen on Valois with the usual devastating results: a series of puns on
Faisceau and the undignified French term for the posterior, *fesses: fesso,
fessistes*, and so on. A satirical song, "Le Dictateur-en-bois" (The
Wooden Dictator) was sung at Valois by camelots when they saw him in
the street. Valois, his wife, and his children were followed in the streets by
jeering royalists, obscenities were shouted at his window at night, he received obnoxious letters and phone calls, and someone urinated in his
mailbox.[42]

These attacks made a tremendous impact. Valois had a prickly sense of
honor and was proud of what he considered his scrupulous integrity. It
made him furious to see his good name publicly impeached. His wife and
children were also upset at seeing the family name dishonored, especially
by an old friend like Daudet, and their reaction only incensed Valois more.

At first, he was so upset that he became physically ill. Within a few weeks, however, he regained his fighting spirit. His January 15 counterattack, while it did not abate his fury, revived his confidence. Valois's indignation was also political. These former colleagues could have no doubts about his honesty. The campaign was premeditated calumny: a cold-blooded attempt at moral and political assassination. He considered such methods unacceptable. He was also surprised to see them used by his former collaborators, an impression shared by others who knew both Valois and the Action française. [43]

Nevertheless, this judgment was not wholly correct. Daudet, for one, probably believed all that was said against his former friend. Moreau and some others believed little of it, but considered the campaign necessary or simply went along, as Valois had done on similar occasions. With Maurras, who led the campaign, outright lying was less common than what Marc Bloch has called the acceptance of "an illusion, which gratifies the interest of the moment." Moreover, when the royalists reasoned that Valois's actions, directed against the Action française, had to have their origin in the Sûreté, they followed the same reasoning as Valois with Etienne Bernard-Précy. This egotistical illusion was shared by most in or around the Action française and would remain a part of Valois's political consciousness. The cloak-and-dagger atmosphere that bathed the activities of all political extremists helped keep it alive. Valois came close to understanding this when he explained Moreau's behavior as the result of a collective madness that considered the Action française so important that leaving it was a crime justifying anything, adding that he too had shared this malady. [44]

The royalists' behavior differed chiefly in its vindictiveness. Though he sometimes lost his temper, Valois maintained a certain nobility even in his sharpest attacks on Maurras. He tried to respect his enemies, making a salute to their prowess part of his code of chivalry. Paradoxically, it was Valois who had the more conservative polemical style and the royalists who were closer to the more virulent forms of twentieth-century propaganda commonly associated with fascism.

The violence and single-mindedness of the royalist attack left scars on even a seasoned campaigner like Valois. For the rest of his life, he was acutely sensitive to any hint of personal attack and saw a campaign of calumny behind every unflattering allusion. And there would be many, since the royalist campaign made the questioning of Valois's honesty a permanent element in his career. The campaign did its greatest damage among the Faisceau's right-wing competitors, placing additional obstacles in the way of a nationalist coalition. It also caused a temporary drop in Faisceau morale and may have slowed the membership drive.[45]

FASCIST PROGRESS IN THE FIRST HALF OF 1926: FROM VERDUN TO REIMS

To keep up morale, Valois threw himself and the Faisceau into a flurry of activity. In late December and January, meetings were held for various corporations. Sectional meetings were organized in Paris and its suburbs. Valois himself addressed a group of cadres to reassure them about the royalist campaign. In addition, with Arthuys and Barrès, he continued to address successful gatherings in major provincial cities: Reims on January 10, Bordeaux on the 20th, Verdun on the 21st.[46] The activity paid off, with new *légionnaires* averaging fifty a day in mid January. The corporations did even better and enough left the UCF to threaten its demise.[47]

To show the public that the Faisceau was alive and growing, Valois organized another monster rally at the Salle Wagram on February 10, reserving a second room for the expected overflow crowd. He made his point: two thousand people came, the royalists did not risk a disturbance, and the meeting provoked a new increase in recruitment. Valois was nevertheless constrained to discuss money, explaining that certain financial interests, unable to control his social program, had withdrawn their backing. This would become a familiar refrain. Valois asked the fascists to contribute, and ensure the independence of their movement. The financial crisis was of short duration. Friends brought funds, and Coty was forced to cough up what he had promised. The organization was far from broke, and Valois was able to go ahead with the major event of February: the pilgrimage to Verdun on the 21st.[48]

The mass meeting at Verdun was the first of three Valois planned, moving westward across France: the second was to be at Reims, the third at Meaux, near Paris. If the third coincided, as was expected, with the height of the political and financial crisis, the way would be open for a "March on Paris." The geography of these meetings combined the great sites and anniversaries of the war, crucial to Valois's propaganda themes, with the area where the Faisceau had its best initial local results. By mid February, Chateau-Thierry boasted 190 members, Soissons 700 to 800, and Reims 300. All over the region, Faisceau agents found widespread antigovernment feeling and sympathy for their cause. One explanation was the nationalist and patriotic, but not monarchist or traditionalist, opinions of the area. More immediate considerations were also at work. The end of payments to war victims hurt local commerce; and reconstruction had been accompanied by numerous tales of waste and corruption. By holding his rallies between the Vosges and Paris, Valois added the results of these local discontents to his Parisian troops.[49]

The rally was set for February 21st, the tenth anniversary of the main German attack on Verdun. The meeting was also a pilgrimage to the battlefields and the Ossuary at Douaumont. With an ecumenicism unusual on the French right, the fascists invited Catholic, Protestant, Jewish, and even Muslim divines, all with the approval of the bishop of Verdun.[50] More serious was the fascists' plans to organize a public procession on Sunday afternoon to the military cemetery at Verdun, despite the mayor's insistence that he wanted no public demonstrations or processions. The local left responded with a vigilance committee: Communists, Socialists, Ligue des droits de l'homme, and so on, who insisted on their own procession. The mayor and the prefect finally gave in, permitting both processions but insisting on separate itineraries. As the prefect wrote to the Sûreté in Paris, he was not overly delighted with this solution, fearing that it would only emphasize the relatively small support of the left.[51]

The "Journée nationale de Verdun" opened the night before at 8:00 P.M. when Valois, Arthuys, and a small group of légionnaires began a vigil at the Douaumont Ossuary. Valois was relieved at 10:00, but a group of légionnaires volunteered to spend the entire night. On Sunday, over five hundred of them engaged in a shorter morning vigil. Tricolor flags were solemnly delivered to the new provincial sections and sky blue standards to the companies. All swore fidelity to their fallen comrades. The ceremony deeply moved Valois, who had spent most of the war at or near Verdun and had participated in the giant battle of February 1916. Most of the légionnaires had also fought at Verdun and surely they, like their leader, were overwhelmed "by the memories that rose up from the soil." That afternoon the Faisceau held its main meeting at the covered market. The assembly of over three thousand officially adopted the "Verdun Program" calling for the dissolution of parliament, a temporary dictatorship, corporative representation, rational organization of the economy, and a solution to the financial crisis with consolidation of the debt in a stable currency. The meeting over, Valois led the légionnaires, three abreast, through the streets of the town to the military cemetery. A sympathetic crowd watched and even followed the fascist procession. The fascists placed a wreath on the tomb of the seven unknown soldiers, where the antifascist committee had recently left its own red-ribboned memorial. The Journée was an unqualified success. Even the weather cooperated, and the fascists had come in the expected numbers. Every commune in the department of the Meuse was represented, and delegations hailed from as far away as St. Nazaire, Bordeaux, Périgueux, and Marseilles. The competing antifascist demonstration barely assembled 250 people.[52]

During the week before the rally, Valois tried to prepare the readers of the *Nouveau Siècle* for the fact that the ex-Communist Delagrange would soon join the Faisceau. At the time, the notion of a Communist turning fascist was not a familiar one. The Faisceau was a predominantly right-wing organization: especially the rank and file, who were for the most part more socially conservative than the leadership. To most French rightists, talk of recruiting, or working with, Communists generated considerable anxiety, further excited by Maurras's charges on this score. Even the social gap was enormous. Delagrange could not behave in nationalist as he had in Communist circles.[53]

By the end of 1925, Delagrange, still a municipal councillor, had become suspect in Communist circles, and in January he was fired from the direction of the red cooperative of Périgueux and accused of having stolen the group's funds. Valois concluded that the charge was unfounded, and no legal action was ever taken. By the end of January, Delagrange had been expelled from the Communist party. On February 4th, he saw Valois in Paris about joining the Faisceau, but formal membership was put off until after the Verdun rally.[54]

Delagrange received a high salary, and the Faisceau helped him buy a house in the Paris suburbs, but the leadership wanted to try him out before giving him major responsibility. Accordingly, the corporations stayed in the hands of Pierre Dumas and René de la Porte, while Delagrange became technical councillor. The former mayor's first public trial was a March 21 Wagram meeting. After extensive coaching by Dumas and his friend Countess Thibaut de Chasteigner, the ex-Communist succeeded in winning the sympathy, if not the enthusiasm, of the better part of the audience of three thousand. Valois and a few other leaders were enthusiastic, hoping Delagrange would be another Léon Jouhaux and create a powerful corporative federation. Delagrange's compromises did not neutralize the internal opposition. Some of the industrialists who helped pay the bills, irritated by the former mayor's tendency to refer admiringly to Lenin and Trotsky, doubted the sincerity of his conversion. Older members resented the newcomer and his publicity. The opposition to Delagrange marked the beginnings of a right wing within the Faisceau that was hostile to what it considered the organization's steady drift to the left.[55]

Delagrange proved less useful than expected. Valois wanted him to undertake a campaign in the heavily Communist Paris suburbs. The drive would be at once political (to attract Communists and Socialists), corporative (to bring in workers), and regional. In April, at a meeting of the Faisceau's ruling directory, Delagrange obtained a promise of one million francs (of money that had not yet come in, it is true). But the lethargic former mayor did little more than attend those meetings he had to address. Although he enticed away a handful of low-level Communist functionaries and workers, he produced none of the mass defections Valois had hoped.[56]

Others were working harder, and the organization continued to grow. From March through May, the number of new *légionnaires* held steady at about 50 per day. Recruiting in the corporations varied between 70 and 150 per week. Total membership was probably between 25,000 and 30,000 by the end of April. Another positive fact was that the Jeunesses patriotes were now drawing away from the royalists and again flirting with the fascists.[57] Most of the gains were in the provinces. In the two months after the Verdun rally, attention continued to be directed to the east. Now fascist propagandists crossed the prewar frontiers into Alsace and Lorraine, hoping to take advantage of the discontent created by the Cartel's clumsy attempt to change the religious regime of this Catholic area. Valois spoke in mid April in Mulhouse, Strasbourg, and Metz, before going on to Lyon. Results were mixed. In Metz only about 65 people had joined by the end of April, while Mulhouse counted 200 fascists.[58]

Though membership continued to grow, some old members were already losing interest. By March, in one Parisian section, only half the *légionnaires* showed up, despite a special letter of convocation. In April, a leader reported to a meeting, from which half of his section was absent, that a new group had been formed to contain the expanding membership. *Légionnaire* impatience was visible in Paris by March 1926. These men had signed up for action and received speeches and counsels of patience instead. Many wanted some public display of force, and a group approached the leadership with a request for a public procession in Paris in March. The leaders did what they could, promising that H-hour of D-day might be sooner than they thought and urging them to practice going to each other's houses so that liaison would be smooth at the critical moment. Though most still went along, this problem would get worse instead of better.[59]

Valois understood the need for clear issues and demagogic formulations but wanted them to reflect real dangers. Anything else served the plutocrats by diverting public attention. In May 1926, he found an issue to his liking. In April and May, Briand and Finance Minister Raoul Péret were fighting another exchange crisis. The suggestion was made that some of the gold reserves of the Bank of France be used as a fund for maneuvering on the exchanges. The bank was hostile to the idea and so was Valois. He needed no prompting, however. To him, the gold reserves were the last solid support of the franc, and this scheme was just another plutocratic attempt at the financial assassination of France: both a symbolic and a real alienation of the French national patrimony.[60] Valois also wanted to educate his followers in an area that, though vital to him, was ignored or misunderstood by many *légionnaires*: the Faisceau's economic and social program.

Valois combined both goals at the next Salle Wagram meeting on May 21, when over 3,500 people heard him give a forthright exposition of his most socially advanced points. He defended high salaries and effective bargaining power for workers, capsuling his argument in an arresting image: it was the British trade unions who had saved the Empire by successfully pushing for ever-higher wages. Though he was frequently applauded, Valois received the best response when he explained the attack on the Bank of France's gold reserves and called on the *légionnaires* to oppose, by force if necessary, any withdrawal of gold from the bank. Here at last was the invisible made visible. The mysterious maneuverings of plutocrats and financiers were replaced by an attack on a tangible object that in turn, apparently, could be defended the way the veterans had defended the soil of France. The *légionnaires* leapt to their feet shouting and waving their arms. Within three days, the walls of Paris were covered with fascist posters. "Alert:" they began, "The last Guarantee of the franc is in danger," but as talk of using the bank's reserves subsided, the fascists halted their campaign. Again, Valois had done the Bank of France's work.[61]

By this time attention had shifted to the second Journée nationale in Reims. By April the Socialists and Communists of the Marne had organized an antifascist committee that covered the east of France with posters proclaiming: "We will block the road to Reims," just the sort of publicity the fascists liked. Valois kept the date of the gathering secret to keep the government, the royalists, and the left in the dark, and to make ready enough money and members to guarantee success. The date was not disclosed until June 5th, when it was set a mere three weeks later, for the 27th. In mid June, all Faisceau sections held meetings approving the Verdun Program, generally by acclamation, and choosing delegates (actually volunteers) to go to Reims.[62]

At the same time, Communists from the Marne and neighboring departments, as well as the Paris area, tried to attract the maximum number of their people to their countermeeting, especially members of the Association républicaine des anciens combattants, the Communist veterans' group, whose members, organized into paramilitary defense units, would be on hand to oppose the *légionnaires*. Local Communists hoped that the authorities, fearing violence, would ban both groups. Nevertheless, fascists and antifascists both got authorizations, though not for processions. The government even sought, without success, to bar the fascists from wearing their blue uniforms outside the meeting rooms.[63]

The fascist meeting began a little after 1:00 P.M. Billed as the first Assemblée nationale des combattants, des producteurs et des chefs de familles, it was a mixture of a party congress, one of the Etats-Généraux meetings, and a Wagram rally. About 1,500 delegates had been selected by fascist organizations. In addition, delegates, for the most part nonvoting ones, were invited from veterans' organizations and the nationalist leagues, excluding the Action française. Despite these last-minute attempts to bring in outsiders and invitations to the citizens of Reims, the meeting represented the movement, not the public. Valois marched to the hall between two columns of *légionnaires*, their hands raised in salute. When he entered the hall, he received a thunderous ovation from the audience of ten thousand, two-thirds of them in fascist blue. Opening the meeting, he declared that the crowd in Reims represented half a million Frenchmen. One hundred thousand (including families) would have been a more reasonable figure.

The assembly was asked to approve seven resolutions: both the *franc-* and *salaire-or*, two assemblies (one corporative and the other regional and familial), and a sovereign state independent of and above the representative assemblies. The *combattants* were to inaugurate this new government through the national revolution. The last resolution called on the *combattants* to form a national militia to put the program into effect and to meet again, when called by the Faisceau, on the banks of the Marne, there to appoint the leader and create the institutions of the new regime, which Valois baptized the République des combattants et des producteurs. This abandonment of the movement's earlier constitutional neutrality went both unpublicized and unnoticed.

The resolutions were accepted by acclamation, with only a few questions and observations from the floor. The assembly lasted over four hours, which were taken up largely by general political speeches unrelated to the resolutions. Arthuys, for example, was brilliant, demagogic, and irrelevant, but quite effective. The language of the speakers was tough, the promises bold. Closing the afternoon's deliberations, Valois stated that at the next meeting, the goal would be "the one you know."[64] The promise would be hard to keep.

Across town, the antifascists held their own meeting. About three thousand attended, mostly Communists, though the local branch of the SFIO also gave its support. The speakers included the Socialist (and much later fascist) deputy Marcel Déat and the young Communist deputy Jacques Duclos. By 6:00 P.M. both meetings were over, and the bulk of the visitors, fascists and Communists, started home.[65]

Both groups were now free to circulate in Reims, and that is when the trouble began. Valois wanted to avoid incidents, and he had ordered the *légionnaires* not to bring their canes or other arms, but the order was not always obeyed, and some members of the guard may have been armed with canes. The Communists—several hundred members of the ARAC from Paris, Reims, and the surrounding area—came well armed and in an aggressive mood.

In the afternoon, two separate incidents between small groups of fascists and Communists developed into a full-scale brawl as each side rushed in reinforcements. The opponents wielded canes and nightsticks and threw bricks and rocks at each other and at the police. After about ten minutes, the gendarmes succeeded in separating the fighters. Several policemen were injured, one seriously. The police then isolated and escorted the remaining demonstrators to their trains, trucks, or cars. Even the trip back to Paris saw incidents between the men in red and those in blue. The *commissaire* in charge of the police for the day had few illusions. Only chance, he stated in his report, had prevented the loss of life.[66]

These incidents did not upset Valois. The fighting had been limited; his men had done creditably, he felt; and his opponents had failed to disturb his day at Reims. He and his followers were encouraged by the sight of their massed strength. The resolutions and promises may have convinced some members that the conquest of power was not far off. One good sign: contingents from both the Jeunesses patriotes and the powerful Association nationale des anciens combattants had attended. Reims showed that despite uncertain financial backing and the vigorous opposition of the Action française, Valois had made himself the leader of a large, well-established movement. For Valois, Reims was a *journée historique* in his *révolution nationale*. Actually, it marked the high point of his influence.[67]

THE *NOUVEAU SIECLE*

One of the major factors giving visibility to the movement was the *Nouveau Siècle*, a daily after December 7. Printed on six pages during the week and eight pages on Sunday or for special editions, the *Nouveau*

Siècle described itself as a newspaper of oriented information. Valois hoped to avoid the major weakness of the *Action française*, which did not carry enough news to be the sole paper of its readers.[68]

The first page of the *Nouveau Siècle* mixed news with fairly subtle commentary and doctrinal discussions, usually oriented to current events. A major article, usually by Valois or Arthuys, filled the first two or three columns. The rest of the page was given over to news, with the exception of a short daily column in italics, capped by the fascist shield and usually signed by Barrès. Space was always left for the savage daily article on parliamentary maneuvering by Léopold Marcellin, who signed himself "The Witness." In February, after a public resolution of their quarrel over the role of the bourgeoisie (see chapter 4), Valois gave René Johannet a front-page column.[69] The rest of the paper combined news and features, including serialized novels, reviews, and sports reportage. Page 5 was frequently reserved for major speeches or Faisceau notices.

Three pages were added to the Sunday edition. *La page des métiers* carried economic and corporative news. *La page des combattants* dealt with the veterans and their associations. Last came the *page de la famille*. Alongside advice columns and fashion articles, this offered rebus and crossword puzzles and a kind of comic strip entitled "Fanfan et Marinette." Fanfan was an orphan boy. His mother had died when he was three, and his father had perished "gloriously" in the war. He was joined by an orphan girl, Marinette, and a dog, Poilu (doughboy), found at the front by his father. The two worked as shepherds for a stone-hearted old peasant, Père Cailloux. The strip mixed familial, patriotic, and religious piety. Fanfan was shown on his knees on the straw of the stable in homage before the relics of his father—helmet, haversack, and Croix de guerre.

Valois tried to stay out of the day-to-day running of the *Nouveau Siècle*. Arthuys, as political director, watched over the paper's line and wrote a large share of the polemical articles. Technical aspects of editing were in the hands of Jacques Roujon. This division of responsibility led at first to some conflict. Valois wanted shorter articles, and was not above cutting some down to size. Valois's injunctions, like the short pieces he gave the weekly *Nouveau Siècle*, showed a more modern sense of propaganda emphasizing simplicity and economy. A sympathetic observer like Henry Poulaille, however, did not consider three- and four-column articles too long and felt that the *Nouveau Siècle* was, journalistically, well run.[70]

Valois got his way. Articles in the daily were shorter than those in the weekly *Nouveau Siècle*. Their tone was lighter, more forceful, more plebeian. The entire paper got a face-lift: a bolder, more modern-looking typeface and a front page graced with photos of popular heroes like fliers.

Probably to its disadvantage, but in conformity with political usage, the *Nouveau Siècle* was used to pay off friends. After the break with the royalists, two journalists were fired, while two friends of Coty's from the *Figaro* became editors. One, Gilbert Charles, had previously written for the weekly *Nouveau Siècle*. The other was an Italian (who would become controversial), Umberto Ferrini.[71]

A new daily needed a major promotional effort. The fascist campaign was considered dangerously modest in Parisian press circles. Perhaps for this reason, initial results were disappointing. Valois had hoped to distribute 300,000 copies, but the printing quickly settled in at about 200,000. The number given to hawkers had to be steadily reduced over the first week as the percentage sold held steady, at 40 percent. This *bouillon* was quite high, even for a new paper. Hachette fared no better in distributing the paper.[72]

The rest of December was just as dismal. Hachette continued to sell fewer than half of its copies. By January, printings had been reduced to 40,000, about half of which were unsold. The January 15th issue with Valois's replies to Maurras excited no more interest. The weekly *Canard enchaîné* satirized the *Nouveau Siècle*'s poor showing and appeals to the Arc de triomphe by calling it "the unknown newspaper."[73]

In February, the situation improved slightly, and the print run was raised to 50,000, with over half sold. As the Faisceau grew, the number of subscribers mounted slowly throughout the year. But subscriptions, which started well under 20,000, probably never went over 40,000.[74] Hachette's Paris sales remained unimpressive. The daily average for March was about 1,300. Results in the provinces were better. In its first few months, the *Nouveau Siècle* was even fashionable in the Nord and the Pas de Calais. One reason was Valois's contacts. Another was that few other national partisan papers made much of an effort to penetrate France outside of Paris. The results were, nonetheless, bad enough for Valois to attribute them to sabotage by Hachette on orders from Horace Finaly.[75]

Finaly or no, sales were disastrous. An April plan for a second launching was abandoned for lack of funds.[76] Instead, the Sunday edition was reduced to six pages. The paper's small circulation would not have been a problem if Valois could have afforded to subsidize it for two or three years, but he could not. The minuscule sales by Hachette and the inability of subscriptions to surpass Faisceau membership meant that the *Nouveau Siècle* was a party journal read by the already-committed, not an important nationalist daily, like the *Action française*, with influence outside its own group. Thus, when the Faisceau fell on hard times, the paper went down with it, ceasing daily publication on December 4, 1926.

The finances of the *Nouveau Siècle* cannot be considered apart from those of the movement as a whole. Despite Valois's claims that they were administered separately, there is evidence that funds deposited with the *Nouveau Siècle* were really intended for the Faisceau. The paper and the movement lived as much as possible on credit and amid continual financial crises. In the difficult business of paying bills, the handful of dedicated contributors—largely Valois, Arthuys, André, and Van den Broeck—shifted their funds and credit where they were most needed. A budget presented to the stockholders of the Société française d'informations politiques, économiques et sociales in March 1926 showed matching credits and debits of 2,808,814 francs. The credit side, however, included almost a million francs in "launching expenses," as well as large debts owed to the paper by the Faisceau and the Etats-Généraux movement. A police analyst guessed that the budget actually represented a loss of two million francs. Some limited points can be made, however, about *Nouveau Siècle* finances. The contribution of a million and a half francs by Coty during 1926 was the financial rock upon which the paper rested. Without it, it is unlikely the *Nouveau Siècle* could have survived. The total capital absorbed by the daily was probably about eight million francs. During the same period, the *Action française* had an operating deficit of about one million francs a year.[77]

One form of revenue was visible: advertisements. The daily *Nouveau Siècle* ran about three-quarters of a page of ads. Serge André's Spidoleine products regularly appeared in small ads scattered across the paper. The largest campaign included half- to full-page ads for Urodinal, a product that allegedly cleaned the kidneys and relieved the gout. This and several other patent medicines had their publicity paid for by a Dr. Graux, apparently a Faisceau supporter. An interesting case was posed by the almost daily large ads for Dunlop tires. Dunlop was a British company operating factories in Montluçon and Moulins. These advertisements had already begun in the weekly *Nouveau Siècle,* and by November 1925 they attracted the attention of a police correspondent, who suggested that, as Dunlop benefited from French hospitality, the company could be led to stop its support of the *Nouveau Siècle*. Nevertheless, the ads continued.[78]

FAISCEAU ORGANIZATION

Alongside the staff of the *Nouveau Siècle* stood the Faisceau. The movement was officially led by a five-man directory, with Valois as president, Arthuys as vice president, Barrès, André d'Humières, and Serge André.

The Faisceau consisted of four groups. The first and most important were the veteran-oriented *légions*. The Faisceau des corporations was Valois's corporative and economic group. The Faisceau civique contained all those, including women, who were not in the other organizations. The Jeunesses fascistes, open to young men under twenty, apparently consisted chiefly of a few hundred Parisian students.[79] This organizational division had limited significance. Membership overlapped, and while members of the corporations were supposed to deal with professional problems and *légionnaires* were often called up for guard duty, members of the other groups did little except occasionally come to meetings.

Among the leadership, personal influence was more important than title. Valois's most intimate advisor, Arthuys, shared in most political decisions and in the analyses of the balance of plutocratic forces preceding them. The only area Arthuys appears not to have influenced was that of general ideological and world-historical musings, Valois's specialty. The only man able to affect these was Philippe Barrès, who became Valois's closest confidant after Arthuys. One reason was the emotional support he gave Valois, who was very upset over the royalist campaigns. Bourgin, on the other hand, despite his closeness to Valois, never influenced Faisceau politics.

Directly underneath these men were those who kept the sometimes cumbersome fascist machine running. D'Humières handled "organization": scheduling travel, renting halls, and seeing to it that fascist nuclei were active and audiences present when party orators descended on a provincial town. The Reims meeting, when he had to work against considerable administrative hostility, was a tour de force. Valois's only complaint was that d'Humières was not economical, but this would not be a problem until the latter half of 1926. Serge André had the thankless task of managing fascist finances. Despite his closeness to Valois, however, he was without influence on general policy. The corporations were run by René de la Porte and Pierre Dumas. De la Porte was the ideologue and politician, Dumas the administrator and organizer. Delagrange held little power.

Though Valois talked a great deal about action, the most common action engaged in by the Faisceau was talking. Although it might be argued that circumstances left little alternative, Valois deliberately avoided the aggressive demonstrations and disruption engaged in by the royalists and Jeunesses patriotes. Nor did the kind of economic and syndical action he preferred become possible. Thus, one of the Faisceau's most important resources was its team of orators. Valois was obliged to be the first of these, and, from the fascist point of view, this was unfortunate. Though an experienced speaker and good with hostile crowds, Valois was far from being a Hitler or Mussolini. He resorted to demagoguery regretfully. He had a distaste for selling important ideas with cheap tricks, and his speeches tended to be long and technical. He wanted his listeners to appreciate the logic of his economic and social positions. Often his enthusiasm held the interest of the audience, and when he was in good form, he could bring down the house. When his energy level was lower, however, or the audience not properly prepared, Valois could be downright boring. Arthuys made a good foil for his leader. Frequently applauded, he stood and spoke in a military manner, spitting out his phrases like bullets. His speeches were demagogic, accusing the plutocrats and thumping down on the politicians. The third of the Faisceau's prestige speakers was Barrès, but, despite his gifts as a writer, his delivery was flat and monotonous.

But Valois, Arthuys, and Barrès could not often be spared from Paris or speak to less important gatherings. This job was usually taken by Marcel Bucard, who was, as d'Humières put it, "a mouth."[80] Bucard traveled across France delivering variations on an immensely successful speech. Addressing veterans, he passed quickly from the vulgar to the sacred and thence to the pathetic, bringing tough-talking combat veterans to the edge of tears with images like that of the fallen comrade offering his bayonet from his outstretched skeletal arm. Another orator with a promising future was Philippe Lamour, a brilliant young lawyer who represented the fascists in their legal battles. Forceful and aggressive, he spoke in an occasionally sarcastic style. Delagrange added a plebeian element to the Faisceau's rhetorical mix.[81]

CORPORATIONS, WORKERS, AND COMMUNISTS

The Faisceau des corporations was one of the Faisceau's most original features and the one dearest to Valois. Its twin tasks were the organization of the economy and the recruitment of workers. The results in both cases were modest. However, the corporations grew swiftly in the early weeks of the movement, many recruits coming from the UCF (among them that group's most active members). Valois's fascist corporations remained vital, with new adherents averaging over 50 a week throughout 1926. In the fall of that year, they were one of the few fascist enterprises not only still growing but exceeding their earlier results, averaging over 100 a week in October. For Paris, the police estimated 2,500 corporatists in April, and the national organization grew to about 10,000 by the end of 1926. In the fall, the fascists made plans to set up autonomous regional units guided by a national technical council.[82]

Although impressive for a right-wing party, these numbers did not necessarily translate into economically influential groups. A healthy percentage of corporatists were *légionnaires* who joined as a formality. Fleshing out the organization meant appealing to both the workers and their employers, while tapping the latter for contributions. In theory, syndicalized mutual constraint would yield high wages and low prices. Valois promised profits to employers; for workers, the *salaire-or* and the eight-hour day (the latter for those who wanted it).[83]

In practice, conflicts were more stubborn. A meeting was planned in June for the town of Torcy, but the workers of the local chocolate factory were on strike, and one of its directors was a member of a group from which the fascists were seeking funds. Unable to devise a solution, the fascists cancelled their meeting. Nor was it easy to please the businessmen by themselves. In an interview with Marcel Bucard, the secretary of the Comité des forges of the Loire insisted that little could be done to improve the efficiency of their ironworks, and that the only way to increase production would be to extend the work week from fifty to fifty-four hours. Bucard replied that the Faisceau stood behind the eight-hour day and favored bonuses to increase production. Such honesty did not make for a rich organization.[84]

For workers, Valois backed social insurance and the *salaire-or*. The standard of living he promised was shown in a cartoon in the issue of the *Nouveau Siècle* edited for the campaign in the Parisian suburbs. A worker, or employee, in cap and jacket stood with his wife and children in front of a small house and a car. The legend read: "No longer a dream, this will be a reality."[85] In the summer and fall of 1926, local sections were told to emphasize the recruitment of workers. Some of the more active centers like Bordeaux and Strasbourg made considerable efforts in this direction. The Bordelais attracted a handful of stevedores and other workers, but the result was to bring them to a café, where the leaders bought them drinks and cigars. Such tactics represented the sort of condescending attitude Valois had always resented and were not going to create a mass movement.[86]

Even when former leftists like Valois, de la Porte, or Dumas were involved, the fascists had to overcome numerous obstacles. Most workers displayed the same suspicion of right-wing groups Valois had encountered for years. Many doubted he was serious about the *salaire-or*, suspecting that it was a device to return salaries to prewar real values. The fascist name created additional problems, since leftist opponents could always enlist some of the many antifascist émigrés or describe what the fascists had done to organized labor in Italy.[87]

Valois sought to overcome these obstacles through a series of regional campaigns. Delagrange's poor results in the Paris suburbs have already been mentioned.[88] For months Valois had avoided the Nord for fear of pitting his young organization against Désiré Ley and Eugène Mathon, who had sided with the Action française. Later, he decided that if the local capitalists were hostile, one could concentrate on the workers. Opportunity knocked in June when a former Communist, Henri Lauridan, offered to join up. Before his expulsion from the Communist party, Lauridan had been secretary of the Union des syndicats unitaires du Nord.[89] In the spring and summer, Delagrange worked with Lauridan in the Nord, though the latter's reputation for corruptibility did not help. In October, Delagrange returned to the Nord, while an assistant, Jean Bardy, toured the east. The former mayor only produced promises, whereas his young colleague organized two new groups and won over twenty-six railroad workers. Propaganda and recruitment could continue, he reported, only if more money were available. It was not.[90]

Valois sought not only workers but Communists. When Henri Lauridan followed Delagrange into the Faisceau, Valois's hopes rose. In October, a Communist municipal councillor from Gennevilliers, Jean Gombault, joined and was hired by Serge André. In Bordeaux, a fur-worker named Rauline, former leader of a Communist combat group, was sent to Paris as a prize catch. Though encouraging, these recruits were isolated. Rauline and Lauridan were both already out of the Communist party when they turned fascist.[91]

The difficulties of working among unionized workers can be seen by the attempt made by the director of a Parisian construction company, Pierre Darras, by early 1927 one of the few corporative leaders still active. Darras hired unemployed nonunion workers and enrolled them in his corporation. His old workers, members of the CGTU, responded with a slowdown. Management then tried to fire them a few at a time, but violence ensued. Darras sent six new men down, but when the workers discovered that they had no union cards, they did not let them work. Darras then fired the whole crew, but, fearing reprisals, his new hirelings refused to work, and he had to admit defeat. Police agents described Darras's efforts as the recruitment of *jaunes*. Valois's impression was the same, and he condemned Darras's methods.[92]

The fascists concentrated on certain industries because recruits came more easily in them or because of their strategic importance. Banking and the stock exchange were still a priority area, but de la Porte accomplished little more than reconstituting the old corporation. A newer, smoothly functioning group was the 350-member Corporative Union of Engineers. The definition of the profession tended to exclude both workers and bosses, an anomaly in fascist corporatism. Valois also took considerable interest in the Insurance Corporation, which sought to defend the industry against threats of a state monopoly. Valois was in touch with the directors of some of the larger companies and cynics suggested that organizing the employees would only help him squeeze the companies. He had little success, and a well-publicized December meeting of the Insurance Corporation attracted no listeners.[93]

The Insurance Corporation, like the Banking Corporation, was directed toward white-collar workers, where left-wing syndicalism was traditionally weak. This was not the case with the Transport Corporation, a focus of working-class recruitment in the second half of 1926. In June and July, a campaign was directed at workers from the Société des transports en commun de la région parisienne (STCRP). The Communists sent spokesmen to the fascist meetings, but the corporatists attracted over two hundred members from the STCRP and a nervous response from L'Humanité. Promising results were also achieved with railroad workers. Several hundred railroad men may have been recruited, largely in the department of the Seine, north and east. A fair percentage may have been middle-level employees like station chiefs and their assistants. One reason for the attention to transportation workers was Delagrange's past as a railroad man; another, as the fascists admitted, was the strategic role these workers could play in a general strike. Edmond Schiffmacker, leader of the Strasbourg fascists, bragged to his men that the Faisceau already (in September) controlled seventeen railway stations. If the number was probably inflated, the intent was plain.[94]

Workers remained between 10 and 20 percent of the fascist corporations' membership. The corporations contained a variety of class and professional groups, differing from the légions only in the absence of military and landowning elements. There were owners and directors of enterprises, managers, and a large number of engineers and other technical personnel. The Faisceau attracted shopkeepers and artisans especially in the provinces. On the lower end of the social scale, there were more salaried employees and white-collar workers than blue-collar ones, and virtually none from heavy industry. The occupational mix leaned heavily to the technical professions (engineers, architects, etc.) and finance (bankers, insurance agents, accountants). These middle-class groups, to which fascist ideology has often appealed, also reflected the technical and financial biases in Valois's thought. Police reports suggest, however, that despite all the obstacles, workers were getting the fascist message, and that increasing numbers were becoming interested. Given time, and the money that bought time, this nucleus could have been expanded.[95]

FASCIST FINANCES

As with recruitment, so with all aspects of Faisceau activity: the limiting factor was money. The basic cause was Valois's decision to start his campaign without reserves. The Faisceau and its daily paper were expensive. The *Nouveau Siècle* absorbed close to 8 million francs and the Faisceau may have drained over 2 million more. Monthly operating deficits for the fascist organization averaged 100,000 francs, and, though the Verdun meeting was cheaper, Reims cost 500,000 francs. Valois's decision to pay the *salaire-or* to the *Nouveau Siècle* staff and the 54-person Faisceau bureaucracy was expensive. While the franc fell in the spring and summer, this meant a constantly increasing drain. But even the recovery of the franc after July hurt, because Valois, expecting continued inflation, had covered himself by buying pounds. To most observers, fascist operations were wastefully conducted.[96]

The most consistent donors were the leading fascists: Valois, Arthuys, André, and Van den Broeck. The next most important contributor was a banker, Jean Beurrier, who came to Paris in 1923 and bought his way into the Union syndicale financière. A shoe manufacturer from Paris named Mayer was a major backer and, along with an engineer named Salomon, one of the few Jews with a visible position in the Faisceau. Their presence, as much as the Italian example, helped explain Valois's avoidance of anti-Semitism.[97]

Coty was the most important outside donor, having given a million and a half francs and constantly promised more. Close behind him came the brandy-making family of Hennessy-Martel. The Hennessys, who would take a more active role in right-wing politics in the 1930s, may have given Valois over a million francs. To avoid political complications, François-Marsal gave his contributions through Van den Broeck. Funds also came through Marcel Pescaud, who distributed money for the private railroad companies. The fascists' hostility to a state monopoly was probably a sufficient attraction. The Printemps department store contributed in the movement's first weeks but soon withdrew its support. In Paris commercial circles, Taittinger was far more popular than Valois.[98]

The financial history of the Faisceau and *Nouveau Siècle* was one of periodic, barely surmounted crises, the publication of the daily *Nouveau Siècle* on December 7 marking the conquest of the first. Valois's daring seemed to pay off as new contributions came in. But when expenses ran higher than expected, another crisis developed in early February. Accordingly, he launched the first of many ambitious collection campaigns. These changed none of the economic realities of the Faisceau. Large contributions continued to come in as before, irregularly and on the whim of those who could afford them. Modest donations demanded so much effort that the net gain was small. The subscription lists in the *Nouveau Siècle*, like those in the *Action française*, were juggled.[99]

By April, the financial situation had improved, and it remained good throughout the spring. Reims upset the delicate balance. Unable to raise the necessary funds in advance, Valois found himself faced with 320,000 francs of debts, due July 1. A generous friend paid these, but money remained short, and for the first time Faisceau operatives were paid late. Money problems plagued Valois throughout the fall. In September, he halted aid to provincial propaganda delegates, and in October, he made a heroic attempt to lick his financial problems through a loan campaign. The goal of ten million francs would have given the fascists needed breathing space. Valois toured the country, meeting with industrialists. Funds came in, but not enough. Finally, Valois was forced into the ultimate economy measure: the daily *Nouveau Siècle* was discontinued on December 4.[100]

PLANS FOR POWER AND THE PARLIAMENTARY CRISIS

Looking over the Faisceau's money problems, d'Humières opined that such an organization had to achieve its goals in a matter of months. He had run the organization for almost a year; it was up to others to take power. Many fascists felt the same way. Some joined expecting action, which could mean anything from demonstrations to the conquest of the state. Others expected the Faisceau to take power by itself or in conjunction with other right-wing groups. This attitude was supported by the rhetoric of the leadership. What were the *légions* if not a fighting organization? Some officers, sympathetic to Valois and Taittinger, expected the *légionnaires* to serve under their command in coming civil disturbances. The *légionnaires* themselves became restless by early spring. Eventually the truth had to be admitted. Valois never intended to throw his troops into battle against the government. As long as a government had the will to stay in power, Arthuys insisted, no force could remove it. Barrès added that nothing could be gained by fighting with police or soldiers in the street. A police correspondent, writing in June 1926, concluded that the fascists had no plans for an armed rising: they had not stockpiled arms or ammunition. Nor was Valois counting on a military coup. He had always argued that the most important organs of control in a modern state were not the military.[101]

Valois's solution came out in a discussion with a senior police official. Baiting Valois, the official insisted that the police were prepared to deal with any disturbances or attacks. Valois replied, "And if you are not given the order?"[102] Valois was counting on the disintegration of the government. His arguments were familiar. Inflation bred more inflation. The irresponsibility of parliamentary institutions would keep cabinets changing until the franc collapsed. Put another way, Finaly and the plutocrats intended to destroy the franc completely, which would bring severe social disturbances.

That would be the Faisceau's moment. *Légionnaires* were told: "Rendezvous on the day the franc reaches zero." The *légions* might be necessary to defeat a communist revolt, along with the corporations who could help break a general strike. Valois hoped to avoid a break with legality and, if possible, street violence. The Action française insisted that fascism had been successful in Italy because Mussolini was called to power by the king. France did not have a king, Barrès countered, but it had a president of the Republic. Valois wanted to create a shadow government that at the moment of crisis, would possess more support than the government. Hence the importance of attracting a large membership and showing it off at Verdun and Reims. Implied in this was a social and economic organization. The generalization of the *franc-or* would show the powerlessness of the government in one of the essential attributes of sovereignty, the regulation of money.[103] Valois was forced like the royalists whose inactivity he had often criticized to wait upon events.

For some time, however, it looked as if these were coming. During the year, finance ministers were juggled as the Cartel des gauches majority disintegrated. Shortly after the birth of the Faisceau, in November 1925, the government of Painlevé (who was his own finance minister) gave way to a set of Briand governments. But Briand had four finance ministers and by June, when Joseph Caillaux took over the ministry for the second time, the situation looked bleak. The franc had fallen to over 170 to the pound sterling, and any solution seemed blocked by the inability of the deputies to agree on a program.

Caillaux stalled, waiting for the report of the committee of experts called by an earlier Briand government. Published on July 4, the report condemned advances from the Bank of France, and called for restoring confidence (i.e., hostility to the Cartel's fiscal measures) and a stabilization backed by foreign loans. Though the *Nouveau Siècle* saluted the experts for criticizing parliament's financial management, it argued that the budget deficits implied by the plan would only provoke more inflation. When Caillaux adopted the major lines of the report, one of its weaknesses became apparent. Long-term foreign credits would have to come from the United States, requiring the ratification of the recent war debts repayment agreement. Repayment, however, was very unpopular, especially among veterans. This gave Valois another opportunity to link his veteran and financial themes. The Faisceau backed the huge veteran protest demonstration on July 11, as the financial and parliamentary crisis was reaching its climax.[104]

In June, Valois began flexing his muscles in preparation for a possible seizure of power. On the 14th, he saw Millerand to invite him to Reims, but also to sound him out on a possible dictatorship. Millerand indicated his disapproval. A few days earlier, addressing a packed meeting in Paris, Valois boasted that he had spoken to a group of left-wing deputies and proposed the formation of a faction of antiparliamentary deputies. The fascist leader mixed promises with threats. The deputies would do well to give up gracefully: the fascists would take account of their gesture.[105]

In July, the crisis headed rapidly for a climax. On the 16th, with the pound at 202 francs, Caillaux asked for delegation of legislative powers on financial matters. On the 17th, in a dramatic gesture, Herriot left his chair as president of the Chamber to attack Caillaux's request. Rumors in political circles, to which Valois presumably had access, claimed that Herriot had made his move on orders from Finaly and the iron magnate François de Wendel, while Louis Marin, who also attacked Caillaux, was said to be pushed by Wendel. Attacked from left and right, Caillaux lost the vote and resigned.[106]

President Gaston Doumergue asked Herriot to form another cabinet, but Herriot and his finance minister, Anatole de Monzie, were overturned upon their initial presentation to the Chamber on July 21. The fall of the Briand and Herriot governments took place in an atmosphere of panic and widespread discontent. The pound soared to 222 francs, prices fell in the stock market amid rumors that the Communists were planning a demonstration or even a general strike. Parisians booed Herriot and other deputies and attacked some foreigners, and on the 21st a hostile crowd formed in front of the Palais Bourbon. At fascist meetings, the fall of the Herriot government was acclaimed. Even the deputies became nervous.[107]

Arthuys and Valois stayed in Paris to monitor the crisis, but their only move was to announce their readiness to assume power.[108] Doumergue, however, had other options. On the 23d, Poincaré formed a Cabinet of National Union, and on the 24th, as confidence returned, the pound declined to 199 francs. On the 27th, Poincaré obtained his majority, and on the 31st the Chamber voted his tax package. The crisis was over.

Later in 1926, when it had become obvious that the fall of the Herriot government had been the high point of the crisis, Marcel Bucard reproached Valois with not having made his move. The fascist leader answered that a seizure of power would have provoked the rumored general strike, something with which their organization was unprepared to deal. A fascist coup might have brought the entire left together against it. Almost two years later, in his memoirs, Valois claimed that, as he mixed with the crowds in front of the Palais Bourbon on July 21, and from a taxi on the Pont de la Concorde, he saw undercover policemen manipulating the crowd. He recognized the agents because they were taking directions from a police official he had met at a party. The agents, he claimed, encouraged the crowd to demonstrate against Herriot but quickly dispersed it after the fall of the cabinet.[109]

Valois was also constrained by his own expectations of catastrophe. While things were going well for the government, it was a bad time to act. When, on the other hand, the position of the authorities was worsening, one had but to wait for the last obstacles to crumble. This is what happened in July 1926. For a few weeks, the political situation remained troubled. Valois undoubtedly kept up hope for a time and tried to maintain it among his followers several months longer. By November 1926, however, his major preoccupation shifted to holding his organization together.[110]

For the fascists, taking power meant the national revolution, the dictatorship of the *combattant* acting under a responsible leader. But the dictator was never named. Fascist leaders titillated their audiences while maintaining an ambiguous position. On the one hand, they argued, only events could reveal the leader: who could have selected Joan of Arc, Napoleon, or Foch in advance? On the other hand, they sometimes suggested, the name of the future dictator was being concealed to spare him ridicule or assassination.[111]

Was Valois the intended ruler? This was the view of the royalists, who lampooned the idea in the song "The Wooden Dictator." It was also the opinion of some police agents.[112] Nevertheless, this does not seem to be correct. Not only was the leadership of the Faisceau collegial, but Valois indicated his willingness to share power with any group, royalists and Communists excepted. He never asked for power for himself but stressed that the Faisceau would provide a "team" to solve the financial crisis and take the responsibilities of power. Nor did fascist militants seem to have felt their leader would become dictator. Privately, they thought that General Charles Mangin, whom Valois had approached in 1924, had been allotted this role, but that after his death only General Maxime Weygand was a serious contender. Valois did not take a modest view of his own importance. Certainly he put himself on the level of Mussolini or Lenin, but only as a world-historical figure, not as a personal dictator;[113] and the importance of the dictatorial positions of Mussolini, Hitler, and Stalin was not as apparent in 1926 as it would become later.

Yet in October, Lamour and Delagrange, at separate meetings, proposed Valois as the dictator. Present at the second meeting, Valois responded with a gesture of negation, and in his speech stressed that the coming national dictatorship should be of elites, not of one man. While Valois may have been sending up a trial balloon, it is more likely that these gestures were based on the intrigues of his subordinates. Besides, Valois had other preoccupations. He was trying to organize his movement for survival under what he called "the chloroform of Poincarism."[114]

SURVIVING POINCARE: THE ITALIAN CONNECTION

Valois did not expect the former president of the Republic to impose his will on parliament. Like his predecessors, Poincaré was controlled by the plutocrats. Further, raising the franc to close to its prewar value would damage French trade relations, causing widespread unemployment, a concern shared by Léon Blum and technicians at the Bank of France.[115] Besides, there was still the possibility that Poincaré would lose his majority, reopening the crisis.[116]

But Poincaré posed problems. Though fascist ideology clearly condemned the parliamentary right as it did the left, the sympathies of the average fascist were with the right. Concerned about Poincaré's popularity, especially in the east, from which the fascists drew so many of their militants, Barrès pressured Valois to support the government of national union. In some local sections, the leaders declared that, not wishing to prejudice the work of national recovery, the Faisceau would refrain from public political activity. Valois's response was to maintain his position that only a dictatorship and the *franc-or* could save France, while claiming that the powers delegated to Poincaré were parliamentary fascism and accounted for his success.[117]

The Faisceau continued to grow as fast as it had in the spring. By October, new *légionnaires* were getting cards in the 60,000 series, though the actual number was lower, since some numbers had been left open for the provinces. Total Faisceau membership may have reached 60,000 by November. Recruitment was slower in Paris than in the provinces, where the fascists' natural base had not been reached in all areas.[118]

At Reims, Valois had promised his followers they would meet again on the banks of the Marne. Most expected a meeting at Meaux, perhaps on the anniversary of the battle of the Marne, the 7th, 8th, or 9th of September, but it became apparent by August that this date would not be met. Instead, on September 5, 150 blue shirts joined in Meaux with members of other *ligues* at commemorative ceremonies. Valois could not organize another *journée nationale* if it were not more important than the one before. The major problem was money. Talk of a Meaux meeting continued for several months, but as time passed, the reality was postponed.[119]

To keep his public interested, Valois held another meeting in the Salle Wagram on October 5. Over 2,500 came to hear him, Arthuys, and Delagrange attack Poincaré. Concluding his address, Valois turned to his audience and cried out: "Who made the victory?" The audience responded: "We did." "Who then will save France, and who will take power tomorrow?" asked Valois. "We will," the massed voices answered each time. The meeting had become more sophisticated; bands played and lights went on and off as the orators took the podium. The audience was enthusiastic, and the fascists were well satisfied. Their public was loyal and, in some quarters, growing.[120]

The next step was a still larger meeting. The easiest issue to exploit against the Poincaré government was the ratification of the unpopular repayment accords on France's debts to Britain and the United States. Nonratification, however, dictated a Continental, rather than pro–Anglo-Saxon, foreign policy. This fitted the pro-Italian tendencies of Valois's fascism. In fact, during the summer and fall of 1926, he had been increasing his contacts with Mussolini's state.

By borrowing the fascist name, Valois associated his movement with a foreign force whose actions might prove embarrassing. As a self-proclaimed nationalist, he could be charged with following in the footsteps of foreigners, if not of treason. Valois was the first to wrestle with the contradictions of a fascist internationalism. He insisted that French fascism was independent of the Italian party, that they were parallel branches of an international movement.[121] That was true. The Faisceau was an off-shoot of the Action française, not of the Italian *fascisti*. Nor did Italian fascist doctrines play a significant role in the development of Valois's ideas. Nevertheless, there were continual contacts between the two groups.

The foundation of the Faisceau was greeted with pleasure by the Italian colony in Paris. Valois and the Fascio of Paris displayed the utmost discretion, avoiding open contacts. Italian observers were, however, present at the inaugural meeting, which received laudatory notice in the transalpine fascist newspaper, *L'impero*. In Italy, the response was more open. The daily *Nouveau Siècle* received a wide distribution, and many Fascist party officials bought subscriptions. French government agents claimed that an agreement had been made between the two groups for the publication and diffusion of the paper. The Italians continued a sympathetic curiosity. When the Faisceau held a meeting in Annemasse, near the Swiss border, members of the Fascio of Geneva attended.[122]

Valois, who was becoming aware that not all fascists were revolutionaries, chose his contacts carefully. In April 1926, he introduced Delagrange and Dumas to a left-wing fascist, Ambrosini, who had worked for a fascist-syndicalist paper in Rome. Officially independent of the Italian government, Ambrosini ran an "Italian revolutionary syndicalist group" in Paris. In fact, Ambrosini was probably an Italian agent. The first of a series of joint meetings was held, with little publicity, on April 10. As the meeting ended, however, a raincoat was stolen, and the French concluded that the thief was a member of Ambrosini's bodyguard. There were no further contacts.[123]

Shortly after, Van den Broeck introduced Valois to an Italian journalist recently arrived in Paris, Esposito. Valois expressed his interest in regular discussions with the Italians. In July, Esposito answered that the Italians were willing to discuss monetary matters. An August trip fell through when Valois insisted on having the talks begin on the French side of the border. A second attempt was arranged for September 10. After some difficulties, Valois and Arthuys met Esposito and an Italian official at the border station of Chiasso. The party went on to Milan, where the French fascists met with Arnaldo Mussolini, brother of the Duce, and other *fascisti*. The two sets of experts disagreed on monetary policy. Valois and Arthuys objected to Italian revalorization, which would only, they argued, make a French stabilization harder. Worse still, by raising the prices of Italian goods in world markets, it would create industrial stagnation in Italy, leaving the country prey to Anglo-American finance.[124] Valois and the president of the Italian fascist corporations, Edmondo Rossoni, discussed the possibility of holding an international fascist corporative conference in Geneva. Valois also considered sending some of his followers on study trips to Italy.[125]

Upon his return to France on September 16, Valois threw himself into plans for the reorganization of the Faisceau and further cooperation with the Italians. There was so much coming and going of Italians around the Faisceau offices that it was said that Valois took no important decision without contacting the Italian embassy.[126] The rapprochement was ill-timed, since Franco-Italian relations were not at their best. When Valois was in Milan, word arrived of yet another attempted assassination of Mussolini, this one, also, apparently linked to antifascist émigrés in Paris. The French public, on its side, was upset about the demands of Italian extremists for Savoy, Nice, Corsica, and Tunisia.[127]

It is difficult to get a precise idea of Valois's involvement with the Italians. Certainly, there were contacts, but the major question of whether the Italians paid Valois remains. He denied receiving so much as a centime from any non-French source. Nevertheless, a French agent in Italy reported that he had been assured that the leaders of the Faisceau were receiving funds from their Italian comrades. Another agent reported that an informant, "Charles," claimed he could provide evidence of collusion, and that the incriminating documents were in the Italian embassy safe. When the backers and finances of the Faisceau were summarized for Poincaré, however, no mention was made of Italian funds. Any Italian contribution would had to have been quite modest. Buying French journalists was commonplace, and Mussolini did more than his share. But his money was better spent on well-read conservative dailies. Nor was the overthrow of the French government a likely policy. Police records show that the many Italian agents in France were busy watching the thousands of immigrant workers and political exiles. And Mussolini kept excellent relations with the *Journal*, the daily recently purchased by Horace Finaly. In later years, however, Mussolini supported both the Austrian Heimwehr and Bucard's Francistes.[128]

Valois needed the Italians for his next event: a giant meeting against the Washington accords and for the Latin bloc, set for November 2d at the Cirque de Paris. A major novelty was his decision to share the podium with representatives of sister Latin states: Leopold Reuhl for Belgium, Ibañez de Ibero for Spain, Pequito Rebello for Portugal, and the futurist Filippo Marinetti for Italy.

The speakers confined themselves to bold but vague phrases against the plutocrats and in favor of the *combattants* and the Latin bloc. Valois argued that a Latin bloc was necessary to counterbalance the Anglo-Saxons and their financiers. It thus went hand in hand with firmness on war debts. The audience of over four thousand, while it did not fill the Cirque, was impressive. The band played the national anthem of each speaker, and Valois brought the house down when he exchanged the Roman salute and fascist cry with representatives of the Fascio of Paris. Two hundred members of the Jeunesses patriotes attended with their insignia. Many put themselves at the service of the fascist guard; a new wave of conversions from the Jeunesses seemed to be in the offing. [129]

Valois seemed to have an issue and the momentum necessary to survive Poincaré. This, however, failed to take account of the deterioration of Franco-Italian relations and of Valois's most resolute opponents: the royalists. The meeting itself was followed by a rash of border incidents as the French and Italian press helped raise the international temperature. In this climate, on November 6, Maurras printed the letter of a recent Faisceau deserter, Jacques Debu-Bridel. Apparently upset by Valois's pro-Italian policies as well as by friction with the *Nouveau Siècle* staff, Debu-Bridel had resigned and returned to the Action française. He wrote Maurras a letter charging Valois with having sold his movement to the Italians. Debu-Bridel claimed that Umberto Ferrini and Esposito were Italian agents, that Valois went to Geneva and Italy to receive funds, and that he took his orders from the Italian embassy. His proofs were remarks he had overheard Ferrini making on the telephone in Italian. Moreover, he claimed that after Valois's trips, the material situation of the newspaper improved dramatically. (It did not.) Debu-Bridel never produced any serious evidence in support of his conclusions, but this did not keep them from being endorsed by Maurras, who accused Valois of treason. [130]

The fascists were stunned that Maurras took Debu-Bridel seriously. Considered incompetent, he had been the whipping boy of the *Nouveau Siècle* editorial staff. Their answer was to deny the charges (although without refuting Debu-Bridel's points) and accuse Maurras of serving international finance through the intermediation of de Monzie. [131]

Maurras continued his campaign, only exacerbating the international situation. The French government accused the Italians of interference in French politics. Valois, receiving warnings that the police had proof of his collusion with the Italians, became concerned that he might become the victim of a sensational newspaper campaign or even prosecution based on a forged document. The plutocrats seemed willing to risk war to break his campaign to create a Latin bloc. Accordingly, he decided to lance the abscess with a physical attack on the Action française. He obviously wanted to cow the royalists and slake his anger. Valois argued, however, that by taking illegal action, he would show he was unafraid of publicity or court action.

Valois had been itching to do something since the Salle d'horticulture incidents, but he had been dissuaded by his lieutenants. Now the threat of international complications overcame these hesitations. Further, the resources of the Faisceau and the Action française were sufficiently similar for each to know the other's financial state. Both were suffering from the revival of confidence in the government. Valois's conclusion was that there was not enough money for both groups. An attack, he hoped, would kill the Action française.[132]

On December 12, Valois gave Maurras an ultimatum. If the campaign were not ceased within forty-eight hours, action would be taken to make it cease. The following day, Arthuys and two other fascists sent a threatening letter. It concluded: "You are going to shut up, and immediately, or we will shut you up." The royalists, of course, dropped none of their charges—not that Valois expected them to. For several days, he had been planning retaliation. After elaborate precautions to maintain secrecy, on Sunday, December 14, Valois sent his *légionnaires* against royalist headquarters, 12 rue de Rome. Shortly after 7:00 P.M., while Valois waited with the bulk of his men, over thirty fascists entered the building. Over twenty ran up the stairs, opened the doors, and began turning the rooms upside down. As Valois had intended when he chose that time, few royalists were present, under a dozen, including Maurice Pujo, Daudet, and Bacconier. He also knew that Maurras was absent. This did not stop his office from being a target of the *légionnaires*, who rushed in crying: "Chez Maurras." Daudet locked himself in his office and remained undisturbed. As the brawl developed, an unidentified fascist (both groups refused to make identifications for the police) bounded up the stairs carrying a pistol against orders. His gun went off in front of a door, triggering a volley of shots from the royalists behind it. Two fascists were injured, one lightly and the other seriously: a bullet punctured a lung. Valois considered the fascist who started the shooting an agent-provocateur. He also felt, rightly, that it was a miracle no one had been killed. The blue shirts accomplished their mission quickly. When the police arrived, most of the fascists were gone.[133]

Valois was delighted with his handiwork. After eleven months to the day, he had avenged the royalist attack on the Salle d'horticulture. He also hoped he had sounded the death knell of royalist influence. Maurras was in the middle of a much more serious fight with the pope, who objected to an organization enjoying much Catholic support being run by a self-proclaimed atheist. The attack, however, drew the royalists together in anger and provided an ideal distraction from the more serious religious problem.[134]

The fascists suffered most. Some members had always felt that Valois spent too much time on polemics with the royalists. Others had chosen the Faisceau because they disapproved of brawling. Valois had already lost those who liked camelot stunts, and now he lost those who did not, provoking a rash of resignations and defections by financial backers. The rue de Rome expedition sealed the fate of the daily *Nouveau Siècle*.[135] A year after the foundation of the Faisceau, Valois's dreams of taking power were more remote than ever, his daily gone, and his organization cracking.

SIX

The Faisceau, III

Falling Left

The Faisceau, after growing rapidly in 1925 and 1926, declined even more quickly in 1927. The most important reason was the improvement in French finances and public confidence wrought by Poincaré. The decline and fall of the Faisceau paralleled Valois's own move leftward, but this latest shift on his part began, not when the Faisceau was near collapse, but at its zenith, and with a purely political problem, Valois's monarchism.

DOCTRINAL SHIFTS

Valois's position as a monarchist outside the Action française became increasingly awkward. Polemics with the royalists pushed the fascists into increasingly antimonarchist positions. After one exchange in February 1926, Bertrand de Lur-Saluces left the group he had so recently joined, taking other provincial royalists with him. At the same time, the pressures of antiroyalists like Philippe Barrès and Marcel Delagrange only increased. Valois knew, as many Frenchmen did not, that relations were not always good between the Action française and its titular leader, the duc d'Orléans. The Pretender knew Valois well and disapproved of the personal campaigns against him. Throughout 1926, Valois hoped to steer him into a break with the Action française. Initial results were encouraging. In February the Pretender wrote a former *ligueur*, now in the Faisceau, implicitly disavowing the attack at the Salle d'horticulture and calling for the cooperation of all nationalists; and Valois read the text frequently at public meetings. But the duc d'Orléans died in April, and the new Pretender, the duc de Guise, took no public stand.[1]

In the weeks before and after the Reims gathering, Valois tried to interest rightist politicians like Alexandre Millerand and André Tardieu in his projects. The answer was the one he had received from Poincaré in 1923 and Sorel in 1908: Frenchmen were not interested in a dictator, and even less in a king. Partly as a result, Valois began republicanizing his movement. He closed his national assembly at Reims by baptizing the movement the République des combattants et des producteurs. On July 14, Bastille Day, the *Nouveau Siècle* carried a long article celebrating the French Revolution as a renewal of elites. But Valois had not cut his ties to the Pretender. In July, in the face of continuing Action française polemics, Valois wrote the duc de Guise to ask if he approved the royalists' charges. The duke maintained his neutrality, and Valois asked for an audience in Belgium in August. There, Valois declared that he would no longer attempt to restore the monarchy and that he did not believe the French people wanted a king or would tolerate a regime without popular support. When he left Brussels, he felt liberated personally and politically.[2]

The liberation remained private, however. There were many royalists and Bonapartists among the fascists, and Valois still hoped for help from the Pretender. On November 6, after being accused of treason by the Action française, Valois again tried to involve the duke. The latter's neutral response was the last straw in Valois's relations with the house of France: along with the raid on the Action française headquarters, which alienated his remaining royalist sympathizers, it cut Valois's last ties to monarchism. At the first annual Fascist Congress in January 1927, the Faisceau officially "entered" the Republic.[3]

Valois insisted that a prince was a person, not a principle, and that loyalty was based on services rendered. With ill-concealed bitterness, Valois asserted that the duke had had an excellent recent opportunity to take a stand for justice. There was truth in the charge by Jean Brière that Valois abandoned the monarchy from anger and disappointment.[4] It would be fairer to say that Valois acted from a mixture of motives. Disappointments with allies reinforced the questioning of his assumptions.

This shift was accompanied by others, elaborated in articles in the *Nouveau Siècle* in 1926 and published in *Le Fascisme* in January 1927. Valois began by redefining fascism. Gone was the eternal resistance to the Barbarian. Now, paying homage to Maurice and Philippe Barrès, Valois defined his movement through the equation nationalism + socialism = fascism. Not only did he take Boulangism as a precursor, but socialism, replacing the more ambivalent syndicalism, sounded closer to the republican left. The change went further. Valois explained that fascism was the culmination of a process, begun by the French Revolution, that was creating the modern state. Liberal parliamentarianism was bankrupt and only fascism combined the participation of nationalism with the justice of socialism. Valois also adopted Enrico Corradini's characterization of fascism as surpassing, but not negating, democracy, liberalism, and socialism.[5]

Gone was the concept of the Revolution as an ahistorical triumph of anti-France (or the *quatre états* or the plutocrats). Now it was a renewal of elites who had ceased to fulfill their role. This took Valois back to his positions of 1906. However, by stating that these elites had failed to adjust to the demand for a new, industrial state, he placed himself further left than he had been in twenty years. Valois also defined fascism as the move ment by which politically conscious members of the working class would enter the government, just as the Revolution had marked the political entry of the bourgeoisie. This historical model represented a close parallel to the Marxist interpretation he had once refuted. Combined with the familiar insistence on technical progress and high salaries, this sense of historical development created a relatively left-leaning fascism, as distinct from the right-leaning fascism of 1925, with its links to French reactionary and royalist traditions.[6]

FASCIST INTERNAL POLITICS

These changes were accompanied by the rise of Paul-Charles Biver. Then in his thirties, Biver was an engineer, decorated for bravery (like so many fascists) who had risen to vice president of the fascist metallurgical corporation.[7] Biver was given the job of pruning the bureaucracy and reducing expenses. Valois had been trying to trim costs since August 1926, with varying degrees of success. Expenses for speakers were cut, and some already approved were not honored, with predictable effects. In December, clerical workers were laid off, and on January 1 many of the central office personnel were fired; the rest had their salaries sharply reduced. In addition, the *franc-or* clause was modified, eliminating the minimum in paper francs, crucial in light of the revalorization of the franc. Many important fascists saw their salaries cut by 40 percent. The deficit was reduced from 900,000 francs on December 31 to 300,000 a month later, when salaries, in arrears for months, were finally paid on time.[8]

A storm of recrimination burst upon Valois. If he were not so stubborn with benefactors like Eugène Mathon and François Coty, there would be money enough for all. These economy measures, added to the disappearance of the daily *Nouveau Siècle*, boded ill for the movement, and many began to make their own plans. Pessimism was not limited to the center. The fascists of the Nord were demoralized, and those of the east had been almost totally inactive since Poincaré had taken over the government. Everywhere, many feared that between half and three quarters of their membership would not renew their cards. Even Valois showed signs of strain.[9] The morale of the eastern cadres was further weakened by the maneuvers of Philippe Lamour and Marcel Bucard. By late 1926, these lieutenants had become as critical of Valois as he had been of Charles Maurras. Their response was to contact Coty, who backed a "dump Valois" movement.

Coty's million and a half francs came to an end in the late fall of 1926. For months he and Valois had been negotiating over continued support for the Faisceau. The major stumbling block was Coty's support for the ratification of the Mellon-Béranger debt repayment accords. Aside from Valois's own convictions, his veteran support made compromise impossible. Coty also wanted a more anti-Semitic line, and Valois had long come to the conclusion that such campaigns were diversions from the real issue. Valois preferred a weekly to a "cotydien."[10]

All this promised to come to a head at the First National Fascist Congress, January 22–24. Valois drew out his opponents by declaring that the congress would discuss elections, suggesting he was ready to abandon his revolutionary projects, perhaps even run for parliament. Valois's opponents hoped to group those still loyal to the Pretenders, royalist or Bonapartist, with those against any hint of electoralism. This negative majority, led by Bucard and Lamour, would dethrone the "Chef." Compared to a seasoned campaigner like Valois, however, his opponents were amateurs. All problems were postponed to the final session. There Valois filibustered for four hours, raising and refuting every objection and carrying his own vaguely worded compromise resolutions. The Faisceau would not participate in the elections or join an electoral group, but would not exclude attempts to influence the elections through tactical alliances. The execution of the policy was entrusted to a Fascist Supreme Council dominated by Valois and his more trusted associates. A week later the council delivered the new "party line." To affect the elections, without participating in them, the fascists would form vigilance committees with other nonelectoral groups tending toward the formation of a "youth bloc." A few weeks later, Valois publicized his break with the monarchy.[11]

Valois admitted much to his followers. Yes, most of them had joined expecting, as he had, a quick victory. But the enemy had taken cover behind Poincarism; a war of attrition was necessary. Fascism, which would dominate the century, might take decades to win. Gone was the program of "action" around which Valois had gathered the bulk of his supporters. This shift was disguised by enough rhetoric to give Valois the free hand he sought. Such a "parliamentary" solution, however, provoked individual defections, encouraged by the fascists' dimming prospects. Shortly after the congress, Valois forced out Pierre Dumas, whom he discovered in secret correspondence with Mathon. Franz van den Broeck, who had made himself scarce for weeks, took the occasion of Valois's break with the Pretender to resign on principle. The Action française decided that former fascists could reenter the Ligue after appropriate signs of contrition. The two main conspirators, Bucard and Lamour, were permitted to remain in the Faisceau.[12]

THE LAST MONETARY CAMPAIGN

Valois had run out of neither optimism nor ideas. He sought to revive his position with another monetary campaign. Since the restoration of confidence in fall 1926, catastrophic inflation no longer threatened. The question became whether to stabilize at the current rate of about 150 francs to the pound sterling or continue revalorization toward the franc's prewar (and still legal) value. Most of the French public (especially the *rentiers*), and thus most politicians, including Poincaré, were in favor of revalorization.

On the other hand, since the report of the government's committee of experts in June 1926, the leading financial specialists of the Banks of France and Algeria were opposed to revalorization. Unless accompanied by automatic salary reductions (a political and social impossibility), a rise in the franc above its internal purchasing power would create unemployment in France, while raising the prices of French goods in foreign markets; the English case was there for all to see. In the months after Poincaré took over, many businessmen had come round to this view, followed by organized labor.[13]

Valois took his stand with the stabilizers and against the revalorizers. But, in contrast to his earlier campaigns, he entered the lists as the battle was drawing to a close. By 1927 the Bank of France had effectively stabilized, obliging a reluctant Poincaré to approve the purchase of gold and foreign currencies to halt the rise in the franc. Though Poincaré was not officially convinced, he had already opted for prosperity over revalorization.[14]

Though aware of the argument based on export prices (since he had used it against Italy), Valois chose more familiar explanations, such as the artificial losses provoked by deflation. These would lead to a treasury crisis and a new bout of inflation. Revalorization was promoted by the pluto-crats and Horace Finaly, who would again benefit from the manipulation of the exchanges. Nor was this unrealistic. At the Bank of France, Charles Rist reported in October 1926 that an international consortium had formed to play on the rise of the franc and profit by further raising the franc with Poincaré's help. Valois also hoped either to attract business sup-port or to take advantage of the unemployment already developing in the Paris suburbs. Between the lack of money, bureaucratic inertia, and gen-eral demoralization, the only responses were Pierre Darras's attempt at company unionism and a newspaper campaign to expel foreign and colo-nial workers.[15]

Valois also revived his old panacea, the *franc-or*. Disingenuously, he argued that a money of account would permit stabilization or a gradual re-valorization, since in either case businessmen would be protected from monetary fluctuations. France could have two currencies: one for produc-ers, the *franc-or*, and one for *rentiers*, paper francs. Finally, Valois argued that the current stability was at the mercy of a parliamentary crisis. The *franc-or* would make it permanent.[16]

On February 13, Valois informed his readers that he and Arthuys, act-ing as representatives of the Ligue du franc-or, had been granted an au-dience with Poincaré on the 19th. Valois was in a difficult position. Some fascists blamed him for not attacking Poincaré more vigorously (as he had once blamed Maurras), while Barrès and his friends urged support for the Lorraine statesman. Valois's response was to offer his cooperation in the interests of France. Poincaré was in a stronger position. Shortly after the appointment was set, he received a lengthy report prepared for the occa-sion by the police. Its conclusions were simple: whatever influence Valois had had in the past, he and his organizations were finished politically, out of money, and rapidly disintegrating. This assessment was certainly not unrelated to the "icy" reception Valois and Arthuys received.[17]

Besides giving his unasked advice, Valois called for a second Semaine de la monnaie to examine the problems of stabilization and revalorization. He quickly found a president in Octave Homberg, a colonial financier and leader of the campaign against the Washington accords.[18] The organizing committee included few holdovers from the first Semaine. The three vice presidents were Valois; the deputy Georges Bonnet, a long-time proponent of a gold-based money of account; and another deputy, Louis Germain-Martin. The reporters included an assortment of deputies (François Piétri, Lucien Lamoureux, Jean Hennessy, and André François-Poncet), professors drawn largely from the law faculties, and a few businessmen. The secretariat was made up of André Fourgeaud of the Ligue de la république, Jean Beurrier, and René de la Porte. Absent was any participation by the Bank of France, François-Marsal, or the government.[19]

The Semaine was set for May. In the meantime, fascists were to sell their monetary program to the country. Again, Valois stressed the political importance of monetary questions to uncomprehending *légionnaires*, tying it to a demagogic appeal for a "franc de la victoire." On the new stabilized currency, Marianne should be replaced by the *combattant*, an unarmed foot soldier protecting agriculture and industry. The usual preparations were made for another Salle Wagram meeting on April 5.[20] The strategy had shifted. Instead of trumpeting the national revolution, Valois retreated toward the more ambiguous formulae of the Etats-Généraux. Invitations only spoke of monetary concerns and omitted the fascist letterhead. Though the audience of 1,200 roared its approval when the recently recruited Henri Lauridan offered his life for the Faisceau, it showed much less interest in the monetary discussions that followed. Such themes could not rouse the same interest in April 1927 that they had in June 1926.[21]

At the second Semaine, the revalorizers were as solidly defeated as the inflationists had been in 1922. A strong majority also voted to permit reckoning and contracts in a gold-based money of account. The government never sanctioned the *franc-or*, and neither was it ever widely used in France. Nevertheless, when Poincaré and the Bank of France legally stabilized the franc in June 1928, Valois claimed that he and the second Semaine had been major causes. While the opinions expressed by the professors and businessmen of the Semaine helped Poincaré's decision, the positions of the Bank of France and the CGT leader Léon Jouhaux were more important.[22]

The second Semaine de la monnaie brought to an end the series of monetary campaigns begun in 1919. During these years, Valois developed and consistently applied the same principles. He echoed the ideas of the more conservative financiers of his time, their hostility to managed currencies and worship of the gold standard. Valois took a more advanced position in 1927 when he recognized, as many public figures did not, that revalorization would create insuperable economic problems. In French monetary politics, Valois and the Bank of France were always on the same side, though often in opposition to the government. From 1921 through 1926, Valois's activities were principally directed against fiduciary inflation, and he insisted on the repayment of the bank's advances to the state. The bank showed its appreciation by offering its financial support for Valois's corporative ventures, as well as backing the first Semaine de la monnaie. Of course, his was only one among a number of enterprises receiving the bank's favors. Valois's major contact was Jules Décamps, head of the economic studies department at the bank, who apparently kept the governor, Robineau, informed.[23]

In 1926 and 1927 Valois and the Bank of France favored stabilization. But Valois had lost his backing. Robineau was replaced in June 1926, and when Décamps was killed in an automobile accident in August, the new governor, Lucien Moreau, put in his own man, Pierre Quesnay. Moreau and Quesnay, along with Charles Rist, now made monetary policy. Moreau cultivated journalists and politicians, but Valois was never one of them. Nor was Moreau on good terms with Homberg; and the second Semaine de la monnaie was not even mentioned in the former's memoirs. One cause was the change in personnel, another, Valois's recent political campaigns.[24] Valois had been a faithful ally, but the bank neither bought nor owned him. Equally undeniably, he was often manipulated by individuals at the bank, who leaked information for his campaigns as appropriate.

FIGHTS WITH COTY AND THE ROYALISTS

But Valois had other battles. In March and April, Coty and Désiré Ley stirred up a journalistic storm over an alleged communist plot in France. Valois considered it a replay of the red scare of 1924, and a British ploy to lead Western Europe into war with the Soviet Union to save the British Empire in Asia. Valois now also considered Coty a British agent. Valois attacked the anticommunist campaigns in a series of articles, culminating in a May 1st piece clearly designating Coty as the culprit. Great Britain, the perfumer had written, was the supreme rampart of the West; without it, France and Europe would crumble. Valois spread the quotation across his front page. Here was an insult to the *combattants* of the Marne, implying they needed British tutelage. It was also an occasion for the invocation of Joan of Arc.[25]

The recently canonized saint became the focus of Valois's campaign against Britain and the red scare. Valois announced another meeting/pilgrimage for May 22 at Domrémy, to show respect for Joan of Arc, hostility to England, and the eternal vigilance of the French soldier guarding the Rhine. He believed in the danger of war and wanted to show the world that Frenchmen were not about to fight Russia under British direction. He also wanted to embarrass Coty and win back the confidence of his troops.

A crowd of five to six hundred attended the parade and indoor meeting. By meeting Coty on the terrain of nationalism, rather than social policy, Valois gained an advantage with his militants. The anti-British campaign was sufficiently popular among rank-and-file fascists to place Coty's agents, Bucard and Lamour, on the defensive. In the middle of the campaign, on May 15, Bucard was quietly forced out of the Faisceau.[26] Compared with Reims and Verdun, Domrémy marked a retreat. Not a step on the road to the national revolution, Domrémy, like the annual processions of the Action française, was more concerned with entertaining the membership than with taking power.

Meanwhile more and more fascists simply ceased attending meetings. By May 1927 two-thirds of the peak membership of about sixty thousand may have become inactive. In the east, many centers were dormant. In the Nord, Valois was criticized for Poincarism, while in Bordeaux the police reported that the "bourgeois" members of the local Faisceau had lost interest.[27]

As his organization languished, Valois was diverted to a set of legal battles. In September 1926 he had publicly challenged the editors of the *Action française* to sign a statement reiterating their charges against him as director of the two corporations that ran the Nouvelle Librairie nationale and the *Nouveau Siècle*. In French law, writers sued for libeling private citizens could only defend themselves by proving the truth of their charges if those they attacked applied for the credit or savings of the public. Valois's challenge was not accepted, and he began proceedings against Daudet, Maurras, Pujo, Jacques Debu-Bridel, and Joseph Delest, administrator of the *Action française*, asking for 200,000 francs in damages. The royalists responded with countersuits demanding 2,700,000 francs, hoping that, at the worst, the two condemnations might cancel each other out.[28]

The cases were heard together by the XIIᵉ Chambre Correctionelle in June 1927. Valois anticipated the hearings with a mixture of relish, because he knew the royalists could not prove their charges, and anxiety because he lacked confidence in his own lieutenants. Valois feared that one of Coty's agents, like the recently resigned Bucard, might create an incident during the proceedings. Worse still, Lamour, the principal attorney, might betray his boss. Partly as a result, he was assisted by another fascist lawyer, Jacques Marx.[29]

The hearings were almost a personal triumph for Valois. Neither Maurras nor Daudet appeared. The royalist evidence was meager at best. Provincial members, brought to Paris to explain that their addresses had been stolen, were confronted by Lamour with copies of their correspondence with the Nouvelle Librairie nationale. Mme. Vatatzi, the widow of Valois's old employer in Russia, took the stand to show the absurdity of the charge that her husband would have brought him from France to make him a police agent. Despite aggressive cross-examinations, the only point the royalist counsel established was that the editors of the Nouveau Siècle split up large sums into smaller ones on their lists of contributors. His insistence exasperated Valois, since in doing so the fascists were protecting Coty, whose gifts did not even show up on the royalists' lists. The court threw out all the royalist complaints, ruling that Valois was excused by the harshness of the polemic against him and had avoided defamation. The court also found for Valois in his own suits, awarding 25,000 francs in damages from the defendants, who were also fined. However, the judges denied Valois's request for publication of the judgment in the Action française. Valois published the court proceedings himself, but in the absence of publication of the judgment in the royalist daily, he could not inform its readers of it.[30]

EVASION

Valois was still a practicing Catholic, a politically useful point given the royalists' struggle with the Church. These considerations may have influenced his decision to make a pilgrimage, on foot, to Lourdes in late July. All Valois told his readers was that he was acquitting himself of an old debt, and that this was the first summer in several years that he had had the time.[31] Psychologically, the trip seems an evasion. Valois wanted to get away from politics. Like his adolescent travels, this shorter trip also gave him time to rethink his intellectual positions, producing some of his later projects. For the Faisceau, it was destructive. On his own admission, Valois left his organization penniless and demoralized.

Valois was accompanied by his eldest son, Bernard, on foot; his younger son Philippe, on a bicycle; and a number of fascists traveling by car. The party left Paris on July 20. After two hundred kilometers, Valois stepped on a nail and then aggravated the wound by walking on it for two days. While Bernard continued on foot, his father went on by car, meeting him nightly to sleep in a barn or a tent.[32]

While the leader was away, de la Porte was left to pay the bills and quiet complainers. Marcel Delagrange and Pierre Darras tried to split the corporations off from the Faisceau. Delagrange was too preoccupied by his own sexual intrigues to accomplish much, but Darras led his construction corporation out of the Faisceau. Delagrange was dismissed in September upon Valois's return. None of the movements to dump Valois could find an acceptable replacement. Of the two figures with sufficient stature, Arthuys remained loyal and Barrès quietly withdrew.[33]

NEW DIRECTIONS AND NEW ALLIES

During the second half of 1927, the fascist leader started casting about for new allies—on the left. This was a process that would continue for the rest of his life, during which he would define himself as a man of the left. In 1927, Valois was abandoning fascism and provoking the dissolution of the Faisceau. Locked in combat with the Action française and Coty, where else could he turn but to the left? And, if the royalist battle with the Holy See reinforced Valois's Catholicism, it also associated him with the democratic Catholics. Valois made continual overtures to Marc Sangnier and his friends, though with little success. Valois had better luck in Radical and Radical-Socialist circles. He seems to have always maintained some contact with Joseph Caillaux or his agents. The fascist invasion of the rue de Rome was applauded in *La Volonté*.[34]

Valois sought an alliance with young Radicals grouped around three small newspapers, *La Volonté*, *Le Rappel*, and *Paris-Phare*. Like Valois, these men wanted to replace the parliamentary Republic with a system that would both strengthen the executive and provide for syndical or economic representation. Some, like Henry de Jouvenel, had been calling for an economic parliament when Valois was mounting his campaigns for the Etats-Généraux. These were the groups Valois hoped to enlist in his "youth bloc." Throughout the late spring and summer of 1927, he advertised his interest in joining a republican antiparliamentary federation. The Faisceau would not enter the electoral process, but it could support a larger group that did.[35]

His offer was taken seriously by two leaders of small groups: Charles-Albert and Pierre Dominique. Charles-Albert had been Valois's colleague years before on *L'Art social*, and Valois had always treated him with respect. After the war he founded a small group, L'Ordre nouveau, which called for the integration of syndicalism into a strengthened state. Pierre Dominique was a medical doctor and founder of the Club Camille Desmoulins, whose program Valois claimed, in *Le Fascisme*, with only slight exaggeration, was "in the purest fascist spirit." It called for the replacement of parliament by a Committee of Public Safety and eventual convocation of the Etats-Généraux. The new Republic would be based on syndicalist and regional principles. Finally the club sought to base itself on veterans and workers. Dominique admired the functioning of both the Bolshevik and Italian Fascist parties and linked them to the Jacobins and Committee of Public Safety of the Revolution. Though it was the prototatalitarian aspects of the Jacobin example that most appealed to Dominique, since he evoked the French Revolution, he considered himself a "pure" republican.[36]

The purity of Valois's republicanism was a major issue. In June 1926, Dominique had opposed Valois's national assembly at Reims, not because of its antiparliamentarianism, but because of its reactionary and antirepublican connections. Dominique conceded that Valois's program had many good points, but insisted that neither he nor the Faisceau were acceptable partners. Valois had been a royalist for twenty years and had built the Faisceau with royalists, Bonapartists, and other reactionaries. Until the new republican proved himself, authentic republicans were justified in keeping their distance.[37]

Charles-Albert came to similar conclusions. In his article "And Why Not a Left Fascism?" he argued that the new party he sought should resemble a left fascism, whether or not it bore the name. Charles-Albert found the Faisceau program appealing, arguing that it represented *a* fascism (and not *Le Fascisme* as Valois said). While this fascism had good points, Valois linked it with Italian Fascism, which was totally unacceptable. The objection was cogent; Valois could define *fascism* as he wished, but he could not talk away the Italian example.[38] The message was clear. To be accepted, Valois would have to jettison fascism in word and deed.

Valois spent the rest of 1927 de-fascisizing his movement. In June he founded the Club du nouveau siècle in imitation of the republican clubs of Paris. Even the meetings represented a sharp break in political style. Valois's fascism had been characterized by grandiose public gatherings, replete with bands and banners. The pilgrimages, usually accompanied by vigils, were focal points of his national revolution. The new club meetings, where Valois exchanged arguments with his contradictors, were in many ways a more important sign of his political evolution than doctrinal statements. Equally symbolic: when Gustave Hervé held his own Salle

Wagram meeting in November to launch a National Socialist party, Lamour made a critical speech, and fascists in the audience got into a brawl with Hervé's guards, who were allied with the Jeunesses patriotes.[39]

Changes in meeting style were accompanied by structural changes in the Faisceau organization. The legions had served as a manpower pool for guards at a few Salle Wagram meetings and an even smaller number of pilgrimages, whose relative rarity did not put too much strain on the légionnaires, mostly mature men with jobs and families. Calling them up once a week for the Club du nouveau siècle was another matter, especially as the number of willing légionnaires was steadily shrinking. In November, Valois decided that only war veterans could be légionnaires, turning the legions into a dead-end structure. To guard meetings and for liaison within the Faisceau, Valois created the all-volunteer Gardes bleus.[40]

Ever since the daily Nouveau Siècle had folded in December 1926, Valois had been raising money for a new one. Realizing, however, that he could never relaunch a full-featured daily, he tried another tactic. Parisian newspapers could not really compete with provincial ones for information, he argued. Local papers gave readers the news they wanted most, earlier. In addition, the cost of wire services and correspondents was so great that newspapers could not live on their own revenues and had to be subsidized. Valois's solution was to create a two-page national daily. Devoted exclusively to doctrine and commentary, the paper would have no wire service charges, no correspondents, and no advertisements. Valois finally brought out his daily on December 1, 1927. The new paper featured a column called "Tribune libre," open to young reformers willing to engage in a dialogue with Valois. The revived daily Nouveau Siècle was the vehicle for his new political orientation.[41]

It had already become clear to Valois that the fascist name and connection were his greatest problems. In September, Robert Cornilleau, the Christian Democrat of the Petit démocrate, suggested that since Valois had cast off so many of his Maurrasian illusions it was perhaps time for him to drop the fascist label as well. Though Valois had welcomed Italian representatives at the Cirque de Paris in November 1926, he was not entirely satisfied with his Latin colleagues. Convinced that revalorization would put them under the control of British plutocrats, Valois wrote an article in August blaming Italian monetary policy for that country's economic and financial problems.[42]

As Valois made his orientation increasingly clear, fascists continued to melt away. In July, Valois noted that not all previous statements were sacred: the doctrine was redefining itself and "errors" would have to be eliminated. In September, he described the continuing crisis as salutary; those who did not belong would go.[43] Some fascists decided to stay and fight. Again the battle took place at the annual Fascist Congress, February 24–26. Valois threw down the gauntlet by suggesting that the Faisceau make contact with the Socialist party and participate in the upcoming elections.[44]

At the congress, Guéguen, head of the Rouen Faisceau, led the loyal opposition, those who wanted Valois to go back to the policies of 1925 and 1926. Henri Lauridan and Philippe Lamour tried to drum up opposition in the corridors. Fascists asked that the paper be renamed "Journal du Faisceau des combattants," and that its columns be reserved for members. But the greatest disturbance came when Valois suggested that the Faisceau put forward candidates in the upcoming election for propaganda purposes. This had been one of Valois's major complaints against the royalists, and the Faisceau had always trumpeted the purity of its antiparliamentarianism. Valois insisted that, if successful, the candidates would resign. Nevertheless, the suggestion raised a storm. Lauridan, Lamour, and Guéguen argued against it with the support of the majority of those in the room. Valois took note of the antiparliamentarianism of the congress and promised that instructions would come from the Supreme Council. He reestablished his situation by asking all those who wanted a living Faisceau to stand. The whole room rose, applauding.[45]

The problem remained, however. During the congress, Valois published an article explaining that there were two fascisms, one popular and the other plutocratic. Henceforth Mussolini's black shirts were in the enemy's camp. Valois also began the exclusion of his opponents within French fascism. At the meeting of the Supreme Council following the congress, Lauridan was evicted from the Faisceau. Valois's opponents made one more attempt at the next meeting of the Supreme Council in March. In the course of a bitter debate, Lamour made public his various charges against Valois, arguing that he had failed as leader of the Faisceau. The majority of the council gave Valois its confidence and voted to exclude Lamour, transform the Faisceau into a closed *ordre moral,* and work toward the formation of a Republican Syndicalist party, which was finally created in June.[46]

After the March meeting, Lamour, Lauridan, Guéguen, and a few other regional leaders voted Valois's revocation as president and founded the Parti fasciste révolutionnaire. Coty's *Figaro* published their press release, but the party melted away soon afterward. Bordeaux, one of the last remaining sections, broke with the center in June, renaming itself the Club Montesquieu. Of the figures who had helped Valois found his movement in 1925, only Bourgin, Arthuys, and de la Porte were left. The new Republican Syndicalist party was founded by a few former fascists, along with nonfascists like Charles-Albert and André Fourgeaud. The Faisceau was dead.[47]

SEVEN

The Years of Respectability

The year 1928 found Valois on the left. At the age of fifty, he began his political life anew. Since the Radical journalist known as Alain, it has been an accepted fact of French politics that denying the right/left distinction marks one as a man of the right, just as the leftist is characterized by his proud assumption of his label. Valois broke many rules of French politics, but he observed this one. As a rightist, he had often sought to transcend the left/right dichotomy. On the left in the 1930s, he regularly trumpeted his allegiance and castigated those who crossed the "line of demarcation."[1] By 1930, he had earned a place on the French left.

But what place? And on which left? Valois was associated with virtually every fraction of the French left of the 1930s, from the Radicals and Socialists to the Communists and Trotskyites. Yet Valois remained an independent, outside the major organizations of the left, but seeking to influence their policies, and involved in most of the debates that divided the French left during the last decade of the Third Republic. Paradoxically, his independence, rather than isolating him, facilitated cooperation with a large range of leftists, who turned to him when they needed maneuvering room vis-à-vis their own political groups.

The disintegration of the French political system that Valois had predicted during the 1920s actually occurred in the 1930s. Its dual catalysts were the depression and the rise of Nazi Germany. Both events were central to the development of Valois's thought during the last decade of peace. Valois's ideas in the 1930s were not a complete rejection of his earlier, rightist positions. His new plans were built dialectically on preexisting foundations, giving them an unusual combination of utopian reach with hard-headed practicality. He felt intensely the challenges facing French society; and as he grappled with the issues dividing Frenchmen, he cast them in a sharper, often highly original, light.

By mid 1928, Valois's situation looked bleak. The Faisceau had come crashing to the ground. He was deeply in debt; and the *Nouveau Siècle*, for which he had sacrificed so much, had finally been destroyed. His ambitious attempt to bring fascism to France left him many enemies, including Maurras and Coty, the man responsible for the demise of the *Nouveau Siècle*. Added to the natural suspicions of Valois's newly acquired leftist comrades, one would expect his first years among the "parties of movement" to be difficult. Almost the opposite was true. Valois's first years on the left, from 1928 through 1932, were ones of widespread acceptance, moderate influence, and considerable material prosperity: they were the years of respectability.

This respectability came from a happy marriage between what he offered and what certain segments of the French left were seeking. At the end of the second decade of the twentieth century, the French left was bitterly divided and largely stalemated. The Communist party was politically isolated, declining in numbers, and suffering from severe (and barely legal) government repression. The electoral fortunes of the Socialist party were progressing, but its political line was stymied by the twin rejection of illegal action and ministerial participation. The resulting immobility tried the patience of many within *la vieille maison;* and these frustrated men were looking for new strategies and new forums to promote them. Even among the well-established Radicals, Young Turks sought to modernize the program of their aging, and essentially conservative, party. Valois was well suited to serve all these groups. Anything that served the rethinking, or better still, the reorganization of the French left, also served him. Hence, his support for all manner of reformers.

PUBLISHING AND POLITICS: ANTIFASCISTS
AND COMMUNISTS

Two instruments were in the hands of the former fascist. One was salvaged from the wreckage of his rightist enterprises, the former Nouvelle Librairie nationale, renamed the Librairie Valois. The other was a new creation, the *Cahiers bleus*. Published from August 1928 to May 1932, the *Cahiers* was a small-format periodical averaging slightly over thirty pages an issue. The pace of publication gradually quickened from approximately two to over three per month: one hundred nineteen issues over almost four years. Most *Cahiers* were devoted to an essay on a subject combining topical and theoretical interest, followed by short notices by Valois or his associates on current events or the progress of their enterprises. No precise circulation figures are available. But, perhaps more important, the *Cahiers bleus* were generally well received in French journalistic and literary circles.[2]

Backing up the *Cahiers* was the Librairie Valois, Valois's publishing house. Articles in the *Cahiers* often turned into books by the Librairie. In October 1928, the royalists dropped the charges they had filed against the Librairie and sold their shares. But the change had been expensive. The old right-wing contracts (and volumes) had to be liquidated, new clienteles created. At the same time, like all of Valois's enterprises (and like Valois himself), the publishing house had to pay its share of debts from the *Nouveau Siècle*. This was accomplished by 1931. The Librairie took a loss in 1927 and 1928, but in 1929 its debts were amortized by a reduction of the capital, which was then more than restored by new contributors. By 1930 the Librairie was in the black and publishing faster than before.[3]

The achievement was as much political as financial. Valois's new allies supported his publications and vice versa. Valois was particularly proud to publish antifascist Italian exiles in France like Pietro Nenni and Francesco Nitti: an excellent way of proving his break with fascism. In July 1929, the *Cahiers bleus* published "The Failure of Fascist Syndicalism," by the socialist Nenni. Other *Cahiers* followed, on Francesco Nitti's prison experiences, and on the Italian press and finances. Calling fascism "a formidable intellectual fraud," Valois began a series on Italian affairs, a gesture not without risk. The American publisher of Nitti's work had already been threatened, as Valois noted, and a few years later two similar Italian exiles were murdered. As reparation for having given credit to the fascist idea in France, Valois published *Finances italiennes* in 1930. After condemning fascism and dictatorship, he argued that Mussolini's monetary revaluation was economic folly, and that his discouragement of emigration deprived the Italian economy of needed foreign exchange, while his simultaneous encouragement of population growth for war was a danger to peace.[4]

If Valois's relations with Italian antifascists signaled a break with his past, his dealings with French communism consummated his separation from old friends. The Communist party's policy of "class against class," its opposition to French imperialism, and its calls for military disobedience had almost completely isolated it within the French political community. The persecutions by the right-center governments of the time excited little indignation outside the far left. But the Communists were good business. Valois wrote a preface to the French translation of Stalin's work on the Five Year Plan, published late in 1930, one of the Librairie's best-sellers. Years later, when relations with the proletarian party had soured, Valois argued that he had made a good deal of money for the Soviet Union.[5] But the Communists had made a lot of money for him too.

Valois evinced considerable sympathy for the Soviet experiment. Yes, there had been violence, but the important question was what a regime did with the productive capacities of men. In this respect the commissars had already surpassed the tsars. What appealed most to Valois was not so much the revolution, with its utopian goals, as the creation of a new system of production. After all, it was Valois who briefly characterized "the organized economy" as "nothing other than socialism itself." Valois's productivism matched that of the Soviet leader. The *Cahiers bleus* portrayed the new Soviet petroleum center in Baku in glowing terms, just as their editor approved the tendency of Soviet films to foreground work and construction instead of individuals. Not that Valois ignored the negative. The Red Army and the GPU were not permanent solutions, he argued; and the Soviet Union had not yet conciliated individual initiative with collective organization. The *Cahiers* also published critiques of the Soviet system and Marxism. But Valois was optimistic. Individual incentives were necessary, but the Russians were reintroducing these; in time, the standard of living of the Soviet worker might improve, and the dictatorship fade away.[6]

Perhaps more important, between the French government and the reds, Valois chose the latter. The government's persecution of Communist organizations was "illegal" and "unjustified." Valois had never taken the right's anticommunist panics seriously. To him, it was the capitalist nations of western Europe who planned war against the Soviet Union. The Communists had frightened them by showing that an economy could function without private property. The great powers also hoped to make Asia safe again for Western imperialism.[7]

These Western plots against the proletarian state had been disarmed, Valois argued, in the recent trial of the industrialists in Moscow. At these trials, which prefigured Stalin's later, and more famous, purge trials, influential figures in the Soviet economy admitted to having organized industrial sabotage at the behest of French agents and in preparation for an eventual war.[8] Though some doubted the testimony, Valois accepted it. For Valois (and many other radicals), such tales of treason were indicative of the way the world worked. Equally important, he had suspected Coty since 1927 of pushing for war against the Soviet Union. To the editor of the *Cahiers,* the trial of the industrialists was the pendant to that of Louis XVI. As the trial of the French king had discredited the principle of hereditary monarchy, that of the Russian saboteurs would the principle of hereditary private property. The Moscow proceedings had created a new legal principle (essential to a new eco-social system): that it was a crime to attempt to reestablish private property. Putting his publishing house at the service of his convictions, Valois printed the translated trial transcript with his own introduction.[9] Though Valois's positions were never Marxist-Leninist, he found himself not only working closely with the Communists but consistently supporting them in French politics.

Nothing better shows the isolation of the Communists than the reactions Valois received. His fellow traveling excited more indignation in publishing circles than had his adoption of the fascist label five years earlier. The most colorful reaction came from the distinguished French ambassador poet Paul Claudel, who sent an outraged letter asking Valois to cease relations, concluding: "If you still possess an ounce of honor and Christian sentiment, I ask myself how you can place your hand in the hands of these monsters."[10]

More than honor was at stake, since Valois's enemies used his Communist connections against him. The attack began in *Le Correspondant,* a conservative Catholic journal, with the suggestion that Valois's books could not pay for themselves, and that the Communists might be picking up the tab. The charge was pounced upon by all those who wanted to embarrass him. Valois also received a private warning; if he did not stop supporting the Communists, the banks would be closed to him.[11] Such rumblings prefigured later conflicts. Before 1933, however, Valois was still on cordial terms with the two major parties of the French left, the Radicals and the Socialists, his most important hunting grounds during the early years of the decade.

PUBLISHING AND POLITICS: RADICALS AND SOCIALISTS

Between 1928 and 1931, Valois lavished more attention on members of the Radical party than on any other group. As the former fascist headed leftward, the ideological territory of the center-left Radicals was congenial. These years marked the apogee of a group of reformers in the Radical party known as the Young Turks, with some of whom Valois had been publicly flirting since 1927. Valois nurtured unrealistic hopes for this middle-class party, whose essence belied its name, hopes spawned in part by the party's recent modernization and expansion.[12]

Valois recognized that the Radicals lacked a clear economic doctrine but made of this weakness a strength. The Socialists, who knew the modern economy better, were paralyzed by its complexities. The Radicals, once they acquired the right conceptions, would be more open to action. Valois hoped to graft his ideas onto the Radicals' less-encumbered ideological trunk.[13] The Radicals, who alternated between center concentration and alliance with the noncommunist left, were, between 1928 and 1930, opting for the second of these. More important (and uncharacteristic), they were out of office. As the Republic had seemed beautiful under the Empire, the Radicals could look radical out of office.

Valois called the Radical Congress of 1929 a "creative revolution." Its achievements? The party, resisting ministerial temptation, rejected a coalition of centers for a union of the left. More promising for the future, Valois thought, were positions taken by leading Radical politicians. Herriot urged peace and European federation, while the titular leader of the party's Young Turks, Edouard Daladier, attacked the plutocrats (he would later invent the phrase, "the two hundred families"), and called for a new state to dominate them. But Valois's hopes were really based on the Young Turks, consisting largely of younger Radicals who wanted to update the party's program. His influence over some young men was such that the Socialist Marcel Déat characterized them (referring to Radical headquarters on the rue de Valois) as "twice Valoisians."[14]

Again the Cahiers and the Librairie were the means. Calling the 1929 Radical Congress a "creative revolution" was a plug for Pierre Dominique's La Révolution créatrice, which had been published by Valois in December 1928. Valois also promoted Jean Luchaire, a representative of Briandist pro-Europeanism who was close to the Radical party, and the young journalist Bertrand de Jouvenel, son of the politician and diplomat Henry de Jouvenel. Between 1928 and 1931, the latter contributed three major works to the Librairie Valois and a project for the joint European development of the colonies (an idea dear to Valois) to the Cahiers bleus.[15]

De Jouvenel, Luchaire, and Dominique were all under thirty when Valois published them, and all three exploited generational themes. De Jouvenel rightly called Valois "the publisher of our generation." Valois's contacts with all three waned as the thirties progressed. If the paths of Valois and these young Radicals crossed, they were, as Valois recognized, going in opposite directions. He was headed away from fascism, they toward it. Luchaire ended as a collaborator; de Jouvenel and Dominique were leading figures in Jacques Doriot's Parti populaire français.[16] Valois maintained better relations with another young Radical, Gaston Riou, whose Europe, ma patrie (Europe, My Fatherland) he published in 1928. Riou remained one of France's leading democratic proponents of Europe-wide federation. Another promising young Radical in Valois's orbit was Pierre Mendès-France, who displayed even then an opening to socialist and syndicalist viewpoints unusual for his party.[17]

In May 1931, Valois drew the conclusion of the effective defeat of the Young Turks: the Radicals would not carry out his revolution.[18] By 1932, he was turning his attention to the Radicals' sometime allies, the SFIO. Rarely did Valois feel the Socialist party lived up to its historical responsibilities. For him, the Socialists understood the complexity of the capitalist economy, and hesitated because they had no replacement for the capitalist motor of individual incentive. They needed not bolder action but bolder thought, doctrinal renovation. Valois encouraged those soon to be known as the neosocialists. The issue that provoked the neosocialist schism was ministerial participation. For Valois, however, the question was not whether to enter the government, but what to do once there. At one point, he hoped that the reformists might enter a government and then be forced by the party's left-wingers to transform the economy.[19]

Though Valois cooperated with other neos, like Barthélémy Montagnon, his closest involvement was with the movement's theoretician, Marcel Déat. The Librairie published Déat's *Perspectives socialistes* (Socialist Perspectives), considered the Bible of neosocialism. For several years, Valois and Déat kept up a close intellectual relationship, Déat joined for a time in Valois's projects, and Valois never lost his respect for the mind of the socialist philosopher. Though Valois never adopted Déat's distinction between ownership and control over the means of production, the former fascist appreciated Déat's break with the party's Marxism on this point. The neosocialist's pragmatic activism also appealed to him. Valois was not one to wait for the inevitable collapse of capitalism.[20]

Déat and Montagnon also crossed Valois's path on their roads to collaboration. Young Turks and neosocialists were touched by the fascist temptation associated with the current of ideological renewal that swept through the parties of interwar France. By the time the rightist options of the neos were visible, however, Valois was well to their left, vigorously attacking their "neofascism." Their fellow traveling with Valois reflected only slightly any residual fascism in his positions. The factors that led many of these individuals to collaboration (marginalization or losses in political infighting; nonconformism; impatience) brought them, at an earlier stage, to Valois.[21]

But Valois supported more loyal Socialists. He favored the constructive revolution group, led by the socialist, syndicalist, and historian Georges Lefranc. This faction, whose manifesto the Librairie published in 1932, asked the Socialist party to exchange its overreliance on parliamentary activity for greater attention to cooperatives, syndicalism, and other forms of economic organization. These were positions Valois could approve. They had little influence within the SFIO, however.[22]

Valois's chief effect, between 1928 and 1932, was to encourage the ideologically and politically marginal elements in the Socialist and Radical parties. He sought to maneuver within, and around, Radicals and Socialists to goad them into changing the economic and social organization of France. Neither party was ready for decisive action before the middle 1930s. In the meantime, the former fascist played the role of proponent of ideological innovation and federator of malcontents.

PROLETARIAN LITERATURE

Valois had his greatest impact during these years on a literary school, and with a lone anarchist. The literary school was that of proletarian literature, the anarchist, Henry Poulaille. Poulaille's background was in many ways similar to Valois's. He, too, was of modest origin and had earned his living through a series of odd jobs before getting an office job with the publisher Grasset.[23] And both cherished the memory of the prewar writers Lucien Jean and Charles-Louis Philippe.

In the last days of 1929, Valois saw an article by Poulaille on Charles-Louis Philippe in the philo-communist literary journal *Monde*. Enthusiastic, Valois invited the anarchist to contribute a *Cahier* on Philippe and "proletarian literature," which appeared in March 1930. Valois liked what he read. The Librairie published Poulaille's weighty tome on proletarian literature, and the anarchist was entrusted with a series and a new journal. This new journal, given the Valoisian name of *Nouvel âge littéraire*, appeared from January 1931 through the end of that year.[24]

Poulaille published novels, stories, and poems by a host of writers, chiefly of working-class origin. To Poulaille, proletarian literature meant the writings of those who worked with their hands and that expressed the realities of their lives. He rejected the populists, bourgeois who took the common people as their subjects, as well as the communists (who had their own concept of "proletarian literature"). To limit proletarian literature to texts expressing the historical role of the working class seemed to him both dogmatic and a confusion of proletarian literature with literature *about* the proletariat. Marxism "had no role to play in the artistic domain." In fact, nothing could be further from a positive hero than the characters of Lucien Jean or of Charles-Louis Philippe's *Bubu de Montparnasse*.[25]

Valois's conception was a bit different. Though he willingly adopted the phrase "proletarian literature," he preferred "literature of producers." For Valois, proletarian literature exalted the values of work and creation, unlike the old literature that favored those of war, parasitism, or idleness. He therefore considered himself a proletarian writer and asked Poulaille to publish his play *Journée d'Europe* in the collection. Poulaille declined, explaining that Valois was an editor and publisher, hardly a proletarian (Poulaille had long ceased to be one himself, but that was another matter). Valois took the rebuff in stride and published the play later on his own. He supported Poulaille against his critics because of shared literary tastes and the conviction that Poulaille was opening a breach for the new literature he sought.[26]

What brought the project to a standstill, however, was lack of money. Years later, Poulaille opined that he might have "financially assassinated" the Librairie Valois. *Nouvel âge littéraire* was published first at 3,000, then at 2,000 copies per issue. No more than 700 of any number ever sold; and subscriptions topped at 305. The deficit after one year of operation was 160,000 francs. Nor did the book collection, Les Romans du nouvel âge, do better. Its sales were often under fifty per work, and the series represented a loss of 250,000 francs for 1931 alone. Valois was obliged, by 1932, to call a halt to the entire enterprise.[27] The reasons? In addition to the mediocrity of much of Poulaille's material, his own literary politics, excluding both bourgeois and communist, conservative and Marxist, narrowed his audience.

The prosperity Valois had laboriously built up by careful management and the revenue he gained from his economic and social works were sacrificed at the altar of his literary ambitions. Valois never blamed Poulaille. Instead, he attributed the poor reception of proletarian literature to the hostility of critics, and his mounting difficulties with the Librairie to that of Hachette and the banks. The whole episode was typical. A great burst of enthusiasm, unlimited credit (intellectual and financial) given to a project, and then surprise when the great breakthrough failed to materialize.[28]

THE PARTI REPUBLICAIN SYNDICALISTE

The Parti républicain syndicaliste (PRS) was founded in June 1928 out of the debris of the Faisceau and the converts of late 1927 and early 1928. The most important of these were Charles-Albert and the Christian democrat Henry le Hoc. Many provincial Faisceau leaders, like Auguste

Lajonchère of Lyon and Jean Barthet of Toulouse, continued their careers in the PRS. The party's founding manifesto contained 108 signatures, and it is unlikely that its membership ever topped a few thousand. The membership was drawn largely from the petite and middle bourgeoisie: technicians, engineers, small entrepreneurs, teachers, and other civil servants. Members hailed from the Paris area, the Lyonnais, and the Southwest. One of the major differences from the Faisceau's recruitment pattern was that no member of the prominent Bordeaux section followed Valois into his new formation. During the following years, the remaining Faisceau notabilities left the movement, de la Porte in 1929, Bourgin in 1930, and Arthuys in 1931.[29]

Though Valois had dropped his categorical objection to electoral activity, the size of his party kept his ambitions modest. The PRS ran candidates in municipal and cantonal elections and participated in parliamentary bielections as a propaganda exercise. The *Cahiers bleus* were quick to celebrate when a party member was elected mayor of some commune, but the PRS conquered no major fiefs. Valois was thus also continually fishing for allies. For a time, he hoped to use the club movement in Paris and the generational theme to federate a group of youthful nonconformists behind him. Hence the section in the *Cahiers* devoted to the *jeunes équipes*. Valois soon discovered, however, that the generational theme was a double-edged sword, as younger men turned it against him.[30]

The syndicalist part of the party name was more important than the republican. Major attention was devoted to economic organization, complementing the wooing of left-wing intellectuals through the *Cahiers* and the Librairie. PRS members were originally expected to donate a minimum of unpaid labor to the party's organizations, an obligation soon reserved to active voting members.[31] Valois and the PRS sought an activity that would help them live up to the syndical part of their name and, they hoped, transform French society at the same time. That project was the development of the Southwest of France.

ELECTRIFYING THE SOUTHWEST

Valois had always had a predilection for the Southwest. Though from the Ile de France himself, he knew the region between the Garonne and the Pyrenees better than any other part of France. He had garnered extensive support there as royalist and fascist, had passed through the area on his 1927 pilgrimage to Lourdes, and had summered there for several years. Valois was convinced the Southwest had a brilliant future. Hydroelectric power from the Pyrenees would transform the region and eventually all of France. This "white coal" was the energy source of the future, clean and abundant. Toulouse was already the center of the youthful aviation industry, guaranteeing its forward-looking orientation. Valois's first idea was to develop the entire Garonne basin and make Toulouse "one of the capitals of electricity." Electrification would spread to the countryside and to agriculture; electric transportation would revive the thermal resorts of the Pyrenees. The project was conceived with the help of the Toulouse section of the PRS, one of the largest and most active outside Paris.[32]

By 1930, Valois decided to begin more modestly, with the commune of Saint-Gaudens (Haute-Garonne). This town of seven thousand inhabitants had been, for several years, Valois's summer vacation spot. Saint-Gaudens was centrally located, was well served with transportation, and had good weather for all-year flying. Most important, Valois had won the backing of the local notables, including Eugène Azémar, general councillor and president of the chamber of commerce. With him came the mayor of Saint-Gaudens, the president of the Toulouse chamber of commerce, Courouleau, and Mlle. Elizabeth Verguin, the Saint-Gaudens landowner with whom Valois had been summering. Members of the Society to Enhance the Value of Saint-Gaudens were to be repaid with founders' shares in the other corporations to be created. To kick off the town's development, Valois proposed a new boulevard, a corniche with the finest view of the Pyrenees in all of France, which would attract tourists, vivifying the entire economy. How to pay for it? Valois wanted the owners of the land in the boulevard's path to donate their property in return for shares in the new company. They would benefit from the increase in land values created by the newly revealed panorama, an increase that could be the source of the credit needed for construction.[33]

The boulevard project was entrusted to a Real Estate and Tourist Society of Saint-Gaudens, run by Courouleau and Henri Clerc. Clerc (later to play a role at Vichy), was a leading PRS militant and president of the French Association of Thermal Spas. Valois raised two million francs, one-third from himself and his associates, half from a Saint-Gaudens family (apparently the Verguins), the rest from other local interests. The transformation of the Southwest seemed well on its way.[34] In the Toulouse suburb of Muret, PRS militants created a syndicalist development project with the support of the Socialist mayor and deputy, Vincent Auriol.[35]

Though cooperative in inspiration, the Saint-Gaudens project was organized on capitalist principles. Valois expected that as success spread outward from city to region, from region to country, all of France would be converted to his principles of economic organization. In another example of his "utopian" mind-set, he counted on the persuasive power of a successful example. He also still hoped to use French businessmen to eliminate capitalism in France.[36] For a time, this did not seem completely absurd. Within a year, he announced the purchase of some of the land along the route of his projected boulevard. Construction was beginning, and the first portion of the panoramic road would be inaugurated in August 1931.[37]

But the boulevard was never completed, and the project came to naught. Valois frequently sought to interest businessmen in his projects. At such times, he forgot he was also a politician. If he could see the long-term implications of his activities, so could others. And a man who had moved within barely three years from fascism to philo-communism was not necessarily the most reliable business partner. The attack began in September 1930, when the influential Radical newspaper La Dépêche de Toulouse warned of the dangers of working with such an enemy of the republic. But the suspicions of the republicans were no match for the rancor of the royalists. That same September, the royalist L'Express du Midi began a series of attacks on Valois, referring to him jeeringly as "the dictator." A few weeks later, the Express triumphed: Valois's societies were falling apart. In fact, partially as the result of the concordant attacks of a local banker (who claimed that Valois had been convicted of fraud), three members of the society resigned, including the influential Azémar. Valois managed nonetheless to hold the society together and plan construction for summer 1931.[38]

In 1931, however, the situation worsened. One reason was a trip Valois took, from January through May 1931, to the French island of La Réunion in the Indian Ocean. He left to slake his wanderlust and make some badly needed money. On the island, Valois reorganized the affairs of an old friend and former Faisceau member who ran a sugar and rum factory. He must have been prosperous, since Valois's fee was several hundred thousand francs.[39]

While Valois was away, his enemies organized. In Saint-Gaudens, some banks, backed by two local newspapers, withdrew their support. The reason: Valois was a notorious communist. During summer 1931, copies of the article from Le Correspondant were posted around Saint-Gaudens. Some of the local businessmen tried to force Valois out of the society, but he controlled too many shares. By 1932, the "capitalist" members resigned and declined to pay in the last quarter of their subscribed capital. These withdrawals strangled Valois. He had already spent a million and a half francs, most of this to purchase land and begin construction, and he was forced to turn over the unpaid obligations of his investors to the construction company as partial payment. Throughout the rest of the decade, it was all Valois could do to keep his Saint-Gaudens societies afloat. His chief concern was to liquidate the mortgages his group had taken out on their land to pay the balance due the construction company. Later attempts to raise money for this purpose only led to further conflicts between Valois and his backers.[40]

Valois was quick to blame the plutocrats and the iron magnate François de Wendel. The Toulouse militant Sammy Beracha compared Valois to the Saint-Simonians. Like him, these nineteenth-century socialists had combined ambitious social theorizing with a taste for great economic realizations.[41] What Beracha forgot to add was that the Saint-Simonians had been nonconformists during the July Monarchy and influential businessmen during the Second Empire. There was a certain naïveté in Valois's expecting the leading forces of French society quietly to let him transform the economy.

The Saint-Gaudens venture closed the period of Valois's respectability. Never again would he work so closely with businessmen, government officials, and local notables. The entire project testified to his political flexibility from 1928 to 1932. Other than the royalists and politicians of the nationalist right, there was almost no group he was not prepared to court. This opportunism paralleled Valois's ideological evolution. Even in an intellectual development as shifting as his, these were years of transition, a period when his rightist certitudes were gone, but satisfactory new leftist ones had yet to be found.

IDEOLOGICAL DEVELOPMENT: GROPING LEFTWARD

Valois always explained that he had abandoned the left as a young man when no one could explain how the factories would be run after the revolution. But Valois did not return to the left in 1928 because he had found the answer. He broke with the right, he admitted, once he saw that it would never overthrow the plutocrats or create a new economy.[42] During his first period on the left, Valois's principal intellectual burden was the justification of the position he had already taken politically: that the future of human society lay with the ideals of the French left.

Valois's ideological evolution from 1928 to 1932 went through two stages. The first found its clearest formulation in *Un Nouvel Age de l'humanité* (A New Age of Humanity), Valois's major work of 1929. *Un*

Nouvel Age is probably the least systematically argued of Valois's works, frequently looking backward to refute earlier positions or settle ideological accounts. Themes only adumbrated in that work were elaborated during a second phase, expressed in two books written during his trip to La Réunion and published in 1931: *Economique,* a reformulation of his economic theories, and *Guerre ou révolution* (War or Revolution), a confrontation of the related problems of culture and militarism. [43]

From 1925 to 1927, Valois strengthened the historical, diachronic aspects of his thought, for example, by turning the French Revolution into a progressive event, and by arguing that fascism would mark the entry of the working class into political life. Yet his conceptions remained bound by the same Quintonian pessimism. The law of the equivalence of effort would keep man's nose to the grindstone despite technological improvements, just as the eternal barbarian required the eternal *combattant*. Now, in 1929, however, Valois argued that humanity was about to enter a genuinely new age.

Valois now decided that scientific developments created new economic forms, necessitating new political and juridical structures. [44] Technological progress was not a new fetish for Valois. But from a secondary aspect of historical development (which would not change the eternal laws of society), it became its chief motor. This position is close to Marxian historical materialism. But Valois felt that he corrected Marx on a significant point. Valois argued that Marx failed to recognize the role played by intellectual developments. This role was crucial for generating scientific progress and creating the political and juridical forms the economic transformations required. Valois's critique was based on an overly schematized view of Marx, but the difference in emphasis had important implications. The autonomy of the spirit meant that new political forms would not automatically follow economic ones. If the twentieth century did not create the new political and juridical forms that the age demanded, a long period of revolution, war, and general decline could follow. In his own imagery, the world was in labor and there were two possibilities: birth or miscarriage.

Thus, Valois's leftist optimism was qualified by a continuing pessimism, a position he would maintain for the rest of his days. Historical movement was not necessarily "progressive for all peoples and all times." The example of the Dark Ages after Rome still threatened. The role of the thinker (that is, Valois) was correspondingly magnified. Again we see the "utopian socialist" mind-set: much anguish would be spared—potentially even all violence—if the voice of reason was heeded and the right solutions were implemented. [45]

Although he evoked other technological developments, Valois zeroed in on one. The new age linked socialism and electricity. Electrification socialized production by making the producer dependent on an outside energy source, whether property relations recognized this or not. The controllers of energy sources could tax producers. Valois expected an economy based on electricity to eliminate many of the evils of industrialism and produce smokeless progress (as in the Garonne basin).[46]

The 1929 book included a second new principle: the law of the elimination of parasitisms. Since, by the law of least effort, men tried to reduce their labor, they likewise sought to cast off parasitical classes, groups who lived from the labor of others. Introducing a diachronic element into a static system, this "law" projected Valois's economics into history and outlined a progressive human self-emancipation, placing Valois firmly on the left. By naming them parasites, Valois redefined the roles of certain social groups. The king, the *combattant*, was no longer essential to production. At most, the warrior permitted others to work and support him, while protecting them from competing parasites. Nor did command alone, unless accompanied by technical or managerial activity, possess economic value or deserve remuneration.[47] Rethinking command reflected the move from right to left, transforming the value of institutions like monarchy and aristocracy, which Valois had once praised.

Redefining classes meant redefining history. The Ancien régime had essentially been military parasitism, and the French Revolution was the first major attempt to throw off this yoke. The revolutionary bourgeoisie had thus acted as a productive or, in Valois's new language, "technical" class. Its error was to have abandoned this position and to have transformed itself (along with elements of the old aristocracy) into a new parasitic class, based on the hereditary right of command in the economy. Valois repeated his earlier arguments that working-class resistance had forced the owning class to return to its technical vocation, adding that it was Sorelian revolutionary socialism that had dispelled the chloroform of the bourgeoisie. Nevertheless, the bourgeoisie continually sought to reform itself as a parasitic plutocracy.[48]

But Valois had long ago found the solution to this problem: so organize society that the owning and managerial class was caught between the pressure of the workers and an independent, incorruptible government. This was the schema of *L'Economie nouvelle*, and the goal of his royalist and fascist corporatism. Such a solution was now unacceptable because Valois no longer recognized the right of private ownership of the means of production. This is what he meant by the heredity of economic command:

only those born into the upper classes had any real chance to rise to leadership positions in the economy, there was no "career open to talent." Valois's critique was clearly shaped by his own social resentments. Capitalist wealth was illegitimate because the real source of the riches of modern production lay in scientific advances. Valois reserved his strongest language for the contrast between the fortunes of businessmen and the modest incomes of scientists, characterizing it as "a violent injustice." In place of Marxist exploitation, Valois substituted his own, and instead of a labor theory of value, a scientific theory of value.[49]

Hence, despite his avowed socialism, Valois's primary identification was not with the working class but with another group, the technicians. This group, drawn from the workers and a few bourgeois, ran the economy, and deserved the corresponding recognition and power. The terms *technician, technique,* and *technical* are ubiquitous positives in *Un Nouvel Age,* signifying modernity, efficiency, and justice. This identification with a middle group reflected itself in the way Valois set off workers' and capitalists' institutions, not as positive and negative poles but as two sides of a dichotomy to be transcended. The mental structure was not barbarians versus legionaries, but "neither London nor Moscow." For example, there were two "technical states": the United States and the Soviet Union. The plutocrats who ran the United States rewarded productivity and had invented the policy of high salaries. Yet their economy would eventually run aground for lack of an organized working class. The Soviet Union had given the state to a class of technicians, but its failure to differentiate rewards could eventually bring it to grief. Similarly, workers who thought that the expropriation of the capitalists would save them the necessary technical revolution were as mistaken as capitalists who thought they could eliminate working-class pressure. Valois's views were not without condescension. If the technician served the people, he did not want to be "crushed by a blind mass." Such appreciations echoed those of the Faisceau period. So did prejudices still visible in Valois's 1932 play *Journée d'Europe,* whose "positive hero" was a war-veteran technician trying to keep the owner of a factory from selling out to international plutocrats. Similarly, the Republic was an unguarded house invaded by two groups: "red guards" seeking to take over governmental functions through union and political pressure, and employer syndicalists trying to organize the economy for their own benefit.[50]

By this last group, Valois meant those technocratic industrial leaders like Ernest Mercier, Jean Coutrot, and Henri de Peyerimhoff, who sought between the wars to make French industry more productive, more mod-

ern, and better organized. While Valois always admired these men, his cooperation with them was never more than intermittent. Even as a fascist,
he had kept his distance from Mercier's right-wing Redressement français.
These technicians served the plutocrats, and their syndical plans left no
room for the necessary working-class pressure. Valois always distrusted
these representatives of the French *haute bourgeoisie*, and in later years,
he would be among their most vigorous opponents. Class resentments
joined with doctrinal considerations in keeping Valois from supporting
France's leading modernizers.[51]

Alongside the familiar idea of a syndically and regionally organized
chamber, Valois called for a sovereign assembly to represent the people as
a whole. Despite some vague comments about the producer's spirit that
would inform his new legislature, Valois did not show how his new parliament would evade the vices of the old one. The civic assembly, as Valois
called it, would select the economic planning committees and choose the
technicians to run the enterprises. These last would negotiate with representatives of the various syndicates, and they would be removed by the
government if their administration were not profitable. But how would
these director/managers be rewarded? Valois did not think that glory
would work for all but a very few, or for brief periods of enthusiasm. Yet
the recently converted leftist was clearly uncomfortable with the idea of
private profit. Surrounding his conclusions with a cloud of temporiza-
tions, Valois called for some distribution of profits to the organizations responsible for them, and to their managers. Though Valois called this socialism, it retained much capitalist logic.[52]

Many of these ideas were similar to other nostrums circulated between
the wars in France—plans designed, like Valois's, to cure France's political
and economic ills. The idea of two assemblies, one civic and one syndical
(really economic), had been suggested by Bertrand de Jouvenel, and there
were many among both big labor and big capital who wanted to set up
some kind of formal economic representation alongside the parliament.
Valois also suggested a new kind of syndical just price. Bargaining between themselves, syndicates would arrive at equivalences between products based on the amount of effort that went into their production. This
idea was similar to Déat's social price. Both represented attempts to maintain a price system while eliminating the unfairness considered implicit in
the capitalist one.[53]

The year 1929 also saw the appearance of another principle, new to
Valois's analytical universe: freedom. All his previous thought was based
on necessity and constraint. But freedom was now a criterion of progress,

essential to the disinterested scientific inquiry underlying industrial advance.[54] Scientists, the saints of the modern world, were the only group who could be relied upon to motivate themselves.

The other new variable was culture, increasingly important through its association with one of Valois's oldest concerns, the problem of war. Valois had begun his intellectual career with a justification of force as the father of work. In *Un Nouvel Age de l'humanité*, he denied this role to the *combattant*. In 1931, he explained why. It was not true that "the man with the whip" created work. Work was the product of love. The mother first sought food and nourishment for her newborn, and her mate, "in the fever of love," aided her. *Le Père* replaced *L'Homme qui vient*. But the other founding myth of *L'Homme qui vient* survived. Early men were cannibals, which explained war. War, like cannibalism, which was its simplest form, was a parasitic alternative to work, not the basis for work but its opposite.[55]

But other figures from *L'Homme qui vient* also came back to haunt the newly antiwar Valois. The biologist René Quinton had penned a Social Darwinist celebration of war based on his own experiences in the 1914–18 conflict. Though Quinton died in 1925, his *Maximes sur la guerre* (Maxims on War) was published in 1930. Quinton celebrated the heroic virtues and explained that man's risk in war was the counterpart to woman's in childbirth—a form of selection and one of the fundamental mysteries of life. Valois's response showed his embarrassment. Quinton was still a great scientist and a noble soul, not an armchair hero (Maurras was intended here). Nevertheless, his positions were not science but Nietzscheanism and had to be kept from once more "poisoning youth." Valois's only substantial arguments, however, were that man had evolved to a stage in which he no longer competed through bravura, but through work, and, more aptly, that Quinton was confusing competition between species with that between individuals.[56]

Valois's argument was now evolutionary. History was the struggle between the creative principle of work and the parasitic one of war. Thus, everything that Valois had earlier said about the parasitic and productivist principles was redefined in terms of war versus work. Earlier societies represented the dominance of warrior elites; and the French Revolution was the first attempt to throw them off, an attempt frustrated when the Revolution turned to militarism to defend itself. The bourgeoisie compromised with the aristocracy and maintained the "regalian" warrior state. Even the bourgeois principle of private property was militaristic, since it was an extension of the right of territorial property, itself based on conquest. This redefinition produced radical formulations. The state was militarist in nature. The proof: its claim to dispose of the lives of its citizens without their consent. All political parties, including the Socialists, were still firmly within this militarist reality.[57]

As with the state, so with the economy. The international economy, Valois explained, in an essentially Leninist argument, was based on the expropriation of raw materials from non-European populations, their processing in Europe, and their resale to the original populations. Some of the resulting profits were distributed to white European workers. The whole system depended on force, on the right of war.[58] Valois had not changed his appreciation, formed as a young man in the Indies, of the role of force in international trade, he had simply changed his judgment of it.

Valois refused to condemn war on sentimental grounds. The spectacle of death and combat had not sickened him, he wanted his readers to know. War was stupid. As long as the primary source of energy for production had been animate (human and animal), conquering populations made sense. But now that the major sources of energy were inanimate, as Valois correctly noted, far more energy could be created through scientific and technical advances than could possibly be conquered. (This left out the possibility of going to war for raw materials, a problem that would become important later.) Further, it was no longer a minority that fought, and the masses of material necessary meant that only war profiteers came out ahead. The French had won the war, only to be obliged to bring in Czechs and Italians to till their soil. Like most French veterans, Valois had concluded, if in his case somewhat tardily, that the destruction of the war outweighed its outcome.[59] Gone was the "spirit of victory."

Despite its inanity, war was still possible, indeed certain, if a revolution did not sweep away existing conditions. These bred war as a tree produced fruit. For Valois, the problem was not just the treaty of Versailles, which seemed calculated to stimulate vengeful feelings among the vanquished, but the principle of national sovereignty itself. But the world of ideas, of culture, also carried war in its bosom. The French Revolution failed because it did not replace militarism with a new culture of producers. For virtually all previous high culture was militarist in origin, nature, and function. This was as true of polite gestures and the rules of society as it was of literature and the arts. All promoted traits useful for war, command, or intrigue among the ruling classes. Even the originally distinct bourgeois culture had become largely subsumed into a new, heavily aristocratic militarist culture. Valois cited the case of the Panthéon, that temple to nineteenth-century secular civilization, next to which he lived and worked for most of his life. Almost without exception, its heroes were either warriors or saints and orators, equally divorced from production. The argument was genetic: since so much French culture was military (really feudal/aristocratic) in origin, so it still was in nature. To work for peace, one had to separate oneself from what passed for high culture in France, indeed from all residual respect for the "bandits," the perpetrators of "murder, theft and pillage" who peopled traditional history. Even revolutionaries like Proudhon had not gone far enough. Although the anarchist had seen that the workman would replace the warrior, he had still expressed his admiration for the warrior ideal.[60] Valois could have said as much of Sorel, but did not.

Such a position was profoundly radical. Reverence for French arts and letters was part of the secular religion of all French intellectuals, including leftist ones. Part of Valois's motivation was an attack on Maurras and his cohorts, who traded in the classical literary ideal. But there were stronger cleavages at work. Valois went further than those who criticized the traditional educational reliance on Latin and Greek. He argued that the education he had received in the popular *école primaire* was superior to the lettered one doled out to the upper classes in the *lycées*. Valois had carried this resentment since adolescence. If there was an insult guaranteed to drive him to fury it was *primaire*.[61] Now the distinction was part of his system.

A new culture was in formation, a "reversal of values." This reversal, of course, was as much Valois's as humanity's. For him too, to paraphrase Burke, the age of chivalry was dead and that of technicians and economists had taken over. These positions explained Valois's high hopes for Poulaille and proletarian literature. But in culture, as in economics, Valois did not attribute all virtue to the proletariat. The new values should be those of work and production in the largest sense, not those of proletarian class struggle. Proletarian literature had taken the lead because manual workers were less tempted by the parasitic values of the upper classes.[62]

Abolishing militarism within one society left the problem of invasion. It would not do, however, for the revolution to create its own army. The close relationship between war, culture, and social structure meant that the new army would poison the revolution. Valois's solution at this time was a nonmilitary defense, an "international hygiene service" to destroy aggressors with the help of the latest scientific techniques—but without heroism. The service would be run by scientists, who would approach their problem as if they were exterminating insects. This and the spread of the revolution to neighboring countries were Valois's only answers in 1931. Even he could see they were unsatisfactory.[63]

The sea voyage that produced *Guerre ou révolution* also saw the completion of *Economique*. Though relatively brief, this work fulfilled two functions, fusing the perspectives of *Guerre ou révolution* and *Un Nouvel Age de l'humanité* and restating Valois's theoretical economic positions. Eight of *Economique*'s twenty-one chapter headings enunciated economic "laws." Valois's arguments were so deductive that they make those of competitors in system-building (like Marx or Comte) seem totally empirical by comparison. *Economique* was the most thoroughly biological of Valois's works. Not only was economics treated as a branch of biology, all of Valois's thought was cast in this same biological mold. Biology, economics, world history—all were one and the same.

Valois began where he had as a young man, with the progressive cooling of the globe. Man played a special role, Valois had explained, through his capacity to create artificial organs or protections against the cold. The middle-aged Valois distinguished between tools, which complemented the actions of muscles or other organs, and machines, which acted as artificial organs. This distinction gave a biological meaning to the industrial revolution. If tools were a mark of humanity, only industrial man was fully human. Man's technological progress was part of a plan on the part of nature (*life* was Valois's term) to transcend the limitations not only of the present physical environment but also of unforeseeable future "catastrophes." Hence, some intelligence directed organic activity, and this intelligence had to be "intracellular" in nature.[64]

Valois's purposeful intracellular intelligence resembles Bergson's *élan vital*. Nevertheless, Valois was probably not directly influenced by the distinguished philosopher. Even when comparing Quinton to his fellows, Valois only mentioned Darwin; and apparently his only reference to Bergson was a hostile one made as a young rightist. If Valois had been aware of the parallels between his and Bergson's arguments, he would have added an appropriate "critique," as he did with Marx.[65]

This does not mean that there was no filiation between Bergson and Valois. Georges Sorel, a great admirer of Bergson, had been a major influence on the young Valois. But the biological sociology of *Economique* was far from the pessimistic heroism of Sorel. Instead, Valois explained that economics was an extension of biology, or, more properly, of physiology. If physiology was the propagation of life within organisms, economics was its "rigorous, external prolongation." The rules governing both kinds of activity, the economic and the physiological, were the same; the economy became more efficient as its mechanisms approached those of the organism.[66]

Adapting his favorite concept, Valois explained that physiological activity was the result of the mutual constraint of organs. Two important consequences followed: (1) since constraint was internal to the organism, and along with it a system (related to reproduction) for the creation of surpluses, there was no need for external constraint to explain production; (2) the whole idea of a master was biologically invalid.

Valois overturned the traditional organicist defense of social hierarchy (e.g., the head must command the feet). It was not the metaphor to which he objected. But the traditional organicists had reversed the process, he argued. Their misapprehension that the brain commanded in the body was an application to biology of their erroneous social views. The brain, Valois insisted, was not the ruler and did not make the crucial organic decisions. The organs determined that certain activities were harmful, that the stomach needed food, that the muscles were tired, and so forth. They transferred this information to the brain, which totaled it up like a statistical bureau, made it conscious, and relayed the decisions to the executing organs. Human actions resulted from "the tumultuous deliberations of the organs, of which only a part reached consciousness."[67]

The organs were the instruments of more fundamental actors, the cells. The motor of all biological, and hence economic, activity was cellular energy, "equally distributed throughout the human body." Its supreme command was an obscure force emanating from the cells themselves. As intelligence was intracellular, so, also, were the reserves of energy that made economic activity possible. The human body was "a great, egalitarian, cellular republic" where decisions came from "a kind of permanent assembly."[68]

The social implications were obvious: political and economic democracy. Moreover, since energy originated with the cell, the ideal social system would maximize individual autonomy. Valois did not draw the radical, almost anarchist, implications of this principle immediately, nor those of one of his other modifications. The law of least effort no longer stated simply that men sought the least effort and the least pain, they now also naturally strove for the "greatest enjoyment and self-expression."[69] Alongside the continuing psychology (and therefore sociology) of constraint, was a bio/sociology of individuality, whose practical role would grow when Valois revised his social models again in the middle 1930s.

In the meantime, Valois's plans for the new society remained vague. The mutual constraint of organs in the body would be matched by some sort of mutual constraint between producers and the coordinating economic brain of society. Valois also fudged on the question of property. Private property tended to reduce waste, but this was more than made up for by the superior technological dynamism he associated with public enterprise. (Saint-Simonian assumptions were associated with a dim view of French entrepreneurship.) Thus, some kind of public ownership would probably have to be combined with a system of limited or temporary private property.[70]

Intellectual freedom, which was economically necessary, also meant the elimination of counterproductive superstitions and utopias. These last were now dubbed a third product of the law of least effort. Men used illusions or dreams to distract themselves from the pain of physical exhaustion, rather than applying the law of the intellectualization of effort and devising new tools. The purveyors of these systems were also parasites. Progress demanded, therefore, the elimination of these belief systems. Valois's discussion could implicate either Christianity, Marxist socialism, or even the Action française. He only drew the conclusions for socialism.[71]

It is easy to note the cruder aspects of Valois's thought, like the naïveté of his organic analogies, or his continuing ignorance of classical economics (his new refutations of the law of supply and demand were no better than his old ones).[72] Distinguishing between related historical processes, however (while recognizing their common basis), meant that the development of social property, for example, would not necessarily eliminate parasitism, even less assure freedom. His analysis also provided a conceptual flexibility that made it easier for Valois to change his analysis of the Soviet system, for example, or to correctly assess the dynamism of Nazi Germany.[73]

The conceptual apparatus Valois developed during his early leftist years served him well in the tumults of the later 1930s, especially when combined with his robust realism and almost proverbial willingness to change his mind. Its lacunae would be filled during the turbulent years of the mid 1930s, when Valois both took a secure position on the far left of the French political spectrum and completed the construction of his revolutionary leftist blueprint for French society.

EIGHT

Everything Is Possible

For a time, many Frenchmen (even, briefly, Valois)[1] thought that the Great Depression would remain an American affair, or at least that the less modern French economy would be spared. By 1933, however, the depression was taking its toll of unemployment, government deficits, and social distress. It sharpened the polarizations in French society and opened a new era of mass political mobilization. On the night of February 6, 1934, French veterans and rightists, like those Valois had once led, rioted against the Daladier government, widespread corruption, and the parliamentary regime. In reaction, the major leftist parties—Socialist, Communist, and even Radical—formed the "antifascist" coalition known as the Popular Front. A Popular Front electoral victory, France's first Socialist-led government, and a wave of quasi-revolutionary strikes followed in 1936.

The years 1933 through 1937 witnessed tremendous political upheaval. On the left, the Communists shifted abruptly from antimilitarism to flag-waving support for a strong defense. The Socialists confronted for the first time the realities of government, and the Radicals found themselves in the often uncomfortable position of being allies of the two proletarian parties. On the right, the traditional parties were threatened by newer, more radical organizations. As France became increasingly polarized, the political atmosphere took on the tone of incipient civil war.

Valois backed the Popular Front movement and, with reservations, its electoral coalition. Fundamentally, however, he belonged to the left opposition. In the debate then raging on the French left, he was one of those who felt that the Popular Front triumph should lead to a revolutionary transformation of French society—one of those for whom "everything was possible."[2] Valois was thus often allied with other members of the radical left excluded from the Popular Front's dominant Socialist-Communist alliance. These included the Trotskyites (briefly in the SFIO), Communist dissidents like Jacques Doriot (before he moved to the right) and Albert Treint, as well as minority groups within the Socialist party like the Gauche révolutionnaire, the revolutionary pacifist group led by Marceau Pivert.[3]

What distinguished Valois most among the left critics of the Popular Front was the utopian temperament that led him to formulate blueprints of the new society (and plans for how to get there). Valois insisted that revolution was neither an exercise in verbal persuasion nor a seizure of political power but the creation within the old society of the forms that would structure the new one. To this end, his publishing and journalistic activities should be syndicalized, the Librairie Valois transformed from a private corporation to a cooperative.

FROM LIBRAIRIE TO COOPERATIVE

By mid 1932, Valois and Henry Poulaille had bankrupted the Librairie Valois. Poulaille moved on to greener pastures. Valois decided that the problem lay with the French publishing industry, which he had long considered to be in the grip of plutocratic forces. He turned in 1932 from his old solution of syndical organization to cooperation partly because the latter promised what he lacked most: capital.

The *Cahiers bleus* ended in May 1932, and Valois replaced it with a new journal, supported by a new set of organizations and a partially new group of backers. The result was a transformation of Valois's political formations from a party with supporting press to a set of interlocking cooperatives. The new periodical was called *Chantiers coopératifs* (Cooperative Worksites). Valois preferred *Nouvel Age* (a title he would adopt later) but agreed to the new title to please those attracted by the cooperative principle. The term *chantiers*, at least, appealed to his sense of ongoing construction. Twenty-one large format issues of *Chantiers* appeared irregularly from May 1932 through May 1934. *Chantiers* was the organ of a series of cultural cooperatives. The journal was supported by its own cooperative, and readers were encouraged to add shares (at one hundred francs each) to their subscriptions. Valois's more original idea was the Compagnie d'organisation rationelle (COR). Founded in September 1931,

COR's announced task was to sell technical plans to new cooperatives, but its chief role was that of holding company and financial manager for Valois's enterprises.[4]

Valois also revived his old ambition to free the French publishing industry from the grip of Hachette. This had been the purpose of the Maison du livre français, but he had ceased major work for the Maison in 1925, and, finding himself persona non grata to this collection of bourgeois publishers, had resigned from the board of directors in 1932. In its place, he created a Maison coopérative du livre to coordinate the sale, distribution, and marketing of the books of leftist publishers. As he saw it, the French book industry was divided between Hachette, which held the lion's share of distribution, and a condominium of Larousse, Plon, and Colin, who controlled the Maison du livre français. These two groups, and especially Hachette, were rationalizing publishing and threatening cultural dictatorship. Six presses joined within a month. The Maison coopérative was installed, along with COR and *Chantiers*, in a new locale at 6bis rue de l'Abbaye,[5] which remained the center of Valois's activities throughout the decade.

The cooperative format, Valois explained, brought together individuals with their contributions of labor or savings. Experience, however, had taught Valois not to rely on his followers. To bankroll his network of cooperatives, he was counting on a project called the "New Encyclopedia."[6]

Like its eighteenth-century counterpart, the New Encyclopedia was to embody a revolutionary culture—to sum up existing knowledge while pointing the way to the future. More important, through the sponsorship of some of the left's leading organizations, the Encyclopedia would represent a guaranteed income for Valois's publishing ventures. The project had originated in 1927 with some of France's most distinguished academics, including the scientist Paul Langevin of the Collège de France, the anthropologist Lucien Lévy-Bruhl, and the left-wing novelist Jules Romains. In 1931 Langevin and the Socialist politician Albert Thomas entrusted the project to Valois. Léon Jouhaux brought the backing of the CGT. Even the Communists showed interest. Langevin, Lévy-Bruhl, and Romains would supervise intellectual matters, while Valois would handle printing, advertisement, and distribution. The Encyclopedia also promised prestigious recruits for Valois's co-ops. Among the proselytes for 1932 was Langevin himself. That same summer, however, Albert Thomas died, and the dossier fell into the lap of Anatole de Monzie, the new minister of education and an old enemy of Valois's. The latter had, among other things, accused the Radical politician of conspiring with Maurras, and had subpoenaed de Monzie to testify about it in court. De Monzie backed a competing project by the historian Lucien Febvre, to be handled by Larousse. Valois went to see his old foe twice, to no avail. Valois called de Monzie's project a usurpation and vowed to continue his own cooperative encyclopedia, but his leftist backers soon withdrew.[7]

Valois was forced back on his own resources. These were sufficient to continue *Chantiers*, but little more, especially since Valois continued to make enemies. In 1932, he refused an offer of collaboration from Hachette, and from that moment, he claimed, he found it increasingly difficult to get credit. The demise of the Encyclopedia provoked the withdrawal of the other left-wing presses in the Maison coopérative, which in 1934 was forced into bankruptcy, bringing the Librairie Valois down with it. Valois had to liquidate his publishing house, paying off outside shareholders at 60 percent. His own investments were almost completely lost. Already, in 1932, Valois's Bureau de presse et d'édition had been forced into bankruptcy. The Librairie Valois was replaced by Editions liberté, but this new cooperative could never support Valois's less profitable ventures as the Librairie had.[8]

Langevin was not the only new recruit. Other personalities who now took central roles in *Chantiers* included the journalist Joseph Dubois and the socialist *lycée* professor Gustave Rodrigues, both of whom would become increasingly important. The neosocialists Marcel Déat and Barthélémy Montagnon were also on the masthead, along with the syndicalist Georges Mer, while among financial contributors was the industrial modernizer Jean Coutrot. Finally, Edouard Berth, Valois's old friend and fellow Sorelian, also began occasional participation in the publications of the rue de l'Abbaye. Valois still had important contacts. The cooperative idea took on a highly visible role in his projects. Syndicalism was decadent in Europe, he argued, because it had ignored cooperation; and if economic planning was the great Soviet contribution, cooperation was the equally essential Western achievement.[9]

A clearer change was Valois's attitude to Christianity. Valois maintained his faith after his break with royalism, and after that with fascism and the right in 1927 and 1928. If intellectual inertia was one explanation, political expediency was another. After the papal condemnation of the Action française in 1926, Valois trumpeted his loyalty to the Holy See; and this allegiance aided his overtures to left-wing Catholics like Robert Cornilleau. In the early 1930s, however, Valois deepened his ideological leftism. The author of *Guerre ou révolution* and *Economique* (both published in 1931) distanced himself from some Catholic positions, but neither text departed from the position he had taken in *Un Nouvel Age de l'humanité* in 1929: that society should remain neutral on matters of religion. By 1933, however, all pretense of neutrality was cast aside. One either was for Voltaire and Proudhon or for the Bible.[10]

Valois now explained that, though he had continued to live as a Christian in the moral sense, he had long ceased to believe in Catholic dogma. This idea, that much of his Catholicism was merely conventional, cannot be accepted for 1927 or before. A pilgrimage to Lourdes in fulfillment of a vow was hardly the behavior of a skeptic. His faith had been real, and he seems to have lost it sometime between 1927 and 1930. More important, Valois now concluded that Christian values had not been historically and were not now progressive. The ancient Greeks had seen that machines could liberate humanity and set thought on a scientific path. Christianity created a bifurcation in human development by promoting worldly renunciation. Not surprisingly, across Europe the Church was siding with fascism and reaction.[11] Valois's ideological anticlericalism undid the last of the changes that had marked his shift to the right in his twenties. Not that he indulged in anticlerical polemics; Valois now simply considered Christianity part of the old culture holding back social progress.

Valois's publishing ventures were moving leftward as well. Much in *Chantiers* smacked of ideological compromise. So, in May 1934, Valois changed his paper again, adopting the messianic name he had been cherishing since 1928: *Nouvel Age*. The first issue appeared in June, and more had changed than the title. The paper was the product of a "workers' cooperative," including Valois, Gustave Rodrigues, César Chambrun (a former Socialist deputy and professor, who died in November), Edouard Berth, Francis Delaisi, and Joseph Dubois. Delaisi never played a major role, while Berth divided his allegiance between *Nouvel Age* and *La Révolution prolétarienne* (whose relations with *Nouvel Age* were not always smooth). More useful supporters included Pol Gandon, a lower-level administrator with the PTT; André Saint-Lagué, professor and member of the advisory National Economic Council; and Maurice Weber, lecturer at the Ecole de Sèvres. As Valois progressed leftward, his support shifted from business and technocratic groups to intellectuals and members of the educational professions, who have traditionally played a large role in the French left. This testified both to his ideological radicalism and his increasing estrangement from the centers of economic power.[12]

To protect himself in his new, more combative, role, Valois created a novel arrangement for *Nouvel Age*. The cooperative that produced the paper neither financed it nor controlled its capital. The Société coopérative des amis de *Nouvel Age* (SCANA), a consumers' cooperative, was the association of readers who paid the producers' cooperative. In other words, the cooperative with the money, SCANA, did not control the paper, while the cooperative that did had no money. An opponent suing for defamation could not put *Nouvel Age* out of business by seizing its operating capital. The producers' cooperative had none. Suing Valois would be like trying to get blood out of a stone.[13] While not legally foolproof, this system afforded a great deal of protection.

Since the demise of the *Nouveau Siècle*, Valois had wanted a new daily; and that was his original intention with *Nouvel Age*. As so often, expected funds were not forthcoming. So *Nouvel Age* began as a weekly, not to become a daily until two years later, during the sit-down strikes of June 1936.[14] Even then, Valois could not really manage daily publication, however. *Nouvel Age* appeared five to six times a week, with additional breaks for major holidays or midsummer. When money ran short, the paper returned temporarily to weekly service, as in much of 1937. For the most part, however, Valois put out close to two hundred issues per year through the spring of 1940.

He managed this feat through a novel system of distribution and a bare-bones format. *Nouvel Age* was only sold to subscribers and not available in kiosks in Paris or the provinces. Individual sales meant using Hachette, which Valois opposed for the usual political reasons. He was also convinced that using Hachette was economically ruinous, since papers lost money from the charges for returning unsold copies. A paper could not live on its own resources. Only politically motivated contributions or advertisements (distributed by Hachette's ally Havas) could fill the gap. Economic and political independence went hand in hand. Though attempts were made to sell *Nouvel Age* at selected Parisian newsstands, Valois chose survival over circulation.[15] The size of the paper held expenses down: two pages, one large sheet printed on both sides, with more pages for special issues, weekend editions, and so on. Editorial costs were also low. Valois did most of the work himself, aided by his daughter Marie. As the years wore on, the strain showed. He appealed to his readers to send funds so that he could hire professional editors and take a much-needed rest. Money came, but never enough to hire professionals.[16]

Nouvel Age started in 1934 with fewer than a hundred cooperators and the subscribers from *Chantiers*. Valois estimated that seven thousand subscribers or a thousand cooperators would cover the costs of the daily. Only a little more than half these figures were achieved. Valois also wanted 100,000 francs for launching expenses, but by mid 1937, he had only

67,000. He published the paper as a daily anyway, and deficits were made up by loans from Valois and a small circle of supporters. Though the finances of the daily improved (along with the frequency of its appearance), as the war approached, Valois and other lenders sought reimbursement, and financial appeals remained a permanent fixture.[17]

Valois also wrote most of *Nouvel Age*. A typical issue featured a short front-page editorial signed *Nouvel Age*, but generally written by Valois after consultation with his collaborators. Most of the rest of the front page was usually shared between an article (or articles) by Valois and a major piece by Gustave Rodrigues, the second most important commentator at the rue de l'Abbaye. Page 2 was dominated by a review of the press signed "Outis," in context a transparent synonym for Valois. On many Saturdays from June 1937 through February 1939, Valois's space was taken by the radical leftist school teacher Régis Messac, who organized either a cultural page or a review of the foreign press. This pacifist, anti-elitist intellectual replaced Poulaille as cultural expert. The daily *Nouvel Age* was designed to complement, not replace, informational newspapers, but its frequent publication permitted Valois to stay on top of unfolding events.

Nouvel Age's influence outstripped its modest circulation. One reason was its preferred clientele: leading militants and other activists in left-wing political, syndical, or professional organizations. For a wider audience, Valois prepared special issues on current crises or major programs. These were sold individually, or distributed at cost, in the provinces by local militants, and in Paris by paid hawkers. Over sixty thousand copies of some of the more popular numbers were disseminated in this way.[18] As these numbers suggest, Valois still played a significant role on the French left.

NEW AGE, NEW PROGRAMS

Two forces shaped Valois's social and economic formulations between 1933 and 1937: the continuation of trends in his thought from the early 1930s and the Great Depression. Both were visible in monetary policy. By 1933, the prosperity accompanying the Poincaré stabilization of 1928 had foundered on the rock of worldwide depression, a deficit loomed, the franc was threatened, and monetary policy was again in question. May 1933 saw Valois working for a third Semaine de la monnaie along with well-known leftists like Francis Delaisi and Vincent Auriol. Though Valois treated the third Semaine as a continuation of the first two, his support had changed. The first meeting was fully backed by the Bank of France, and even the second, in 1927, still had the support of the monetary institution. In 1933, however, when Valois approached bank officials, they explained that they preferred that monetary issues receive as little public discussion as possible. The business groups that had supported the first two Semaines were replaced by a series of cooperatives and other leftist organizations. The left-leaning Radical Edouard Daladier, then prime minister, also contributed financially to the Semaine, though this fact was not widely publicized. Several ministers were present, and some embassies sent observers. Valois had not burned all his bridges.[19]

The Semaine, which met from May 30 to June 2, directed itself almost exclusively to international trade. The conclusion: gold was to blame; its maldistribution was "strangling international exchanges." Governments should cease using gold to back currencies, balance international exchanges, or make payments between nations. Gold should only be a measure to compare one monetary unit with another. While this solution, something like the gold-exchange standard, might have simplified a French devaluation, it would not have helped the French economy, which was suffering from the discrepancy between domestic and world prices. The Semaine also adopted the recommendation of one member to set up an international compensation office and agreed to study Valois's suggestion for an international money of account to facilitate it,[20] a transparent reformulation of the *franc-or*.

As social turmoil within France increased, Valois continued work on his plans for the future society. By the middle of the decade, he had arrived at a complete blueprint: a society based on the law of least effort, which was self-regulating and based on egalitarian and anti-authoritarian principles. Added, however, was an economic-historical dynamic linking the growing problems of capitalism with the essential features of the new society.

Valois began with the problem that had troubled his youthful leftism: once the constraints of capitalism were eliminated, how would workers be obliged to work, or, to use his new vocabulary, how would the dynamism of production be assured? Valois wanted to recreate what he called the "automatism" of the economy—that is, the way individual self-interest came together for the common good and the ability of the market to direct investment and production while eliminating the incompetent. These virtues Valois now recognized in the free-market system, though he argued that they had died with the old individually controlled economic units. He never gave a more vigorous exposition of the virtues of laissez-faire than in these years when he sought the complete elimination of property in the means of production.[21]

Valois had already rejected industrial democracy, but he also criticized the Soviet solution of authority as unsocialist and inefficient. He reserved his sharpest scorn, however, for the "wait and see" school, who acted, he argued, as if the problem would be solved by "some operation similar to that of the Holy Spirit, which gave the apostles, on Pentecost, the gift of tongues by means of flames that descended onto their heads." Socialists would have to take man as nature furnished him. In another context, Valois spoke of man as created by "nature and history." Biological and social evolution might eventually produce a majority of men and women working without constraint. But revolutionaries would have to deal with humanity as it was and would remain for some time. The criticism was apt: one could seek to create the new socialist man, but one would have to use the old one to do it.[22]

Valois had already sketched the solution in *Economique*. Putting organizational flesh on the bones of his organic analogy, he now planned for mutual constraint between consumers' and producers' cooperatives. Local associations of consumers would consult with producers' groups and name the heads of factories and farms. The economic leaders would be responsible to the consumers, who would demand the highest possible level of production and replace the director if he failed to satisfy them. The director would then, of course, seek the maximum from his workers, who would, however, be syndically organized and keep the right to strike. Unable to exploit his workers, the director would have to seek increased production through technical advances, always Valois's goal. Consumers would receive production bonds (actually money), which they could spend as they chose, creating the appropriate demand and complete consumer sovereignty. Starting with the same assumptions as liberal capitalism, he projected a system that aped it in many ways. From the conflict of egoisms would come the common good, with consumer power deriving from organization, not competition. With this elegant solution, Valois reconstructed his earlier rightist mutual constraint in conformity with his new leftist assumptions. Neither an independent sovereign nor even a true government were necessary any longer, only a series of boards for economic coordination.[23]

The most important new element was the hierarchy of consumer co-ops. But by the late 1930s, Valois was no longer using the term *cooperative*. Instead, he now spoke of *consumer syndicalism*, castigating French syndicalists for concentrating on producer syndicalism while allowing the equally vital consumer variety to languish. This was a new type of "integral syndicalism."[24] With characteristic activism, Valois exhorted his followers to organize local consumers' syndicates. They could begin by negotiating preferential terms from local merchants in return for a union label. Eventually one or more of these might be persuaded to turn their stores into purchasing co-ops. Despite a few local starts, no real consumers' syndicates were created.[25]

Yet the new age marked a clean break even from cooperative principles. For Valois now moved toward a truly communist system by severing pay from work. He made this jump by assimilating a new economic and social model, known as "abundance," the contribution of Gustave Rodrigues.

Abundance was, first of all, an explanation of the Great Depression. On his own, Valois had not gone far on this point, speaking only of a capitalist inability to plan rationally, or an ill-explained crisis of overproduction.[26] For Rodrigues, however, the depression was caused by technological progress. As industry became more capital-intensive, the share of its product generated by labor constantly diminished, and salaries did likewise, if not absolutely, at least in relation to production. It then followed that the workers, as an aggregate, could never afford to buy their own products. As productivity increased, the money supply could not keep up, and prices spiraled downward. Laying off workers only made the situation worse. The depression was thus a progressive, not a cyclical, phenomenon.

The economic system of "exchange" had to be replaced by "distribution"—that is, the provision of goods without reference to the economic value of the work performed by the members of society. Salaries, profits, and a market for labor would all have to go. Exchange, Rodrigues explained, was based on scarcity. The abundance created by modern industry could only be distributed. Thus, "abundance" was both a technological/economic fact and an economic/social system.[27]

Although based on a misconception of capitalism—the more technologically advanced an enterprise, the greater the marginal productivity of its workers, and hence their salaries—"abundance" did offer an explanation of the crisis of overproduction and underconsumption facing all advanced economies in the 1930s. And it did so without resorting to the Marxian concept of surplus labor, which Valois never accepted.[28]

But the term *abundance* also maintained its primitive meaning and its association with liberation from constraint. Though Valois occasionally repeated his old principle that technical progress replaced physical effort with an equivalent mental effort, he now argued that the new society of abundance would liberate the human personality. Invoking the Aristotelian idea that men could only be truly free when others (like slaves) performed their work for them, Valois explained that machines would be the slaves of the future, liberating men for their complete development and creating an "integral humanism."[29]

Abundance meant new rights. In place of the right of property came what Rodrigues dubbed "the right to life," revoking the principle that only those who worked could eat. The "Droit à la paresse" (right to leisure), treated semi-ironically by Marx's son-in-law Paul Lafargue, was now possible, according to the doctrinaires of the rue de l'Abbaye. With his taste for definitions, Valois elevated the right to life to the founding principle of the new society. Since abundance was the product of socially produced technological progress, all human beings were "indivisible co-inheritors" of the wealth and productive forces of the planet. This, and not services rendered, justified their rights.[30]

But Rodrigues, whose "Droit à la vie" organization joined the rue de l'Abbaye cooperatives, was neither the doctrine's originator nor its sole claimant. Within Valois's own circle, Joseph Dubois developed its economic core before 1934. The idea was in the air because by 1933 another writer, Jacques Duboin, had also formulated the "abundance" doctrine as an explanation for the depression and a model for the future. Abundancists were also legion in the Pivertist wing of the SFIO, of which Rodrigues was a member. With competing theorists came competing organizations: Duboin's Le Droit au travail (The Right to Work) in 1933 and two other small abundance leagues, Dynamo, a group of production-oriented technicians, and JEUNES, led by Jean Nocher. A relationship of competition and cooperation quickly developed among the abundancists.[31]

Could these groups be brought together, and could they be enlisted in Valois's projects? The Nouvel Age organization and Rodrigues's Droit à la vie joined with JEUNES, Duboin's Droit au travail, Dynamo, and two other small leftist groups, the Front social and the Club pour et contre of Jacques Rozner (now with Valois) to form an abundance front in July.[32] By September, however, the front was in shambles, as all groups other than Nouvel Age and Droit à la vie withdrew. For the next several years, Valois and the other abundance leagues accused each other of stealing their ideas and washed one another's dirty linen in public. Even Joseph Dubois broke openly with the rue de l'Abbaye. In the spring of 1939, Nouvel Age and the other groups again moved toward cooperation, but revived polemics would have doomed any joint plans even if the war had not intervened.

Valois insisted on a decentralized economy, whereas JEUNES, the Droit au travail, and Dynamo were willing to see the distribution of abundance within the existing structure of French society, perhaps strengthening the government's role in managing production and distribution. For Valois, this would mean a dangerous authoritarian control of the economy. Abundance could not function, he insisted, without his parallel pyramids of consumers' and producers' cooperatives and a decentralized consumer sovereignty as economic motor. To stress this point, Valois penned a special number on the autonomous "commune" as essential to human freedom and economic dynamism. By declining to endorse Valois's postrevolutionary organization, the other front members refused to isolate themselves from the leading groups in French society and join Valois on the far left of the political spectrum.[33]

Valois could not work with other modernizing, production-oriented groups because of his position on the left fringe of the Popular Front. He also felt that the fascist danger in France lay, not in uniformed, flag-waving rightists (he knew only too well the limits of their power), but in the threat of a government takeover of the economy in cahoots with leading plutocrats and their technician assistants. Such a takeover could as easily be achieved with leftist politicians as with rightist ones.

FROM THE 6TH OF FEBRUARY TO THE POPULAR FRONT

In the middle years of the decade, many in France seemed ready for a revolution. To some, the riots of February 6, 1934, came close to being what Valois, as a rightist, had always sought: a nationalist, popular, antiparliamentary revolution. In fact, the leaguers and veterans who burned buses and clashed with police on the Place de la Concorde had no revolutionary plans. All they achieved was the familiar shift from a left-center to a right-center parliamentary majority.

But the 6th of February was a potent myth. By concretizing the "fascist" danger, the Paris riots galvanized the left into new activity, creating the Rassemblement populaire, which grew into the Popular Front electoral coalition. By the time this alliance had won the 1936 parliamentary elections, French society was severely divided between "antifascists" on the left and "anticommunists" on the right. This turmoil offered opportunities for Valois, as it did for all nonconformists.

By February 11, Valois had put out a special issue of *Chantiers*. After an initial run of ten thousand copies sold out, twenty thousand more were quickly printed.[34] For the editor of *Chantiers*, the events of the 6th of February were neither a spontaneous riot nor a failed insurrection, but the culmination of a long-maturing plot. "We accuse," Valois trumpeted, à la Zola, "the banks and trusts of having organized the fascist riot." The veterans and leaguers of the 6th of February were dupes, their role to provide enough cadavers to discredit Daladier and the Radical government. The job completed, they could go home. The Stavisky scandal? An orchestrated pretext. Stavisky's activities were minor compared to the organized raiding of the economy by the real masters of France.[35]

Valois's view of fascism was an exceptionally nuanced one for the time, as befitted a former practitioner. Then as now, interpretations of fascism revolved around the relationship between fascist movements and capitalism. Valois scorned those who considered this new phenomenon the last gasp of a dying capitalism. Fascism, he warned, was a young, dynamic movement. It represented the attempt to solve, through authority, problems of economic organization that capitalism could no longer solve through the market. It was carried by a new elite of proletarian origin, eager to replace the decadent representatives of the bourgeoisie. With their proletarian cadres and youthful vigor, fascist regimes, like Hitler's recently installed National Socialism, were a serious threat to France.[36]

Plutocratic agents had helped fascists to power, but they did not always control them. Valois saw the fascist states as the scenes of struggles between the new leadership and older economic ruling groups. Valois saw Italy dominated by conservatives and nationalists, yet he at times thought that Hitler's Germany might evolve into an equally undesirable authoritarian socialism. Such fascism was not likely in France. It could not come from nationalist leagues like the Croix de feu, the Jeunesses patriotes, or the Action française. To be successful, Valois insisted, fascist movements had to be born on the left, with a popular base. Only Jacques Doriot, former Communist and genuine proletarian, possessed, briefly, this potential.[37]

Yet there was another fascism, safe, plutocratically controlled. To create such a tame fascism, the banks and trusts first tried a "left fascism" by encouraging Déat and the neosocialists, who broke with the SFIO in 1933. Since 1933, Valois had been involved in a budding leftist coalition known as the Table ronde, which brought together reformists and others interested in a constructive, nonparliamentary socialist movement, including the leading "neos." Déat's intentions might be excellent, Valois argued; his plan would produce a plutocratically dominated corporatism—effectively fascism. The middle classes were dying and would never support a real attack on capitalism. Controlling the state would avail little if the plutocrats dominated the economy. When another "neo" sang the praises of "authority," Valois apostrophized him: "I've traveled that road! . . . that solves absolutely nothing." Any appeal to authority automatically led to fascism, which was why the trusts backed the neos.[38]

How was one to fight plutocratic fascism? Not by defending "democracy" and "the Republic"—that is, the existing regime. For Valois, parliament and the parties were finished, and the antiparliamentary sentiments of the masses were one of fascism's strongest weapons. The only solution was a "syndical republic."[39] Yet once electoral conquest was ruled out, what would the institutional basis for the revolution be? Valois came up with a familiar solution: the Estates-General, now representing syndical and other leftist or cooperative groups. Valois found the formula being used by the CGT but swiftly took it over as a replacement for his own "syndical constituent assembly," exploiting it heavily in the latter months of 1934. For a time, the Table ronde also favored these leftist "Estates."[40]

If the Estates-General had a "twenties" ring, so too did a group Valois now courted: the veterans. Former soldiers of the Great War, whether nationalist or communist, were probably the largest single contingent in the 6th of February riots. Since that night, their dissatisfaction with the political system had not abated. For a few months it looked as if the veterans might serve the revolution. On March 24, the national council of the Conférence nationale des anciens combattants, an umbrella organization of veterans' groups, called for the dissolution of the Chamber and the election of a new one based on proportional representation, along with public control of credit and other reforms.[41]

Valois exulted. The action of the *combattants* (again, he preferred this term to *anciens combattants*) could lead to a syndicalist constituent assembly. Ten years ago, Valois reminded his former comrades in arms, he had called upon them to join him against the plutocrats, and many had followed him. They had one last chance to play a political role. Again, Valois argued the uniqueness of the war experience. The World War I fighters had proven their devotion to the collectivity, and that men could live in essentially communist conditions, outside hierarchies of income. (Gone was the parallel between military and professional hierarchies.) The *combattants* had no economic role, but they might give the opening signal of the revolution. "I will not conceal," he added, "that this is also my personal wish." As one of Valois's critics noted, his appeal to the veterans had something of the smell of the Faisceau about it. Valois also feared that if the veterans did not join his revolution, they would serve the other one. Leftists must repeat to satiation that behind the leaders of the nationalist and some veterans' leagues were the magnates of French finance and industry. He attacked Jean Goy, leader of the rightist Union nationale des combattants on the 6th of February, noting that Goy had been paid by Ernest Mercier in 1925 to found the Front républicain. Mercier received his own article. Valois now considered him the principal liaison between the trusts and veterans' groups, and a prime organizer of the 6th of February.[42]

In May, the Union fédérale des combattants invited other groups to join it in a sweeping reform project, asking for responses by July 8. At the same time, the more conservative Union nationale des combattants also threatened political action. Proposals circulated for common action between the Union fédérale, the neosocialists, and the CGT. Acting through a recently founded umbrella organization, Valois accepted the Union fédérale's invitation. Some pacifist veterans' groups also expressed interest. The July 8 deadline produced no more than another set of veterans' meetings.[43]

By late summer, attention shifted from groups to plans. "Planists" felt that the best way to pull their national economies out of the depression was to coordinate economic activity through a government-sponsored plan. Planism represented, therefore, an opening to the socialization of the economy. Most of all, planism was an activist faith, refusing to let the depression cure itself through the laws of the market and out of the hides of the unemployed. Planism thus also saw itself as a barrier to fascism.

In the late 1920s and early 1930s, Valois had drafted and promoted plans for coordinated investment, both regionally (the southwest) and internationally ("Eurafrica"). He also considered planning a key element in the new society, though the coexistence of a centralized plan with the anarchistic, quasi-market mechanisms of Valois's future society was not unproblematic. In the France of the 1930s however, planism was associated primarily with the Belgian socialist Henri de Man. In March 1934, Valois gave a very sympathetic presentation of de Man and his Plan du travail.[44]

In late 1934, however, Valois reversed positions: the major plans—those of de Man, many in the CGT, and the neosocialists, as well as most projects for nationalizing banking or credit—were all part of a new plutocratic plot, another attempted "left fascism." In fact, the first of the plans, that of "the 9th of July" was drawn up by a collection of technocrats, modernizers, and social reformers identified with both the right and the left of the political spectrum, under the patronage of the leftist writer Jules Romains. This was followed shortly by another plan created under the leadership of Valois's former collaborator (now heading toward fascism) Charles-Albert. Valois attacked the 9th of July plan for its opposition to the right to strike for civil servants, and repeated à propos of Charles-Albert's scheme his arguments against a centralized, state-controlled economy.[45] More fundamental for Valois were a series of suspicious similarities. Both the 9th of July and CGT plans called for a national economic council to control credit, with employers' and workers' representatives. Not only did this legitimize the employers, it threatened to give them, and the banks, even more control over the economy.[46] A socialist plan should be revolutionary, not revive a flagging capitalism or strengthen the state. This was also to be the core of Valois's disagreement with the Blum government.

The trusts wanted corporatism to save capitalism and increase their opportunities for exploitation, Valois argued. Nationalization of the banks or credit would put the economy into their hands and usher in a fascist state. If this could be brought about by the left, all the better. Valois also came up with a new interpretation of de Man, whom he now saw as a left-wing Machiavelli who had been in the plot from the beginning; the Flemish socialist's ideas were an idealist regression to pre-Marxist positions.[47]

When, in January 1935, the center-right politician Pierre-Etienne Flandin proposed to institute some of the planists' recommendations, Valois labeled it "an economic 6th of February," an attempt to nationalize credit in the service of industrial capital.[48] By this time, other leftists had also come out against the plans, and even the CGT officially distanced itself from its own plan. Valois credited his resolute action with foiling the plutocratic plot. His organizations did play a role in stirring up latent opposition to a highly controversial set of propositions. He also got the CGT-sponsored Conférence des plans to adopt revolutionary goals. The controversy over planism helped consummate breaks with many reformist socialists, like Georges Lefranc. And when former friends like Déat found themselves accused of consorting with the enemy, they were quick to rake up Valois's unsavory past. The battles of 1934 commenced a set of polemics, in which Valois was constantly defending himself against charges of excessive political versatility. The watchword of the budding Popular Front was *antifascism*. Was it appropriate for the barely repentant inventor of French fascism to give lessons in revolutionary purity?[49]

These enmities were increased by Valois's fight with the Fédération nationale des coopératives. In 1932, Valois tried, without success, to enlist the support of the Fédération nationale and its director, Ernest Poisson. Only after Valois threatened to create his own bank did Poisson direct the federation's Banque des coopératives to grant him a credit line of 200,000 francs. The Maison coopérative du livre quickly used the first 8,000 francs and directed its members to deposit their funds with the Banque des coopératives. In late 1933, however, the bank refused to release the balance of the credit, an act Valois attributed to his recent political evolution. In

April 1934, the Banque des coopératives was forced to suspend payment; its director, Georges Lévy, had invested its funds in a private business that had gone sour. Valois's conclusion? The bank's discomfiture resulted from its capitalist methods, those of the old reformist cooperative movement. A new, revolutionary cooperation would have to take its place. A democratic, cellular approach would have blocked such irresponsible administration. New democratically organized cooperatives should assume the bank's debts, and the leadership of the federation must be replaced with new blood.[50]

It soon turned out that Poisson had founded the Banque des coopératives to cover a deficit in his wholesale operation and that the bank had passed this deficit along through false bookkeeping. Since this fact was known to the Bank of France, Valois concluded, Poisson and Lévy were at the mercy of the plutocrats. In late 1934 and early 1935, Valois worked to get Poisson voted out at the next federation congress. Poisson demanded immediate repayment of the advance to the Maison coopérative du livre and accused Valois (falsely) of attacking the bank because he could not re-pay it. More difficult to refute was his more general charge that Valois was an extortionist and a blackmailer who had made his career by pulling money out of one clientele after another, which explained his striking po-litical evolution. Poisson's attack was all the more damaging since it sup-ported similar charges by others in the syndicalist and socialist move-ments. *Nouvel Age* complained that the old royalist calumnies were being circulated and demanded proof, all to no avail. Such charges followed Va-lois everywhere he made enemies on the left. Partly as a result, despite Valois's damaging information, Poisson emerged strengthened. At the federation congress in Dijon in 1935, Valois was not allowed to speak. He must have seemed a troublemaker to most, handing out his special issues at the entrance to the congress and quarreling with the guards who tried to throw him out. At about the same time, Valois's own Maison coopéra-tive du livre was forced into legal bankruptcy by a cooperative bank. The decision was appealed and a replacement organization set up, but Valois's prospects for aid from the cooperative movement were nil.[51]

The major issue defining Valois's position on the left, however, was his opposition to war and militarism. In June 1934, over a year after the es-tablishment of the Third Reich, Valois called those seeking to prepare France for conflict "criminals and madmen." Valois tried for a journalistic *succès de scandale* by adding a personal dimension: he returned his order of mobilization, indicated his refusal to serve, and resigned his commis-sion as a reserve officer. This gesture, redolent with anarchist defiance, was designed to clear up any ambiguities that might have remained from his militarist past. The issue of *Nouvel Age* in question was put on sale at Paris newsstands, and later issues chronicle Valois's subsequent dealings with the military and his deliberately provocative behavior. The authorities expressed regret that, given Valois's age (he was then fifty-eight), all they could do was revoke his commission.[52] Valois argued that if war could not be prevented by a timely revolution, the international conflict should be turned into a revolutionary war.

More significant in the French context, Valois opposed any war preparation, moral or material. Almost no one in the France of 1934 looked forward to a repetition of the bloodbath of 1914–18. In that sense, the entire political class was pacifist. On the left, resolute antifascism was combined with a sincere desire for peace. The problems were essentially two: did the international fascist danger justify a change in the traditional antimilitarism of the French left? And what was the best way of dealing with Hitler—compromise, or opposition and a military buildup? Many tried to avoid the unpalatable choices as long as possible. Others, like Blum, decided early on that Hitler could only be met with force, whether this led to war or an armed peace.[53]

With his "revolutionary" strategy, Valois joined those whose opposition to war was not weakened by their antifascism. Normally, this would have included the French Communists, the staunchest of antimilitarists. But they had shifted to strong support for French rearmament. The resulting political realignment left Valois in opposition to the Communists, and clearly to the left of the developing Popular Front coalition. But it also brought him some potential allies.

Stalin's May 1935 declaration approving French military preparation created a storm among antimilitarist French leftists. Valois's reaction was direct: "The Third International is dead! Long Live the Fourth International." Since Stalin had abandoned the revolution, Frenchmen would have to act without their Russian brothers.

Soon, however, the Soviet Union became an object lesson in the dangers of state socialism. In the absence of a system of motivation, an increasingly brutal authoritarianism was economically necessary. The cult of personality also came in for severe criticism. One article was entitled: "Duce, Duce! ou le divin Joseph Vissarimovitch" [*sic*]. Finally, reversing his position from that on the trial of the industrialists, Valois condemned the purge trials as a bloodbath motivated by Stalin's paranoia and the logic of his system. The Communists replied in kind. Among other charges, they told militants privately that they had proof Valois worked for French intelligence.[54]

Opposition to the new Communist tactic would have to come from those who considered antimilitarism more important than proletarian unity. For Valois, unity should be for the revolution, not for the *union sacrée* (as the national unity of World War I was called). As a result, the rue de l'Abbaye became a focal point for a coalition of the noncommunist revolutionary left. Responding to the initiative of the left-wing teachers' union, the Fédération unitaire de l'enseignement, Nouvel Age became the center of a group that included the French Trotskyites and La Lutte finale, a mini-party led by the dissident communist Albert Treint.

At the same time, another coalition formed around the journal *La Révolution prolétarienne*. Robert Louzon, the principal figure behind *La Révolution prolétarienne*, was a leading Sorelian who, unlike Valois and Berth, had never wavered in his leftist faith. Though wary of Valois, Louzon and his friends agreed to bring together the two groups at a conference to be held in Saint-Denis. This working-class town was the turf of its popular mayor, Jacques Doriot, who had just been expelled from the Communist party. He and his followers, baptized the "Rayon de Saint-Denis," were still on the left, but hostile to Moscow. Antimilitarism was an ideal position for them.[55]

Valois's participation quickly became controversial. At the first meeting in June, Nouvel Age agreed to leave its leader's name off the opening documents, on the understanding that the rue de l'Abbaye and the conference would have the right to choose its delegates. At the second meeting, in July, the conflict exploded. Valois was roundly attacked by an anarchist group, but the delegates voted that Nouvel Age could appoint whom it wished, and Valois won a seat on the resolutions committee. This did not silence his opponents. The anarchist Jules Chazanoff, known as Chazof, and the *Révolution prolétarienne* mounted newspaper campaigns against the former fascist. Valois had consistently acted against the interests of the working class and syndicalism. The final argument was self-fulfilling. If Valois's conversion were sincere, he would not seek a leadership role in the revolutionary movement, since it was evident that his name created difficulties. The *Révolution prolétarienne* group withdrew from the conference, and Doriot's "Rayon," followed suit, even though they had voted with Nouvel Age.[56]

More was at issue than personalities. Louzon and his comrades feared that what had started as an antiwar coalition risked becoming a new revolutionary party. *Nouvel Age* was not completely wrong in its charge that the *Révolution prolétarienne* sabotaged the conference when it could not control it. Valois continually complained of the passivity of revolutionary groups in France. His attempts to push them into action, however, disrupted their comfortable live-and-let-live ways.[57]

Another attempt at coalition-building had thus failed. But there were still other allies for Valois's revolutionary pacifism—in the Socialist party. Like other Frenchmen, the Socialists were divided between their concern with growing German power and their desire for peace. Not all adopted Blum's philosophy of military preparedness and national union against the fascist threat. Within the SFIO, the revolutionary pacifist opposition was best personified by Marceau Pivert, secretary of the 15th section of the Socialist party. No sooner did the Saint-Denis antiwar conference collapse, in October 1935, than Valois announced his entry into the Socialist party's 15th section. Valois's acceptance by the section followed weeks of negotiations, during which he had to overcome the opposition of those who doubted his leftist purity. Other sections objected to the new member, however. In December 1935, the federal council of the SFIO Federation of the Seine voted not to admit the former fascist. The clinching argument came when an opponent read aloud a 1912 article by Valois vilifying Jaurès and appearing to countenance his murder.[58]

Valois's entry into the Socialist party would probably not have made much difference. Notwithstanding his rejection, he continued to maintain excellent relations with its Pivertist wing; and he would certainly have been expelled from the SFIO, as Rodrigues was, during the party's purge of leftists in 1937 and 1938.[59] But Valois's failure underlined his continuing separation from the groups that were creating the most important leftist alliance of the interwar years, the Popular Front. While Valois had failed to build his revolutionary coalition, others had built their own, antifascist, one.

THE POPULAR FRONT

The Popular Front left Valois ambivalent. He was suspicious of any coalition that included groups like the neosocialists or politicians like Herriot, and he had little faith in the established political parties. Yet Valois knew that opposing the Popular Front would be political suicide. The popular enthusiasm behind this new political alignment was too great to ignore. The stated tactic of the rue de l'Abbaye would be to support this new movement in hopes of changing it from a *popular* front to a "revolutionary" one.[60]

Valois also noted that the Popular Front attacked the Bank of France, Rothschild, and François de Wendel, but said not a word about Horace

Finaly, "the man whom no one dared to name." The movement was being used by this occult master of the press and backer of the parliamentary left. Once the left government had done its work, it could be overthrown, like Herriot in 1926.[61] Valois also thought he knew its task: devaluation. It was not only, as Valois reminded his readers, that the plutocrats alternated between deflation and inflation/devaluation as successive ways of despoiling Frenchmen. A devaluation would also soon be economically necessary. The progress of abundance pushed down prices. Only periodic devaluations would permit investment. But devaluations would not even work as a palliative, since technological progress was constantly accelerating. There were, of course, other, better reasons for devaluation, to lighten the debt burden on the French government and to lower French prices abroad. Valois recognized, at least, that the former problem was serious. Hence the plutocratic plan: make the Popular Front responsible for the devaluation, and, if the international situation soured, use the same leftist alliance to reestablish the *union sacrée*. What are you going to do, Valois asked the leaders of the Popular Front, when you take power and find the cashbox empty? Turn to the Bank of France and be strangled as in 1926? His solution: upon coming to power, the Popular Front government should immediately explain the situation and order a devaluation. This financial breather should be used to establish a socialist economy, for example, by extending credits to cooperatives and businesses not controlled by the trusts.[62]

The Popular Front electoral victory of May 1936 renewed Valois's optimism, as did the strikes and factory occupations of June. But factory occupations solved nothing if they remained a form of pressure; and the Italian example showed what could happen if they were not followed up. Socializing the occupied businesses opened the familiar question of how to run them. Valois took the opportunity to break with the Trotskyites, who preached worker control, while nonetheless defending these heretical communists against repression by the new Socialist government. There was truth to Valois's contention that the factory occupations did not lead to socialization because the workers lacked a sense of how to run industry.[63] More generally, this failure, and the Popular Front's assistance in ending the strikes, reflected the essentially reformist, defensive nature of the Popular Front. From Valois's perspective, the gains of the Popular Front were never as important as the missed opportunities. Unlike so many other chroniclers of the period, he never waxed eloquent over labor breakthroughs, like the first paid vacations.

From the beginning Valois urged the Popular Front government to take more vigorous action. It was not just that, as he echoed Pivert, "everything is possible," but also that, as he immediately added, "everything is necessary." No matter how they had voted, Frenchmen wanted a solution to the economic problems of the hour. If the Socialist-led government did not solve these, Valois correctly prophesied, it would be overthrown. Selected nationalizations and the destruction of the Havas-Hachette press combine were necessary defensive measures, as well as revolutionary goals.[64]

Not surprisingly, but correctly as it turned out, Valois insisted on the primacy of financial and monetary issues. Arguing that the cause of the current difficulties was the hoarding of money, Vincent Auriol proposed enlisting this inactive capital through a public loan and pumping the money into the economy through government spending. In the meantime, the government would live on advances from the Bank of France. Valois's objections were pertinent. Why should capital withheld under a conservative government be made available to a Socialist-led one? Furthermore, relying on advances from the Bank of France forced the government to live from day to day. Barely spoken was Valois's more fundamental concern. Auriol's program would leave him at the mercy of the plutocrats and promote more monetary instability.[65] This was also why Valois never celebrated the Matignon accords. Indeed, a diligent reader of Nouvel Age could remain unaware that they represented the most sweeping wage increases ever granted French workers. For Valois, wage gains unprotected from changes in purchasing power, and in a context of inflation, were so much sleight-of-hand. In fact, he was proven right, inasmuch as rising prices consumed most of the paper increases within months.

Valois triumphed bitterly half a year later when the Blum government announced its devaluation, negotiated secretly with the British and U.S. governments. First the government had soaked the small bondholders, the only ones swayed by the Popular Front mystique, Valois argued. Then it devalued suddenly, permitting big gains by the international financiers who were in on it.[66] As soon as he saw the text of the law, Valois hurried to the Ministry of Finance to propose a 10 to 15 percent tax on international exchange transactions. The technicians explained that they had rejected this idea because they wanted to encourage the repatriation of French capital. The devaluation would not even benefit the Socialist-led government, Valois insisted. Given the government's present indebtedness to the Bank of France, all this devaluation would produce would be "six months of dry bread." Here, too, his pessimism was well founded.[67]

Valois's denunciation was almost a declaration of war against the Blum/Auriol team. For him, monetary manipulations were the social original sin. By the fall of 1936, other issues had already led him to the conclusion that, to use Rodrigues's words, the Socialists were "in the process of ruining a magnificent opportunity."[68] Perhaps the most awesome challenge to the Blum government was the Spanish Civil War. The first reaction of the French government was to prepare an enormous shipment of military supplies for its Spanish counterpart. A violent campaign in the French nationalist press, led by Valois's former friends of the *Action française*, and an accompanying chorus of political protest, changed Blum's mind. He opted instead for a policy of nonintervention, which the Italians and Germans honored more in the breach than in the observance. The French Communist party then used nonintervention as a stick to beat the Socialists, though the Communists knew that the Blum government was secretly continuing to send arms, albeit in smaller quantities, to the Spanish republicans.[69] If Valois was aware of Blum's subterfuge, he gave no evidence of it.

Valois backed full military cooperation with the Spanish government, joining the large percentage of revolutionary "pacifists" who supported intervention in the civil war. He refused, however, to admit that there was any contradiction in his policy, arguing that neither Hitler nor Mussolini would risk war over Spain, where the revolutionary dynamic would work against them. More important, the fascization of Spain was part of an Italo-German plot to surround France. Any step toward its completion increased the risks of conflict. The campaign against intervention also excited Valois's attention. Valois wanted Maurras and the others at the Action française arrested. As he said in a slightly different context, there can be no liberty against liberty; and fascism should be outlawed.[70]

There was one last incident, however, when it seemed that the Blum government might be propelled into more revolutionary action, and action particularly to Valois's liking. That incident was the death of the Socialist minister of the interior, Roger Salengro, who committed suicide on November 17, 1936, after a sustained and particularly vicious campaign in the right-wing press falsely accusing him of desertion during the war. Though this public smear campaign was in many ways typical of the deplorable mores of political journalism in interwar France, Salengro's high position and evident innocence galvanized left-wing public opinion against the press.[71]

The timing was apt since Valois had recently begun yet another campaign against the Havas-Hachette trust. In a clear attempt to separate the Popular Front leadership from its followers, *Nouvel Age* attacked the bondage of the established left-wing press. As Valois put it, "the press is no longer for sale, it is entirely bought," meaning that virtually all the press was controlled by "the trust." Even though their memberships and readerships were sufficient to support the papers, the Socialist *Le Populaire*, the Communist *L'Humanité*, and the CGT's *Le Peuple* had recently signed or renewed contracts with Havas for advertisement and Hachette for distribution. Valois was not impressed by the Blum government's proposed reforms, which only concerned libel law and the disclosure of resources. If the government really wanted to attack the Havas-Hachette combine, it could eliminate the preferential postal and railroad tariffs. A newspaper consisting essentially of advertisements should pay as a catalogue, not as a vehicle of thought. This would eliminate the financial advantages of advertising and free the press.[72]

By the second week of November, Valois seemed to be having some success. The Blum government forced the resignation of Pierre Guimier, one of the chief executive officers of the Agence Havas. The official argument was the incompatibility of Guimier's position on the newspaper *Le Journal* with his role as head of an agency that received government subsidies. Valois was torn between exultation and disappointment. Guimier had been one of his bêtes noires for years, one of those occult masters of the press whom he alone had denounced. "La première charette," he headlined, evoking the tumbrils that had carried victims to the guillotine during the Revolution (and Maurice Barrès's novel *Leurs figures*). But Valois also knew that no journalistic reign of terror was at hand. Guimier was only an employee, and his elimination did little to dent the power of Havas and Hachette.[73]

Salengro's death gave fresh impetus to the anti-Havas campaign. Valois hoped to use the mounting indignation both to push the government into attacking Havas and Hachette and to bring a halt to the slander campaigns against himself. Valois said he understood Salengro's despair at ever clearing his name. Rather than crying over the body of his comrade, Valois insisted, Blum should have used the cadaver to mobilize his public. And, since Blum had come out against calumny, why did he not order an investigation of the way slanders had been, and still were, being spread against him, even within the Socialist party?[74] Though he did not stop the campaigns against him, Valois attracted considerable attention. His first special issue sold out immediately and was reprinted. Perhaps for this reason, the Socialist party, in late November 1936, sent an official to one of the weekly Nouvel Age meetings to defend the government against another of Valois's charges.[75]

Valois had decided by November 1936 that no provocation would move the government into revolutionary action.[76] But it was not just that the Popular Front government would not make the revolution; to Valois, Blum was engaged in the fascization of the economy—the creation of some kind of corporatism or neocapitalism for the benefit of the banks and trusts. This was the same policy Valois had denounced under the rightist governments of 1934 to 1936. Indeed, there were many, some with government connections, who were looking to some kind of corporative solution to the depression. Valois saw any measure to strengthen the state's control over the economy, if not taken in an aggressively revolutionary manner, as part of a conspiracy to complete the economic mutation from individual to state capitalism. This transformation would be at the expense of socialism, democracy, and the economic interests of Frenchmen.

The ire of Nouvel Age was provoked by talk, in August 1936, of a system of "industrial agreements." Valois attacked these as corporatism and attempts to reduce production to consumption—madness from the point of view of abundance theory. Valois blamed this "Trojan Horse" of "economic fascism" on René Belin of the CGT (with whom he would tangle often), Charles Spinasse of the Blum government, and Jean Coutrot. In November and December 1936, harsh phrases rained down upon the readers of Nouvel Age. "Total treason," the paper thundered; "Neo-Capitalism in power." When the Blum government adopted measures including compulsory arbitration, Valois termed them "the most cowardly treason that has ever been organized against the people." When Spinasse nominated Coutrot head of the Centre national d'organisation scientifique du travail in December, Valois screamed that this was turning over the economy to technician-servants of the trusts; and he followed this up with a press campaign against Coutrot, proponent of "economic dictatorship." Fascism was being introduced into France under the cover of antifascism.[77]

The whole gamut of measures was being sold to the Popular Front, Valois argued, as preparation for war against Germany. Valois also slaked his anger on Blum personally. He had always thought of Blum as essentially bourgeois, foreign to the working class, the former rightist explained, but he had held back his judgment since 1927 lest he reflect prejudices from time spent "with the enemy." Now, Valois insisted, he was forced to conclude that Blum had been part of the great plot against socialism and syndicalism since 1932. There was political convenience in Valois's discovery. But Blum represented all that Valois had always detested, and that he had excoriated before the war in Jaurès: he was a bourgeois, an intellectual, and a consummate practitioner of the parliamentary arts. And parliamentarianism, Valois repeated, was the source of all the problems of the socialist movement in France.

However, Valois wanted the Blum government to fall to the left. Hence, despite his lack of sympathy in February 1937 when the cabinet encountered the financial problems he had predicted, Valois advised Auriol to beef up his treasury with a 2 percent loan with a gold-exchange guarantee. He could then, Valois suggested, drive Frenchmen into buying these bonds through renewed inflation, while adopting measures, like the *franc-or*, to protect pensioners and businessmen. Valois recognized that this would not solve the government's long-term financial problems (he considered these insoluble), but it would buy time to work out radical remedies.[78]

When Blum and Auriol found their own solution, Valois termed it "the coup d'état of the 5th of March." Valois noted the banking connections of the technicians whom the government had put in charge of its fund for exchange equalization. This was putting the fox in the chicken coop. Furthermore, the banks only agreed to bail out the Blum government if it abandoned its policy of restoring prosperity by increasing purchasing power. The people would do without while bankers and industrialists profited.[79]

Valois tried desperately to convince his public that antifascism had become preparation for war, that it was neither a revolutionary nor even an anticapitalist policy. French capitalism was not fascist. French capitalists had seen fascism in Germany and Italy slip out of the hands of their counterparts—hence their policy of herding Blum into a *union sacrée*. The whole Popular Front experience was part of an elaborate plot to get the French left behind such a program.[80]

In June 1937, an event changed Valois's analysis, though, when the smoke cleared, he was no more sympathetic to the Blum government than before. Horace Finaly, Valois's bête noire for years, was fired as director of the Banque de Paris et des Pays-Bas. Since this position commanded Havas and Hachette, Finaly had lost control over the French press. Valois's explanation? Since Finaly had (through the Blum government) removed the regents of the Bank of France, the regents had chased him from his position at the Banque de Paris. The combine of François de Wendel, the Rothschilds, and Lucien Moreau now controlled the press and could turn its power against the Popular Front. French capitalism was split into two warring clans. Valois was scandalized when newspapers like the pro– Popular Front *L'Oeuvre* praised Finaly. One must both finish off Finaly *and* fight the Moreau–de Wendel group.[81]

It was in these terms that Valois saw the fall of the Blum government later that month. When Blum requested full legislative powers to stem the exchange crisis, Valois answered that Blum's full powers would be Finaly's rule. A century of socialism would have led to no more than the dictatorship of Finaly and his creatures. Valois was not one of those, there- fore, who blamed the Senate when its refusal of confidence led to Blum's resignation. The failure of the Popular Front government was the failure of the parliamentary system. Valois wanted revolution, Blum to save a re- gime that Valois thought neither savable nor worth saving. The great re- forms of France's first Socialist government meant little to Valois. Only the five-day week seemed to him a revolutionary step, since it broke with the old idea that man was only free from work on the Lord's day.[82]

From February 6, 1934, to the fall of the first Socialist-led government of the Third Republic in June 1937, Valois remained part of the left oppo- sition to the Popular Front. He failed to build alliances with those who shared either his convictions about the coming age of abundance or his revolutionary hopes. Part of this was owing to the suspicions raised by his fascist past. But Valois's failure to inflect the policy of the Popular Front seriously was part of the failure of the whole French revolutionary left in these years. And the major cause of this was the canalization of left-wing sentiment behind a movement that, in terms of the fundamental institu- tions of the Third Republic, was essentially conservative.

Valois did survive, even prosper, in an intensely competitive, and fre- quently hostile, atmosphere. His movement steadily, if slowly, grew stronger. It was in the years of the Popular Front that he succeeded, for the first time since the rich days of the *Nouveau Siècle*, in publishing a daily paper. His uncompromising positions made this far more of an achieve- ment than the expensive fascist daily had been. *Nouvel Age* and the co- operatives of the rue de l'Abbaye remained the bases of his influence and independence.

NINE

War or Revolution

Almost no one in the France of 1937 wanted war. Yet most could see armed conflict approaching. A resurgent Germany remilitarized the Rhineland in March 1936 and sealed the Pact of Steel with an imperialist Italy a few months later. Hitler gathered the fruit of this diplomacy with the annexation of Austria in early 1938. Czechoslovakia would come later that year, while the continuing Civil War in Spain threatened to drag the great powers into the conflict.

Most Frenchmen were torn between instinctive opposition to war and mounting concern. The right was divided between those who wanted France to stand up to Hitler and a group on the radical right, led by Valois's former friends of the Action française, who preached concessions toward Germany and courtship of Italy. While most of these appeasers of the right (like Maurras) lacked confidence in French strength, a noisy minority was motivated by ideological sympathy for the totalitarian experiment across the Rhine. The left was torn between antimilitarism and antifascism. If the contest was between democracy (with all its flaws) and fascism, then resistance to the aggressor combined national interest and social justice. But if avoidance of war remained the first priority, then perhaps an understanding could be reached with Germany, especially since France was not without responsibility for the frustrations of its Teutonic neighbor over the 1919 Treaty of Versailles. Bedeviling the judgments of almost all factions were conflicting attitudes to Stalin's Russia, the chief power supporting vigorous resistance to Hitler.

AGAINST WAR AND FASCISM

As the decade advanced, Valois's principled opposition to fascism deepened into horror. Valois read *Mein Kampf* in the complete (and unauthorized) French translation and urged his followers to do so too. Partly as a consequence, he saw the Nazi regime as portending a new racial conception of humanity, leading to the enslavement of entire populations and the wholesale slaughter of the Jews. This appreciation extended to the concept of totalitarianism (although not the word). Thus, the Soviet system also represented a serious moral regression. Valois was disgusted by the purge trials, by the fact that assassination had become a normal form of political action: "In the name of the race or of the revolution, whole populations are decimated, robbed, deported, tortured, massacred." Although he was a former fascist and decorated battle veteran, Valois was horrified by the direction he saw his century taking. Liberal capitalism might have been unjust, he argued, but its period of dominance compared favorably with the massacres of the present century.[1] Valois was sufficiently familiar with twentieth-century mass politics to see its brutal potential accurately, but sufficiently wedded to the traditional values of Western culture to shrink back from it with horror.

To the veteran of Verdun, it seemed as though almost everyone else in Europe was preparing for war; and he believed plans for the coming conflict were the key to international and domestic politics. The bellicosity of Hitler and Mussolini stemmed from more than their characters or the dynamics of their systems. For the most fundamental level of explanation, Valois modernized an idea he had shared before the war with Sorel and members of the Italian right, explaining now that Germany, Italy, and Japan were driven to war because they lacked necessary raw materials, especially energy. The Soviet Union, the United States, and Britain and France with their empires controlled most of the planet's natural resources. German and Italian policies were aimed against the French and British empires.

Valois insisted on the ambitions of France's Latin sister state (familiar to him from his association with the Italian nationalists), concerned to refute those, like Maurras, who sought an accommodation with Mussolini. Italo-German strategy was to surround France and threaten British and French imperial communications. Support for Franco served both objectives since it also threatened the British at Gibraltar. Similarly, Valois saw Arab restiveness in Palestine as largely provoked by Italy.[2]

But the other powers also thought in terms of war. The USSR sought to push the threat of war westward by provoking a Franco-German conflict. The French Communist party was its agent; and Valois called *L'Humanité* the most warmongering paper in France. Yet Russia was an important, if unsure, ally. Given the instability of the Soviet system and the convergent evolution of the Stalin and Hitler regimes, Valois never excluded the possibility of a Russo-German rapprochement, especially if the Western powers tried to turn German ambitions eastward. His "totalitarian" analysis was in many ways more prescient than the antifascist one of the Popular Front.[3]

The leaders of the "Demo-plutocracies" of France and Britain were little better. Having created the fascist menace through their bumbling, they could think of nothing better than military preparation to meet it, though some plutocratic factions sought to accommodate Hitler. Even the leading democratic politicians, like Blum, had also resigned themselves to war.[4]

ANTIWAR MONETARY POLITICS

For Valois, the coming conflict also guaranteed continuing monetary crisis. France, which had not finished paying for the last war, was already engaging the expenses of the next. Since the economy could not support such a charge, the government was obliged to live off inflation, and the franc was consigned to a speedy collapse.

Valois attacked Georges Bonnet, finance minister in the Chautemps government, which had replaced the Blum cabinet in 1937. The "full powers" granted him meant dictatorship, phoney money, and war![5] But Valois also had to educate his public, to repeat the points he had drilled into the blue shirts of the twenties. The decline of the franc was caused neither by capital flight, as leftists argued, nor by foreign bankers, as rightists claimed, but by monetary inflation. Monetary manipulation was even more necessary now that the progress of abundance had rendered normal capitalism unprofitable. By the same token, exchange controls, a favorite idea of the left, were useless, their revival one more attempt to make Finaly economic dictator.[6] From 1937 through the first months of 1939, Valois maintained his pessimism about the franc. "Once again, 'hideous bankruptcy,' " he headlined in January 1938. A few weeks later, he explained that money was coming to the end of its historical role. The demonetarization of gold was one more sign of the death of the system of exchange. Valois was no kinder to Paul Reynaud, who assumed the economic reins in the fall of 1938. Monetary chaos was right around the corner.[7]

Setting aside the problem of war preparations, Valois recognized that the government could only make up its deficit through increased taxes.

But in the current climate, they would overburden production. Instead the government should take its cut before products were sold. Businessmen could produce up to 60 percent more goods if there were consumers for them. The government would take this surplus as a tax; it could then create money by drawing bills on the goods it now owned and discounting these through the Bank of France. Valois recognized that this was similar to pump-priming schemes he had denounced as inflationary. His proposal was not, however, he argued, since the new francs would be backed by merchandise. How the government would dispose of its goods without further depressing demand he did not face directly. Indeed, if the government were to use these goods itself, this would be close to the deficit financing of rearmament to which state after state was turning. But Valois expected his scheme to take France out of capitalism. Government prepurchase would bypass the market, forcing the government to create a distributive economy.[8]

But Valois did not expect any French government willingly to adopt his revolutionary cure or to abandon the addictive drug of inflation. In the meantime, Frenchmen would have to be defended and the plutocrats forced to cede power. Syndicats of savers, retirees, and other "users" of the franc should defend their rights. In October 1937 he announced gold bonds sold by a *caisse coopérative* (cooperative fund). These bonds, available only to members of the rue de l'Abbaye cooperatives, were payable either in gold or in the number of paper francs equivalent to the gold value of the original investment: the *franc-or* for savers. The gold bonds would permit Valois's co-op members to protect their savings. In the long run, however (and contrary to Valois's claims of the 1920s), no money of account could keep the capitalist system afloat. It would simply force the plutocrats to declare bankruptcy. Further, a 5 percent commission charged to bond holders would not only defray the costs of the *caisse* but also help support the Nouvel Age movement. Of course, any other pecuniary advantages resulting from handling this new capital also accrued to Valois's enterprises.[9]

The gold fund turned out to be one of Valois's most popular creations. On one day, over seventy thousand francs were invested. By the end of the year, the *caisse* listed assets of 354,615 francs, with a declared value of 35,729 gold francs. Soon Valois had to defend the *caisse* against leftist critics who wondered why he was organizing a flight from the franc, and whether a leftist militant should be in the banking business. If the CGT had organized such a service, the banks would have lost power long ago, the former blue shirt retorted. Controlling the economy was more important than seizing the state, Valois had been insisting for twenty years. Here was a good example.[10]

Results were so good that Valois proposed a *caisse coopérative à stock d'or*, a gold-based cooperative fund with savings and checking accounts whose revenue would be divided between the depositors and the movement. In September 1938, after the Munich crisis created a further panic, Valois opened his gold fund accounts. Again, results were excellent. In November, Valois announced short-term deposits of 114,655 francs and long-term investments of 464,512. By the end of February 1939, as war clouds gathered on the horizon, the respective figures stood at 96,913 and 644,391 francs.[11] In this climate of inflation and mounting insecurity, there were few other ways of indexing savings while maintaining some liquidity; and this one added ideological virtue to self-interest.

Valois's cooperative gold fund only served savers. For most Frenchmen, a far better issue was the protection of their earning power. In May 1938, Valois began a campaign for the *salaire-or*. Over twenty thousand copies of a special placard/issue were distributed by Nouvel Age militants all over France.[12]

PONTIGNY AND THE REFORMIST SCANDAL

Just as the monetary crisis derived directly from war preparations, so too, for Valois, did the movement for syndicalo-patronal cooperation associated with the name of Pontigny. For several years, this former Cistercian abbey had been the site of a series of seminars, called *décades*, under the leadership of Paul Desjardins. One of Desjardins's major concerns was social and economic reform; and Pontigny had become linked with the kind of reformist socialism represented by the neos. Valois went to Pontigny for the first time in 1929, when Desjardins responded to the gift of a copy of *Un Nouvel Age de l'humanité* by asking its author to the annual "decade." He wanted Valois to collaborate with Henri de Man, who was fast becoming one of the leading spirits of the Pontigny circle. Valois came that summer, and he returned in 1931 and 1932. By 1932 Valois decided that Pontigny was not for him; and he purposefully left in the middle of the proceedings.[13]

Valois boycotted further *décades*, and he broke with de Man in 1934, but he did not make an issue of Pontigny until 1938. What provoked his wrath then was a meeting of Swedish syndicalists and patronal representatives with their French counterparts. The Swedes had worked out a system of collective bargaining and labor-management cooperation. At

Pontigny, the Scandinavians showed off their social wares while French syndicalists clinked glasses with their class enemies.[14] This was waving a red flag at the bull of the rue de l'Abbaye. For Valois, Pontigny was an attempted debauching of French syndicalism, a way-station on the road to pluto-fascist state capitalism, and another form of war preparation. He also took the opportunity to launch a campaign against the reformist wing of the CGT.

First of all, Valois noted, the Pontigny meeting had been organized by Auguste Detoeuf, a modernizing businessman and proponent of coordinated capitalism. Behind Detoeuf lay Mercier, and therefore Finaly. In a more serious charge, Valois accused the participating French syndicalists of treason. By working toward corporatism and social peace, he insisted, they violated the Charte d'Amiens, the founding document of the CGT. Of course, this revolutionary constitution had long been honored more in the breach than in the observance; and some CGT members were happy to declare themselves in favor of social peace. But if syndicalists no longer believed in replacing the owning class, Valois countered, they should admit as much and publicly support corporatism, as he had done years ago.[15] The *décade* of 1938 also brought out some of Valois's more personal notions. Pontigny was a *mauvais lieu*, a zone of moral danger, a kind of political brothel where naïve working-class militants were surrounded by all the trappings of upper-bourgeois society. Amid the glitter and gentility, the proletarian lost confidence in himself, his politics, and his class. Morality was also sociology. Pontigny proved Sorel right in his concern to preserve the working class from bourgeois contamination.[16]

The attack on Pontigny consummated the break with the reformists of the CGT and SFIO. Valois had already caught Léon Jouhaux's right-hand man, René Belin, the previous December spreading stories that Valois had sold out to the banks. Belin's reply to Valois's anti-Pontigny campaign was basic, and appropriate for all the attacked reformists. "Search the past of those who scream of treason," he urged. "They are the ones who have most betrayed." Valois and Belin sued each other, starting a set of legal battles that continued down to the war. Belin's sharp reactions are the best index to the impact of Valois's campaigns among French syndicalists.[17]

For the leader of the rue de l'Abbaye, however, the issue was greater than the soul of the CGT. The favorable comment on Pontigny from the establishment *Le Temps*, Col. François de la Rocque, and other conservatives showed that the *décade* was the visible part of a far larger "autumn plot." The silence of the French Communists showed that they too were in the game. The goal, of course, was always the same—to prepare the country for war. Valois claimed, as usual, to have aborted the conspiracy. His continual campaigns against class cooperation and corporatism made life difficult for French economic and social reformers of both left and right.[18]

THE EMBARGO

The central dilemma remained what it had been in 1931: "War or revolution?" But, what if war preceded revolution? At first, Valois believed the coming war would create a revolutionary situation. The aggressor would launch major air attacks without warning. In fact, both states would probably have their planes in the air so quickly that it would be impossible to determine who struck first. More important, these attacks would disrupt economic and political activity. All over France, communities would find themselves cut off from the world, thrown back on their own resources. If properly prepared, Valois's local supporters could organize a new economy, which could spread contagiously to the rest of the country. The new struggle would combine war and revolution.[19]

The Spanish Civil War showed Valois his error. The good (bad?) news was that cities, indeed countries, could survive sustained aerial bombardment. The horrors of the next war would not, of themselves, create the revolution. And this was a game France would not win. The superior dynamism, the purer militarism, and the popular elements in the fascist states would give them victory. The plutocrats, who had lost virtually every battle since the Treaty of Versailles, would lose this one too. Though Valois's technical arguments were often flawed, he sensed quite early that the divided France of the late 1930s would not repeat the heroic effort of 1914–18.[20]

Valois rejected both sentimental pacifism and revolutionary defeatism. War was the combined product of human nature, with its parasitical and aggressive tendencies, and social organization. Goodwill and mutual understanding were powerless against such forces. As for the revolutionary defeatism of the Gauche révolutionnaire, Valois had known for years that this would simply open France to its enemies. Finally, even if the revolution preceded the war, it might not spread to all belligerents. A revolutionary France would still need some kind of defense, though a nonmilitarist one. But was this not squaring the circle? For Valois, social problems were never insoluble. The revolutionary engineer (the image was his own) simply had to find the proper technique.[21]

In September 1937, Valois found his solution: the embargo. Five-sixths of the oil used outside the United States was produced by, or under the control of, countries favorably disposed to France—Britain, the United States, the USSR—and trusts like the Anglo-Persian and Royal Dutch companies. One could not make war, especially the modern mechanized variety, without fuel. Between them, Germany, Italy, and Japan lacked enough oil for sustained combat. If the democracies of the world (plus the USSR) could block oil shipments to the Axis powers, the threat of war would be ended. The embargo was a perfect formula. It avoided the use of military force, it represented the victory of the economic over the military, and it was based on the root cause of conflict, the unequal division of raw materials.[22]

Of the antifascist powers, only France (along with tiny Belgium) controlled no significant petroleum resources. But Frenchmen were "the raw material of battle," Valois argued. If British plutocrats were persuaded French soldiers would not fight, they would have to consider a nonmilitary option. The "embargo" was not a "boycott," an attempt to cut off all economic relations. The embargo, designed to turn the populations of fascist states against their leaders, would only deny hostile states the sinews of war. Starving the Axis would rally the people round their dictators. The gap between possessing and nonpossessing nations could only be ended by making Europe a joint economic consortium. Renouncing war meant renouncing force and European rule over the colored peoples of the planet.[23]

European unity, the end of empire, eventual equality for black and yellow: these meant a revolutionary reconstruction of the international order. But the embargo implied as great a set of changes within France. Capitalists would not freely give up the profits of sales to the Axis. They would have to be forced to do so by syndically organized Frenchmen. Here was a dream Valois had cherished since his royalist days; producers, acting through their economic organizations, forcing political decisions on the plutocratic masters of France. Since damming up the free flow of international commerce would wreak havoc with the laissez-faire system, averting war had to be part of a larger economic and social construction. Though Valois was really calling for a revolution to prevent war, his opening wedge was a relatively simple and appealing program. As he put it, the syndicate of murderers was already formed; would the syndicate of owners be permitted to sell them the raw materials to prepare the massacre?[24]

Prospects seemed excellent. The remnants of the Saint-Denis antiwar coalition had been reactivated as the Conférence permanente contre la guerre. Participating now were Albert Treint's La Lutte finale; members of Marceau Pivert's Gauche révolutionnaire; the Trotskyite Parti d'unité prolétarienne; the Ligue internationale des mères; and a few small anarchist associations. Valois and Gustave Rodrigues converted the administrative commission of the Conférence permanente to the embargo in September 1937. Nouvel Age was back in a leadership position in the antiwar movement: another pacifist association, the Rassemblement international contre la guerre, also adopted the slogan "No fuel for the warmakers," and the embargo was on the program of an antiwar conference in Brussels in October.[25]

All these groups came from that same noncommunist radical left with which Valois had been flirting since the mid 1930s. As such, they remained marginal to the French political system. Much more significant, therefore, was the opening to the Rassemblement universel pour la paix. The RUP was a mainstream leftist organization made up largely of Communists and fellow travelers, with close ties to the Popular Front. Valois and his men distributed tracts at the RUP meeting in Paris in late September, and the congress unanimously called on the member governments of the League of Nations to organize boycotts of all essential materials against the Axis powers, virtually Valois's program.[26]

Support swelled throughout the autumn of 1937. Leftist groups ranging from veterans and professional associations to the powerful Parti ouvrier belge adopted the no-fuel program. Valois's occasional ally Marcel Déat also came out for an oil embargo. Meanwhile, Valois added iron, nickel, and cotton to his list of strategic materials by the time the Conférence permanente contre la guerre met again in November 1937. The following month, Valois called attention to Franco-American control over bauxite sources. The organizations of the rue de l'Abbaye distributed hundreds of thousands of tracts and special issues. In December the SFIO adopted the slogan "No oil, no fuel." On the 5th, the Conférence permanente contre la guerre distributed fifty thousand tracts in Paris. A group of France's most distinguished leftist professors also went on record for the embargo. Former rivals and occasional allies were climbing on the bandwagon.[27]

None of this dispelled Valois's sense of urgency. The oil card would not last forever, he had warned in October. By the end of 1938, the Axis might well solve its petroleum problem. He was all the more frustrated when his budding embargo movement ran into trouble in January 1938. First, Treint bolted the movement with his followers. Next, the RUP refused to join in a projected antiwar conference; and as Valois received an onslaught of attacks from leading syndicalists and journalists, the rue de l'Abbaye was rocked by a series of internal revolts. Valois crushed the internal opposition and replied to his critics, but his momentum was lost.[28]

The reasons for this collapse were familiar. Behind the simple idea of halting supplies to the warmongers of the world lay Valois's revolutionary program. And the leader at the rue de l'Abbaye never denied himself the opportunity to attack enemies like the Communists. During the last year and a half of peace, Valois defended his embargo against two groups of critics. One consisted of the pure pacifists, who feared the embargo would provoke war. Valois answered that as long as the Axis powers had not completed their strategic preparations, the embargo would block, not hasten, the conflict. If natural resources were really the problem, some pacifists argued, why not share them equitably, including colonial possessions. The modern world was economically indivisible, and no power could be economically independent, Valois replied. Germany, Italy, and Japan had sufficient access to natural resources for peaceful purposes. Only in the context of war were they resource poor. Compromise was impossible. But so was capitulation! Valois refuted the idea of letting Hitler unify Europe. Nazi hegemony would not bring peace, Valois pointed out; subject races would eventually revolt, and the Axis powers would fall out among themselves.[29]

If Valois was too bellicose for the pacifists, he was too pacifist for the proponents of military preparedness—for those who, whatever their judgment of the usefulness of an embargo of strategic materials, also believed in rearmament as precaution and deterrent. He attacked these proponents of "pacifist cannons and machine guns," like Paul Rivet, head of the Comité de vigilance anti-fasciste. If they were not planning for war, why did they support the arms buildup?[30]

As the months passed, it became increasingly difficult for Valois to combine vigorous antifascism and absolute nonviolence. The embargo would take time to work. In the meantime, the country would have to be defended against a lightning attack based on existing oil stocks. If the Maginot line were not occupied, Valois explained, Hitler would "enter without knocking." At first Valois argued that air attacks on open cities should be met with economic ostracism. By early 1939, however, he and Rodrigues admitted that air defense would be necessary, though it should not be accompanied by attacks on the aggressor's territory. Finally, Valois had long argued that, to be effective, the blockade would have to be accompanied by a certain naval "police" action—at the least, blocking the Suez Canal. Though he would not admit it, Valois was willing to appeal to force. Too willing for some followers. In March 1939, Régis Messac resigned, protesting that Valois and Rodrigues were becoming nationalists and militarists. His solution of peaceful propaganda only earned Valois's ridicule. But Messac had a point. As the war approached, Valois's positions increasingly resembled those of the pro-war leftists he criticized.[31] And his militarization of the blockade portended later choices.

THE RACE AGAINST WAR

Valois saw himself in an increasingly desperate race against approaching massacre. In 1938 the Nazi Führer set the pace. The embargo idea was still advancing, though at a speed that left Valois discouraged. In February 1938, the RUP organized a rally for an embargo on strategic materials, but only against Japan. At this rate ("six months late"), the race to halt the Axis would be lost. Hitler's absorption of Austria in March only increased Valois's sense of urgency. His first response, however, was to reassure his readers. Hitler could still be stopped. In a remarkable analysis, Valois explained Hitler's tactics. Hitler only moved against an adversary when he had achieved an overwhelming, crushing advantage. He was thus perfectly willing to pursue his goals in increments. For the same reason, the Nazi leader was also not about to seek a general war as long as the odds seemed close. There were lessons to be learned from Hitler and Mussolini—the difference that force of will and popular dynamism could make. The bankers and politicians of France and Britain did not have the people with them. Germany, Italy, and the Soviet Union had only achieved their successes by eliminating their former ruling personnel. Frenchmen could bring dynamism back to their side by adopting Valois's revolutionary program.[32]

As Valois saw it, the dictators had not completed their preparations. Hitler still needed Hungarian wheat and Rumanian oil. And as long as Catalonia held out, the French could invade Spain through this antifascist pocket. Arming the Spanish Republicans thus also delayed war. Valois developed a new political framework to accompany his embargo. The solution was European federalism, he insisted, and he organized a committee for a United States of the Peoples of Europe. At one hundred francs each, the committee sold "European passports" identifying their holders as "citizens of Europe" (and raising money for the rue de l'Abbaye).[33]

"The European War Will Not Take Place," Valois headlined a few days later, echoing the title of Giraudoux's 1935 play *The Trojan War Will Not Take Place*. There was unintentional irony in this evocation. In Giraudoux's pacifist production, war occurs despite Hector's diplomatic efforts and an agreement to return Helen to the Greeks. Doubts were gnawing beneath

Valois's optimistic exterior. On March 17, *Nouvel Age* insisted that it would continue to oppose war, "even if it wins the race against us."[34]

Valois's European campaign was not just opportunism. The former fascist saw how Hitler played on the clavier of European national sentiments. To refute him, one would have to elevate the debate beyond the constricting national claims of Central Europe. Valois was consciously preparing for the next act in the European drama: Czechoslovakia. As early as the end of March 1938, Valois explained the nature of the threat. Hitler would not attack Czechoslovakia directly, and the French guarantee would probably be useless. Instead, the Germans would seek to dislocate the multiethnic state—splitting off the Slovaks, or the Sudeten Germans, or both. What would France do if Hitler merely took the Sudetenland, Valois asked? He repeated his warnings later that spring and summer. The greatest risk of war was not from Hitler (who wanted one, but only when he was ready) but from the democracies. If despite everything, the Nazis attacked Czechoslovakia, the allies must not respond with war, Valois insisted, but with a complete economic break. Better still, why not overthrow Hitler peacefully while there was still time?[35]

The Sudeten crisis, which culminated in the Munich conference, dominated *Nouvel Age* in September, as it did most of the French press. Once Hitler had Prague, Valois explained, the route was open to Rumanian oil. By October or November, Hitler would have enough men to crush the Czechs. French and English troops would not be ready until the spring. Thrown back on economic measures anyway, the allies should adopt a strict military defensive, break economic relations and assist in the overthrow of the fascist regimes.[36]

Later that month, Valois explained why a lightning German attack on France should not be feared. The Maginot line would protect the Franco-German border; and if the Wehrmacht attacked through Belgium, the French army, its right flank protected, could easily outmaneuver the invader. The German force would be exposed to a devastating attack on its flank, "unless it could advance with such an extraordinary impetuosity, that it is hard to conceive of it." French leaders did not see the technical problems inherent in modern warfare, Valois insisted; "obsessed by the memory of 1914, [they] saw a German army, motorized this time, sweeping down on Paris at one hundred [kilometers] an hour."[37]

Of course, this is almost precisely what happened less than two years later; and Valois did not significantly modify his assessment during that time (though he did add an important caveat). How did Valois, who correctly estimated Nazi dynamism and military skill in general terms, go so wrong on particulars? That his error was widely shared is not enough of an explanation. Valois was usually willing to challenge accepted wisdom, and he of all people believed in the almost miraculous transformative potential of new technology. The explanation lies in the overwhelming importance Valois gave to the control of strategic materials and the economic potential of the belligerents. On this he was right in the long run. But he confused the long run with the short, the strategic with the tactical. In so doing, he, along with most other Frenchmen, failed to appreciate the new relations of time and distance.

Valois should not have been surprised by Neville Chamberlain's policy of appeasement. He had noted the political difficulties in refusing self-determination to the Sudeten Germans; and he predicted that the plutocrats, who feared war, would be bluffed by Hitler, who did not. Nevertheless, Chamberlain's initial concessions infuriated Valois who called them "plutocratic treason . . . to save the dividends of Anglo-French imperialism." French hesitations Valois ascribed to the contest between the Franco-Russian pro-war and Anglo-French appeasement factions. More practically, he warned that concessions would only excite the Führer's ambitions.[38] Chamberlain's concessions at their first, Berchtesgaden, interview did lead to increased demands at the second meeting in Bad Godesberg. This time, however, the Führer was asking too much, the immediate occupation of the Sudetenland, and the British and French resisted. The French and Czechs mobilized, and war seemed imminent.

Valois desperately tried to avert panic. "Everything is possible," he headlined; "Neither war nor capitulation, the blockade, the blockade! THE BLOCKADE." Nevertheless, he feared that Hitler might have gone too far to back off, that Chamberlain might have tricked him into an overly aggressive policy. Valois expected war. Instead he got Munich. *Nouvel Age* made the Allied concessions the basis for an almost nationalist campaign. The Allied leaders were "cowards and capitulators," Munich "the most shameful defeat of our history." It would deliver all of Czechoslovakia to the Nazis and open the route to Rumanian oil and Ukrainian wheat. And it was stupid, because the Allies had held the strategic advantage; the Italians, among others, were not prepared to fight.[39]

Though Valois understood the basis for Allied hesitations, he chose conspiratorial over structural explanations. The slight differences between what the British and French had refused at Bad Godesberg and what they accepted a few days later at Munich proved that the whole crisis had been orchestrated. Its purpose was to frighten public opinion into accepting the surrender of Central Europe to Germany. But the Allied arms buildup showed that Britain and France were really preparing for war. The idea that Chamberlain and Daladier might want peace, but fear war, did not enter into Valois's calculations. Instead he concluded that the British wanted war, but later. From his perspective, this was madness; while the Allies gained time, the Axis gained strategic advantages. Hitler was invited to turn his ambitions against the Soviet Union—a dangerous policy, Valois had been suggesting for some time, since it could easily provoke a Hitler-Stalin pact.[40]

Valois blamed the pro-war party of Paul Reynaud and Georges Mandel, the "capitulation" group of Daladier and Georges Bonnet, and the old-style pacifists, especially those grouped around René Belin and the reformist wing of the CGT. They had wanted self-determination for the Sudeten Germans, but they had denied it to the Czechs, Valois reminded them when Hitler absorbed the rest of Bohemia a few weeks later.[41] The struggle for the embargo was, thus, also a struggle with domestic political rivals. Valois's sharpest battles were fought not with the pro-war groups of left and right but with pacifists and appeasers at both ends of the political spectrum. It was chiefly with these that he became embroiled in court battles, making 1938 the most litigious year of his career.

In May, Charles Laurent, secretary of the powerful Fédération des fonctionnaires, called Valois "a chameleon, who had passed, to support himself, through all the nuances of the political rainbow." Particularly incensed because he had had amicable relations with Laurent from 1927 through 1933, Valois sued for damages. The battle was even more bitter with Belin, one of the most important reformists in the CGT. Since at least 1936, Belin had been trying to persuade Valois's followers (notably Rodrigues) that the former fascist was a tool of the banks. In December 1937, Belin repeated the charge in front of an audience. Belin refused to recant (or duel), so the editor of Nouvel Age threatened to sue. To Valois's fury, Belin made insinuations without giving him a clear legal case. In one long attack, Belin referred only to "Mr. Damages and Interests," mocking Valois's penchant for lawsuits. Valois called Belin a "left fascist," for his state-capitalist schemes, and referred to him as René-Basile Belin, invoking the literary symbol of calumny he had previously used for Maurras. After Munich, Belin joined the munichois, those who supported compromise to preserve the peace. For this, and his previous support for rearmament, Valois labeled him a pacifist with airplanes. When Belin sued, the editor claimed he did so to block the criticism of his peace policy. Valois also sued Belin's sometime friend, Christian Pineau, a corporatist modernizer who had at different times worked with former Faisceau members and even with Valois during the early 1930s. More recently, Pineau had sent out a circular denouncing Valois's gold-bond schemes. Pineau accused Valois of living off journalistic blackmail and crooked accounting procedures.[42]

Legally more threatening was the fight between Valois and his former comrades at the Action française. In December 1936, Maurras sued Valois over his charge that he was an agent of the Havas-Hachette press combine, asking for one million francs in damages. Valois quickly reminded his readers that he had organized *Nouvel Age* to be litigation-proof. But the Action française sued both Valois and "the company that exploits *Nouvel Age*." Valois was no more able to prove his charges than the royalists had been years before. In May 1938, the court found against him and SCANA, ordering insertion of the verdict and one hundred francs damages. Valois refused payment and denied that SCANA was liable, daring the royalists to order the seizure of his person to force payment. They responded by trying to seize SCANA's postal checking account. Valois shifted this into the name of COR. In December 1938, the royalists convinced the postal administration that checks sent to COR but marked for SCANA could be seized for damages and recovery costs. Valois sued the postal administration.[43]

On top of all this, Valois became embroiled in litigation with disgruntled members of his own organizations who, frustrated over his refusal to give them more say, tried to retrieve some of the financial contributions they had made to the cause. All in all, *Nouvel Age* reported in December of 1938, Valois and the rue de l'Abbaye were involved in fourteen separate court cases. Valois was wrong when he saw these as a coordinated attack, but correct when he noted they were a serious drain on his time and money.[44]

In February 1939, the Pineau, Laurent, and Belin cases went to trial. Almost everyone had slandered everyone else, and no one could prove his charges. Valois won his cases against Laurent and Pineau, but lost Belin's case against him. Other litigation, of course, went on.[45] Much of the bitterness of these battles stemmed from the fact that Belin, Maurras, and their respective allies were the mainstays of the *munichois* of the left, on the one hand, and the appeasers of the right, on the other. It was this that kept them and Valois at each other's journalistic throats up until, and in the case of the royalists after, the outbreak of the war.

NEITHER WAR NOR CAPITULATION

The Munich agreement was greeted with relief by most Frenchmen. A significant minority, including the Lyon syndicalist and pacifist Léon Emery and CGT reformists like Belin, considered it a victory of public opinion

over the dangerous inflexibility of some Allied leaders.[46] *Nouvel Age* rejected this position, as it did its logical extension, French concessions on
colonies, now being suggested in some leftist circles. If you need a slogan,
Valois counseled, try "Tunisia for the Tunisians, Ethiopia for the
Ethiopians."[47] Similarly, the rue de l'Abbaye supported the Communist-
led strikes against the government's restrictive decree laws at the end of
November 1938 and denounced the compulsory dissolution of the Communist party. Valois criticized those leftists who opposed the strikes out of
support for the government's peace policy. These included not only Emery
but also Gaston Bergery, whom Valois correctly assessed as being on his
way to fascism.[48]

The editor of *Nouvel Age* still urged the embargo. Hitler's chances in
an armed conflict were greatly improved and it was folly to continue with
a war strategy. Valois was increasingly bitter over the lost opportunities.
An embargo would have been easy to implement in 1937, but by now the
tactic had lost half of its potential efficacy. The oil advantage over Japan
would also soon be gone. In another year, an embargo would be almost
useless. Economic warfare would have to be supplemented by political and
psychological weapons. The citizens of the Axis countries still wanted
freedom, Valois asserted, and Hitler's racism could be used to turn the
peoples of the earth against him. This would be especially true of the col-
onized races, if France took the lead against imperialism.[49]

Any attack on Nazi racism would have to deal squarely with anti-
Semitism. Since the Dreyfus Affair, the Jewish "problem" had been a
right-wing issue in France, and Valois had thus given it scant attention
since joining the left. As the war scare mounted during the Munich crisis,
however, he felt it necessary to refute the anti-Semitic pro-appeasement
argument that French Jews were pushing for war to avenge their German
brethren. Valois's reply was simple: there were Jews, and important Jewish interests, on both sides.[50]

In mid November, after the giant pogrom of Kristallnacht, Valois
published a series of articles on "the Jewish problem," the most detailed
treatment he had given the issue since his reactionary days before World
War I. As a former anti-Semite, Valois sought to convince, not denounce,
the followers of this doctrine. The Jewish problem was not a figment of
the anti-Semitic imagination. There was a Jewish problem of sorts in contemporary capitalist society, though there would be none in his new society. Using a politically chosen parallel, Valois explained that the Jews
and the Jesuits sought, like all well-organized groups, to conquer the centers of economic and political power. They were simply the most success-

ful. To deny this, or the connections both groups enjoyed with powerful financial groups, "was to deny the light of day." The success of the Jews excited the envy and "social hatred" that always faced material success under capitalism.[51]

But there was more to the Jewish experience, for Valois. What the anti-Semites objected to most in the Jew was that he was not "at home" anywhere, that his rights did not stem from conquest or physical occupation. To Valois this was a virtue. The Jews were one of the few groups who had put their energies into the arts of peace rather than those of war. As a former reactionary, Valois understood clearly the association of the Jews with the transcendent, progressive aspects of modern European civilization. As a revolutionary leftist, he integrated this understanding into a new analysis. The anti-Semite wanted to take back by force what the Jew had gained through economic activity.[52]

Earlier cycles of anti-Jewish activity had usually ended in compromise. But Hitler's anti-Semitism would not pass so easily, Valois warned. It was both the founding doctrine of the Nazi state and a personal obsession: for the Führer, "the extermination of the Jews was a divine mission." Hence, too, Jewish bellicosity was madness. Echoing Hitler's sinister prediction (but from opposite motives), Valois argued that a European war would be "a catastrophe for Israel" and appealed for the support of French Jews. Valois had always seen the Jews as torn between justice (the prophets) and wealth (the golden calf). To choose the first meant, for Valois, breaking ethnic solidarity with bankers like Lazard and Rothschild. He criticized the organizer of the International League against Anti-Semitism, Bernard Lecache, for refusing to part with his powerful allies. There was no more a natural solidarity of Jews with Rothschild than of Lorrainers with de Wendel, Valois insisted.[53] The Jews had but two choices, revolution and the overthrow of Hitler, or massacre. Nevertheless, Valois's impression of European anti-Semitism was sufficiently strong for him to argue that, in either case, the Jews of Europe would have to be resettled. He avoided mentioning Palestine, though he was well aware both of Zionism and of Arab resistance to it.[54]

For Valois, Jewish bankers acted no differently than their gentile colleagues. Both groups were divided between two suicidal policies: preparation for war, and concessions to Hitler. But the most immediate danger in the last weeks of 1938 came from the appeasers. On November 24, *Nouvel Age* began a blistering attack on Georges Bonnet, foreign minister and leader of the appeasement faction. Valois excoriated Bonnet for preparing a Franco-German agreement that was to include a free hand for the Reich in the Ukraine. In Valois's strategic terms, this was folly. But it was also criminal. Bonnet's backers, Lazard and Rothschild, were willing to sell the poor Jews of East and Central Europe down the river to buy off "Hitler, the executioner of the Jews." To prevent a new Munich, Valois rolled out his biggest journalistic cannon. Georges Bonnet had been an ally back when Valois was fighting inflation in the 1920s, and Valois had always considered him a skilled financial technician. Now Valois described the minister of foreign affairs as intelligent and servile: "Anything would be permitted against him" in the name of humanity. On the back page, he returned to the charge: "Georges Bonnet takes on, at the present, the figure of a state criminal. I weigh my words." Others did so as well, but Valois failed to provoke a legal response from the government.[55]

As the year came to a close, Valois found the ideal target for his anti-appeasement campaign: Anatole de Monzie. This old enemy was minister of public works in the Daladier government and gave every appearance of carrying on his own private negotiations with the German government. Valois discovered that de Monzie had held a series of conversations in Berlin with Goebbels the previous July. These, he now argued, explained everything that had happened since. As befitting a man against whom he held so many grudges, Valois's attack on de Monzie was both personal and political: de Monzie was venal and driven by uncontrollable passions, for example, for women—the opposite of Valois's personal morality. Valois tried to keep the heat on de Monzie, who denied discussing foreign policy with Goebbels, and on Bonnet, whose own secret negotiations came to light in February 1939.[56]

The problem was to mobilize support behind his solutions before it was too late. On October 15, 1937, the rue de l'Abbaye organized a national conference to discuss a United States of Europe. Representatives of anarchist groups, and of the Catholic leftists at *Esprit*, spoke in favor of unity. Jean Coutrot, the modernizing capitalist whom Valois had successively worked with and denounced, also played a role. Coutrot wanted a strong France to deter aggression, but the concept of deterrence did not exist for Valois. One only armed for war.[57]

Lacking a coalition, Valois tried his own device for mobilizing public support, a "national consultation" on war and peace. He chose a neighborhood (the fairly bourgeois fifteenth arrondissement of Paris) and flooded it with sixteen thousand copies of the *Nouvel Age* questionnaire, a collection of twenty-three very leading questions. Did the receiver want war? Did he want to overthrow Hitler? Would he not prefer to overthrow the Nazis without resorting to arms? Valois distributed the ballots in December 1938, hoping for a 3 percent response. The respondents would become the leaders of their arrondissement—for *Nouvel Age*. Even this goal was not attained, and Valois quietly let the matter drop.[58]

In February 1939, Valois still defended his antiwar, antifascist policy. An embargo, though useful, would be less effective, especially if the fascists succeeded in Rumania. Looking forward to a time when the economic edge might evaporate completely, Valois suggested that the conflict could become an armed peace. Then the societies with the superior economic organization (the democracies, if they adopted his program) would outlast their enemies. Valois feared, not unreasonably as it turned out, that if the current opposition between plutocratic strategies continued, France would be divided between war supporters and pacifists, a miserable condition in which to enter a war.[59]

THE FALLING CURTAIN: GEOPOLITICS IN EASTERN EUROPE

As spring crept over a rapidly arming Europe, Valois updated his economic and military prognoses. He also had to deal with a piece of bad news, the German-Rumanian economic accord of March 1939. "Grave," he called the situation it created, "but not desperate." He kept reassuring his readers that there was still time. A long period of eco-political maneuvering was beginning. Even with Rumanian oil, the Nazis did not have enough fuel for sustained combat. France had already entered a period of military stalemate, "neither war nor peace." The powers would struggle for the control of strategic materials; there might be naval battles. If one side garnered the necessary resources, however, a strictly military conflict might even be superfluous.[60]

Valois also reassured his readers when rumors of a German plan to attack through Holland surfaced in March: the Maginot line would protect the French flank. There was a danger, however. The Wehrmacht now had enough oil for a lightning attack. This could be successful *if* the French did not maintain strict military vigilance. In any other circumstance, and especially if misguided pacifists persuaded the government to relax its guard, Nazi troops would flood the hexagon. Nothing, not even aerial bombardment, should tempt the government from the combination of military defense and economic offensive. The new economy would be created, "under fire," if necessary. As he had for the previous war, Valois predicted a long struggle, during which the belligerents would match economic potentials. The difference was that for World War I, Valois had projected a technical-military contest. Now he saw the competition in economic and social terms. But how could France build a new economy with most of its young men guarding the borders? Some kind of rotation was necessary, and for Valois, it was obvious that it should be organized syndically. An additional benefit would be keeping the economy in civilian hands. Valois considered the military organization of economic activity in the Great War to be the perfect example of an inefficient state-run economy.[61]

Though his program amounted virtually to war, Valois continued to distinguish it from armed conflict. As he put it, victory was certain, so long as France avoided going to war. But by the spring of 1939, Valois had become increasingly concerned that Britain had now opted for armed conflict. French warmongers—repentant *munichois*—also worried him. There was no greater danger to peace, Valois warned, than these former compromisers. In effect, Hitler's absorption of Czechoslovakia, followed by other fascist land grabs in Europe, had reduced the sentiment for compromise and the audience for pacifism. The pacifists who remained were now more Hitlerite agents, whether conscious or unconscious, than genuine peacemakers.

Valois charged Maurras (using the royalists' old phrase) of acting "in the service of Germany." He made two charges against his former "*maître*." First, inasmuch as Valois and Berth had both known about Italian ambitions in Tunisia before the war, if Maurras was working with Mussolini, he must already have conceded the colony, or more. Second, why was the *Action française*, which had led the campaign against German infiltration before World War I, now so silent about Nazi activity in France?[62]

In April, Valois became concerned with Poland and the Soviet Union. He thought Britain's military guarantee to Poland a good thing, which might possibly lead to a diplomatic defeat for the Axis. But, Valois cautioned, it was crucial that any major moves in Eastern Europe be made in cooperation with Russia. If not, Stalin would look to Hitler for his security. A Russo-German pact would give Hitler all the raw materials he needed; and those who worked against good Franco-Soviet relations, Valois insisted, were "cretins or traitors." Nevertheless, Valois did not believe that Danzig would lead to war. The important area was the Mediterranean, but Germany was not ready to strike there yet.[63]

On June 23, Valois, for the first time perhaps, lost confidence in the future. What provoked this was the news that, as Franco-Russian negotiations foundered, a German trade delegation was on its way to Moscow.

Valois sought to put on a brave show in the face of this bad news. Russia could never be more than a mediocre supplier for Germany. The psychological edge might still be with the democracies. Nevertheless, his resignation was obvious. "There is never a catastrophe for men who wish to live," he argued. The new age was perhaps not around the corner. His cadets would see it; and "we, too, perhaps." Nor is it a coincidence that in the coming weeks, Valois began talking about publishing the third volume of his memoirs. He sensed that an era was coming to an end, both for himself and for France.[64]

Valois was pessimistic about Poland. The Slav state could not survive the opposition of either Germany or Russia without the determined support of the other. But this was "a hypothesis one would prefer not to have to think about." Valois was also beginning to suspect that the Anglo-French military guarantee to Poland might leave the Allies with two equally unacceptable alternatives: capitulation or war. These possibilities haunted Valois's summer. He considered the former catastrophe, a new Munich, more likely, reassuring his readers that, despite government warnings, there would be no war. As for heading off either option through an embargo, Valois ill concealed his pessimism. One must try to do what was right and necessary, he urged, even if the chances of success seemed thin.[65]

In the past, when things were going badly, Valois had looked to the long run. He did so again in the summer of 1939, talking about the great revolutionary transformation taking place across the globe. Valois cited the work of Frédéric Joliot-Curie and the potential of atomic power. The use of such incalculable power for military purposes was something he never discussed, if he imagined it. If the short term looked increasingly bleak, Valois kept his faith (at least in writing) in the liberating possibilities of technology.[66]

At the same time, however, he became increasingly concerned that Hitlerite agents in France would disarm the Maginot line, leaving the way open for a German blitzkrieg, or that the same result might come from civil war. For this reason, and to slake his frustrated anger, Valois published a special issue of Nouvel Age in July: sixteen pages against Charles Maurras and the Action française, dubbed the leader of "the Hitlerite press in France." The arguments were familiar (Maurras the servant of the plutocrats and of Havas). What had changed was their context. With anti-German feeling mounting in France and Maurras (while anti-German) still resolutely antiwar, it seemed possible to tar the old royalist with the antipatriotic brush he had used so often against others.[67]

The Molotov-Ribbentrop pact of August 23 did not come as a shock to the readers of *Nouvel Age*, as it did to so many other Frenchmen. Valois had made many extraordinary predictions, but this one was strikingly accurate. From one point of view, the Hitler-Stalin pact made Valois's situation easier. He had struggled with the contradiction of supporting a Franco-Soviet alliance while condemning Stalinism. The political choices were now clearer. "We must overturn all the totalitarianisms," Valois wrote, and he evoked Bakunin by referring to the Molotov-Ribbentrop treaty as the "knouto-Germanic pact." The Soviet and Nazi regimes had been evolving toward each other. Only anti-Semitism really distinguished them, and a kind of anti-Jewish policy seemed to be operative in Moscow anyway. These structural affinities made a political accord between the USSR and the democracies more difficult than one between the two dictatorships. Nevertheless, Valois still castigated the plutocrats for having maneuvered so badly during the past decade.[68]

The material disadvantages of this situation were compensated by political advantages. The British and French could pose as the liberators of humanity—provided they made their own (Valois's) revolution. For the Poles, Valois held out no hope. Their country would be divided again, and militarily there was nothing Britain or France could do about it. Again Valois looked to a long struggle, and again he urged an embargo. He also saw new opportunities. If Britain and France were forthcoming about sharing raw materials, Italy and Spain could be detached from the German-Soviet coalition.[69]

Valois also began a campaign to win over the followers of the Communist party. War could be prevented, Valois assured any Communists who would listen, if they would help support an embargo. In any case, Valois wanted to be prepared. *Nouvel Age* declared that it was looking for a suitable locale in the outer suburbs. When the article explaining this search appeared, however, it was heavily censored. The war Valois had feared for so long had descended upon France.[70]

TEN

Revolution or Defeat

Although a bitter blow, the war was hardly a surprise. True, the strategist of the rue de l'Abbaye had not expected a war over Poland. But after the Molotov-Ribbentrop pact, Valois, like most Frenchmen, could see the imminence of conflict. For a decade he had warned that war would be an unmitigated tragedy. But the beginning of the war was not catastrophic for the men and women of *Nouvel Age*. Valois had predicted Poland's fall, and the "phoney war" that ensued looked a lot like the "armed peace" already described by the sage of the rue de l'Abbaye. All that had changed was the declaration of war. Valois's program: extend the blockade and create the distributive economy. If the Maginot line were guarded, and the dictatorships outclassed through his revolution, France and liberty could still triumph. This program was the major argument of Valois's *Prométhée vainqueur, ou, Explication de la guerre* (Prometheus the Victor, or, the Explanation of the War), written in the last months of 1939.[1]

A new urgency replaced the old one. The race had been against war, and the preventive was the blockade. Now the remedy was revolution, and the race was against defeat. Partly by design, partly through the contagion of the national ambience, Valois presented his ideas in a more patriotic and national, less radical and socialist manner. War even brought out the emotional militarism hiding beneath the veteran's reasoned pacifism.

REORGANIZING FOR WAR

Mobilization brought problems. Gustave Rodrigues was assigned to a *lycée* in the provinces, and all Valois's other collaborators, except Jacques

Rennes, were called up for military service. As so often in the past, Valois paid with his person, putting out a two-page weekly *Nouvel Age* almost single-handed. It was late November before Rodrigues resumed regular contributions. By January 1940, Valois had collected enough staff and funds to make the paper "daily" again—that is, to print four to five issues a week. He maintained this rhythm until the fall of France in June 1940.[2]

The war gave a new direction to Valois's cooperative drive. In August 1939, he set about organizing a new base of operations, outside Paris. This would be more than safer office space: it would be a complete agricultural community, a *domaine* where families could be settled and the wounded treated. The Nouvel Age "commune" would be a consumers' cooperative; production could still be centered in a nearby town. Though Valois could not say so explicitly under wartime censorship, he was reviving an idea from 1936. In the chaos of war, the new society might be created by initially isolated units—with a new feudal manor in response to a new breakdown. Valois's *domaine* would include vegetable gardens and a farmyard for raising fowl. His apocalyptic visions led this radical modernizer back to the ideal community envisaged by nineteenth-century utopians.[3]

By mid September, Valois had his site, a 75-acre farm about fifty miles southwest of Paris, near Orléans. Members of the Nouvel Age cooperatives were invited to buy shares (at from 5,000 to 25,000 francs) in the new Société immobilière des amis de Nouvel Age (SIANA). A month later, all the places in the first *domaine* were spoken for, and Valois began to take reservations for a second. Within a few months, he promised, the first commune would be operational and the offices of *Nouvel Age* would move there. This rural exodus was to be associated with the evacuation of Nouvel Age members and businesses from the northeast to areas farther from the traditional German invasion route. Should the Nazis attack before this time (an event Valois declared unlikely), installation would be rushed.[4]

The commune in the Orléanais never opened. By the time of the German offensive in May 1940, all that had been prepared was space for the Nouvel Age crew, and the orderly evacuation Valois had hoped for was replaced by panic-led exodus. Valois's most popular projects were those that appealed to the fears, rather than the hopes, of Frenchmen: his gold fund and his rural refuge. Indeed, he complained, when he had proposed a village cooperative before the war, no one had listened. But if war was again to be the mother of revolution, Valois was determined to assemble its offspring.[5]

Finances were looking up. The war had cost *Nouvel Age* about a thousand subscribers, but another thousand replaced them; and running the paper as a weekly for several months also saved money. Over a hundred new cooperators joined, and the treasury was so healthy that *Nouvel Age* amortized almost all its commercial debt and began the payment of its private obligations, many to Valois.[6]

WAR AIMS/PEACE AIMS

Before the war, Valois had chosen antifascism over pacifism. Now he made the point more explicit. Did the pacifists prefer life to death? There was no life in Dachau. "If I had to choose between two fates, I would prefer to risk my life, arms in hand, in open battle, than to . . . die like an animal under the blows of a Hitlerite or Stalinist killer." He would fight for his country. That it was also that of liberty was an added justification.[7]

Valois disagreed with those like Churchill who hoped to detach Stalin from Hitler. The two totalitarianisms were linked by more than chance, Valois argued, reiterating his points about the convergent evolution of the Soviet and Nazi regimes. Progressing from excuses to a virtual mea culpa, he admitted to having misjudged the Russian Revolution. It was no real revolution, he now declared, just an exchange of many owners for one. He had undervalued the French Revolution, the former fascist admitted, because he had never really understood the importance of liberty. As a description of more than half his adult life, the remark was surprisingly apt and unusually frank. And if he had underestimated liberty, Valois continued, it was because as a Frenchman he had never been denied it. The two hundred families of London and Paris were preferable to the murderers of Moscow and Berlin; and the war would force the democracies to create the new society.[8]

Russia needed careful treatment. Valois faulted those who, at the time of the Russo-Finnish war, sought military operations against the Soviet Union. One could not make war against Russia, he insisted, remembering Napoleon but forgetting World War I. Instead, the Allies should defeat Germany and create a united Europe from the Atlantic to the Vistula. A Europe of abundance would eventually provoke the necessary changes in the Soviet sphere: in effect, containment plus peaceful coexistence. Since the totalitarian allies were rivals, in the short term, what weakened one strengthened the other. Valois also revived a fear from his reactionary years: a "savage onslaught of Germanism and Slavism" against the West.

But German Ostpolitik might separate the Aryan state from its Mediterranean ally. In September 1939 and March 1940, *Nouvel Age* campaigned to win Italy from the Nazi alliance. Valois appealed to his former fascist comrade in arms. Referring back to their "European" conversations of 1926, the former blue shirt expressed his sympathy with Mussolini's revolt against the democracy and socialism of that time. Though he could not approve the Italian leader's subsequent evolution, Valois appealed to him as a former socialist to help found a new Europe. As the first country to seek a new order, might not Italy be the first to try a genuinely European solution? The editor of *Nouvel Age* insisted that Mussolini could only be won over by offering Italy its place in a European federation, and dusted off his Eur-African scheme for the development of the southern continent as a replacement for Italy's imperial ambitions.

Though Valois considered his offer a long shot, for him the founder of Italian Fascism had always been more than a modern condottiere. If the left-wing militant could emerge from the leader of the Faisceau, was not the revolutionary socialist still buried within the Italian dictator? And Fascist Italy, unlike Nazi Germany and Stalinist Russia, was not really a totalitarian state, despite original impulses in that direction. But if Valois correctly gauged Italian political and social realities, he underestimated the appeal of raw dynamism and the cult of violence in Mussolini's Fascism, probably because they had always been limited in his own. Valois was clearly speaking through his own conceptions when he adjured Mussolini to break with Stalin, "who represents today, with modern technology, the barbarian invasion against that Roman world that you wanted to call back to life." By late spring 1940, Valois brought his campaign to a close. Echoing his judgment of Franco-Soviet cooperation, he insisted that although chances had been slim, the game was worth the candle.[9]

That is, if played by Valois. As always, the editor of *Nouvel Age* was suspicious of other attempts to curry favor with dictators. During these same months, Valois attacked his former *maître* as an Italian agent. Maurras's positions seemed admirably synchronized with Italian ones, and news traveled back and forth between Rome and royalist headquarters in Paris with disturbing speed. Maurras, however, was doing the same thing as his former lieutenant, and from the same motives. Both were desperately trying to keep Mussolini out of the anti-French coalition, and both were appealing to what they considered values shared with the Italian dictator. Their wartime battling testified to the continuing sharp divisions within the French political elite.[10]

If Maurras's sympathies with Mussolini's Italy were common knowledge, so was his hostility to Germany. But even here, Valois smelled a rat. Seeking to avoid what he considered the principal fault of the Versailles settlement, Maurras had begun a campaign for the breakup of Germany.

To such balance-of-power arguments, Valois replied by stressing the economic necessity of a federated Europe, and with an appeal to French pride reminiscent of the 1920s. "Are you afraid of being submerged by the German mass?" he asked his countrymen. "If so, you are ripe for the abyss into which exhausted peoples fall." Finally, to refute the claim that the German spirit was responsible for Hitlerism, Valois published eloquent German unemployment figures from before and after the Nazi takeover.

Under the circumstances, Valois averred, threatening to grind up Germany was treason; and Maurras had deliberately mounted his campaign to facilitate Nazi propaganda. Proof? The royalist's articles were immediately cited across the Rhine as signs of French annexationism. Valois did not believe in coincidences. Further proof that Maurras was now working consciously for the Nazis were prewar royalist contacts with Paul Ferdonnet, the French turncoat who worked for the Germans on Radio Stuttgart, and similarities between the campaigns of the *Action française* and those of the traitor.[11]

Particularly frustrating for the neopatriot of the rue de l'Abbaye, the censor was determined to keep him from settling scores with the old man of the Action française. Articles denouncing Maurras as a leader of the Hitlerite forces in France were regularly blanked out, as was an entire special issue. Valois protested and resorted to subterfuges and innuendos. Only in March 1940 could he finally print his "documentation" of Maurras's treason. Some months earlier, however, Valois had been allowed to present his material to the magistrate investigating the Ferdonnet affair. Valois also criticized the censors for covering his attempts to explain that France faced a long war. A quarter of a century earlier, they had censored similar passages from *Le Cheval de Troie*, and he had been right then. More important, Frenchmen would be more willing to make the necessary sacrifices if the government did not hide potential difficulties.[12]

But Valois ran into more serious problems with the French authorities. His offices were searched in his absence, and the government suppressed a private newsletter for Nouvel Age cooperators. This latter episode was apparently related to something more ambitious: Valois's last attempt to put together a revolutionary coalition.

THE LAST COALITION

In *Nouvel Age*, Valois always maintained the optimism that was almost official in wartime France. To his more dedicated followers, he sang a different tune. From the beginning of the war, Valois distributed a private newsletter to Nouvel Age cooperators in which he was considerably less optimistic. For years, Valois had been saying that the plutocrats had lost every major battle in Europe since World War I. What reason was there to suppose they would successfully prosecute the new war? Certainly, the actions of the French government in 1939 and early 1940 were not impressive. It was essential to replace it. Such arguments attracted the attention of the authorities, and the newsletter was banned.[13]

Valois was trying to arrange a broader coalition than any since the Faisceau. Before the war, he had opened a dialogue with Philippe Barrès, whose patriotic antifascist strategies approached his own, and who was an important source of information in campaigns against Anatole de Monzie. In the dedication to *Prométhée vainqueur*, reprinted in *Nouvel Age* in January, Valois listed Barrès in a carefully balanced set of names running from a "royalist writer" to a "socialist miner." The only other important "new" names were Henri Clerc, with whom Valois had been flirting politically for years; Jacques Maritain, the distinguished Catholic philosopher; and Jean Coutrot. All were identified as supporting the *Nouvel Age* war goals of liberty, human dignity, and European federation.[14] Valois had reached back across the multiple political way stations of his career for a new *union sacrée*. His new coalition meant reaching out to two major groups, for some years outside his political circles: traditional Catholics and big business.

Though unwilling to drop his materialist critique of the Christian ethos, Valois had sought alliance throughout the 1930s with like-minded Catholics. Now, he suggested that Catholics could work with the atheists of Nouvel Age to create a society based on human dignity, leaving metaphysical questions open. In the name of the humanism that had always attracted Valois in Christianity, the former believer sought to rally Catholics against the totalitarianism threatening the West.[15]

More difficult to justify was Valois's renewed attempt to ally himself with the modernizing, technocratic branches of French capitalism represented by Coutrot (to whom Valois soon added Auguste Detoeuf). In recent years, he had strongly criticized these proponents of "economic dictatorship." Now they were "revolutionary capitalists" who realized that the days of the market system and independent national economies were over, and were ready for a new social system and a united Europe. If capitalists led the movement for a new Europe, who would refuse to work with them?[16]

The editor of *Nouvel Age* evoked the fraternization of classes in the July Revolution of 1830: the coalition Valois now envisaged would include "graduates of the *grandes écoles*, aristocrats, bourgeois, and merchants, . . . [renewing] an alliance interrupted for a century." This was a sharp change from Valois's previous, largely negative vision of the July Revolution. Not that his interpretation of the "reign of the bankers" had changed completely: it was chiefly that the people were stronger now and would not be duped a second time. Without discarding his fundamental vision of French history (little changed in his peregrinations from right to left), Valois amended his assessment of the reign of the financial powers against which he had dedicated his life. The early democrats of France were the elite of the working class, but they had barely been able to read and write; "occult oligarchies" had provided the economic expertise democratic governments lacked. A greater defense of plutocracy Valois would never give.[17]

Just as World War I softened many of Valois's radical-right positions and led him closer to the French mainstream, the early months of World War II moderated his radical leftism. Partly this was opportunism, partly the contagion of the patriotic atmosphere. Making his positions more socially inclusive also meant stressing the continuities over the ruptures in his career. It was not a coincidence, therefore, that in 1940 the former fascist announced his willingness once again to sell his earlier right-wing books, those he had tried to keep out of circulation since his great political sea change in 1929.[18]

Valois restated his eco-social program in the most reassuring way possible. Property would not be eliminated, it would be generalized. Many Frenchmen already held savings accounts; the principle should simply be extended to the entire population. Hierarchies would be maintained in production, but submitted to the control of an egalitarian society of consumers. The directorial function in business would be preserved. Current employers would not accede to this function automatically as a class. But many, Valois suggested, perhaps even most, could retain their positions. Only time would tell. Valois sought to convince French bourgeois that a revolution, his revolution, could be a smooth, unthreatening transition to a better society for all.[19]

Such reassurances testified to the disparate nature of Valois's coalition. He and capitalist technicians like Coutrot were farther apart than his rhetoric implied. By late April, Valois announced plans to publish a joint daily paper in October. Only the neocapitalists, he explained, had not yet given their agreement. In peacetime, this alliance would probably have gone the way of so many others. Indeed, in the beginning of June, Valois publicly

broke with Coutrot.[20] By then it was too late for recriminations: the battle
of France was being lost.

FROM THE PHONEY WAR TO THE FALL OF FRANCE

As in World War I, Valois argued that France would have to organize for
a long war. His solution was also similar: organize the army syndically.
By this, Valois meant the introduction of market forces and individual initiative into the economic services of the armed forces. Citing his own experience between 1914 and 1918, the veteran explained that soldiers ready
to offer their lives for their country did not normally pay much attention
to their matériel. Products delivered free of charge were wasted; and many
of the best items never made it out of the depots. Instead, Valois suggested
soldiers be given an allowance, as under the Ancien régime, and be permitted to keep any savings. Furthermore, they should be encouraged to
practice a trade in their spare time, or to pursue technical training. Workshops and cultural centers could be set up near military bases. The increase in production would serve everyone, and although such a system
might not work for frontline troops, it certainly could be applied to the
rest of the nation in arms. Valois's aversion to economic bureaucracies
thus led him to a solution that might seem too daring for today's economic
neoliberals.[21]

What was good for the army was good for the country. Rather than demand sacrifices through taxation and rationing, the government should
organize the population syndically and then demand whatever proportion
was necessary, a quarter or a third, for the war effort. With such incentives, everyone would organize for most efficient production. The shift
from the policy combining syndicalization with minimal consumption that
Valois had proposed during World War I to his new position of syndical
organization fueled by maximal consumption reflected his move from the
pessimistic worldview of the right to the communism and abundance of
the left. Abundance would be the best psychological warfare, whereas the
current system of mixed capitalism and command economy only produced
waste. France must change its social organization "during the war and in
order to win the war." When he delivered this warning in March 1940,
Valois felt that France was running out of time. It was, but not for the reasons he proposed.[22]

Valois's economic logic, which led him to doubt there would be a German invasion, clashed with a nagging fear that the enemy would indeed
come, and that the French not be prepared. For the first six months of the

war, Valois stuck to his basic position that Hitler did not have the wherewithal for a full-scale invasion—unless internal dissension weakened
French defenses.[23] A blocked western front left two possibilities. One (this
was more prophetic than Valois knew) was that one side would develop
tactics to overcome the superiority of the defense. The second was the familiar notion of eco-social competition. True to his economic interpretation, Valois most feared a Nazi invasion of the Balkans aimed at Rumanian
or Black Sea oil.[24]

But the most horrifying events for him during the winter of 1939–40
were the expropriation of Polish property and the systematic degradation
of the Polish people. Again Hitler had shocked the former fascist. For Valois, the Nazi actions were a new descent into barbarism. By seeking to re-
arrange the ethnic map of Europe, to extinguish whole peoples, the Germans were returning to the age of the barbarian invasions. They risked
creating "blind hatreds" that would last for generations. Valois apologized
for his uncustomary display of emotion. He had never liked either "the
indignation and anger of the right [or] the sentimentality of the traditional left [and] the gross exploitation of human suffering" characteristic
of L'Humanité. All were substitutes for action. This, as much as his genuine horror at the behavior of the Nazis, showed the relatively rational,
utopian character of Valois's thought. Even as a fascist, demagoguery had
never come easily to him, and what he feared most in the ominous beginnings of Hitler's racial program was their capacity to stir up an unquench-
able cycle of destructive passions.[25]

As the winter of 1939–40 waned in western Europe, Frenchmen began
to ask themselves where, or indeed whether, the Germans would strike. In
March and early April, Valois repeated his argument that inasmuch as
they only had a three-month supply of gasoline, the Nazis would be unable to invade France. He went so far as to declare that the economic
blockade had made a blitzkrieg attack through Belgium and Holland impossible. But he noted the possibility that the impatience of the German
people, strained by wartime privations, might force Hitler into a desperate move.[26]

The World War I veteran was less optimistic about political affairs. In
February 1940, Nouvel Age finally received a press card for the Chamber
of Deputies. On March 21, Daladier was replaced by Paul Reynaud. For
Valois, the fall of Daladier resulted from the pressure of former French
munichois, whose goal was a compromise peace with Germany. Nor did
the Reynaud government, swollen by the kind of parliamentary compromises that Valois always thought disastrous for action, inspire much

confidence. And the same pro-Hitler group that had overthrown Daladier, led by François de Wendel, was now trying to unseat Reynaud. But Reynaud was a capitalist, "capable of self-renewal," and Valois gave him conditional support.[27]

When, on April 8, the Reynaud government announced the mining of Norwegian ports to block iron shipments to Germany, Valois gave a hearty "bravo." This was the way he had always conceived the war, a struggle to keep raw materials out of the hands of France's enemies. The swift German invasion of Denmark and Norway that followed brought out a more complex, and more traditionally militarist, response. Valois gave the government his most masculine advice: "Act"; but, quoting Hamlet, he added: "The rest is silence." When the British Navy defeated a German force in the North Sea, Valois told his readers how he and his collaborators had listened to the military communiqués and the French, British, and Norwegian anthems: on their feet, in silence, overcome with patriotic emotion. The Germans were good at elaborating planning, Valois admitted, but French and British troops had superior maneuvering ability. Rodrigues went further toward World War I *bourrage de crâne*. The allies were winning, he explained, because free men fought better than slaves. Both positions were a far cry from Valois's 1930s pacifism, his disquisitions on the need to avoid the contagion of militarism and heroism. The instincts of the World War I *poilu* revived in the aging leftist militant. Early in the Norwegian campaign, *Nouvel Age* warned that the battle might produce "surprises." The government should explain all the imponderables to the French people, Valois argued, to free itself from the pressures of an overly optimistic or pessimistic public opinion. Later in the month, when the Allies were forced to withdraw from Trondheim, Valois lectured his readers on the need for discipline and patience. The war would have its ups and downs.[28]

Underneath such determined optimism, Valois was increasingly irritated. The fight for the iron route showed he had been right all along. Imagine what could have been saved if the government had listened to him in 1937 and 1938. "We are furious at having been right," he wrote angrily. "We beseech you" listen to us now, that is, before it is too late, he urged. Despite the menacing tone, however, Valois still did not expect an attack on the western front. When Blum suggested that German successes in Norway augured ill for the defense of Belgium and Holland, Valois answered that Hitler had no interest in attacking those countries. The Scandinavian campaign confirmed Valois in his resource-oriented view of the conflict. The Germans still did not have the wherewithal for an attack on France, he declared again in late April.[29]

In the late spring of 1940, Valois's more immediate battles were legal. He was still litigating with the Action française over its attempt to collect from SCANA and COR. In April, Belin won his libel cases against Valois and was awarded 55,000 francs. More serious, Valois received fines totaling 3,300 francs. On May 9 the Préfecture de police sent an agent to collect. Nonpayment would bring a month in prison. The agent would be back in a week, at which time he would take Valois into custody.

Valois was desperate. He did not have the money. He appealed to his readers, to the members of parliament, and to other journalists. Was this any way to treat the enemy of Hitlerites and Stalinists, the man who had led the campaign for the blockade? No one came to his aid, however, and Valois came to an agreement with the court. To raise the money, he agreed to sell those of his titles that still possessed commercial value.[30]

Valois received written notice from the Préfecture on May 10, 1940, the day of the German attack on Holland. At first, Valois did not comprehend the full significance of the air attack on France's northeastern flank, though he was impressed with what Hitler could do with airplanes. "The man . . . has imagination," he concluded, but thought a "general assault" was still beyond the Führer's means. By May 21, however, as the Wehrmacht sliced through French defenses, Valois came to terms with the full implications of the German offensive. The French patriot began by thinking the unthinkable and drawing the conclusions that less than a month later would independently be expressed by Charles de Gaulle: "If, by an inconceivable concourse of the worst misfortunes, the battle of France should be lost, the universal war against German totalitarianism would not be lost. It will continue." If the French did not learn the techniques warfare now demanded, Valois concluded prophetically, they would "suffer under the German yoke until the day when [they] are liberated by the universal coalition." As Rodrigues added shortly afterward, the war would not be short whatever happened. France would still have its colonies, its navy, and part of its army.[31]

What provoked this early determination? Valois could see the astonishing superiority of the German war machine. Defenses were "swallowed up" far faster than he had thought possible, the veteran admitted.[32] He also seems to have retained enough contact with French military circles to have a fair idea of the bewilderment reigning among those in charge. Added to his oft-stated judgment of the inferior dynamism of the French ruling elite, this provided a good basis for his pessimism. But the editor of *Nouvel Age* also clearly feared an armistice. With his antennae always out for the agitations of French Hitlerophiles and compromisers, he certainly knew of the maneuvers already begun in favor of one.

Valois saw his country in a desperate situation and struggled for a solution. He sought to repeat what he had always considered the tactical breakthrough of the *Cheval de Troie*. The new Trojan Horse, Valois concluded, was the airplane. In the Low Countries, Hitler had already shown how men could be dropped behind enemy lines with gliders and parachutes. But this technique could be taken a lot farther. Thousands of men could be dropped deep within enemy territory. Such tactics would use a lot of fuel, Valois argued, another advantage for the Allies.[33]

Nevertheless, Valois did not attribute Nazi successes exclusively to military tactics. Treason and psychological warfare alone could explain the speed with which defenses had crumbled, he argued. Furthermore, like many of the French officers whose narrow-mindedness he excoriated, Valois was slow to grasp the implications of the new tactics of coordinated armored warfare. By the end of May, he realized that only tanks backed by airplanes could block the German advance, but he seemed unaware that France did not possess the formations necessary for such warfare. Yes, he admitted, Reynaud was right to insist on the need for these units, but this only made oil more crucial. At no time did the author of *Le Cheval de Troie*, a book dedicated to the tank, mention either de Gaulle or his German emulators.[34]

For the editor of *Nouvel Age*, the problem went to the essence of Third Republic France. He combined a frequently trenchant critique of the stalemate society with his own resentments. Frenchmen should "cease giggling" about the military abilities of "Corporal Hitler." Nazi successes in arms, and in social organization, Valois argued, came from their superior dynamism. The Nazis had swept away the old elites and brought in new leaders. The French would lose as long as they clung fearfully to the old ways and the old elites, as long as they remained timid and conservative. You cannot inspire the army, Valois insisted, "by telling it that it is fighting to save the old world, the world of Latinity, of Christendom, of [17]89 and of September 4, [1870]." A new vision was needed, one of a "creative and conquering intelligence giving its law to a new world, above the old laws of steel and gold."

As fear rose in Paris, *Nouvel Age* made a desperate attempt to goad the French people into a bolder, more aggressive stance. They should trust in their own energy, not the exhaustion of the enemy. There was no point crying over the good old days, which, "whether one liked it or not, would never come back." The Wailing Wall was in Jerusalem, the paper wrote, and was not made for "the proud Gaul, whose blood should still be flowing in our veins."[35]

In some of the most forceful writing of his career, Valois let out years of pent-up resentment. When it came to building a new world, no diplomas were necessary; "there was no special school," explained the self-taught Valois. The government should call upon the fifty or so true men of action in France, men "who had been marking time in this country, without profit for the Republic, and whose actions, utilized in time, would have warded off the blow." The "occult powers" favored the mediocre in public life and kept out the talented. Anguished patriotism and personal resentment ran hand in hand. Valois desperately wanted to do something, for he had little confidence that the country could make it without him.[36]

Valois gave his support to the newly modified Reynaud government of May 18. Here was a stripped-down war cabinet ready for action. One other of his compliments was less sincere. He welcomed Marshal Philippe Pétain's appointment as vice president of the Council of Ministers, saluting his "legendary energy." More cynically, he argued that bringing Pétain into the ministry should prevent Reynaud's opposition from using the name of the glorious old soldier against the government and its policy of war to the finish.[37]

Was Valois aware of the dangers of taking an opponent of this policy into the government? An attentive reader of Nouvel Age would remember that when certain reactionary circles had touted Marshal Pétain as the savior of France before the war, Valois had noted that Pétain had been unduly passive during World War I and had evidently not really understood modern warfare. Valois had spent most of World War I in the Verdun sector, had lived through the great battle of that name, and had described Pétain in appropriately lyrical terms in his memoirs. His later judgment was unusual for a veteran of Verdun, but not, as events would show, inaccurate.[38]

The fortunes of Allied arms did not improve. On May 26, King Leopold III of Belgium, refusing to follow his government into exile, capitulated to the Germans without warning his allies. This sudden "treason," as the French press unanimously qualified it, gave the coup de grâce to the battle of Flanders. For Valois, the behavior of the Belgian monarch demonstrated the crucial role of long-prepared treachery. The French Army could have maneuvered behind the tank-proof Maginot line, Valois insisted. Its error had been to abandon prepared defensive positions and charge hastily into

Belgium, where it was struck, ill-prepared, by the German motorized offensive. But who had called desperately for the French Army?: King Leopold, who less than three weeks later exposed the French to defeat by his precipitate capitulation. This explanation made light of the strategic blunder of General Maurice Gamelin, who had not been obliged to come to the immediate aid of the Belgians. But Valois preferred the ultimately prophetic explanation of treason provoked by fear of revolution and the unknown.[39]

Behind the "ex-king of the Belgians," as Valois now called him, was his political evil genius, Henri de Man. De Man was, indeed, a close advisor of Leopold's and the only major Belgian politician to back his decision. De Man had been the star of Pontigny, the spiritual father of neosocialism; and this new juncture gave Valois the ideal opportunity to settle accounts. Here was proof of what he had warned of for years: a plutocratic-inspired conspiracy progressing from social treason to national betrayal. Valois filled the final issues of *Nouvel Age* with denunciations of de Man. He reminded his readers that as early as 1934, he had predicted that the Belgian socialist was seeking a dictatorship with royal support. Valois took care to excuse those Pontignards who had since shown themselves to be French patriots, notably Paul Desjardins and Marcel Déat: an ironic judgment given both Déat's earlier appeasement and later collaboration with the Nazis.[40]

Defeat through betrayal meant that the French had not been beaten in a fair fight. The battle that should have been waged on the Franco-Belgian border would now be fought on a new line from Montmédy to the sea, Valois argued. French armored units would be pitted against their German counterparts. If Valois knew that French troops were now badly outnumbered and lacked mobile armored units, he did not say so. He thought the situation desperate, sending a special appeal to "a certain number of personalities" to lead a movement to bring new blood into the French government. More important, Valois insisted that his readers should plan for the worst. Whatever happened, the war would go on. France was only "the first army fighting . . . in the avant-garde of humanity."[41]

The last issue of *Nouvel Age* was dated June 8–10, 1940. On the 10th, the French government left Paris; on the 14th, the German army entered. The Wehrmacht quickly swept past Valois's refuge in the Orléanais. On the 16th, Reynaud, who wanted to continue the war, was replaced by Pétain, who promptly asked for an armistice. Less than a month later, on July 10th, in the French resort town of Vichy, the National Assembly turned over all powers to Marshal Pétain. The Third Republic was dead.

Valois had opposed this regime for virtually all his adult life. It died, among other things, from a fundamental conservatism he had always condemned. In 1931 he had told his countrymen to make a revolution or submit to another war. They had chosen not to make the revolution and had received the war. Then Valois had warned them to make a revolution or lose the war. Again, inaction had received its brutal sanction.

Some marginal political figures (including former associates of Valois's), the losers in the Third Republic's political battles, felt that France had been defeated for failing to heed their warnings. Many of these now formed the new leadership at Vichy. Yet others, more radical, headed the collaborationist circles in Paris. But Valois could take no pleasure in the demise of the parliamentary republic, first and foremost because it had been purchased at the cost of the defeat of France. Perhaps more important, Valois could see nothing good in the political changes wrought by the defeat. Unlike Maurras, he found in them no "divine surprise." Unlike many of his countrymen, Valois had preserved his faith in a new world that would be more, not less, democratic. And of one other thing he also remained sure: whatever the vicissitudes of the war, the new society he dreamed of would not be created in the shadow of Nazi guns.

ELEVEN

Occupation and Resistance

Defeat changed the lives of millions of Frenchmen. Many were separated from their loved ones as prisoners of war. Jews and other "undesirables" were herded into camps; many were sent to their deaths. As the Occupation continued, there was forced labor service, armed resistance, sabotage, and brutal repression.

Valois had known difficult living conditions during World War I. He had always been proud of his capacity to endure physical hardship. For years, he had boasted that he was conspiring, usually openly, against the powers that dominated French society, frequently against the government itself. But the very tolerant Republic never even tried to take away his freedom. This would not be the case under Vichy. During World War II, the eternal opponent paid the price of his radicalism. His first incarceration was in a French prison. The second, in Bergen-Belsen, led to his death.

FIRST RESISTANCE AND FIRST IMPRISONMENT

The disorganization of invasion and occupation increased Valois's dependence on members of his family. During the *drôle de guerre*, his daughter, Marie Valois, had taken over larger responsibilities in the Nouvel Age secretariat. Valois had had high hopes for his eldest son, Bernard, but he never played an important part in his father's enterprises. During the war, this role was taken over by the cadet, Philippe, whose sickly constitution spared him military service.[1]

Valois left Paris ahead of the German Army on June 10, 1940. The exodus took the life of his last true intellectual collaborator. Fleeing the Nazi hordes, Gustave Rodrigues managed to reach Biarritz in southwestern France. A Jew, he wanted to cross the border into Spain. But, for some reason, his wife refused to go with him, and the idealistic socialist threw himself off a cliff in despair. When Valois heard the news, it only added personal sadness to a season of tragedy.[2]

Sadness was not desperation. As Valois headed south, he instructed Philippe to move the Nouvel Age archives to what he had hoped would be the relative safety of Poitiers. But the Wehrmacht moved too fast for this plan. Valois reached Morocco by the time the armistice was signed on June 22, and established himself in Casablanca. His first hope was to publish *Nouvel Age* there, free of German control. With typical optimism, he threw himself into political conspiracy. He made contact with the Pretender, the count of Paris; with a group of officers, many of them rightists; and with a few former Nouvel Age people. While Valois's specific goals at this time remain obscure, his activity was certainly directed against the Vichy government. News of his activities soon reached the French military governor, and Valois was arrested and imprisoned in the civil prison in Meknes in December 1940.

This did not stop his activity. He established a correspondence with his last private secretary at Nouvel Age, a young leftist named Roger Maria, and with his help, continued his series of confidential circular letters from his Moroccan prison. In March 1941, Valois was transferred to France, to the military prison in Clermont-Ferrand.[3] Mme. Valois moved to that city to be near her husband, and Roger Maria, who was stationed in Vichy, passed himself off as Valois's godson, visiting his former boss on Sundays. At the prison, Valois found an old friend, Pierre Mendès-France, whom he had published in the heyday of the Librairie Valois. A few months later, Mendès-France escaped from prison and from France, and published an account of his imprisonment.

Mendès castigated what he termed Valois's scandalous treatment. Though Valois was in ill health, he said, he was treated like "the most despicable common law prisoner. They did not take his distinguished war record into account, and at first would not even grant him the officer's regimen." Mendès may not have known that Valois had resigned his commission a few years earlier. Roger Maria's recollections were different. He considered his master's conditions altogether correct. Valois even operated a kind of political and economic academy within the prison.[4]

Mendès-France believed that Valois's arrest had been provoked by his old enemy, Charles Maurras, who thus "took revenge fifteen years after quarrels that he alone had not forgotten." Maurras was perfectly capable of such revenge, especially since he and Valois were still locked in battle when the Germans marched through France. Valois's obsession with the old monarchist was also alive, but by the same token he would not have told Mendès about any Moroccan plots if he expected the younger man to make them public.

A similar ambiguity surrounds Mendès's conclusion that Valois's arrest was particularly ironic since he was vigorously anti-Gaullist. That Valois had little sympathy for de Gaulle is likely, but for Mendès-France, writing in 1941, a Gaullist was anyone who remained anti-German and willing to continue the struggle against Nazism, a category that included Valois. Painting Valois as an innocent victim of Vichy helped protect him, while blackening his jailers. During the war, however, Valois showed a lack of sympathy for the Allied governments and a mistrust of any "liberation" carried out by their armies.[5]

In April 1941, Valois was freed, apparently for lack of evidence. He and his wife first moved to Lozanne in the suburbs of Lyon, the largest city in the still-unoccupied zone and the capital of the French Resistance. In the Val d'Ardières, six kilometers south of Beaujeu, in the Beaujolais, Valois found an old mill that had been turned into a resort hotel. The war had dried up business, and many of the local resorts were bankrupt or up for sale at greatly reduced prices. The cooperative gold fund had suspended formal activity on September 9, 1939, although clients who requested re-payment during the occupation received part of the value of their hold-ings. Philippe, who was watching over the headquarters at the rue de l'Abbaye, had access to the gold coins purchased by the fund. Given the often precarious finances of *Nouvel Age*, these coins, or other proceeds from the fund, may have helped purchase the resort at the Val d'Ardières.[6]

There in the hills of the Beaujolais, Valois set up his island of peace in the middle of war. He kept his own sheep, goats, and chickens and worked in his own garden. In the France of the Occupation, when food was ra-tioned and comfortable bourgeois drove to the country to buy black mar-ket food from peasants, having one's own supply of fresh meat and veg-etables was a luxury. Nor was Valois alone. Besides his wife and Roger Maria, his household included his son Philippe (who also went back and forth to Paris), his daughter Marie and her husband and two children, and a female cousin with her children. Writing, working in his garden, surrounded by his family, Valois was happy in the Val d'Ardières. To Philippe, it seemed that he had returned to the Jouarre of his childhood, to that "garden full of flowers and light."[7]

RESISTANCE IN THE BEAUJOLAIS

Valois's hotel was an ideal location for political activity, near enough to the Resistance center in Lyon, but sufficiently out of the way to avoid close, regular surveillance by either the Vichy police or the German forces that occupied the so-called free zone in 1942. Valois knew he could not go underground; he was too well known, his face too recognizable. He would have two lives, one public and legal, the other secret. Accordingly, he notified the Vichy authorities of his residence at the Val d'Ardières and of his desire to retire from active politics and exploit the remains of his stock from the Librairie Valois. He was no longer young, his imprisonment had been debilitating, and the idea may have seemed reasonable to the authorities, who left him largely undisturbed for three years.[8]

Valois was not, however, the sort of person to be content with tending his own garden. The best cover for clandestine activity was a real business. If the legal activity made money and supported the illegal one, all the better. The Librairie continued to bring in a profit. Valois sold the remaining copies of many works, including some from his right-wing period. For many titles, demand outstripped supply.[9] To alleviate the national food problem (created by German requisitions), Vichy encouraged people to start their own gardens. To aid them, Valois edited a monthly bulletin on small gardens. The bulletin, which contained real advice on crops, methods of cultivation, and so on, ran at a profit, and was the perfect cover for clandestine communications. Roger Maria kept the files, using colored tabs to indicate which of the subscribers received the other, clandestine, publications of the Val d'Ardières.[10]

Visitors were always dropping by, and at times the former mill became an economic and social studies seminar. Many of Valois's most important collaborators were previous unknowns, men who, if they had supported the Nouvel Age co-ops, had not held visible positions in his organizations. Nevertheless, some *Nouvel Age* veterans, like Maurice Leblanc, Pol Gandon, and Jacques Rozner, stayed in close touch. Others who had separated from Valois over the years were reunited in a kind of *union sacrée* of the Occupation. Régis Messac, whose pacifism was destroyed by the Occupation, rejoined Valois's circle; and André d'Humières, the old rightist and Faisceau organization man, became one of Valois's major financial backers.

Auguste Lajonchère of Lyon was a regular collaborator, and his wife helped to run off some of Valois's clandestine publications on a duplicating machine.[11]

As always with Valois, even practical activities had revolutionary implications. Thus, he tried to turn his government-sanctioned gardening organizations into a network of cooperatives dedicated to food production and distribution. In January 1943, he founded the Société d'études immobilières et agricoles (Real Estate and Agricultural Studies Corporation), whose capital of 50,000 francs was subscribed by Valois, his Val d'Ardières cooperative, d'Humières, and seven other of his new local organizers. The company's function was to buy land that would then be leased to local gardening and distribution co-ops. The group made plans to buy land, including plots in the departments of the Drôme and the Dordogne. Valois also sought to redirect his St. Gaudens land to his new projects. Food production and distribution co-ops were created across the formerly unoccupied zone, as well as in Paris and the Nord.[12]

Valois hinted to a correspondent that once better informed, he would see the "relations . . . between the needed revolution and the organization of gardening." In November 1942, Valois was again predicting military stalemate. This time, however, the silence of arms could lead to a breakdown of order, especially if the Communists led an insurrection. In the resulting chaos, Valois's food co-ops could play a crucial role, becoming the cells of the new society. The expected shortages would increase their influence with the population. Even the demagogic slogan was ready: "Our revolutionary duty is to maintain French vegetables in French hands to nourish French energies." As the war continued, Valois sought to add a chain of cultural cooperatives (really book dealers and newsagents) to his vegetable ones. He traveled throughout the formerly unoccupied zone, followed closely by inspectors from the Renseignements généraux. In Marseilles they called him in for a half-day interrogation but, faced with his documentation, concluded his activities were innocent. Valois's advice to his local organizers: allay suspicion by holding meetings in the town hall itself.[13]

This revolutionary project was not Valois's only subversive activity. In what was virtually a third line of action, he worked with the French Resistance. There is no evidence that Valois took part in any military action, intelligence-gathering, or sabotage. He found an appropriate activity in the growing discussion within Resistance circles about the causes of France's predicament and how to prepare for a new, stronger, more just French society.

Valois led a discussion group and edited a clandestine periodical, *Après*, associated with the organization known as Combat. As the leading non-communist organization in the Resistance, Combat offered an acceptable haven for Valois's consistently anti-Stalinist line. At least three numbers of *Après* appeared, one written solely by Valois, the other two clear compromises between his positions and other currents of the noncommunist left. Through these publications, Valois played a major role in the formation of Resistance ideology. Through them, also, he was linked to the national coordinating center of the Resistance in Lyon.[14]

FINAL FORMULATIONS

Valois's writings under the Occupation were published in forms ranging from the fully legal, and hence censored, to the pseudonymous and clandestine. For the censor, he wrote *La Fin du Bolchévisme: Conséquences européenes de l'événement* (The End of Bolshevism: European Consequences of the Event), completed in late June 1941 and published a few months later. For the Resistance, in the late summer of 1943, he wrote "La France trahie par les trusts" (France, Betrayed by the Trusts), which was published clandestinely in *Après*, signed "Adam."(A careful reader could have guessed the identity of its author, however. Who else would have explained that, unlike the other right-wing leagues, the Faisceau of Valois and Barrès fought the trusts?) "Comment finira la guerre, ou la vraie révolution," written between late 1940 and 1942, was produced on a duplicator sometime in the latter year. While still in prison in Morocco, Valois had begun his definitive explanation of the meaning of life and history, *L'Homme devant l'Eternel* (Man before the Eternal). A first draft was completed in the Val d'Ardières in June 1943. Never revised, it was published after the war.[15] Valois submitted "Comment finira la guerre" to the Vichy censor, and when it was refused, tried unsuccessfully to arrange publication first in Switzerland, then in newly liberated North Africa. Both it and *L'Homme devant l'Eternel* were run off on a duplicator. While this form of publication was perhaps illegal, it was not really clandestine, since Valois signed both works and offered them to his followers, along with *Fin du Bolchévisme*, in widely distributed circular letters.[16]

Valois wrote *La Fin du Bolchévisme* soon after his release from prison. The German invasion of the Soviet Union on June 22, 1941, provided the occasion; within a week, he completed a fifty-page essay on the implications of the dramatic new turn in the war. Valois could not say all he wanted under Vichy censorship, but he seems to have sinned essentially by omission. Not only do none of the positions diverge from Valois's intellectual evolution, but writing something he did not believe, under his own name, would risk confusing his followers throughout France.[17] He used a politically acceptable denunciation of the Soviet system as the wedge for the introduction of his more controversial ideas.

The title was itself a prediction. Though Russia could not easily be defeated on its own soil, Valois argued, the shock of the Nazi invasion would destroy the Soviet system, ending the chapter of world history begun in October 1917. Valois generalized this collapse through an extension of his totalitarian analysis. To his earlier assimilation of Nazism to Bolshevism, he added all the wartime governments, including the Western democracies. Fear bred imitation. The bourgeoisies of Europe supported fascism against communism, and to beat the reds, their opponents adopted their methods: total control over the economy and society and the single party. War preparation and the conflict itself had done the rest. The plutocracies of the West had been forced to adopt the same total state control: "There is no longer a single democracy in the world," he averred—not even Switzerland. Thus the collapse of the state economy in Russia would threaten every other regime. No other system, neither the Italian, the German, nor even the American, offered a replacement for a defunct statism. As usual, Valois also threatened catastrophe. The disintegration of the Soviet empire would send large numbers of people into chaotic movement. And Europe could not be organized viably without Russian raw materials (when, in November 1942, Valois admitted having misjudged Russian resistance, he shifted his catastrophic scenario to one provoked by a Communist uprising).[18]

Valois's solution of 1941 was neither original nor practical: an academy of social and economic research in Switzerland where experts of all nationalities could create the new system. This was the one he had long proposed, which he now defined as combining the centralized direction demanded by modern industry with the liberty required for human endeavor. The new system must also be universal; there could not be a plurality of economic regimes any more than there had been under liberalism. France, temporarily out of the war, could lead the movement for the new society.[19]

Valois made a number of tactical concessions. He did not specifically denounce either Nazism or Vichy (he spoke of the "still unnamed events of June and July 1940 in France"). He described Hitler's role as the elimination of national boundaries and the last vestiges of economic liberalism from the European continent. Finally, *Fin du Bolchévisme* was larded with denunciations of Marx, who was responsible, through the Soviet economy, for poisoning Europe. Valois focused his criticism on what he called the Marxist conception of a society of producers, which demanded economic dictatorship. He praised Marx's conception of history—the idea that the evolution of economic forces dictated new social regimes.[20]

The most striking shift was also the most apparently Vichyite. Valois was neither anti-German nor pro-Allied. It was not just that he sought to position himself, as he put it, above and outside the conflict.[21] He wrote as if there were nothing important to choose among the contenders for power in Europe. Gone was the insistence on the democratic elements in the demo-plutocracies. Gone too were his earlier distinctions between the survival of civilized values in the West against the regressive and brutal barbarism of Nazism and communism. It would be tempting to attribute these omissions to the circumstances of publication, especially since Valois avoided speaking in detail about either the fascist or the Western systems. Nevertheless, this fundamental unwillingness to take the side of Allies was even more clearly reflected in his other clandestine publications. The opening pages of "Comment finira la guerre," written in 1942, stressed a Russian and Japanese "Asiatic" danger, and Stalinist control over events, but saw no solution coming from the Allies.[22] In both private and circular letters to his followers, Valois insisted that France must not choose among the belligerents, none of whom had anything to offer, and criticized "Gaullists of the right and the left" for their insistence on a military solution.[23] In "La France trahie par les trusts" in 1943, Valois repeated his blanket condemnation, but shifted his emphasis from state control of the economy to the ubiquity of "the trusts," a term that now largely replaced *plutocracy* in his vocabulary. Further, when explaining the past twenty years, he placed less emphasis on Stalin's alleged control over events and more on the trusts. Some changes from earlier writings represented the filling in of deliberate omissions, others changed perspectives between 1941 and 1943.

The only major difference between the trustified systems of the West (and the Axis) and that of the Soviet Union, Valois argued in 1943, was that one was based on a hereditary social class and the other on a co-opted corps of officials. In both cases the economy was run by a single central committee, and state and trusts were really one and the same. In more sweeping terms than ever before, Valois denounced the trusts' control of all aspects of French life, from the economy to the parliament, the administration, the police, and, of course, the press. What had started as producers' cartels a century earlier had become a form of government.[24]

As he had in *Fin du Bolchévisme*, Valois put the Russian Revolution at the center of his account of the modern world. His insistence on the power of the trusts returned him to formulations of his reactionary youth. English trusts were responsible for Kerensky, but the October Revolution had been financed by American and Jewish trusts. Valois was careful to explain that these plutocrats did not act to spread Judeo-Bolshevism, as the anti-Semites claimed, but to gain access to markets closed to them by the tsarist government. (The argument would not, however, have disconcerted an anti-Semite.) But not only did the Soviet rulers close their economy still more firmly to the trusts, their program of state capitalism backed by terror made the leaders of the trusts themselves fear for their lives.[25]

Valois associated these familiar maneuverings with a new conspiracy, the *synarchie*. This new name was attached in the minds of many Frenchmen (in and out of Vichy) with an alleged conspiracy of high-level technocrats and politically minded businessmen operating behind the scenes of the Vichy government. The grain of truth behind the charges was the rise to power of a coterie of technocrats in Pétain's government from 1940 to 1942. Rumor of a synarchic conspiracy spread rapidly in the France of 1941 and 1942; for some opinion makers, like Roger Menevée, it became a lifelong obsession. The Occupation widened the appeal of the kinds of conspiratorial explanations that Valois had long favored.[26]

Whether as the "Mouvement synarchique d'empire" or the "Convention synarchique révolutionnaire," the conspiracy of *polytechniciens* and others against democracy, parliamentarianism, and syndicalism had allegedly begun in 1922 or 1923. The leader of this evil band was Valois's occasional ally, and more frequently enemy, Jean Coutrot. Others included Henri de Peyerimhoff, René Belin, and other Vichyites. Through the synarchic conspiracy, Valois identified the technocratic modernizers, with whom he had flirted and quarreled for years, with the plutocratic menace.[27]

Structurally, the notion of the synarchist conspiracy changed nothing in Valois's outlook. The French defeat had been engineered to free the German army for a Western crusade against the Soviet Union. Valois stuck resolutely to this explanation, repeating it in the later sections of *L'Homme devant l'Eternel*. That he did so was ironic given the eloquence with which he had earlier castigated the lack of dynamism in French society, the conservatism of its military establishment, and the record of consistent plutocratic failure. But it was also Valois who had predicted that the Germans could not successfully invade, *unless* the Maginot line were undefended. Wounded national pride was probably decisive in the triumph of conspiracy over structural explanation.[28]

To Valois's way of thinking, a German victory demanded extensive preparation. Using anticommunism as bait, the trusts supported the pro-German campaigns of Pierre Laval, André Tardieu, and Pierre-Etienne Flandin, even turning the notoriously anti-German *Action française* to their positions. It was also necessary to penetrate or divide all elements of French society. The Cagoule, a right-wing secret society, worked on the army; sometime Prefect of Police Jean Chiappe on the police. The Librairie Valois was given the works of most of the future collaborators: Jean Luchaire, Henri Clerc, Bertrand de Jouvenel, and Marcel Déat, among others. Only half successful on February 6, 1934, the synarchists had to keep Pétain in reserve and settle for Gaston Doumergue. Though the Communists generally worked to counter this conspiracy, many events of the 1930s were created in parallel by both groups. The Popular Front was backed by the Soviet Union to stir up Franco-German conflict, and by the synarchists to discredit the French left as belligerent. Similarly, the Spanish Civil War was for the synarchists part of the outflanking of France, and for the Russians the beginning of war between the fascists and the Western powers.[29]

Final preparations for the French defeat began in 1936. The warnings of France's best generals were kept from the public. To be sure of a French defeat, the trusts put in the weakest man they could find, Daladier, confident he would choose the least competent of French generals. The Parisian economy was deliberately disrupted by an ill-planned economic evacuation, and the capital's citizens were sent out on the roads to hamper French troop movements. With half of France on the road, no one could oppose the synarchist takeover. Vichy's "alleged national revolution" (as Valois distinguished it from his earlier project) was direct synarchist rule. By then, however, some of the conspirators had fallen out among themselves; Coutrot was eliminated and forced to commit suicide in 1941.[30]

Valois explained the later history of Vichy in terms of maneuverings between the synarchists and other, more independent agents of the trusts like Laval. By 1942, Valois concluded, the German, French, and American trusts had come together on a new policy. The German trusts were concerned by the seriousness with which Hitler was pursuing his antiplutocratic policy. They now wanted a redemocratized (in theory) Europe to launch against the Soviet Union. Accordingly, the Allied armies would "liberate" France and overthrow Nazism, in the process preventing the revolution that 90 percent of the population now wanted.[31]

Valois's policy was, thus, neither Gaullist nor pro-Allied. Only with difficulty could it be called pro-Resistance. The Allied victory in Sicily and the deposition of Mussolini were caused by means far more political than military, he insisted. It is easy to see how Valois would have interpreted the liberation and the Cold War. As an apparent concession, de Gaulle was not attacked, but to accomplish this Valois barely mentioned the rebel general and avoided discussing the Free French entirely. (Other issues of *Après* were not free of Gaullism; and *Combat* as a whole was pro-Allied.) Valois's preference for the demo-plutocracies seems to have been burnt out in the bitterness of defeat. In *L'Homme devant l'Eternel*, Valois admitted the greater liberty of demo-capitalist societies, but insisted it had been purchased at the expense of a dramatic lowering of public morality. He did not advise attachment to one of the resistance movements. Instead, Frenchmen should make the revolution and create the new economy from the ground up, then and there, before the liberation, by setting up their own local cooperatives. Valois's final political position was ironically close to Pétain's famous statement in June 1944 that the approaching battle did not concern Frenchmen.[32]

The months of imprisonment and precarious freedom from 1940 through 1943 also produced Valois's final theoretical statements. *L'Homme devant l'Eternel*, as its title suggests, was Valois's ultimate intellectual and philosophical synthesis. "Comment finira la guerre" updated his economic and political recommendations.

In apparent reaction to Vichy's praise of Ancien régime corporatism, Valois stressed the superiority of economic liberalism to the guild system of prerevolutionary France. The liberal system had worked splendidly until 1914. It had filled the world with riches, and exploitation of the workers was compensated for by the rise in the standard of living. Valois also refined his abundance theory: falling demand was increasingly serious, since production was more oriented to mass consumption than to luxury goods. He also gave his most detailed description of the functioning of the new economy, down to salary structures, dividends, and compensation for lost property rights. Inequality of revenue was made explicit, the new age would feature a mobile hierarchy. It is not surprising either, therefore, that Valois now saw his new economy as the true successor to liberal capitalism and called it "community liberalism."[33]

But man could not live by bread alone, or at least that was Valois's central argument in *L'Homme devant l'Eternel*. This last of Valois's writings was, more than anything else, an attempt to recast all his thought in frankly religious terms. The tone was sermonesque. Mankind had proved unable to enter the new age because of intellectual inertia and laziness: the law of least effort applied to the world of mental constructs. Only a new religion could usher in, and support, the new society. The utopian modernizer constructed his own version of Saint-Simon's New Christianity. Not surprisingly, it resembled a theologized biology. What Valois called "the Eternal," explicitly evoking the Old Testament, was the force of life, cellular energy itself, essentially Bergson's *élan vital*. Indeed, for the first time, Valois evoked the philosopher of creative evolution, though he did not draw on him directly. He argued that this eternal life force, which he also described as universal energy, was the ultimate, unknowable ground of being, and as such the touchstone for all morality.[34]

This divinized nature was neither purposeless nor diverse. Returning to René Quinton, Valois explained again how man was the chosen vessel in the quest by energy to escape the deteriorating conditions of the globe. Life sought, first, movement from the earth's surface, and finally to escape the planet altogether through space travel. Valois also charged man with the ultimate elimination of parasitism. Our species would learn to take energy from its ultimate source without passing through other plants or animals.[35]

Valois now moralized these biological imperatives. Good was what served the task of sending men into space, evil what blocked it. His religion was the church of interstellar exploration. More than a scientific utopia, this cult solved two problems: that of production and consumption and that of heroism. Valois had long made the desire to consume the basis of his social model of mutual constraint. In the 1930s, he had explained that abundance would extend the ancient Greek dream to all men and permit the full cultivation of the human personality. The Quintonian constraint of potentially worsening conditions was present but undeveloped. Now the pious space program provided a goal for excess production. Men should not work for creature comforts, wasting the energy entrusted to them by life. They should devote this energy to the service of the deified life force ("asceticism in abundance," he called it in another context). A cycle was complete, Valois had harmonized the progress and abundance envisaged by his left-wing project with the constraint and moral discipline of his earliest right-wing formulations—his grandfather's influence, one might say, with that of his grandmother. Though it was obviously the role of the new church to lead the people to sacrifice, a contradiction remained between his religion of space travel based on pious exhortation and his consumption-driven economic model, repeated in *L'Homme devant l'Eternel*.[36]

In Valois's favor was the human thirst for heroism and sacrifice. In a way, he was adapting his psychology to the success of fascism, with its appeal to the heroic and martial virtues, which evidently were also the stuff of the Resistance. He wanted to convince his fellowman, locked in combat across the planet, that the virtues of war could be still better cultivated in peace. For the first time really, despite his earlier *combattant* campaigns, Valois recognized the appeal of war, while reviving the old idea that it had served the purposes of life by eliminating the weak and decadent. True heroism was risking one's life. Previously, this had meant taking the life of another. The hazards of space exploration would furnish the risk of heroism without the brutality of war. The replacement of war with exploration resembles Saint-Simon's substitution of the conquest of nature for the conquest of man. Distinct in Valois's conception is its emphasis on the need for heroism, which he now assorted with references to Nietzsche, as well as Sorel and Proudhon. Valois's interest in space travel also reflected the influence of H. G. Wells, whom Valois labeled one of the founders of the new age. For the first time, also, Valois gave due credit to Saint-Simon, whose positions he had often echoed, but rarely evoked. *L'homme devant l'Eternel* seems the product of wider reading than Valois had had time for in many years.[37]

Valois also evoked Nietzsche in his explanation of human nature. Contemporary man was caught in an intermediate state between his animal origins and his future as a superman. Unlike the topos of half-angel, half-beast, Valois's concept was developmental. Man still had a largely animal nature. The desire to strike out physically at our enemies, Valois lectured his combative compatriots, was a survival of the animal in man. Present-day institutions had to be designed for this far-from-perfect specimen. Unlike our contemporary sociobiologists, Valois argued that with time, new institutions, and the new religion, man would evolve to a state beyond animality, a new kingdom, as different from the animals as they were from plants. Conquering war was more than recognizing its inherent impracticality; it was acceding from animality to superhumanity.[38]

Valois insisted that the new religion, which he dubbed humanism, should be elaborated and transmitted through a set of democratic assemblies parallel to the economic ones. It must displace the outdated cults of Moses, Jesus, Muhammad, Buddha, and Confucius. Yet Valois stressed the continuities with earlier religions, especially Christianity. Part of this was to ease the transition for his readers. But he also clearly saw his space cult outlined in the Bible, much as Christian exegetes found their Messiah in the Old Testament. Was it not curious, he argued, that the New Testament spoke so often of getting to heaven, of storing up treasure in heaven instead of on earth. The parallel works better in French, where *ciel* can mean either the sky or heaven. When Valois invited his fellowmen to *la conquête du ciel*, he knew it had a double meaning. He also considered images like Jacob's ladder exemplary of his vision of man. Valois had been a practicing Catholic from 1905 to the late 1920s. He retained great respect for the Christian virtues and remained marked by the Bible despite his later conclusion, repeated in *L'Homme devant l'Eternel*, that Christianity was an unscientific collection of fables. His religious evolutionism linked his earlier faith to his new ideas.[39]

If Valois sought intellectual closure in his last book, it was at least partly because he sensed his life to be nearing its end. Approaching his sixty-fifth birthday, he assured his readers that, although still full of life, he was nevertheless reconciled to death, the return of his individualized energy to the ultimate source of energy and being.[40]

SECOND IMPRISONMENT AND DEATH

Valois understood that heroism meant risking one's life. Hence, he was not unprepared when, on May 18, 1944, two black automobiles filled with Gestapo agents pulled up at his retreat in the Val d'Ardières. According to one story, a resister in Lyon had been arrested with copies of "La France trahie," and the Germans were looking for a printing press at the Val d'Ardières. Roger Maria believes that someone in Combat deliberately betrayed Valois. If betrayal it was, the source could equally well have been Communists fed up with Valois's militant anti-Stalinism, though during these months the arrest of local resisters was common. Had Valois been warned the Germans were coming, he would have fled into the *maquis*, but the telephones were not working that day, and the Resistance could not call him from Lyon. At the farmhouse, the Germans found nothing. Valois and Roger Maria were arrested.[41]

Valois and his young secretary were taken to Gestapo headquarters in Lyon, nerve center of the German fight against the Resistance. In the courtyard they were met by the infamous director of the establishment, Klaus Barbie. "Ah, here we have the famous Monsieur Georges Valois, the great economist," he taunted his new prisoner. Maria and his boss were interrogated separately. Valois's response was undoubtedly the one he had taught to his secretary: make all the speeches you wish, denounce the plutocrats, but do not give names. What success the sixty-six-year-old had we can only guess. He had learned some interrogation techniques during World War I and was inured to physical hardship.[42]

Still reasonably healthy, though thinner and somewhat weakened, Valois was sent to the work camp at Neuengamme. There he met old Nouvel Age supporters and quickly organized a study group. Despite his inspiration, its membership was subject to constant renewal as new prisoners arrived at the camp and older ones, whose strength was declining, were sent to Bergen-Belsen and other locations, never to return.[43]

Valois's turn came in December 1944. In the overcrowded barracks of Block 5 at Bergen-Belsen, filled with the sick and wretched, he befriended a Dr. Fréjafon, who has left a moving account of his last days.[44] Here, too, Valois became the leader of the group of prisoners. He passed through the barracks each day, comforting the sick and discouraged. In the evenings, after the block was locked, the "most morally painful moment of the day," Valois organized a series of talks. The men crowded around his bunk as he shared some of the hope that came so naturally to him, explaining the march of humanity to the new age. Whatever his reservations about the plutocratically controlled Allies, Valois preached the love of France to his listeners and comforted them with his faith in the inevitability of Allied victory. When the German Ardennes offensive discouraged many, Valois remained publicly optimistic, insisting that it was the last charge of an animal at bay.

To Dr. Fréjafon, however, the old campaigner was showing signs of strain, caused by his almost superhuman efforts to maintain a uniformly cheerful and confident exterior. He was particularly distressed by the renewal through death of his audience. When one especially eager young listener was brusquely sent to the crematorium, Valois could not hide his tears. Other evenings, he would conceal his discouragement when he searched in vain for familiar faces in his audience. Valois explained to a fellow inmate, as he had in his last book, that full humanity meant facing death. But this torture was far worse: the Sisyphean task of winning converts only to see them reduced to ashes.

The physical conditions of life in the camp also took their toll, though Valois, who had developed a certain personal ascendancy even over the German guard, was spared inspections in the snow. He tried nevertheless to take regular exercise, marching on the frozen ground with his ersatz soles clacking as he walked. He also managed, despite the great difficulties this involved, to wash and shave several times a week. The rituals of cleanliness, like those of politeness, were part of what raised man above animality, Valois had taught; and he was not about to let his captors reduce his humanity. For the same reason, what seemed to disturb him most were the worn, unkempt clothes he was forced to wear, and he experienced genuine pleasure when Dr. Fréjafon was able to get him a pair of neat dress slacks.

In the middle of January 1945, Valois was sent to the infirmary for a problem with his thigh. Though the operation was successful, he was too weak to return to the block. As a typhus epidemic broke out among the patients on February 8, Valois remained calm and smiling, continuing his explanation to an *agrégé* fellow-prisoner of the necessary ascent to an organized humanity. On January 16, Valois himself became ill, suffering from chills and headaches. Two days later, he died, after hours of fever-induced delirium. His last words were appropriate to his entire life. When the Russian doctor assured him that he had the flu, he answered: "It had better be only the flu; there will be so much to do soon."

Valois did not live to see the liberation, but his death was one he would have wished. It was a political martyrdom: not the brutal death of a soldier seeking to kill his enemy, but the sacrifice of a militant who had given his last breath for his vision of a redeemed humanity.

Conclusion

If a death can define a life, then surely Valois's does. It tends to refute the most basic charge that can be leveled against him, that his ideological peregrinations were the result of crass opportunism. No opportunistic calculus could explain his decision to risk his life in association with a Resistance whose goals he did not fully share. Valois gave his life for his ideas.

But was there not a less crass form of opportunism involved, a tendency to shift political philosophy when the public associated with it had been soaked dry, or, less cynically, when Valois had concluded that they could not be persuaded to back his projects? Would it be fair to say that Valois took his ideology and alliances as they came and simply moved across the French political spectrum trying to interest one group after another in his plans?

Certainly there was some truth in the charge made by a disgruntled fascist, for example, that Valois publicly abandoned the monarchy out of spite, and because neither the Pretender nor French royalists were of any further use to him. Valois did have a tendency to react politically, even ideologically to personal quarrels, to political disappointments. But this process was largely unconscious, and human. To the degree that Valois's philosophical shifts reflected events, they were also reasoned reactions to the lessons of his political activity. Most important, neither spite nor selfish calculation were behind the major shifts in his life.

When Valois abandoned the radical left in his twenties, there was little to gain by a profession of Catholicism and reactionary royalism. Nothing would have kept him from pursuing a career on the left, especially after the "Revolution Dreyfussienne." In any case, the opportunistic thing to do would have been to switch, not from far left to far right, but to the respectable center left or right, in an itinerary that figures from Millerand to Laval would make famous.

The same is true of his other great sea change, his abandonment of the right and steady drift leftward after the demise of the Faisceau in 1927–28. As I have shown, Valois's own claim that he could have taken power, and that he purposely disbanded the Faisceau because he had come to judge it politically noxious, is not accurate. Poincaré alone removed whatever chances Valois ever had to shake the Republic. But Valois was not obliged by circumstances to move left, and his move leftward obviously contributed to the loss of the Faisceau's membership. He could have stayed on the right; a few compromises on anti-Semitism and international politics would have kept François Coty's crucial financial support, just as a bit more flexibility on social matters could have brought more business funding. The end of the crisis affected all right-wing leagues, the Action française and the Jeunesses patriotes as well as the Faisceau. Like these other movements, Valois could have held on and waited for better times. These surely came after the 6th of February. Or even then, he could have headed back toward alliances with the budding fascistoid modernizing groups of the period. Men like Marcel Déat, Gaston Bergery, Pierre Dominique, and their followers would have welcomed him. Instead, Valois only moved further leftward, cutting himself off from ideological currents that had been sympathetic to him for several years. As to his motivations, we must take him at his word—that he had changed his mind, that if he attacked Déat, Henri de Man, and company, it was because he was convinced they were aiding his plutocratic opponents.

This does not mean that Valois rejected tactical alliances (he did not), or that he was unwilling to tailor his public utterances to circumstances (he was), but simply that he was unwilling to compromise anything fundamental, and that any potential adherent, or donor, could easily find out his complete position on any subject.

Categorizations of an evolution as shifting as that of Valois always run the risk of oversimplification, but one can safely divide his intellectual development into three main phases: reactionary, fascist, and leftist. During the first, his social critique relied on ethnic and national categories, and he held out no prospect of significant social change based on historical evolution. Valois's fascism, especially its later, more left-leaning phase, reduced the importance of national and ethnic thinking, when not eliminating them altogether, while opening up more progressive views of social evolution, especially as tied to technological change. As a leftist, Valois preached changes that were both revolutionary in nature and the product of secular historical development—the new age of humanity. Though his formulations of the 1930s were based on a conception of human nature usually used to justify rightist conclusions (that human nature was and would remain for some time essentially selfish), his conceptions were genuinely leftist. He was universalist, almost completely pacifist, and believed in a coming communist society that would permit total human liberation and personal development and that was based on common ownership and management of the means of production. The most important issue separating his leftism from his rightism was a changed view of history and the possibilities of human development. New views of strikes or of modes of business ownership were consequences more than causes, since Valois tried to carry those benefits he saw associated with private enterprise into his communist society.

In these terms, Valois's fascism occupied an intermediate position. Socially, it was in many ways a passage from his reactionary rightist to his leftist formulations. For the mass of his followers, though not most of the leadership, it was firmly on the right, and that is also the way it was integrated into the French political system. Much of the misunderstanding between Valois and his followers was stemmed from this contrast. At the same time, however, Valois's fascism borrowed a number of ideas characteristic of that phenomenon: mass mobilization, recreation of the camaraderie of the front, and the worship of vitality or even violence.

Anti-Semitism has played a fundamental role in some fascist movements (e.g., Nazism), but has been essentially foreign to others (e.g., Italian Fascism). It has been closely associated with virtually all branches of the traditionalist radical right. Anti-Semitism played a major role in Valois's reactionary period. Time spent with the Action française certainly helped, but Valois's anti-Semitism seems to have developed earlier and was part of the reactionary worldview that brought him to the Action française as much as it was nurtured there. Anti-Jewish politics were absent from Faisceau ideology and tactics. The reason was not just an opportunist appeal to a broad membership. Valois had become convinced that, to borrow a phrase, anti-Semitism was the socialism of fools, that it was irrelevant to the real conflicts in French society and hence a dangerous distraction. That is why he refused to move even an inch in this direction to please Coty. As a leftist faced with the rise of political racism and anti-Semitism, Valois sought an explanation of this phenomenon as a means to

controlling it. He also had a better appreciation of Nazi racism and its hor-
rific consequences than most of his contemporaries.

The worship of violence for its own sake, not simply as a more or less
regrettable means to an end, is a fundamental characteristic of all fascisms. Valois's was no exception. What was exceptional in his case was its
extreme deemphasis. Though Valois sometimes saw a social, or biological,
role for war, this idea was strongest in his reactionary period. The role of
the *légions* was defensive at most; despite some rhetorical ambiguities,
they were not really intended to seize power. A careful study of violence
involving the Faisceau shows that the fascists were almost always acting
defensively, and that the leadership was still more hostile to violence than
the mass of blue shirts. Conquering the street to conquer the masses, Hitler's tactic, was never Valois's. Nor did he cultivate violence for political
propaganda purposes as did both the Action française and the otherwise
far more conservative Jeunesses patriotes.[1] The sole real exception was
Valois's attack on the rue de Rome, which was the product of exceptional
rage and frustration. And, Valois did seem to have a personal dislike for
acts of violence and killing themselves.

Admittedly, this was unusual for a fascist. But Valois's relative deem-
phasizing of violence and his concern for economic and social justice
(which cost him much support) should not lead us to argue that he was not
really fascist. His was one of the earliest European fascist movements; it
both bore the name and publicly linked itself to Italian Fascism. To label
it nonfascist would be to reverse the relationship between historical object
and definition. We must see fascism as a continuum. Valois's Faisceau
represents one of its extremes, fascism at its most socially concerned and
at its least violent.

Does Valois's career show the fundamental unity, or at least the strong
links, between radical right and radical left? On the contrary, it shows the
opposite. On the level of ideas, Valois did not simply draw differing practical conclusions from notions that could be attached, indifferently, to radical left or radical right. As I have shown, Valois was a genuine reactionary
before the war and a genuine leftist after 1930. And these changes did not
come easily to him, but demanded years of rethinking. While trying to
hold his idea of human nature reasonably constant, Valois was obliged to
change his conceptions of history and society, broadly speaking, from
those of the right to those of the left. More than anything else, his intellectual odyssey illuminates the fundamental differences between the
radical-rightist and radical-leftist critiques of modern society. The idea of
a golden age of radical right-left union, whether in the Cercle Proudhon or

the Faisceau, is really a myth propagated by later fascists, fundamentally men of the right, searching nostalgically for an impossible fusion.

This is not to say that fascists or radical rightists cannot be sincere in their social concerns. Valois most certainly was. But, once positions become more developed, either ideologically or practically, one has to take sides. Valois had to, and he did, once on the right, once on the left. His attempts to build a radical right-left alliance both before the war and during the Faisceau period are the best proof of its essential impossibility. One would be hard-pressed to imagine a candidate better equipped by background, sincerity, or seriousness of purpose.

The defense mechanisms of political society in the Third Republic worked well, and one of these was the very real separation between radical-right and radical-left opponents of the regime. The ideological confusions and political alliances that marked the end of the nineteenth century did not survive the Dreyfus Affair. If Valois for a time seemed to be trying to prolong the alliances of Boulangism, others were forced to left or right by the same currents that made his attempts at coalition-building so futile. While Maurice Barrès headed for the right with its cortege of nationalism and conservatism, Valois's sometime mentor Augustin Hamon found his way to the radical left. If the fundamental stability of Third Republic France was its best protection against fascism, the increasing political division between radical left and right also played its role.

Was there naïveté in many of Valois's shifts and positions? Certainly. He was often misinformed, and all those who are neither radical leftists or rightists (and many of those too) will agree that there was a large part of fabulation and paranoia in his political pronouncements. But Valois's willingness to look at political problems from more than one ideological angle, his readiness to challenge accepted political judgments, and his "utopian" insistence on workable, practical criteria for political activity led him to frequently prescient judgments: on socialism, on revolution and the state, on totalitarianism, on the destiny of the radical right and the radical left, on society, work, and the economy. Many of his points are still relevant today as we continue his search for a society that is socially just, that protects the individual, and that leaves room for heroism in the service of humanity. In fact, among our current concerns there seems only one that he did not anticipate, feminism. But even here his contention that forms of the family would have to evolve shows he would easily have added it to his system of human development.

As I write, communism and the state-controlled economy have collapsed across Europe. They are being replaced by a rush to private enterprise, to the market as the ideal form of economic organization. European communism has died of essentially those ills Valois diagnosed as mortal. But the demise of state socialism as a form will not discredit socialism forever. The appeal for a society of justice and belonging, the frustrations with a system of private property and classes are too closely tied to fundamental elements of Western culture to fall into the dustbin of history. They will arise again, and when they do, systems like Valois's, which seek to avoid the pitfalls of state management and preserve the advantages of the market system without abandoning the traditional goals of socialism may well have widespread appeal.

•   •   •

It is nonetheless striking that one of the most common words in Valois's book titles, from *L'Homme qui vient* through *L'Homme contre l'argent* to the final *L'Homme devant l'Eternel*, is *man—l'homme*. Of course, on the most basic level, Valois was referring to himself. He was the man who was coming, who fought the forces of money, and who, in 1943, was facing the Eternal. But in the French of these titles, the individual man becomes man the category (after all he could have entitled his memoirs *Un Homme contre . . .*). Similarly, the pseudonym he chose for "La France trahie," was Adam, the first man, the man alone. When I asked Valois's son Philippe what aspect of his father had been neglected by historians, he answered: his solitude. Despite all his political campaigns and alliances, Valois remained fundamentally in his own consciousness a man alone. His virtual orphaning, the absence of siblings, and the difficult conditions of his early childhood obviously had something to do with this permanent sense of loneliness. Just as clearly it was reflected in his messianic search for community. By the same token, it may have contributed to the ease with which he left communities of political belief, frequently breaking old friendships in the process. Valois was also clearly devoted to his wife and family, but he showed the sincerity of his feelings by keeping them private.

Yet there is obviously more to this focus on "man." For Valois, it was a key conceptual category, one he was much more comfortable with than, for example, worker or even Frenchman. His biosocial models are designed for all men. He thought in terms of the individual and the species, not in intermediate categories like class or nation. It is easy to see in this a naïve bourgeois individualism. By the same token, it is not difficult to understand Valois's unitary individualism in Marxist terms, as the product of his own class background, which partook of both the proletarian and the petit bourgeois and never involved true integration into the working class. This would explain not only his ideological versatility but also his preference for the intermediate class of technicians—except that many firm Marxists have come from petit bourgeois backgrounds. Similarly, Valois's nonproletarian (or more correctly, only partly proletarian) socialism can be seen as the product of a less industrially advanced society, as a position already surpassed by historical evolution. Yet Valois's emphasis on man and consumer, like his concern for the distribution of abundance and the valorization of leisure are strikingly contemporary. His socialism was both non- and postindustrial. In this, it reflected Third Republic France's combination of backward and dynamic economic sectors, of social conservatism and intellectual daring. Valois, the eternal opponent of the Third Republic, was in his own way a faithful mirror of it, of its limitations and its hesitations, its resentments and its conflicts, but also of its unexampled creativity.

Abbreviations

AF	*Action française*
AN	Archives nationales
CB	*Cahiers bleus*
CC	Commissaire central
CdCP	*Cahiers du Cercle Proudhon*
CEG	*Cahiers des Etats-Généraux*
Ch	*Chantiers coopératifs*
CS	Commissaire spécial
GV	Georges Valois
LV	Librairie Valois
NA	*Nouvel Age*
NLN	Nouvelle Librairie nationale
NS	*Le Nouveau Siècle*
PP	Archives de la Préfecture de police de Paris
PP/HP	Personal papers, Henry Poulaille
PP/GV	Personal papers, Georges Valois
RAF	*Revue de l'Action française*
RCIL	*Revue critique des idées et des livres*

Notes

NOTE: Unless otherwise stated, place of publication is Paris. Codings on AN documents have been copied verbatim from the originals.

INTRODUCTION

1. See, e.g., *Le Faisceau de Georges Valois* by the rightist militant Jean-Maurice Duval (La Librairie française, 1979). GRECE militants also told me of their interest in Valois's example. See, too, Allen Douglas, " 'La Nouvelle Droite': The Revival of Radical Rightist Thought in Contemporary France," *Tocqueville Review—La Revue Tocqueville* 4 (Fall 1984): 361–87.

2. See, e.g., Zeev Sternhell, *La Droite révolutionnaire, 1885–1914: Les Origines françaises du fascisme* (Editions du Seuil, 1978) and *Ni droite ni gauche: L'Idéologie fasciste en France* (Editions du Seuil, 1983); Paul Mazgaj, *The Action française and Revolutionary Syndicalism* (Chapel Hill: University of North Carolina Press, 1979); Richard Kuisel, *Capitalism and the State in Modern France* (Berkeley and Los Angeles: University of California Press, 1981; and Robert Soucy, *French Fascism: The First Wave* (New Haven: Yale University Press, 1986). Soucy's chapters on Valois rely heavily, among other sources, on my doctoral dissertation, on which the first half of this book is based. Similarities in organization are attributable largely to this. Divergent interpretations are another matter. Yves Guchet's *Georges Valois: L'Action française, le Faisceau, la république syndicale* (Editions de l'albatross, 1975), based on a Third Cycle doctoral dissertation, was written before the police archives were open and hence makes no use of police reports. The new edition of this work (Erasme, 1990) appeared when my book was already in press. In his later version, Guchet has made relatively modest use of these sources whose general usefulness he contests (see 5–6). Police reports, like other sources, must be used with circumspection. Their systematic examination can, however, provide more information than Guchet suggests. For example, his affirmation that they provide "practically nothing" on relations

261

among the Faisceau leadership (6) would be difficult to justify. Guchet has also, apparently, chosen not to exploit other available sources, especially on Valois's last years.

3. It is noteworthy, for example, that Soucy's reasonably extensive survey of Valois's "Career and Thought" (*French Fascism*, 126–73) confines itself almost exclusively to his rightist period. Even the two versions of Guchet's biography devote a spare one-sixth of their space to the second, leftist, half of Valois's career (*Georges Valois* [1975], 203–46; [1990], 267–319).

4. Sternhell, *Ni droite*, Philippe Burrin, *La Dérive fasciste* (Editions du Seuil, 1986).

5. Jules Levey, "The Sorelian Syndicalists: Edward Berth, Georges Valois, and Hubert Lagardelle" (Ph.D. diss., Columbia University, 1967); Jack J. Roth, *The Cult of Violence* (Berkeley and Los Angeles: University of California Press, 1980).

6. Sorel was neither a modernizer nor a utopian.

7. GV, "Technique," *NA*, Feb. 23, 1940.

8. These modernizers are chronicled for the twentieth century in Kuisel, *Capitalism and the State*.

9. Anatole France, *L'Ile des pingouins* (1908; Calmann-Lévy, 1980), 168.

1. CHILDHOOD AND YOUTH

1. Archives départementales de Seine-et-Marne, 6E 252/15, Commune de Jouarre, mariages, 1875, no. 22; Archives de Paris (Hôtel Saint-Aignan), reconstitution des actes de l'état civil, 7174, acte de naissance, Berthe, Joséphine Evrard; Archives municipales de Paris, no. 9558, acte de naissance 4442, 14ᵉ arrdt., Gressent, Alfred Georges, 4E, p. 64. Valois said that his father opened a butcher shop, but his death certificate lists him as *garçon boucher*: see GV, *D'un siècle à l'autre: Chronique d'une génération* (NLN, 1924), 15–16; acte de décès, Alfred [*sic*] Gressent, no. 2890, Mairie du 15ᵉ arrdt.

2. Archives municipales de Paris, no. 9558, acte de naissance, Gressent, Alfred Georges; personal communication from Philippe Gressent-Valois, July 18, 1987.

3. Philippe opined that Gressent died as the result of a fight provoked by the dubious fatherhood of his son (personal communication from Philippe Gressent-Valois, July 18, 1987); acte de décès, Alfred [*sic*] Gressent, no. 2890, Mairie du 15ᵉ arrdt.; GV, *D'un siècle*, 11, 16–19; Henri Poulaille, *Le Pain quotidien* (LV, 1931), 9–15, which experience is autobiographical; Jean Grave, *Quarante ans de propagande anarchiste* (Flammarion, 1973), 128–29, 143.

4. Personal communications from Philippe Gressent-Valois, July 18, 1987, and July 21, 1988.

5. See, e.g., GV, "La Vertu," *NA*, June 24–27, 1939; GV, *L'Homme devant l'Eternel* (LV, 1947), 128.

6. Personal communication from Philippe Gressent-Valois, July 18, 1987; GV, *D'un siècle*, 16–29; Archives départmentales de Seine-et-Marne, Commune de Jouarre, mariages, 1850, no. 15, and signature of Adjoint du Maire Eugène Frédéric Marteau for 1882.

7. GV, *D'un siècle*, 44–45, 49–50, 56.

8. Ibid., 45–59.

9. Ibid., 27–31; Archives départmentales de Seine-et-Marne, Commune de Jouarre, mariages, 1850, no. 15; personal communication from Roger Maria, July 21, 1988. Cf. Paul Nizan, *Antoine Bloyé* (Grasset, 1933).

10. GV, *D'un siècle*, 40–43. Cf. Henri de Man, *L'Idée socialiste*, trans. H. Corbin and A. Kojevnikov (Grasset, 1935), 136–38.

11. GV, *D'un siècle*, 19, 39, 43, 66, 102; GV, "Le 'Cas,' " *NA*, Sept. 20–27, 1936.

12. GV, *D'un siècle*, 102. The main exception to Valois's dislike of such academics was Hubert Bourgin, a *normalien* who criticized other *normaliens* (see Bourgin, *De Jaurès à Léon Blum* [Fayard, 1938]). Though Valois's frustrations first led him to anarchism, his lack of university training was relatively typical for the European fascist leadership. See Juan J. Linz, "Some Notes toward a Comparative Study of Fascism in Sociological Historical Perspective," in Walter Laqueur, ed., *Fascism: A Reader's Guide* (Berkeley and Los Angeles: University of California Press, 1976), 48.

13. GV, *D'un siècle*, 67–71; see, e.g., Grave, *Quarante ans*, 280.

14. GV, *D'un siècle*, 71, 76–79, 94–95; PP 344, 2.649, "Au Prés.," Feb. 18, 1927; GV, *Basile, ou la politique de la calomnie* (NLN, 1927), 479; GV, *L'Homme contre l'argent* (LV, 1928), 7–8.

15. GV, *D'un siècle*, 150, 152, 155, 161–62, 166–71; GV, *Basile*, 480, 654–61.

16. GV, *D'un siècle*, 72, 85–86, 90, 92, 164–65.

17. English in original.

18. GV, *D'un siècle*, 85, 158–59, 161–71.

19. Ibid., 186–91; GV, *Basile*, 159–60.

20. See, e.g., GV, *Technique de la révolution syndicale* (Editions liberté, 1935), 305, n. 1. Maurice Barrès, *Les Déracinés*, in *L'Oeuvre de Maurice Barrès* (Club de l'honnête homme, 1965), 3:11–364. See also chapter 4 below.

21. GV, *D'un siècle*, 70, 99–105; Paul Desjardins, "Agendas de poche—13 août 1929," in Anne Heurgon-Desjardins, *Paul Desjardins et les décades de Pontigny* (Presses universitaires de France, 1964), 304.

22. GV, *D'un siècle*, 108–10; Xavier Durand, "L'Art social au théatre: Deux expériences," *Le Mouvement social*, no. 91, 13–33. See also GV, "L'Affaire Ferrer en France," in *Histoire et philosophie sociales* (Nouvelle Librairie nationale, 1924), 190–97; Jean Maîtron, *Dictionnaire biographique du mouvement ouvrier français* (Les Editions ouvrières, 1964–), 22:123–24.

23. GV, *D'un siècle*, 118–19. On Pelloutier's involvement with the Art social and *L'Humanité nouvelle* groups, and his positions at that time, see Jacques Julliard, *Fernand Pelloutier et les origines du syndicalisme d'action directe* (Editions du Seuil, 1985), 12–13, 45, 58, 67, 92–98. Delesalle and Pelloutier also worked at the *Temps nouveaux*. Grave disputes Valois's involvement (*Quarante ans*, 339, 352, 355–56).

24. GV, *D'un siècle*, 123–26, 134; Grave, *Quarante ans*, 345–46; G. Gressent [GV], review of F. Schrader, *Des conditions d'arrêt ou d'avortement des groupes humains*, in *L'Humanité nouvelle*, 1897, 499–500; Augustin Hamon, *Les Maîtres de la France* (Editions sociales internationales, 1938); see also Augustin Hamon, *Psychologie de l'anarchiste-socialiste* (P. V. Stock, 1895).

25. GV, *D'un siècle*, 131.

26. See, e.g., the heavily anti-Semitic book by Augustin Hamon and Georges Bachot, *L'Agonie d'une société* (Nouvelle Librairie parisienne, 1889), i–ii, vi, 7–8, 21, 36, 49, 225–26; Auguste Chirac, "Les Discussions sur la Banque de France," *L'Humanité nouvelle*, 1897, 407–26. On Chirac and the populist current, see Patrick H. Hutton, "Popular Boulangism and the Advent of Mass Politics in France," *Journal of Contemporary History* 11 (1976): 87–88. The overlapping of radical right and radical left during these years is a major argument of Sternhell, *La Droite révolutionnaire*.

27. GV, *D'un siècle*, 131–36; Pierre Andreu, *Le Rouge et le blanc* (La Table ronde, 1977), 75; Claude Polin, "La Violence de Sisyphe, ou Georges Sorel et sa logique," in Georges Sorel, *Réflexions sur la violence* (Marcel Rivière, 1972), vii. In Valois's discussion of Sorel, he frequently refers to Sorelian writings that postdate this period (see *D'un siècle*, 134, 137, 207). See also Roth, *Cult of Violence*, 11–23.

28. GV, *D'un siècle*, 111; GV, "Lucien Jean 20 Mai 1870—1er Juin 1908," in Lucien Jean, *Parmi les hommes* (Mercure de France, 1910), v–xi; "La Vie culturelle—Lucien Jean," *NA*, Jan. 19, 1940, 1; Louis Lanoizelee, *Lucien Jean* (Plaisir du bibliophile, 1952), 17–26, 31. Lanoizelée owed much of his documentation to an interview with Valois in 1935 (23).

29. GV, *D'un siècle*, 112; Jean's letters to Valois of June 1898 and July 1910, both in Lanoizelée, *Lucien Jean*, 62.

30. GV, *D'un siècle*, 112–16; Lanoizelée, *Lucien Jean*, 23, 33–38, 61; Durand, "L'Art social," 25, 28. It is questionable whether Jean and Philippe (a clerk) were proletarians, but this is the name of the literary school. See chapter 7 and Henry Poulaille, *Nouvel Age littéraire* (LV, 1930). Jean's letters in Lanoizelée's collection corroborate Valois's account.

31. PP 344, 2.649, "Au Prés.," Feb. 18, 1927; GV, *D'un siècle*, 147–48. Among the literature on the horrors of military life: Lucien Descaves, *Les Sous-offs* (Tresse et Stock, 1889).

32. GV, *D'un siècle*, 66, 191, 206–14; PP 344, 2.649, "Au Prés.," Feb. 18, 1927; GV, *Basile*, 659.

33. GV, *Technique*, 112, 114.

34. GV, *D'un siècle*, 195–96; GV, *Basile*, 160; personal communication from Philippe Gressent-Valois, July 18, 1987; GV, *Le Père: Philosophie de la famille* (NLN, 1924), esp. 74–116. This text, written in 1912 or 1913, probably reflects Valois's ideas on the family in 1905.

35. GV, *D'un siècle*, 147, 172, 186; GV, *L'Homme contre*, 184; GV, "Torpeur," *NA*, Jan. 11, 1940, 2; Maurice Barrès, *Leurs figures*, in *L'Oeuvre de Maurice Barrès*, 4:227–449; Hippolyte Taine, *Histoire de la littérature anglaise* (Hachette, 1895), e.g., 1:xii, xviii, xxxix–xv.

36. GV, *D'un siècle*, 145–46, 204–10; GV, *Technique*, 21–22, 111–12; GV, *La Monarchie et la classe ouvrière* (NLN, 1914), 238–54; "Une agression," *NA*, Mar. 3, 1936. Sorel's deception produced Georges Sorel, *La Révolution dreyfusienne* (Marcel Rivière, 1909). Charles Péguy, *Notre jeunesse* (Editions Gallimard, 1957), esp. 31, 105–21.

37. GV, *D'un siècle*, 210–11; GV, *Technique*, 112. Cf. Hendrik de Man, *Zur Psychologie des Sozialismus* (Jena: Eugen Diederichs Verlag, 1926), 184–85.

38. See, e.g., GV, *Un Nouvel Age de l'humanité* (LV, 1929), 7; GV, *Technique*, 112.

39. GV, *L'Homme qui vient: Philosophie de l'autorité* (NLN, 1923), 41, 51–52.

40. Ibid., 47–50, 67, 182–83.

41. Ibid., 50, 55–56.

42. Ibid., 54–57, 67–69, 80–81, 113–14.

43. Ibid., 69–72, 102–4, 135–36.

44. Ibid., 185–90.

45. Ibid., 203–17.

46. GV, *Technique*, 112; GV, *D'un siècle*, 195–96.

47. GV, *L'Homme qui vient*, 26 (and n. 1), 31.

48. GV, "Préface" to Nel Ariès, "*L'Economie politique et la doctrine catholique* (NLN, 1923), vi; GV, *D'un siècle*, 134–35, 150, 152; GV, *L'Homme qui vient*, 27, 32; GV, "Révision," *NA*, Dec. 10, 1937; GV, "Revue," *NA*, Feb. 7, 1940. Valois may have used Nietzsche's *La Généalogie de la morale*, trans. Henry Albert (Société de "Mercure de France," 1900). Valois limits the notion of humanitarianism as a strategy of the weak against the strong to its social and political implications rather than using it against Christianity as Nietzsche does.

49. GV, *L'Homme qui vient*, 23; GV, *D'un siècle*, 147, 238; Paul Bourget, *Etudes et portraits*, vol. 3, *Sociologie et littérature* (Librairie Plon, 1906), 3–22. This chapter, "De la vraie méthode scientifique," written in Dec. 1905, was probably the one Valois referred to in *D'un siècle*. Whether it came to his notice in time to influence the writing of *L'Homme qui vient* is another question. See also Paul Bourget, *L'Etape* (Librairie Plon, 1902 [?]).

50. Taine, *Histoire*, xxxix, xlix.

51. GV, *L'Homme qui vient*, 59–63; Barrès, *Les Déracinés*, 164–78.

52. Valois stated that he was totally ignorant of Action française doctrines when he wrote *L'Homme qui vient* (ibid., 26, n. 1, 31, n. 1).

53. Ibid., 35–36, esp. n. 2; Linda Loeb Clark, *Social Darwinism in France* (University: University of Alabama Press, 1984), 76–88.

54. GV, *D'un siècle*, 220; Jean Weber, "Les Théories biologiques de M. René Quinton," *Revue de métaphysique et de morale*, Jan. 1905, cited in GV, *L'Homme qui vient*, 37, n. 1; Bourget, *Sociologie et littérature*, 18–19, 129, written respectively in Dec. 1905, and Mar. 1906; Paul Bourget, *Pages de critique et de doctrine* (Librairie Plon, n.d.), 2:142–43, written June 1904.

55. René Quinton, *L'Eau de mer, milieu organique* (Masson, 1904), v–vii, 415–17, 436–38, 446, 450–54.

56. Bourget, *Pages*, 2:142–43; Bourget, *Sociologie et littérature*, 18–19, 129; GV, *L'Homme qui vient*, 36–41.

57. GV, *L'Homme devant l'Eternel*, 59–68. For Valois's 1930s critique of Quinton, see chapter 7, below. Though his conceptions bore some similarities, Valois showed no evidence of ever having read or appreciated Bergson (though some of his contacts, like Sorel, did). Henri Bergson, *L'Evolution créatrice* (Presses universitaires de France, 1969). See also chapter 11 below.

58. GV, *L'Homme qui vient*, 216–18, 224, 227–28; "Préface" to Ariès, *L'Economie politique*, vi.

59. GV, *L'Homme qui vient*, 520.

60. See, e.g., Robert Wohl, *The Generation of 1914* (Cambridge, Mass.: Harvard University Press, 1979), 5–18.

61. GV, *D'un siècle*, 196, 232–34, 236–38.

62. Ibid., 238–43.

63. Ibid., 38, 240, 243–46.

64. Ibid., 253.

2. VALOIS IN THE ACTION FRANÇAISE, I

1. GV, *Economique* (LV, 1931), 17.

2. Henry Poulaille, personal communication, Mar. 25, 1975.

3. Eugen Weber, *Action française* (Stanford: Stanford University Press, 1962), 18–49.

4. AN F^7 12863, F/1655, "D'un correspondant," Paris, Oct. 25, 1915.

5. GV, *D'un siècle*, 250; AN F^7 12863, "L'Action française et les syndicats"; AN F^7 13195, "Préfecture de police," Paris, Nov. 21, 1908; Sternhell, *Droite révolutionnaire*, 277–79, and on the *jaunes*, 245–316. On the royalists' relations with French syndicalists of the left, see Mazgaj, *Action française and Revolutionary Syndicalism*.

6. AN F^7 13195, Arras/1603, Paris, Aug. 10, 1908; Jean Rivain, "Les Socialistes antidémocrates," *RAF*, n.s., 17, no. 185 (1907): 412–18.

7. AN F^7 12863, "L'A.F. et les syndicats." See also Hannah Arendt, *Antisemitism* (New York: Harcourt, Brace & World, 1968), 114.

8. AN F^7 13195, Arras/1603, Paris, Aug. 10, 1908; *L'Accord social*, 98, Dec. 5, 1909.

9. GV, *L'Homme qui vient*, 125–30, 150–52.

10. AN F^7 13195, M/2311, Paris, Nov. 16, 1908. GV, "La Révolution sociale ou le roi," *RAF*, n.s., 19, no. 198, 442–46; 20, no. 200, 109–24; 20, no. 202, 308–23; 20, no. 203, 385–93, all in 1907. GV, "Enquête sur la monarchie et la classe ouvrière," *RCIL* 1, no. 1 (1908): 49–56. GV, *La Monarchie et la classe ouvrière* (NLN, 1914), 65. Maître, *Dictionnaire*, 10:174–75.

11. References are to the 1914 edition of *La Monarchie et la classe ouvrière*, with a new introduction.

12. *RCIL* 1, no. 1 (1908): 50–51. This short introduction by GV to the "Enquête" was not published in *La Monarchie et la classe ouvrière*. *La Monarchie et la classe ouvrière*, 69–71, 96–100, 112, 121–24, 255, 264–66.

13. GV, *D'un siècle*, 118; Lanoizelée, *Lucien Jean*, 36; GV, *La Monarchie et la classe ouvrière*, 217–33. Cf. Emile Para's cooler, "Politique et syndicats," *RCIL* 1, no. 5 (1908): 418–21, and, for a less favorable judgment, but one that agrees on several points, see Jean Grave, *Quarante ans*, 367, 376–77, 460, 525–26.

14. GV, *La Monarchie et la classe ouvrière*, 274.

15. GV, *D'un siècle*, 253–59.

16. AN F^7 12861, "D'un correspondant," Paris, July 27, 1911. In AN F^7 12862: Paris, Apr. 18, 1909; June 16, 1909; June 21, 1909; "D'un correspondant," Paris, Apr. 5, 1911. AN F^7 13195, Nov. 5, 1910. Throughout its short history (it died in

May 1914), *Terre libre* stuck to the position that nothing other than the nationalization of land would end the exploitation of the workers.

17. AN F⁷ 12863, "L'A.F. et les syndicats"; AN F⁷ 13195, "Préfecture de police," Sept. 10, 1908; AN F⁷ 13195, Nov. 5, 1910.

18. Bourget, *Etudes et portraits*, vol. 3, *Sociologie et littérature*, 147. Bainville, "Antidémocrates," *RAF* 7 (July 15, 1902): 121–28; Roth, *Cult of Violence*, 62ff.

19. Sorel, "Modernisme," and GV, "Notes," both in *RCIL* 9, no. 8 (1908): 177–204 and 252–56 respectively. On the *Cité française*, see Levey, "Sorelian Syndicalists," 131–36; on Sorel, Valois, and the royalists, see also Roth, *Cult*, 84–128, and Paul Mazgaj, "The Young Sorelians and Decadence," *Journal of Contemporary History* 17 (1981): 179–99.

20. GV, *La Monarchie et la classe ouvrière*, 9, 193–95; Charles Maurras, *Enquête sur la monarchie* (NLN, 1924), 418; GV, "Pourqoui," *CdCP*, Feb. 1912, 41. This interpretation of French history opposed Valois not only to orthodox Marxists but to Sorel; see Sorel, *Illusions du progrès*, 5, 65–66, 89, 137.

21. GV, "La Bourgeoisie capitaliste," in *Histoire et philosophie sociales*, 415 (this study first appeared in *CdCP*, Dec. 1912). GV, *La Monarchie et la classe ouvrière*, 3–7, 15–20, 193, 199, 318–23. See esp. 199: "Or, depuis plus d'un Siècle, l'action politique du prolétariat français, détournée de ses fins propres, a TOUJOURS servi l'intérêt des Quatre Etats."

22. The first of the two scenarios envisages the revolution from the point of view of an anarcho-syndicalist: the bourgeois have fled, taking their gold with them, and the workers have taken over the factories. However, as soon as any economic exchange takes place, the workers start demanding gold as payment for goods. Those who have gold and connections with the revolutionary movement, the Jews, become masters of the situation. The second scenario involved the revolution as suggested by Jaurès in *L'Humanité*. Jaurès proposed that proprietors might be indemnified with interest-bearing bonds. Valois explained however that these bonds would soon fall victim to speculation. As their prices were reduced by a well-organized panic, the Jews would buy them up and gain a stranglehold over the French economy. *La Monarchie et la classe ouvrière*, 25–43, 90–91, 116–19, 177, 179, 184, 195–99, 207–11, 233–34, 320–23. See also GV, "La Religion du progrès," in *Histoire et philosophie sociales* (NLN, 1924), 25–165; these were the chapters Valois contributed to the book he co-authored with François Renié, *Les Manuels scolaires* (NLN, 1911). In "L'Affaire Ferrer," 169–247, Valois argued that this campaign in favor of a Spanish anarchist was orchestrated by the government. Grave, one of the leaders of the pro-Ferrer campaign, shared some of Valois's suspicions (*Quarante ans*, 458–59). See also Roth, *Cult*, 43.

23. GV, *La Monarchie et la classe ouvrière*, 50–51, 82–90; "Conférence royaliste de MM. Arnal et G. Valois," *Le Nouvelliste*, Feb. 7, 1910; Sorel, *Réflexions*, 97–102.

24. Sorel, *Réflexions*, 101; GV, "L'Etre et le devenir," in *Histoire et philosophie*, 5–24. In 1912, Valois used the Sorelian proposition that the proletariat could push the bourgeoisie into fulfilling a role, but it was the restoration of a nationally minded bourgeoisie that would separate itself from the Jewish bourgeoisie ("La Bourgeoisie capitaliste," 402–5). Sorel agreed with Marx that it was utopian foolishness to speculate on the organization of the future society, while for Valois

this problem led him to foresake the revolution. Valois believed in technical progress, but a "scientific" law robbed this of any social significance ("La Religion du progrès," 57). In addition, Sorel was hostile to the organicist explanations Valois increasingly favored over the years (Clark, *Social Darwinism*, 88).

25. GV, *La Monarchie et la classe ouvrière*, 63; Charles Maurras, *L'Avenir de l'intelligence* (Flammarion, 1927), 17; GV, "Notre première année," *CdCP*, Aug. 1912; GV, "Les Salons, les châteaux, et le peuple français," in *Histoire et philosophie*, 414 (this study was first published in 1912).

26. GV, *La Monarchie et la classe ouvrière*, 196; GV, "La Bourgeoisie capitaliste," 385–86.

27. Cf. La Tour du Pin Chambly de la Charce, *Vers un ordre social chrétien* (Gabriel Beauchesne, 1929), 330–52. Valois reported that a certain D. was forced to resign from an anarchist newspaper after a fifteen-year collaboration because he refused to delete the phrase *sale petit juif* from his text (*La Monarchie et la classe ouvrière*, 80). The anarchist was Paul Delesalle, and the editor Jean Grave. According to Grave, Delesalle quit upon his refusal to allow him to continue an anti-Semitic campaign in the *Temps nouveaux*; their collaboration had, according to Grave, lasted six years (Grave, *Quarante ans*, 355–56).

28. GV, *La Monarchie et la classe ouvrière*, 291–310; GV, "La Bourgeoisie capitaliste," 386–90; GV, "Les Salons," 424–27. Maurice Barrès, *Thèmes et doctrines du nationalisme*, in *Oeuvre*, 5:67.

29. GV, *Le Père*, 17–21, 25–33, 44–47.

30. Ibid., 204–13.

31. Ibid., 52–58. Valois repeated this argument years later in *L'Homme devant l'Eternel*, 190–91. He may have derived it partly from a book by F. Schrader he reviewed in *L'Humanité nouvelle*, 1897, 499–500. Cf. Clark, *Social Darwinism*, 159–71.

32. Levey, "The Sorelian Syndicalists," 33–35, 132–33; GV, *Basile*, 254–55. Edouard Berth's positions at the time of his first contacts with Valois are represented by the central chapters of *Les Méfaits des intellectuels* (Marcel Rivière, 1926), 117–294, written between 1905 and 1908.

33. "Pourquoi nous," *CdCP*, Feb. 1912, 34; "Notre première," *CdCP*, Aug. 1912, 157; AN F⁷ 12863, "L'A.F. et les syndicats." On Lagrange as seen by Andreu and Bernanos, see Pierre Andreu, "Demain sur nos tombeaux," *Combat*, Apr. 1936.

34. Such use of Proudhon was not new, "Proudhon," *RAF* 7 (July 15, 1902): 145–52. After the foundation of the Cercle, the nationalists' use of Proudhon was contested by the university and by Hubert Lagardelle, a former collaborator with Berth and Sorel at the *Mouvement socialiste*. See "Pourquoi nous," *CdCP*, Feb. 1912, 53. On Proudhon's "contradictions," see Robert Louis Hoffman, *Revolutionary Justice: The Social and Political Theory of P. J. Proudhon* (Urbana: University of Illinois Press, 1972), 3–6. Darville [Berth], Henri Lagrange et al., "Déclaration," *CdCP*, Feb. 1912.

35. AN F⁷ 12863, "D'un correspondant," Paris, Mar. 16, 1912; AN F⁷ 12863, "L'A.F. et les syndicats"; GV, *D'un siècle*, 252; René de Marans, "Grandes," *CdCP*, Aug. 1912, 118.

36. *CdCP*, Dec. 1912, 176; AN F⁷ 12863, "L'A.F. et les syndicats."

37. GV, *D'un siècle*, 252; Darville [Berth], Lagrange et al., "Déclaration," *CdCP*, Feb. 1912; "Pourquoi nous," *CdCP*, Feb. 1912, 36–37; Lagrange, "L'Oeuvre," *CdCP*, Aug. 1912, 127–28; GV, "De Quelques," *CdCP*, Jan.–Feb. 1914, 73.

38. GV, "L'Action," *CdCP*, Dec. 1912, 275; *La Monarchie et la classe ouvrière*, XCI–XCII; "Hommage," *CdCP*, Aug. 1912, 111.

39. Vincent, "Le Bilan," *CdCP*, May 1912, 99–103; Vincent, "La Famille," *CdCP*, Aug. 1912, 134–36, 144–48; "Notre première," *CdCP*, Aug. 1912, 162–64; GV, *D'un siècle*, 253; GV, "Préface" to Albert Vincent, *Les Instituteurs et la démocratie* (NLN, 1918), v–xi.

40. Darville [Berth], "Proudhon," *CdCP*, Feb. 1912, 10–13, 16–18.

41. "Réponse de M. Jean Darville," in GV, *La Monarchie et la classe ouvrière*, CXXVI–CXXXI; Berth, *Méfaits*, 57–58, 60–61, 66–67, 73, 96–99; Darville [Berth], " 'Satellites,' " *CdCP*, Dec. 1912, 177–80, 187–88, 194–202.

42. Berth noted with an equal lack of sympathy Maurras's horror of Bergson and admiration for Comte. "Réponse," CXXXIII–CXXXV; Berth, *Méfaits*, 10–11, 52–57, 67, 74–75, 84–86, 99, 162–63, 212, 355.

43. GV, *L'Homme qui vient*, 26. Berth differed from later fascists, among other things, on the nature and extent of the state and the role of the personal leader. There is also no emphasis on a party or movement to incarnate the political ideal. Nor is it argued that Berth's thought was a source for later fascist ideologies, merely that Berth was participating in a pre-fascist or even proto-fascist climate, from which Valois was excluded both by his Maurrasianism and his temperament. For Berth's attitudes to the Jews see, e.g., *Méfaits*, 65, 68, 71; Darville [Berth], " 'Satellites,' " *CdCP*, Dec. 1912, 180. For Berth's later judgments of Valoisian fascism, see *Méfaits*, 39–40, written in 1926. The idea of the Cercle Proudhon as pre-fascism and a link to later French fascism was most clearly expressed by Drieu La Rochelle, "Modes intellectuelles," *Les Nouvelles littéraires*, Jan. 6, 1934, 1–2. Its most forceful statement as regards Valois is in Sternhell, *Ni droite*, 106–7.

44. In AN F^7 12863: "D'un correspondant," Paris, Mar. 16, 1912; "Préfecture de police," May 8, 1912; "D'un correspondant," Paris, Feb. 28, 1913.

45. La Tour du Pin, *Vers un ordre*, 16–47, 267–80; AN F^7 12863, "D'un correspondant," Feb. 28, 1913; AN F^7 12863, "D'un correspondant," Mar. 16, 1912; de Marans, "Réponse," *CdCP*, Jan.–Feb. 1914, 70–71.

46. In AN F^7 12863: "D'un correspondant," Mar. 16, 1912; "D'un correspondant," Feb. 28, 1913; "Préfecture de police," May 8, 1912; "Deux documents," *CdCP*, 1914, 11, 57–60; GV, *D'un siècle*, 256–57; Weber, *Action française*, 79–80; and Valois's flattering eulogy, "Le Colonel," *CEG* 3, no. 17 (1924): 482.

47. GV, *D'un siècle*, 247–48; GV, *La Monarchie et la classe ouvrière*, CLVII–CLVIII; Louis Dimier, *Vingt ans d'Action française* (NLN, 1926), 17–18, 25; "Pourquoi nous," *CdCP*, Feb. 1912, 40; AN F^7 12863, "D'un correspondant," Mar. 1, 1912; "Les Menteurs," *AF*, Dec. 26, 1910; Daudet, "La Journée," *AF*, Dec. 28, 1910.

48. GV, *D'un siècle*, 259–61.

49. GV, "Le 'Cas Valois,' " *NA*, Sept. 20–27, 1936. Cf. André Gaucher, *L'Honorable Léon Daudet* (Editions de la parole française, n.d.), 57–58. After the break with the royalists, the organization was renamed the Librairie Valois. See chapter 6.

50. GV, *D'un siècle*, 262–64; GV, *Le Cheval de Troie* (NLN, 1918), 9; GV, *La Révolution nationale* (NLN, 1924), 9.

51. GV, *D'un siècle*, 262; GV, *Cheval*, 10; AN F^7 13195, Dec. 12, 1925; AN F^7 13195, Apr. 9, 1926.

52. In AN F^7 12863: "Préfecture de police," Jan. 11, 1912; "Préfecture de police," Feb. 21, 1912; "Préfecture de police," March 17, 1912; Dec. 17, 1912; "D'un correspondant," June 12, 1913. AN F^7 13195, "Préfecture de police," Feb. 14, 1912; AN F^7 13195, "Télégramme," 93797/691, June 1, 1912; GV et al., *La Monarchie protectrice des intérêts ouvriers* (Ligue d'Action française, section de Saumur); "Conférence royaliste de MM. Arnal et G. Valois," *Le Nouvelliste*, Dec. 7, 1910.

53. GV, *D'un siècle*, 266–67, 278–84; "Le Poursuivant," *NS*, July 9, 1925.

54. GV, *D'un siècle*, 284; "La Réunion," *CEG* 3, no. 18 (1925): 690.

55. "Le Poursuivant," *NS*, July 9, 1925; GV, *L'Economie nouvelle* (NLN, 1920), 6; PP/GV, Carton No. 2, Dossier "Pièces," No. 0845, Le Général Ebener, Sept. 27, 1917.

56. GV, *Cheval*, 9; GV, *Révolution nationale*, 9; GV, *Guerre ou révolution* (LV, 1931), 12. Cf. Henri Lagrange, *Vingt ans en 1914* (NLN, 1920), 216–18.

57. GV, *Cheval*, 177–232, 306–11.

58. The passage, removed from p. 211 of the 1918 edition, was replaced in "Le Cheval de Troie" in *Histoire et philosophie sociales*, 527. See also, GV, *Cheval*, 311, 233–70. Lagrange had a similar opinion, *Vingt ans*, 216.

3. VALOIS IN THE ACTION FRANÇAISE, II

1. See Dimier, *Vingt ans*, 298–317.

2. GV, *Economie nouvelle*, 10–13, 17–18, 294–301; GV, *D'un siècle*, 274–96. Cf. Nicole Racine and Louis Bodin, *Le P.C. français pendant l'entre-deux-guerres* (Armand Colin, 1972), 78. Even a modernizer like Ernest Mercier called his organization the Redressement français and made its symbol a wounded Gaul rising to fight again. See Richard Kuisel, *Ernest Mercier, French Technocrat* (Berkeley and Los Angeles: University of California Press, 1967), 65.

3. GV, *Economie nouvelle*, 69–75. Valois, who treated liberal economics as a monolithic entity, gave no sources for this judgment, which was probably related to the fact that the subjective theory of value had become relatively well known in the early years of the century (Jan Romein, *The Watershed of Two Eras*, trans. Arnold Pomerans [Middletown, Conn.: Wesleyan University Press, 1978], 372–73).

4. GV, *Economie nouvelle*, 72–73, 78. Cf. J. A. Schumpeter, *History of Economic Analysis* (New York: Oxford University Press, 1968), 188, 601–3.

5. GV, *Economie nouvelle*, 78–82; Schumpeter, *History*, 992–93.

6. GV, "La Valeur et la loi de l'offre et de la demande," in *Oeuvre économique*, vol. 1, *L'Economie nouvelle* (NLN, 1924), 5–76 and esp. 22–23, 25–32, 41–45.

7. "Sorel," *CdCP*, Aug. 1912, 113.

8. Dimier, *Vingt ans*, 224; GV, "L'Etre et le devenir," in *Histoire et philosophie sociales*, 5; GV, *L'Homme contre*, 24–25; GV, *Economie nouvelle*, 114, 164–65; La Tour du Pin, *Vers un ordre social chrétien*, 72–82. The ignorance of economics among members of the French elite has become almost proverbial. See, e.g.,

Stephen Schuker, *The End of French Predominance in Europe* (Chapel Hill: University of North Carolina Press, 1976), 45.

9. GV, *Economie nouvelle*, 26–27.

10. Ibid., 40–60; GV, "L'Etre et le devenir," 5–24.

11. GV, *Economie nouvelle*, 245–52.

12. GV, *D'un siècle*, 268–73, 284–87.

13. GV, *Economie nouvelle*, 81–84, 104–15, 125–29.

14. This is also the thesis of E. Beau de Loménie, *Les Responsabilités des dynasties bourgeoises* (Denoël, 1943–63).

15. GV, *Economie nouvelle*, 97–98; GV, "La Valeur et la loi," 27.

16. Ibid., 52–53, 83–85, 97–98.

17. See, e.g., ibid., 229–33.

18. Ibid., 8–9, 55, 229–34; GV and Georges Coquelle, *Intelligence et production* (NLN, 1920), 14.

19. GV, *Economie nouvelle*, 1–5. Cf. Kropotkin's definition: "L'étude des besoins de l'humanité et des moyens de les satisfaire avec la moindre perte possible des forces humaines" (Pierre Kropotkine, *Oeuvres*, ed. Martin Zemliak [Maspéro, 1976], 50).

20. GV, *Economie nouvelle*, 143–51.

21. Ibid., 124–33.

22. Ibid., 137–41, 152–59, 188–94.

23. Ibid., 86–89; GV, "La Valeur et la loi," 54.

24. GV, *Economie nouvelle*, 177–85.

25. Ibid., 245–59.

26. Ibid., 195–204.

27. Ibid., 205–15; GV, *Cheval*, 245–58.

28. Ibid., 10–13, 284–301.

29. Dimier, *Vingt ans*, 247–50; GV, *D'un siècle*, 247–50; GV, *L'Homme contre*, 9. The defense of workers' syndicalism in his October 1918 talk represented a transitional stage; see GV, *La Réforme économique et sociale* (NLN, 1918).

30. GV, *Réforme*, 4, 47; GV and Georges Coquelle, *Intelligence et production*, 56–58, 95, 97–98; GV, *L'Homme contre*, 11–12. See Charles S. Maier, *Recasting Bourgeois Europe* (Princeton: Princeton University Press, 1975), 74–75. And see Kuisel, *Capitalism and the State in Modern France*, on business's generally lukewarm reaction to the CGP (55–58) and on Clémentel as economic modernizer (37–48).

31. GV and Georges Coquelle, *Intelligence et production*, 107, 124; GV, *L'Homme contre*, 26–28.

32. Ibid., 108–9, 127–30, 187–206.

33. GV, "Le 'Cas Valois,' " *NA*, Sept. 20–27, 1936.

34. "L'Union," *CEG*, Dec. 1923–Jan. 1924, 381; GV and Georges Coquelle, *Intelligence et production*, 171–79; GV, *L'Homme contre*, 14–15, 32–34, 42; GV, "Le 'Cas Valois,' " GV, *D'un siècle*, 292–93. The republican Hachette had long been attacked as monopolistic by the left and, more commonly, by the radical right, including Barrès and Drumont. See Jean Mistler, *La Librairie Hachette de 1826 à nos jours* (Hachette, 1964), 121–36, 308–23; on Hachette's association with the Banque de Paris, see 340–43.

35. GV, *L'Homme contre*, 14, 34–35; "La Bataille," *CB*, no. 119 (May 23, 1932), 3, 5–6.

36. GV, *L'Homme contre*, 32–34; "La Bataille," 7, 12–13.

37. GV, "Les Semaines," *CEG*, no. 4 (July 1923): 307–9.

38. GV, *L'Homme contre*, 40–41; "Les Semaines," 308–9; "L'Union," *CEG*, no. 8, 381; GV and Georges Coquelle, *Intelligence et production*, 68–69.

39. GV, "La Monnaie saine tuera la vie chère," in GV, *Oeuvre économique*, vol. 2, *L'Etat, les finances et la monnaie* (NLN, 1925), 15–34.

40. GV, "La Monnaie saine," 40–43; GV, *L'Etat, les finances*, 40–43, 118–21.

41. GV, *L'Etat, les finances*, 161–64.

42. GV, "La Monnaie saine," 43; *L'Etat, les finances*, 123–26, 176–77. J. M. Keynes was equally severe, accepting Lenin's proposition that the best way to destroy capitalism would be to debauch the money (*Essays in Persuasion* [New York: Norton, 1963], 77–79; essay first published in 1919).

43. GV, "La Monnaie saine," 36, 75–76.

44. Ibid., 44–50, 78–85; GV, *L'Homme contre*, 47–48.

45. GV, "La Monnaie saine," 37, 50–55, 84–87, GV, *L'Etat, les finances*, x.

46. GV, *L'Homme contre*, 39–40, 48–49; GV, "Considérations," *CB*, July 25–Aug. 1, 1931, 23; "Qui es-tu?" *CEG*, no. 11 (June 1924): 647–48.

47. GV, *L'Homme contre*, 50; GV, *L'Etat, les finances*, x; Jacques Arthuys, *Le Problème de la monnaie* (NLN, 1921), and esp. 39–60, 177–89.

48. GV, *L'Homme contre*, 50–51; GV, *L'Etat, les finances*, x, 137–38, 159.

49. "Qui es-tu?" 626–28; GV, *L'Homme contre*, 88; personal communication from Hélène Patou, Apr. 8, 1975; "Le Comité," *CEG*, no. 8 (Dec. 1923–Jan. 1924): 330–34; Henry-Louis Dubly, *Vers un ordre économique et social, Eugène Mathon, 1860–1935* (1946), and esp. 153–58.

50. GV, *L'Homme contre*, 12–13, 23–26; AN F⁷ 12953, A-283, Dec. 19, 1925; Dubly, *Vers un ordre économique*, 19–20, 56–57, 283–84.

51. GV, *L'Etat syndical et la représentation corporative, Oeuvre économique*, vol. 3 (NLN-LV, 1927), 10–11, 14–17; GV, *L'Homme contre*, 51; GV, "La Monnaie saine," 86–88; "La Semaine," *CEG*, no. 8 (Dec. 1923–Jan. 1924): 368; "Qui es-tu?" 631.

52. GV, *L'Homme contre*, 50–51; AN F⁷ 12954, A./1.060, May 27, 1926; Schuker, *End of French Predominance*, 118–19.

53. GV, *L'Homme contre*, 36, 52; "La Bataille," 14–15; "Qui-es tu?" 631.

54. GV, *L'Homme contre*, 52–53; "La Semaine," 368–74; GV and Marie de Roux in *L'Etat, les finances*, 169–84.

55. GV, *L'Homme contre*, 29, 66–69.

56. Ibid., 69–70; Charles Maurras, "Mademoiselle Monk," in *L'Avenir de l'intelligence* (Flammarion, 1927), 237–61; Charles Maurras, "Si le coup de force est possible," in *L'Enquête sur la monarchie* (NLN, 1924), 546–48.

57. GV and Georges Coquelle, *Intelligence et production*, 259–64; GV, *L'Homme contre*, 72–73; "La Réforme," *CEG*, no. 1 (Apr. 1923): 20; Arthuys, "Historique," *CEG*, no. 1 (Apr. 1923): 31–32.

58. "Qui es-tu?" 638, 643–46; GV, *L'Homme contre*, 28–29, 84–86, 363; Claude Bellanger et al., *Histoire générale de la presse française* (Presses universitaires de France, 1972), 3:615; AN F⁷ 13195, Dec. 22, 1925; AN F⁷ 13208, "Le Mouvement corporatif du 'Faisceau,' " Apr. 1926.

59. "Déclaration," *CEG*, no. 1 (Apr. 1923): 1; "La Vie," *CEG*, no. 3 (June 1923): 291–92.

60. "Déclaration," 2–3; "La Réforme," 10–12; Arthuys, "Le Salut," *CEG*, no. 1 (Apr. 1923): 67–68; GV, "Réponse," *CEG*, no. 2 (May 1923): 149; GV, *Etat syndical*, 155–58.

61. "Origine," *CEG*, no. 1 (Apr. 1923): 84–92; GV, "Réponse," 144–153; "La Réforme," 12.

62. Jacques Arthuys, *Comment éviter la hideuse banqueroute* (NLN, 1922), 35–63, 147–90, 211–21, 261–75; GV, *Etat syndical*, 115–25; GV, *L'Etat, les finances*, 195–99, 236–37, 266–67; Arthuys, "Notes," *CEG*, no. 3 (June 1923): 220–29.

63. GV, *L'Homme contre*, 56–57, 70; GV, "Réponse," 148–52; Arthuys, *Comment éviter*, 85–116, 261–75.

64. "Chronique," *CEG*, no. 1 (Apr. 1923): 93–94; "Communications," *CEG*, no. 2 (May 1923): 163–65, and *CEG*, no. 3 (June 1923): 240.

65. F. François-Marsal, "La Politique," *CEG*, no. 2 (May 1923): 97–118, and no. 3 (June 1923): 197–215; Pierre Héricourt, "Les Etats-Généraux," *CEG*, no. 3 (June 1923): 242–46.

66. "Communications," *CEG*, no. 5 (Sept. 1923): 443–44; GV, "La Réponse," *CEG*, no. 7 (Nov. 1923): 168–82; "Communications," *CEG*, no. 7 (Nov. 1923): 183–84.

67. AN F⁷ 13195, Dec. 9, 1925; GV, *L'Homme contre*, 73–77.

68. *L'Homme contre*, 71, 78–79; GV, "Historique," *CEG*, no. 17 (Dec. 1924): 484–85; AN F⁷ 13208, "Le Mouvement corporatif," Apr. 1926.

69. Francis Delaisi, "Les Financiers et la démocratie," *Crapouillot*, Nov. 1936, first published in 1911. For Delaisi's replies to attacks by Romier, see "IV documents," *CEG*, no. 4 (July 1923): 367–74.

70. Paul Painlevé, "Notre semaine des P.T.T.," *L'Oeuvre*, Apr. 14, 1923; "Cahiers des doléances," *L'Oeuvre*, Apr. 18, 1923; Francis Delaisi, "Pourquoi deux semaines," *L'Oeuvre*, Apr. 19, 1923; Francis Delaisi, "Semaine des usagers," *L'Oeuvre*, Apr. 19, 1923; Francis Delaisi, "La Semaine," *L'Oeuvre*, Apr. 28, 1923; Pierre Héricourt, "Les Semaines," *CEG*, no. 3 (June 1923): 247–52; GV, *Etat syndical*, 40–60.

71. GV, *L'Etat, les finances*, 211–20, 328–64. Schuker is in substantial agreement (*End of French Predominance*, 35–36).

72. GV, *L'Etat, les finances*, 269–72, 277–91, 333–40; GV, "Le Mystère," *CEG*, no. 5 (Sept. 1923): 414–32.

73. GV, *L'Etat, les finances*, 325–40, 358–408; GV, *L'Homme contre*, 90.

74. GV, *L'Homme contre*, 80–81, 90; GV, *L'Etat, les finances*, 189–92.

75. GV, *L'Homme contre*, 86–89.

76. GV, *L'Etat, les finances*, 409–16. Cf. Schuker, *End of French Predominance*, 55–56, who does not explain this law.

77. GV, *L'Etat, les finances*, 425–32. This last argument contradicts Valois's earlier contention that businessmen would base their prices on replacement costs and make huge paper profits.

78. *CEG*, no. 9 (Feb.–Mar. 1924): 383–408; GV, *L'Homme contre*, 92–93, 98; Edouard Bonnefous, *Histoire politique de la Troisième République* (Presses universitaires de France, 1968), 3:418–22, who is clearly at a loss for an explanation.

Schuker suggests that Poincaré provoked the crisis to reorient his cabinet leftward, but that François-Marsal was added to provide "balance" (*End of French Predominance*, 116–17).

79. "Une Démission," *CEG*, no. 9 (Feb.–Mar. 1924): 465; GV, *L'Etat, les finances*, 437–49, 542–43; GV, *L'Homme contre*, 85–86, 89, 92–98; GV, "Revue," *NA*, Nov. 20, 1936; AN F⁷ 13194, "Surveillance des ligueurs—4ème journée," Nov. 27, 1925. I have not been able to find reports in either AN or PP on the fight with Bernard-Précy. From the numerous reports on Valois, it is clear that no one in the police believed he had been a Russian agent.

80. GV, "Première," *CEG* 3, no. 15 (Oct. 1924): 290–91.

81. Henri Coston, *Partis, journaux et hommes politiques* (Lectures françaises, 1960), 16; GV, *L'Homme contre*, 71; GV, *Etat syndical*, 121–25; "Les Grandes," *CEG*, no. 9 (Feb.–Mar. 1924): 450–60; Jean-Noël Jeanneney, *François de Wendel en république* (Editions du Seuil, 1983); Schuker, *End of French Predominance*, 224. Cf. Weber, *Action française*, 207.

82. PP 344, 2.649, "La Ligue du franc-or," Feb. 18, 1927, 1–2.

83. Pierre Dumas, "Le Comité," *CEG*, no. 17 (Dec. 15, 1924): 539–40; GV, *Le Faisceau des combattants, des chefs de famille et des producteurs*, tract no. 9, 16; AN F⁷ 13208, "Le Mouvement corporatif," Apr. 1926.

84. "Rapports," *CEG*, no. 17 (Dec. 15, 1924): 545–95.

85. Pierre Dumas, "L'Organisation," *CEG*, no. 17 (Dec. 15, 1924): 499–500; GV, *L'Homme contre*, 44–45, 65.

86. "Le Comité," *CEG*, no. 9 (Feb.–Mar. 1924): 465; GV, *L'Homme contre*, 102–3; Georges Lachapelle, *Elections législatives du 11 Mai 1924* (Librairie Georges Roustan, 1924), 206.

87. GV, *Etat syndical*, 294–95.

88. Arthuys, "La Crise," *CEG*, no. 9 (Feb.–Mar. 1924): 394. This packet of bonds, "the largest volume of long-term government obligations since the end of the war," amounted to approximately thirty billion francs, as large as the annual budget (Schuker, *End of French Predominance*, 134–35, 151).

4. THE FAISCEAU, I

1. On the Faisceau, see Soucy, *French Fascism*, 87–125, 174–95; Sternhell, *Ni droite*, 106–36; Zeev Sternhell, "Anatomie d'un mouvement fasciste: Le Faisceau de Georges Valois," *Revue française de science politique* 26 (1976): 5–40; Jerzy Eisler, "Georges Valois et une idéologie de combattants," *Acta Poloniae Historica* 48 (1983): 133–63.

2. GV, *Révolution nationale*, 34–35, 87–92, 97, 143–50.

3. Ibid., 43–46, 62–67, 79, 98–99, 128–31.

4. Ibid., 67–86.

5. Ibid., 75–76, 86–97; GV, *La Politique de la victoire* (NLN, 1925), 34–48.

6. GV, *Révolution nationale*, 112–19; GV, *L'Etat, les finances*, xi–xii.

7. GV, *Politique*, 27–30; GV, *Révolution nationale*, 104, 111–12.

8. GV, *L'Etat, les finances*, 514–22, 565, 608.

9. Ibid., xxv, xxvii, 518–19, 566–67, 570, 627.

10. Ibid., 519, 564–66, 571.

11. Ibid., 219; GV, "Le 'Cas Valois,' " *NA*, Sept. 20–27, 1936.

12. GV, *L'Homme contre*, 158–59, 247–48; GV, *L'Etat, les finances*, 566; AN F^7 12953, A-684, Oct. 24, 1925; AN F^7 12953, A-9 253, Nov. 11, 1925. In AN F^7 12954: A.734, Jan. 27, 1926; A.-1.060, May 27, 1926; 2.018, June 23, 1926; A/2.020, June 24, 1926; A.-6.488, July 21, 1926; A-2.079, July 27, 1926; A-7.770, Sept. 13, 1926; Jean-Noël Jeanneney, *L'Argent caché: Milieux d'affaires et pouvoir politique dans la France du XXe siècle* (Editions du Seuil, 1983), 128–29, 226–27; Jean Giraudoux, *Bella* (Grasset, 1926). According to Roger Menevée, by sponsoring Standard Oil in France, Finaly placed himself in opposition to François-Marsal and Millerand, who were associated with Royal Dutch (Menevée, "M. Horace Finaly," *Les Documents politiques, diplomatiques et financiers*, 18e année, no. 9 [Sept. 1937]: 416). Jean-Noël Jeanneney, besides noting Finaly's battle with Caillaux, writes: "Les noms de Finaly et d'Homberg restent aujourd'hui encore associés, dans le souvenir des vieux 'boursiers,' comme les deux grands 'animateurs' de la corbeille dans ces années vingt" (Jeanneney, *François de Wendel en république*, 308). Stephen Schuker, who does not mention Finaly, describes Herriot as lacking contacts in the banking world (Schuker, *End of French Predominance in Europe*, 128). He notes, however, that when Clémentel, Herriot's finance minister, tried to gain leverage with the house of Morgan, he threatened to arrange a loan through Kuhn in New York and the Banque de Paris et des Pays-Bas (309).

13. Keynes, *Essays in Persuasion*, 105–8; AN F^7 12953, A.9.253.-, Nov. 11, 1925. According to Schuker, Clémentel, like his predecessors, was trying to circumvent the legal limits on fiduciary circulation to ease periodic treasury crises (*End of French Predominance*, 137–39).

14. Menevée, "M. Horace Finaly," 401–19.

15. GV, *L'Homme contre*, 353.

16. GV, *Révolution nationale*, 20–34; GV, *Politique*, 80–81, 101–4; Jacques Arthuys, *Les Combattants* (NLN, 1925), 85–89, 108–9; "Réunion," *CEG*, no. 18 (1925): 680; "Déclaration," *NS*, Feb. 26, 1925.

17. GV, *Révolution nationale*, 20–26; GV, *Politique*, 5–15. The notion of the French Revolution as a renewal of elites revives one of Valois's arguments of 1906; see GV, *L'Homme qui vient*, 59–60.

18. GV, *Révolution nationale*, 145–60; GV, *Politique*, 17–18, 69–78; Arthuys, *Combattants*, 184–92.

19. GV, *Révolution nationale*, 51–53, 162–79; GV, *Politique*, 16–37, 83–87, 95–108.

20. GV, *Politique*, 65–67; Kropotkine, *Oeuvres*, 191–92; GV, *Révolution nationale*, 135–40. This appendix is similar to the extra, royalist, chapter Valois added to *L'Homme qui vient* (see chapter 1).

21. See, e.g., GV, *Révolution nationale*, 27; GV, *Politique*, 20–30, 41–42.

22. Arthuys, *Combattants*, 82–83.

23. GV, *L'Homme contre*, 118–19; AN F^7 13208, A/1062-SF, "F. van den BROECK D'OBRENAN," Paris, Dec. 5, 1925.

24. GV, *L'Homme contre*, 118–23.

25. Ibid., 66–67, 119–23; AN F^7 13195, Sept. 6, 1924.

26. "La Semaine," *CEG*, no. 18 (1925): 668–71; GV, *Politique*, 124.

27. Hubert Bourgin, *Le Parti contre la patrie* (Plon-Nourrit, 1924); id., *Le Militarisme allemand* (F. Alcan, 1915); AN F^7 13208, F.10.057, Nov. 6, 1925; "Le Nouveau Siècle," brochure in AN F^7 13208; Henri Guillemin, *Charles Péguy* (Editions du Seuil, 1981), 110–12.

28. Coston, *Partis, journaux et hommes politiques*, 537; Hubert Bourgin, "Les Mains," *Faisceau Bellifontain*, Apr. 1926; AN F^7 13208, Nov. 20, 1925; PP 344, 2.649, "Correspondance," Dec. 8, 1925; "Revue," *CEG*, no. 14 (Sept. 15, 1924): 279–80; GV, *L'Homme contre*, 123.

29. See chapter 11.

30. GV, *L'Homme contre*, 129–30, 185–86, 219; "La Réunion," *CEG* 3, no. 18 (1925): 674–711. In AN F^7 13208: "Le Nouveau Siècle," brochure; F.10.043, Paris, Oct. 21, 1925; A.9.469,-, Paris, Nov. 19, 1925; A/1033-SF, Paris, Nov. 20, 1925.

31. GV, *Politique*, 113–30.

32. GV, *L'Homme contre*, 131–47; Bonnefous, *Histoire*, 4:49–55.

33. GV, *L'Homme contre*, 125–27.

34. AN F^7 13195, Dec. 28, 1925; AN F^7 13208, Périgueux, Apr. 7, 1926; GV, *Le Faisceau des combattants*, 16; GV, *L'Homme contre*, 126, 165.

35. GV, *L'Homme contre*, 126–28; GV, *Basile*, 46, 59–60.

36. AN F^7 13208, Feb. 14, 1925; AN F^7 13208, Feb. 21, 1925; GV, *L'Homme contre*, 148–49.

37. GV, *L'Homme contre*, 149; GV, *Basile*, 200–201. In AN F^7 13208: Feb. 21, 1925; A-329, Mar. 14, 1925; "Le Nouveau Siècle," brochure.

38. GV, *Basile*, xxiii–xxiv; AN F^7 13208, Feb. 14, 1925; AN F^7 13208, Nov. 1925; PP 344, 2.649, "Le Nouveau Siècle."

39. AN F^7 13208, A/6382, Dec. 15, 1925; Philippe Barrès, *La Guerre à vingt ans* (Plon-Nourrit, 1924).

40. GV, *Politique*, 113–14; also, Barrès, *La Guerre*, 8–9, 312; Philippe Barrès, *La Victoire au dernier tournant* (Nouvelle Librairie française, 1932), 193–94; Barrès, "Le Secret," *NS*, Mar. 26, 1925; PP 344, 2.649, "Correspondance," Dec. 8, 1925; GV, *L'Homme contre*, 163, 184–85. Valois wrote, after they had separated politically, "Heureux ceux qui travailleront avec Philippe Barrès."

41. GV, *L'Homme contre*, 164, 293–94; "Appel," *NS*, Apr. 16, 1925; "Les Légions," *NS*, Apr. 16, 1925; "La Vie," *NS*, July 23, 1925. In AN F^7 13208: préfet de l'Aisne, July 16, 1925; July 1, 1925; Oct. 8, 1925; "Réunion organisée par les 'Légions,' " Oct. 15, 1925.

42. GV, *L'Homme contre*, 158–59; GV, "La Vérité," *NS*, July 2, 1925; Bonnefous, *Histoire*, 4:90.

43. *NS*, July 9, 1925. In AN F^7 13208: July 1, 1925; A/887, July 2, 1925; July 20, 1925; July 21, 1925.

44. AN F^7 13208, July 20, 1925; Bonnefous, *Histoire*, 4:90–91; Arthuys, "La Petite," *NS*, July 23, 1925; GV, "Le Salaire-Or," *NS*, July 23, 1925, and July 30, 1925; GV, *L'Homme contre*, 183.

45. In AN F^7 13208: A/6.093, July 18, 1925; A/6.245, July 22, 1925; A/6.331, July 23, 1925; July 24, 1925; July 31, 1925; A.7.177, Aug. 26, 1925.

46. AN F⁷ 13208, "Le Mouvement corporatif," Apr. 1926; AN F⁷ 12953, Sept. 24, 1925; GV, *L'Homme contre*, 29.

47. See the letter from M. de X. [de la Porte] in GV, *Politique*, 122–24; GV, *L'Homme contre*, 186.

48. AN F⁷ 12953, Sept. 24, 1925; AN F⁷ 12953, A-684, Oct. 24, 1925; GV, *L'Homme contre*, 158; GV, *Basile*, 69; Thébault, "Chez les," *NS*, July 2, 1925; "La Grève," *NS*, Aug. 6, 1925; Lusignac, "Ce qu'il," *NS*, Aug. 20, 1925; "La Grève," *NS*, Aug. 27, 1925; L.[usignac], "Fin de mois," *NS*, Sept. 3, 1925; L.[usignac], "Fin de grève," *NS*, Sept. 17, 1925.

49. GV, *L'Homme contre*, 163–66; GV, *Basile*, 10, 39–42, 125–28.

50. GV, *L'Homme contre*, 140–44.

51. Ibid., 144, 166; AN F⁷ 12953, F.10.047, Oct. 29, 1925; AN F⁷ 12954, F.10.129, Jan. 4, 1926; AN F⁷ 13208, personal correspondence, Mathon to Cazeneuve, Nov. 25, 1925.

52. GV, *L'Homme contre*, 150–56; AN F⁷ 13208, A.7.177, Aug. 26, 1925; "Le Reveil," *NS*, June 18, 1925; A. Kupfermann, "François Coty, journaliste et homme politique" (diss. for "Troisième Cycle," Paris, 1965).

53. GV, *Basile*, 16–19, 39–42, 59–60, 65–67, 125–29, 163, 298–99, 318–19; GV, *L'Homme contre*, 135–37.

54. GV, *Basile*, 11–12, 42–43; GV, *L'Homme contre*, 166–67.

55. The series began with GV, "La Conquête," *NS*, July 16, 1925.

56. GV, *Basile*, xxiii; GV, "Le Salaire-Or," tract 2, in AN F⁷ 13208; AN F⁷ 13208, Sept. 25, 1925.

57. GV, *L'Homme contre*, 114, 116, 160–63; GV, *Basile*, 26–27, 220–21, 224–33; personal interview, Philippe Gressent-Valois, July 18, 1987.

58. GV, *L'Homme contre*, 166–67; GV, *Basile*, xxv–xxvi; GV, "Après," *AF*, June 19, 1910; Guillemin, *Péguy*, 202–3, 500.

59. AN F⁷ 13208, CS à Roanne, no. 1561, Sept. 20, 1925; GV, *L'Homme contre*, 167–68; Bucy, "Une Journée," *NS*, Oct. 1, 1925; GV, *La Réforme économique et sociale*.

60. GV, *Basile*, 45–48, 59, 69–70; AN F⁷ 13208, Sept. 25, 1925; PP 344, 2.649, Nov. 22, 1925.

61. GV, *L'Homme contre*, 74–77, 159–60; GV, *Basile*, 18–19, 320–21, 442; PP 344, 2.649, Nov. 22, 1925; AN F⁷ 13195, Oct. 16, 1925; AN F⁷ 13208, Sept. 25, 1925; AN F⁷ 13208, Paris, Oct. 25, 1925.

62. GV, *Basile*, 131–32, 296–97; AN F⁷ 13195, Oct. 13, 1925; AN F⁷ 13195, Oct. 16, 1925; AN F⁷ 13208, Paris, Oct. 24, 1925.

63. PP 344, 2.649, Nov. 22, 1925; AN F⁷ 13195, Oct. 16, 1925. In AN F⁷ 13208: A.6.331., Paris, July 23, 1925; Sept. 25, 1925; Paris, Oct. 24, 1925; GV, *L'Homme contre*, 171; GV, *Basile*, xviii.

64. GV, *Basile*, xxviii–xxx; GV, *L'Homme contre*, 171.

65. GV, *L'Homme contre*, 171–74; GV, *Basile*, xxx–xxxiii.

66. GV, "Sur les différents," *AF*, Oct. 11, 1925; Maurras, "Georges Valois," *AF*, Oct. 12, 1925.

67. GV, *L'Homme contre*, 160–61, 173–74, 205–7; GV, *Basile*, xxx–xxxiii, 133, 290–303.

68. AN F⁷ 13208, Oct. 22, 1925; AN F⁷ 13208, Oct. 24, 1925.

69. In AN F⁷ 13208: A.7.177, Paris, Aug. 26, 1925; A.8283, Paris, Oct. 10, 1925; A.9.002.-, Paris, Nov. 3, 1925; Nov. 3, 1925. In AN F⁷ 13209: Nov. 5, 1925; Nov. 10, 1925; Nov. 8, 1925. GV, *L'Homme contre*, 186.

70. The numbers reported vary slightly. Two police reports give 4,000, another added the three locations to give 3,550. Valois privately claimed 5,000. See AN F⁷ 13209, "Réunion organisée par les 'Faisceaux' . . . ," Nov. 11, 1925; four pages, Nov. 11, 1925; Nov. 12, 1925. The *Nouveau Siècle* gave 6,000 and various right-wing papers 5–8,000, "A la salle," *NS*, Nov. 19, 1925; "Revue," *NS*, Nov. 19, 1925.

71. In AN F⁷ 13209: "Réunion organisée par les 'Faisceaux' . . . ," Nov. 11, 1925; four pages, Nov. 11, 1925; Nov. 12, 1925; V.L., Nov. 15, 1925. GV, *L'Homme contre*, 187. For the speeches, see *NS*, Nov. 12, 1925, and for the meeting, "A la salle," *NS*, Nov. 19, 1925.

72. In AN F⁷ 13209: "Les Légions," circular, Nov. 1, 1925; "A.S. de la réunion du 'Faisceau' . . . ," Nov. 8, 1925; "Réunion organisée par les 'Faisceaux' . . . ," Nov. 11, 1925; four pages, Nov. 11, 1925. These numbers, while fair for a new group, were not impressive. The Communist Association républicaine des anciens combattants had brought six hundred marching to the tomb of the unknown soldier in June. See AN F⁷ 13208, "Manifestations dans les rues organisées depuis Avril 1925."

73. AN F⁷ 13208, A.9.232, Paris, Nov. 10, 1925; AN F⁷ 13209, V.L., Nov. 15, 1925; AN F⁷ 13209, Dec. 1, 1925; GV, *Basile*, 87–90. A police informant asked, "Percera-t-il? A-t-il assez d'argent? N'a-t-il pas compté sans les énergies de gauche qu'il conteste systématiquement?" AN F⁷ 13209, Nov. 12, 1925.

5. THE FAISCEAU, II

1. GV, *L'Homme contre*, 187–88; "Le Faisceau," *NS*, Nov. 26, 1925.

2. GV, *L'Homme contre*, 180–81, 188–89; *Le Fascisme*, 13, 155; Kuisel, *Mercier*, 45ff; "A bas," *Ch*, Mar. 1, 1934. In AN F⁷ 13208: Paris, Oct. 22, 1925; Nov. 13, 1925; A.9664, Paris, Nov. 24, 1925; no. 4479, CS, Lille, Dec. 11, 1925. In AN F⁷ 13209, private correspondence, Mathon to Cazeneuve, Nov. 25, 1925; préfet du Nord, Lille, Dec. 3, 1925; Dec. 8, 1925.

3. GV, *L'Homme contre*, 188–91; AN F⁷ 13208, "Effectifs," Dec. 12, 1925; AN F⁷ 13209, Dec. 10, 1925. JP membership for early December was about 5,000, AN F⁷ 13208, summary of Ligue activity. The Action française was credited with 13,500 members for the dept. of the Seine in Apr. 1926, AN F⁷ 13208, A.3359 bis, Paris, Apr. 13, 1926.

4. AN F⁷ 13208, A.9.452, Paris, Nov. 19, 1925; AN F⁷ 13208, A.9664, Paris, Nov. 24, 1925; AN F⁷ 13209, Dec. 10, 1925.

5. GV, *L'Homme contre*, 220–24; GV, *Basile*, 135, 142–44, 149–50; AN F⁷ 13208, Dec. 12, 1925; AN F⁷ 13208, Dec. 15, 1925; AN F⁷ 13209, "Réunion organisée par le Faisceau," Dec. 15, 1925. On violence between the Faisceau and its enemies, see Allen Douglas, "Fascist Violence in France: The Case of the Faisceau," *Journal of Contemporary History* 19 (Fall 1984): 689–712.

6. GV, *L'Etat syndical*, xxii–xxiii.

7. GV, *L'Homme contre*, 174; GV, *Basile*, 5–6, 466; "La Vie," *NS*, Oct. 29, 1925; "La Vie," *NS*, Nov. 12, 1925; "Congrès," *NS*, Dec. 3, 1925; "Un Document," *NS*, Nov. 12, 1925; "A Nos Amis," *AF*, Nov. 10, 1925; AN F^7 13195, Oct. 13, 1925; AN F^7 13195, Oct. 16, 1925; AN F^7 13206, A.7.584.M.D., Paris, Oct. 17, 1927; AN F^7 13208, V.L., Paris, Oct. 24, 1925.

8. GV, *L'Homme contre*, 180; GV, *Basile*, 300–301. In AN F^7 13195: Oct. 13, 1925; Oct. 20, 1925; Dec. 10, 1925. AN F^7 13208, A.8.358, Paris, Oct. 13, 1925; AN F^7 13208, A.9.301.-, Paris, Nov. 13, 1925.

9. In AN F^7 13195, Oct. 16, 1925; Nov. 13, 1925; Paris, Dec. 1, 1925; Dec. 1, 1925; Dec. 4, 1925; Dec. 12, 1925; Dec. 12, 1925 (Pierre Lecoeur); Dec. 12, 1925 (Réal del Sarte). In AN F^7 13208: A.9.301.-, Paris, Nov. 13, 1925; A.9664, Paris, Nov. 24, 1925; A.3359 bis, Paris, April 13, 1926. In AN F^7 13209: A.9269, Paris, Nov. 12, 1925; "Renseignements," Paris, Nov. 15, 1925; Dec. 1, 1925; Dec. 9, 1925; Dec. 10, 1925.

10. GV, *L'Homme contre*, 181–84.

11. GV, *Basile*, 133–35, 165–66; Manouvriez and Mathiex, "A la cour," *AF*, Nov. 4, 1925.

12. "11 Novembre," *AF*, Nov. 12, 1925; "Notre," *AF*, Nov. 26, 1925; GV, *Basile*, xxxv, 73–74, 87–90; AN F^7 13209, V.L., Paris, Nov. 15, 1925.

13. Maurice Pujo, "Les Conditions," *AF*, Dec. 1, 1925; Léon Daudet, "Le Sang-froid," *AF*, Nov. 27, 1925; AN F^7 13195, A.9.629, Paris, Nov. 1925.

14. AN F^7 13208, Dec. 18, 1925; AN F^7 13208, "de la Préfecture de police," Dec. 23, 1925; AN F^7 13209, Dec. 10, 1925; PP 344, 2.649, Nov. 22, 1925; AN F^7 13210, Copy "Centraux d'AF," Paris, Jan. 2, 1926.

15. GV, *L'Homme contre*, 217–18; GV, *Basile*, xv, 304.

16. GV, *L'Homme contre*, 217–18; GV, *Basile*, 33, 302–4, 310, 312, 452–53, 668–70.

17. GV, *L'Homme contre*, 218; GV, *Basile*, 303–7, 312, 667–70, 672–73; "La Nouvelle," *AF*, Dec. 22, 1925.

18. GV, *L'Homme contre*, 189–92.

19. See, e.g., AN F^7 13209, V.L., Paris, Nov. 15, 1925.

20. GV, *Basile*, 292–93, 638; Charles Maurras, "III. Une Exécution," *AF*, Dec. 14, 1925. For French texts of the interviews, see GV, *Contre le mensonge et la calomnie* (NLN, 1926), 44–45.

21. The Action française exploited this in the title of an article: "De l'Action! De l'Action! en voilà. Valois chassé par les étudiants!" *AF*, Dec. 14, 1925; GV, *Basile*, 137; Maurras, "III. Une Exécution," *AF*, Dec. 14, 1925.

22. AN F^7 13208, Dec. 18, 1925. Valois reported a similar "plot," with his own role changed; and stories of impending government action circulated in right-wing circles, "Le Complot," *NS*, Dec. 3, 1925; AN F^7 13209, Nov. 19, 1925. The military countermeasures that confirmed the royalist suspicions may have been the precautions taken at the end of November, AN F^7 13209, gouverneur militaire de Paris, Nov. 23, 1925.

23. For Maurras, see his column from Dec. 15 to Jan. 2 in the *AF*. For Daudet, see: "À qui le tour," *AF*, Dec. 16, 1925; "Le Cas," *AF*, Dec. 25, 1925; "Deux," *AF*, Dec. 28, 1925; "Par le Sang," *AF*, Jan. 2, 1926.

24. AN F^7 13195, Dec. 17, 1925.

25. AN F⁷ 13195, V.L., Paris, Dec. 30, 1925; AN F⁷ 13208, CS, Bordeaux, Feb. 12, 1926.

26. In AN F⁷ 13195: Dec. 17, 1925; Dec. 18, 1925; Dec. 20, 1925; Dec. 21, 1925; V.L., Paris, Dec. 30, 1925.

27. Hubert Bourgin, "Constitution," and GV, "Sur l'agression," NS, Dec. 15, 1925; "L'Agression," NS, Dec. 16, 1925; Hubert Bourgin and Léon de Lapérouse, "La Campagne," NS, Dec. 18, 1925; GV, "Ce que," NS, Dec. 24, 1925; GV, L'Homme contre, 227; GV, Basile, 190–91.

28. AN F⁷ 13195, Dec. 28, 1925; AN F⁷ 13208, Jan. 14, 1926. Typical of the type of veteran Valois was trying to attract was the father of Jacques Laurent. M. Laurent was proud of his wartime service and infuriated by those who preached understanding with Germany. He disliked metics, distrusted politicians, and resented Anglo-Saxon finance, which he considered partially responsible for the fall of the franc. Yet he was anticlerical and proud of both the Revolution and the First Empire. He also disliked the verbal and physical violence of the Action française (Jacques Laurent, Histoire égoiste [La Table ronde, 1976], 65, 118, 210).

29. AN F⁷ 13208, Paris, Oct. 22, 1925; AN F⁷ 13208, Jan. 1926; AN F⁷ 13209, Dec. 5, 1925.

30. AN F⁷ 13208, Jan. 1926; AN F⁷ 13209, Dec. 8, 1925.

31. Maurras, "III. Sur une," AF, Dec. 16, 1925.

32. AN F⁷ 13208, Jan. 1926. A police estimate made sometime after November 1925 gave the JPs 5,000 members, AN F⁷ 13208, summary of Ligue activity. See also Soucy, French Fascism, 39–86.

33. Taittinger was also editor-in-chief of La Liberté, whose director, Camille Aymard, had recently written a book, Bolchevisme ou fascisme? Français, il faut choisir. See GV, L'Homme contre, 180; AN F⁷ 12950, Jan. 28, 1926; AN F⁷ 13208, Jan. 1926; AN F⁷ 13208, "Fusion des Jeunesses patriotes et la Légion"; AN F⁷ 13232, A/1.545.G.C.-6., Paris, Mar. 4, 1926; Beau de Loménie, Responsabilités, IV, 67–69.

34. AN F⁷ 13208, Paris, Oct. 22, 1925; AN F⁷ 13208, -806., Paris, Jan. 11, 1926; AN F⁷ 13209, V.L., Paris, Nov. 18, 1926.

35. The new organization claimed to have recruited 30,000 members by October 1925. In AN F⁷ 13208: Jan. 1925; "Fusion des Jeunesses patriotes et de la Légion"; CC, Rouen, Mar. 5, 1925; A/5923., Paris, Mar. 12, 1925; No. 520, CS, Strasbourg, Mar. 30, 1925; No. 460, Commissariat central de police, Nantes, May 26, 1925; préfet de la Loire inférieure, Nantes, June 25, 1925; Sept. 6, 1925. AN F⁷ 13209, Dec. 18, 1925. See also Soucy, French Fascism, 27–38.

36. "Chronique," NS, Dec. 16, 1925; "M. Antoine Rédier," NS, Dec. 19, 1925; AN F⁷ 13208, "Fusion des Jeunesses patriotes"; AN F⁷ 13208, A.156, Paris, Jan. 9, 1926. In AN F⁷ 13209: Nov. 21, 1925; Dec. 10, 1925; Dec. 16, 1925; Dec. 18, 1925; Dec. 20, 1925. AN F⁷ 13232, Jan. 15, 1926; AN F⁷ 12954, no. 14, CC, Nantes, Jan. 6, 1926.

37. In AN F⁷ 13208: Jan. 1926; Feb. 19, 1926; CC, Rouen, Mar. 5, 1926; No. 378, Commissariat central de police, Nantes, May 15, 1926; Copy of circular, "La Légion Comité de Paris"; "Fusion des Jeunesses patriotes"; AN F⁷ 13210, CS, Lyon, Apr. 21, 1926; AN F⁷ 12954, CC, No. 14, Nantes, Jan. 6, 1926; GV, L'Homme contre, 234.

38. See by Maurras in *AF:* "IV. 'Faisons,' " Jan. 4, 1926; "L'Union," Jan. 13, 1926; "IV. Une Obsession," Jan. 15, 1926; "III. De quelques," Jan. 17, 1926; "Vers l'aveu," Jan. 26, 1926; "III. La Tactique," Jan. 30, 1926. See by Daudet: "Maboule" Jan. 8, 1926; "Le Désarroi," Jan. 16, 1925; "Valois," Jan. 21, 1926; "La Trahison," Feb. 3, 1926.

39. Maurras, "II. Celui," *AF,* Jan. 25, 1926; Maurras, "Constat," *AF,* Feb. 2, 1926. See also GV, *Basile,* 33–36, 81–82, 85–86, 637, 661–66; GV, *L'Homme contre,* 227.

40. *NS,* Jan. 15, 1926.

41. AN F[7] 13195, Dec. 17, 1925; AN F[7] 13195, Dec. 18, 1925. In AN F[7] 13208: Jan. 27, 1926; Jan. 28, 1926; Jan. 29, 1926; Jan. 30, 1926; Feb. 1, 1926; A.-857, Feb. 1, 1926. AN F[7] 13210, Apr. 19, 1926; AN F[7] 13210, April 26, 1926. GV, *L'Homme contre,* 234, 239; "Valois," *AF,* Jan. 30, 1926.

42. GV, *L'Homme contre,* 208, 226; GV, *Basile,* 137; Daudet, "Maboul," *AF,* Jan. 8, 1926; "Une Ovation," *AF,* Jan. 19, 1926. The words of the "Dictateur-en-bois": "Oh! dis chéri, montre-moi ta Dictature! / Dictature! / Oh! comme je voudrais voir ça! / Montre-la / Oh! dis, montre-la! / Mais l'bonhomme en bois s'excusa / D'un air bête! / "Je le'regrette, / La dictature? Je n'en ai pas! / J'suis un dictateur en bois!" (Léon Daudet, " 'L'Etudiant,' " *AF,* Jan. 27, 1926).

43. GV, *Basile,* xiii, 174–77, 190–91, 256, 314–15; GV, *L'Homme contre,* 223–26; AN F[7] 13210, Apr. 26, 1926.

44. GV, *L'Homme contre,* 206–7; Charles Maurras, "IV. Une 'Clé,' " *AF,* Dec. 20, 1925; Marc Bloch, *The Historian's Craft,* trans. Peter Putnam (New York: Vintage Books, 1953), 99.

45. GV, *L'Homme contre,* 226–28; AN F[7] 13210, Jan. 14, 1926.

46. AN F[7] 13208, Jan. 6, 1926; AN F[7] 13209, No. 345, CS, Bordeaux, Jan. 21, 1926; AN F[7] 13209, Dec. 22, 1925. In AN F[7] 13210: Jan. 11, 1926; Jan. 13, 1926; Jan. 14, 1926; Jan. 21, 1926; Jan. 23, 1926.

47. AN F[7] 13209, Dec. 28, 1925. In AN F[7] 13210: Jan. 3, 1926; Jan. 5, 1926; Jan. 19, 1926; Jan. 23, 1926; Feb. 6, 1926.

48. AN F[7] 13209, Dec. 20, 1925. In AN F[7] 13210: Feb. 6, 1926; Feb. 9, 1926; Feb. 10, 1926; Feb. 11, 1926; Paris, Feb. 11, 1926; Feb. 15, 1926; Feb. 19, 1926.

49. AN F[7] 13208, Jan. 6, 1926. In AN F[7] 13210: Jan. 9, 1926; Jan. 19, 1926; Feb. 15, 1926; Feb. 16, 1926. François Goguel, *Géographie des élections françaises sous la Troisième et la Quatrième Républiques* (Armand Colin, 1970), 48–51, 167. For a complete discussion of the Verdun and Reims meetings, see Douglas, "Fascist Violence," 701–5.

50. In AN F[7] 13209: Feb. 3, 1926; no. 147, CS, Verdun, Feb. 9, 1926; copy of circular and timetable, Paris, Feb. 9, 1926; no. 167, CS, Verdun, Feb. 12, 1926; no. 182, CS, Verdun, Feb. 15, 1926; AN F[7] 13209, Feb. 19, 1926; no. 250, CS, Longwy, Feb. 19, 1926; no. 117, CS, Châlons-sur-Marne, Feb. 20, 1926; no. 252, CS, Reims, Feb. 20, 1926; no. 373, CS, Briey, Feb. 21, 1926. AN F[7] 13210, Feb. 13, 1926; AN F[7] 13210, Feb. 19, 1926.

51. In AN F[7] 13209: copy of tract "Comité de Vigilance"; préfet de la Meuse, Bar-le-Duc, Feb. 17, 1926, with attached correspondence; préfet de la Meuse, Bar-le-Duc, Feb. 18, 1926, with attached correspondence; préfet de la Meuse, Feb. 20, 1926.

52. In AN F⁷ 13209: circular and timetable, Paris, Feb. 9, 1926; préfet de la Meuse, Bar-le-Duc, Feb. 19, 1926; Feb. 20, 1926; préfet de la Meuse, Bar-le-Duc, Feb. 21, 1926; no. 207, CS, Verdun, Feb. 21, 1926. AN F⁷ 13210, Feb. 23, 1926; GV, *L'Homme contre*, 235–36. For the official account, see the *NS*, Feb. 22, 1926, 1–2.

53. Beginning with GV, "De Périgueux," *NS*, Feb. 16, 1926. See also AN F⁷ 13210, Mar. 24, 1926.

54. GV, "De Périgueux," *NS*, Feb. 20, 1926. In AN F⁷ 13210: Jan. 27, 1926; Feb. 6, 1926; Mar. 9, 1926; V.L., Paris, Mar. 9, 1926. GV, *L'Homme contre*, 238.

55. AN F⁷ 13208, "Le Mouvement corporatif," Apr. 1926; AN F⁷ 13208, Mar. 19, 1926. In AN F⁷ 13210: Mar. 3, 1926; Mar. 4, 1926; V.L., Paris, Mar. 9, 1926; Mar. 17, 1926; Mar. 24, 1926; V.L., Paris, Apr. 8, 1926; May 12, 1926. GV, *L'Homme contre*, 238; Bourget-Pailleron, "Une Magnifique," *NS*, Mar. 22, 1926.

56. In AN F⁷ 13208: Mar. 19, 1926; Paris, Apr. 12, 1926; May 2, 1926; V.L., Paris, May 26, 1926. In AN F⁷ 13210: Mar. 3, 1926; Mar. 4, 1926; V.L., Paris, April 8, 1926; May 12, 1926; May 20, 1926.

57. In AN F⁷ 13208: "Effectifs," Apr. 10, 1926; Apr. 13, 1926; May 12, 1926. AN F⁷ 13210, Mar. 13, 1926; AN F⁷ 13210, A-3.359bis, Paris, Apr. 13, 1926.

58. AN F⁷ 13208, Paris, Apr. 12, 1926. In AN F⁷ 13209: no. 835, CS, Metz, Apr. 10, 1926; CC, Metz, Apr. 17, 1926; no. 589, CS, Mulhouse, Apr. 27, 1926; no. 1455, CS, Metz, Apr. 30, 1926. In AN F⁷ 13210: no. 6658, CS, Colmar, Apr. 3, 1926; Mar. 4, 1926; Mar. 30, 1926; CC, Mulhouse, Apr. 15, 1926; no. 523, CS, Mulhouse, Apr. 15, 1926; no. 646, CS, Strasbourg, Apr. 16, 1926; CS, Lyon, Apr. 21, 1926.

59. In AN F⁷ 13210: Mar. 4, 1926; Mar. 20, 1926; Mar. 26, 1926; Apr. 16, 1926; Apr. 21, 1926; "Réunion 29ème Compagnie," Apr. 21, 1926.

60. GV, *L'Homme contre*, 240–41; Bonnefous, *Histoire*, 4:131–32.

61. GV, *L'Homme contre*, 240–41. In AN F⁷ 13210: May 21, 1926; May 22, 1926; May 25, 1926.

62. GV, *L'Homme contre*, 233–34; Bourget-Pailleron, "Une Magnifique." In AN F⁷ 13210: Mar. 30, 1926; June 5, 1926; June 9, 1926. In AN F⁷ 13211: CC, Reims, Apr. 1, 1926; Apr. 14, 1926; no. 342, CS, Châlons-sur-Marne, Apr. 20, 1926; CC, Reims, Apr. 23, 1926; no. 728, CS, Reims, Apr. 24, 1926; CS, Châlons-sur-Marne, Apr. 27, 1926; CC, Reims, Apr. 27, 1926; CC, Reims, May 3, 1926; préfet de la Marne, Châlons-sur-Marne, May 3, 1926; CC, May 6, 1926; CC, "Confidentiel," Reims, May 7, 1926; May 18, 1926; CS, Reims, May 19, 1926; CC, Reims, May 29, 1926; May 31, 1926; CS, Reims, June 2, 1926; CC, Reims, June 5, 1926; June 12, 1926; CC, Reims, June 14, 1926; CC, June 16, 1926; no. 2382, CC, Saint-Quentin, June 17, 1926; CC, Reims, June 18, 1926; CC, Reims, June 19, 1926; CC, Reims, June 21, 1926; CS, Bordeaux, June 21, 1926.

63. In AN F⁷ 13211: CC, Reims, June 5, 1926; no. 629, CS, Reims, June 9, 1926; cabinet du préfet de la Marne, Châlons-sur-Marne, June 15, 1926; no. 2382, CC, Saint-Quentin, June 17, 1926; préfet de la Marne, Châlons-sur-Marne, June 17, 1926; June 19, 1926; no. 1055, CS, Reims, June 21, 1926; June 23, 1926; CC, Reims, June 23, 1926; "Interdiction des rassemblements," Reims, June 25, 1926; June 24, 1926; no. 2487, CC, Saint-Quentin, June 24, 1926; June 26, 1926.

64. *Première assemblée nationale des combattants, des producteurs, et des chefs de famille* (NLN, 1926); AN F⁷ 13211, no. 1080, CS, Reims, June 27, 1926; AN F⁷ 13211, no. 1082, CS, Reims, June 28, 1926; *NS*, June 28, 1926.

65. AN F⁷ 13211, no. 1081, CS, Reims, June 27, 1926.

66. In AN F⁷ 13212: June 28, 1926; CC, Reims, June 28, 1926; July 1, 1926. In AN F⁷ 13211: Commissaire divisionnaire, June 30, 1926; note—June 27, 1926, 24H; June 24, 1926; CC, Reims, June 5, 1926.

67. *Première assemblée nationale*, 131–37; GV, *L'Homme contre*, 249–52; AN F⁷ 13212, July 1, 1926.

68. "Le Nouveau Siècle," brochure in AN F⁷ 13208; Bellanger, *Histoire*, 3:324–25.

69. René Johannet, "Fin," *NS*, Feb. 4, 1926. Johannet's column began with Feb. 21, 1926. PP 344, 2.649, "Le Nouveau Siècle," Feb. 18, 1927.

70. Personal communication from Henry Poulaille, Mar. 25, 1975; GV, *Basile*, 55–56; AN F⁷ 13208, A.10.363, Paris, Dec. 18, 1925; AN F⁷ 13208, F.10.112, Paris, Dec. 16, 1925.

71. GV, *Basile*, 56; AN F⁷ 13208, A.10.363, Paris, Dec. 18, 1925; AN F⁷ 13208, Jan. 6, 1926.

72. In AN F⁷ 13208: Nov. 1925; A.8.561.-, Paris, Oct. 20, 1925; Nov. 5, 1925; A.9713, Paris, Nov. 25, 1925; Nov. 27, 1925; A.-9.862, Dec. 1, 1925; Dec. 1, 1925; Dec. 3, 1925; A.9962, Paris, Dec. 4, 1926; Dec. 4, 1926; F. 10102, Paris, Dec. 7, 1925; Dec. 9, 1925; Dec. 10, 1925; A.10.125, Dec. 10, 1925; A.10. 245.-, Paris, Dec. 14, 1925; A/10.166, Paris, Dec. 11, 1925; F.10.123, Paris, Dec. 24, 1925.

73. In AN F⁷ 13208: A.10.391, Paris, Dec. 19, 1925; F.10.117, Paris, Dec. 21, 1925; A.10.621, Dec. 24, 1925; Jan. 9, 1926; F.10.142, Paris, Jan. 14, 1926; F.10144, Paris, Jan. 16, 1926; A.776.-, Paris, Jan. 29, 1926. *Le Canard enchaîné*, Dec. 30, 1925.

74. AN F⁷ 13208, Jan. 9, 1926; AN F⁷ 13208, Feb. 3, 1926.

75. In AN F⁷ 13208: no. 1197, CS, Nantes, Dec. 12, 1925; no. 26691, chef de service, Toulon, Dec. 21, 1925; F.10144., Paris, Jan. 16, 1926; A.2.485, Paris, Mar. 19, 1926; A/2.932, Paris, Mar. 29, 1926; no. 2376, Paris, Mar. 16, 1926; A.2635, Paris, Mar. 24, 1926; A.2150, Paris, Mar. 10, 1926; Sept. 2, 1926.

76. AN F⁷ 13208, Apr. 26, 1926; AN F⁷ 13208, May 2, 1926. The *Action française*, which was selling relatively well in this period, was printing about 100,000 copies, of which 45,000 went to subscribers. *L'Humanité* varied between 100,000 and 160,000 copies (Bellanger, *Histoire*, 3:528, 580).

77. *L'Homme contre*, 151. In AN F⁷ 13208: A.9927, Paris, Dec. 8, 1925; F.10.117, Paris, Dec. 21, 1925; F.10.123, Paris, Dec. 24, 1925. PP 344, 2.649, "Le Nouveau Siècle," Feb. 18, 1927; Bellanger, *Histoire*, 3:524.

78. In AN F⁷ 13208: A.9.424.-, Paris, Nov. 18, 1925; F.10102, Paris, Dec. 7, 1925.

79. AN F⁷ 13208, Mar. 19, 1926.

80. GV, *L'Homme contre*, 289.

81. AN F⁷ 13210, June 11, 1926.

82. In AN F⁷ 13208: "Effectifs," Dec. 12, 1925; May 12, 1926; June 11, 1926; Oct. 31, 1926; Feb. 6, 1926; "Conseil technique du Faisceau des Corporations," Nov. 30, 1926; "Le Mouvement corporatif," Apr., 1926; Oct. 13, 1926.

83. GV, *Le Fascisme*, 67–92.

84. AN F^7 13208, Nov. 30, 1926; AN F^7 13209, no. 1.523, CS, Saint-Etienne, June 14, 1926; AN F^7 13210, June 6, 1926.

85. *NS*, no. 132, May 12, 1926.

86. AN F^7 13209, no. 1448, CC, Bordeaux, June 24, 1926. In AN F^7 13210: No. 4455, CS, Bordeaux, Aug. 14, 1926; no. 1.758, CC, Bordeaux, Aug. 14, 1926; no. 1.779, CC, Bordeaux, Aug. 21, 1926; no. 2098, CS, Strasbourg, Nov. 15, 1926.

87. See, e.g., AN F^7 13209, Dec. 5, 1925 and attached tract.

88. AN F^7 13210, Aug. 6, 1926.

89. In AN F^7 13208: "de la Préfecture de police," Paris, Apr. 12, 1925; June 7, 1926; Paris, July 18, 1926; GV, *L'Homme contre*, 181.

90. In AN F^7 13208: préfet du Nord, Lille, May 26, 1926; June 7, 1926; Paris, July 18, 1926; Oct. 13, 1926; Oct. 31, 1926. In AN F^7 13210: no. 2640, inspecteur de police spécial, Valenciennes, July 22, 1926; préfet du Nord, Lille, Aug. 11, 1926; préfet du Nord, Lille, Sept. 4, 1926; Aug. 6, 1926; Aug. 8, 1926; Oct. 21, 1926; Oct. 23, 1926.

91. AN F^7 13208, Nov. 27, 1926, AN F^7 13210, Oct. 23, 1926; AN F^7 13210, no. 842, CS, Toulouse, July 21, 1926; Maîtron, *Dictionnaire*, 30:131.

92. Darras was invited to hire these unemployed miners by the préfecture de la Seine. In AN F^7 13212: Jan. 18, 1927 (three reports); Jan. 21, 1927; Jan. 29, 1927. GV, *L'Homme contre*, 303.

93. In AN F^7 13208: Paris, Mar. 1, 1926; "Le Mouvement corporatif," Apr. 1926; V.L., Paris, May 26, 1926. AN F^7 13210, Dec. 14, 1926.

94. AN F^7 13210, June 2, 1926; AN F^7 13210, June 3, 1926; R. Leboursier, "Dans les T.C.R.P.," *L'Humanité*, Sept. 26, 1926; AN F^7 13208, Oct. 13, 1926; AN F^7 13208, Oct. 31, 1926. In AN F^7 13210: préfet du Nord, Lille, Sept. 4, 1926; Sept. 26, 1926; no. 752 (?), CS, Strasbourg, Sept. 30, 1926; Oct. 21, 1926. PP 344, 2.649, "Au Prés.," Feb. 18, 1927.

95. See, e.g., in AN F^7 13208: "Effectifs," Dec. 12, 1925; "Le Mouvement corporatif," Apr. 1926; V.L., Paris, May 26, 1926. AN F^7 13210, Feb. 6, 1926; AN F^7 13210, no. 547, CS, Amiens, Mar. 26, 1926.

96. In AN F^7 13208: Feb. 27, 1926; Nov. 27, 1926. In AN F^7 13210: Feb. 19, 1926; July 12, 1926; Sept. 16, 1926; Oct. 5, 1926; Nov. 4, 1926. GV, *L'Homme contre*, 293.

97. AN F^7 13208, "Le Mouvement corporatif," Apr. 1926; AN F^7 13208, A/ 1719-SF, Paris, Dec. 14, 1926. In AN F^7 13210: A/1638 SF, Paris, Oct. 23, 1926; Apr. 8, 1926; Oct. 29, 1926. AN F^7 13212, Jan. 25, 1927; GV, *La Politique de la victoire*, 125.

98. AN F^7 13208, Paris, Dec. 1, 1925; AN F^7 13208, F.10.143, Paris, Jan. 16, 1926; AN F^7 13210, V.L., Paris, Oct. 23, 1926; PP 344, 2.649, "Le Nouveau Siècle," Feb. 18, 1927; Bellanger, *Histoire*, 3:493, n. 3.

99. In AN F^7 13208: Feb. 6, 1926; Feb. 26, 1926; Feb. 27, 1926. AN F^7 13210, Paris, Feb. 11, 1926; AN F^7 13210, Mar. 17, 1926; GV, *Basile*, xxv, 271–72.

100. AN F^7 13208, May 12, 1926; AN F^7 13209, Apr. 26, 1926. In AN F^7 13210: Mar. 24, 1926; June 11, 1926; July 2, 1926; Sept. 16, 1926; Sept. 22, 1926; no. 2.582, CS, Saint-Etienne, Oct. 29, 1926; Oct. 26, 1926; Oct. 28, 1926; Oct. 29, 1926; Nov. 4, 1926; Nov. 22, 1926. AN F^7 13211, May 31, 1926.

101. In AN F^7 13208: F.10.150, Paris, Jan. 26, 1926; May 15, 1926; Nov. 27, 1926. In AN F^7 13210: June 9, 1926; "De bonne source," Paris, June 10, 1926; June 12, 1926; CC, Le Havre, May 30, 1926; GV, *L'Homme contre*, 57–58.

102. GV, *L'Homme contre*, 243–44.

103. AN F^7 13208, May 15, 1926; AN F^7 13208, Paris, July 18, 1926; AN F^7 13209, no. 396, CS, Ecouviez, June 6, 1926. In AN F^7 13210: Apr. 8, 1926; June 9, 1926; CS, Le Havre, May 30, 1926; Oct. 9, 1926.

104. Lusignac, "Le Rapport," *NS*, July 5, 1926, 1; GV, "La Révolution," *NS*, July 6, 1926; GV, "M. Caillaux," *NS*, July 7, 1926; Rigny, "Contre," *NS*, July 12, 1926.

105. AN F^7 13208, June 16, 1926; AN F^7 13210, June 9, 1926.

106. AN F^7 12954, 2.018, Paris, June 23, 1926; AN F^7 12954, A.2.078, Paris, July 27, 1926. On de Wendel's hostility to the Caillaux cabinet, see Jeanneney, *François de Wendel*, 307–12.

107. See, e.g., in AN F^7 12954: A-2.062, Paris, July 19, 1926; A-2.063, July 19, 1926; A/1.450 S.F., July 20, 1926; A-2.070, July 22, 1926; July 24, 1926. AN F^7 13210, no. 2640, inspecteur de police spécial, Valenciennes, July 22, 1926; Bonnefous, *Histoire*, 4:159–64.

108. AN F^7 13210, no. 2640, inspecteur de police spécial, Valenciennes, July 22, 1926; GV, *L'Homme contre*, 259; *NS*, July 18 and 19, 1926.

109. GV, *L'Homme contre*, 257–59; AN F^7 12954, A-2.1063, Paris, July 19, 1926.

110. AN F^7 12954, July 28, 1926; AN F^7 13210, Oct. 9, 1926; AN F^7 13210, Nov. 22, 1926.

111. AN F^7 13209, no. 1322, CS, Bordeaux, Feb. 27, 1926; AN F^7 13210, June 12, 1926.

112. See, e.g., AN F^7 13209, Dec. 18, 1925.

113. AN F^7 13208, July 1, 1926; AN F^7 13208, Nov. 6, 1926. In AN F^7 13209: CS, Vichy, Jan. 16, 1926; no. 1448, CC, Bordeaux, June 24, 1926; no. 1.523, CS, Saint-Etienne, June 14, 1926.

114. AN F^7 13210, no. 12838, commissaire de police, Metz, Oct. 4, 1926; AN F^7 13210, Oct. 6, 1926; GV, *L'Homme contre*, 261, 301–2.

115. AN F^7 13208, Nov. 6, 1926; AN F^7 13210, Oct. 6, 1926; Jacques Rueff, "Préface," to Emile Moreau, *Souvenirs d'un gouveneur de la Banque de France* (M.-Th. Genin, 1954), v–xv; Bonnefous, *Histoire*, 4:243.

116. AN F^7 13210, Sept. 24, 1926; AN F^7 13210, Sept. 27, 1926.

117. In AN F^7 13210: July 8, 1926; Aug. 6, 1926; Aug. 21, 1926; Aug. 24, 1926.

118. AN F^7 13208, "Effectifs," Sept. 24, 1926; AN F^7 13208, Oct. 13, 1926; AN F^7 13210, Oct. 9, 1926; AN F^7 13210, Oct. 16, 1926. The membership numbers given above are larger than those presented by Sternhell ("Anatomie," 23–25). My interpretations of the data are based on an analysis of the complete record of Faisceau activity, the inclusion of temporarily inactive members (since they would probably come out in the event of a crisis) and an examination of the proportions of local members who came out for the Verdun and Reims meetings.

119. AN F^7 13195, commissariat spécial de Melun, Sept. 6, 1926; AN F^7 13195, A/7/.725., Paris, Sept. 8, 1926; AN F^7 13210, Aug. 24, 1926; AN F^7 13211, 8424, "Confidentiel," Oct. 8, 1926.

120. In AN F⁷ 13210: Oct. 4, 1926; Oct. 6, 1926; Oct. 9, 1926. "Le Faisceau," *NS*, Oct. 6, 1926.

121. GV, *L'Homme contre*, 264–65.

122. In AN F⁷ 13208: "Traduction—Renseignements," Jan. 1926; Nov. 18, 1926; Paris, Dec. 5, 1926. AN F⁷ 13209, Nov. 16, 1926; AN F⁷ 13210, rapport spécial Modane, no. 626, Jan. 22, 1926; AN F⁷ 13210, no. 3.098, CS, Annemasse, Nov. 8, 1926; AN F⁷ 13245, March (?) 1926.

123. AN F⁷ 13210, Apr. 19, 1926.

124. GV, *L'Homme contre*, 265–69. Cf. Keynes, *Essays*, 190–91, whose judgment is similar.

125. AN F⁷ 13210, Sept. 21, 1926 (two reports).

126. AN F⁷ 13210, Sept. 24, 1926; GV, *L'Homme contre*, 269–70.

127. GV, *L'Homme contre*, 268–69; Bonnefous, *Histoire*, 4:194.

128. PP 344, 2.649, "Au Prés.," Feb. 18, 1927; PP 344, 2.649, "Le Nouveau Siècle," Feb. 18, 1927; AN F⁷ 13209, A-18.816 (?), Dec. 7, 1925; AN F⁷ 13209, "Renseignements Traduction," Dec. 18, 1925; AN F⁷ 13232, Nov. 1926; Bellanger, *Histoire*, 3:505–6. For the surveillance of Italian agents in France, see AN F⁷ 13245, 13246, 13247. On the Italian international fascism of later years, see Michael Ledeen, *Universal Fascism* (New York: Howard Fertig, 1972).

129. In AN F⁷ 13210: Oct. 16, 1926; Oct. 25, 1926; Nov. 1, 1926; H.C., chef de police du quartier Vivienne, Paris, Nov. 3, 1926; Nov. 5, 1926. "Pour la paix," *NS*, Nov. 3, 1926, p. 1. For the speeches, see *NS*, Nov. 7, 1926, p. 3.

130. See Maurras in *AF*, Nov. 5–12, 1926; GV, *L'Homme contre*, 371; GV, *Basile*, 57–58, 105–20, 164–72, 256–77.

131. GV, "Alliés," *NS*, Nov. 6, 1926; "La Libération," *NS*, Nov. 8, 1926; GV, "Les Complices," *NS*, Nov. 12, 1926; AN F⁷ 13210, Nov. 13, 1926.

132. GV, *L'Homme contre*, 272–74; AN F⁷ 13210, A.-9.600, M/P.4., Paris, Nov. 25, 1926.

133. GV, "Les Complices," *NS*, Nov. 12, 1926. In AN F⁷ 13197: "Au sujet d'un coup de main," Nov. 15, 1926; procès-verbal no. 828, préfet de police, cabinet de M. Rose. AN F⁷ 13210, "Réunion du conseil national," Nov. 15, 1926; AN F⁷ 13210, A-9.600, M/P.4, Paris, Nov. 25, 1926; "Avertissement," *NS*, Nov. 15, 1926; GV, *L'Homme contre*, 272–74, 279.

134. AN F⁷ 13210, Nov. 20, 1926. See also Weber, *Action française*, 219–39.

135. In AN F⁷ 13210: "Réunion du conseil national," Nov. 15, 1926; Nov. 26, 1926; Dec. 14, 1926.

6. THE FAISCEAU, III

1. AN F⁷ 13208, F.10.167, Paris, Feb. 9, 1926; AN F⁷ 13208, CS, Bordeaux, Mar. 15, 1926; AN F⁷ 13209, commissaire de police, Bordeaux, Feb. 26, 1926; AN F⁷ 13209, CS, Bordeaux, Feb. 27, 1926. In AN F⁷ 13210: June 9, 1926; June 19, 1926; Apr. 13, 1926; May 20, 1926. GV, *L'Homme contre*, 184–85, 230; GV, *Basile*, 127.

2. GV, *L'Homme contre*, 248–49, 259–60, 284–86; "Notre République," xxiii–xxxiv; *Première assemblée nationale*, 128–29; *NS*, July 14, 1926.

3. AN F^7 13210, telegram no. 0554/46703 MC, Paris, Nov. 6, 1926; AN F^7 13212, Jan. 18, 1927.

4. Jean Brière, *Le Tartuffe démasqué* (Les Etincelles, [1929?]), 29; "Notre république," xxiii–xxvi. Valois declared that he had mistakenly turned to the monarchy as a young man seduced by Paul Claudel's *Tête d'or* (1889; Mercure de France, 1959), but that he could now see that the play was really pre-fascist and not monarchist. The play is not royalist, and Claudel's grandiose images of youthful heroism, wide spaces, and barbarian hordes were ideally suited to impress Valois's imagination. But Valois's royalism was hardly accidental. If Valois found the king in Claudel, he was looking for him. See "Notre république," xvi–xvii.

5. GV, *Le Fascisme*, 6, 11–16, 21–31, 35–36.

6. Ibid., 35–44, 75, 78–81, 149–53.

7. PP 344, 2.649, "Au Prés.," Feb. 18, 1927; AN F^7 13208, Dec. 9, 1926; AN F^7 13208, Dec. 27, 1926; AN F^7 13210: Oct. 2, 1926; AN F^7 13210, Oct. 5, 1926 (two reports); AN F^7 13212, Jan. 3, 1927; AN F^7 13212, Jan. 8, 1927; GV, *L'Homme contre*, 287–91.

8. AN F^7 13208, Dec. 10, 1926; AN F^7 13208, A.-2.317, Paris, Dec. 8, 1926. In AN F^7 13210: Dec. 3, 1926; Dec. 4, 1926; Dec. 27, 1926; Dec. 30, 1926. In AN F^7 13212: Jan. 3, 1927; Jan. 10, 1927; Jan. 13, 1927; Jan. 19, 1927; Jan. 25, 1927; Feb. 2, 1927. GV, *L'Homme contre*, 287–91, 300.

9. GV, *L'Homme contre*, 291–94, 300. In AN F^7 13208: Nov. 10, 1926; Dec. 14, 1926; Dec. 27, 1926. In AN F^7 13210: Oct. 5, 1926; Dec. 14, 1926; Dec. 21, 1926; Dec. 27, 1926; Dec. 30, 1926. AN F^7 13212, préfet de la Meuse, Bar-le-Duc, Dec. 24, 1926. In AN F^7 13212, Jan. 3, 1927; Jan. 13, 1927; Jan. 22, 1927.

10. AN F^7 13202, A.-2.317, Paris, Dec. 18, 1926; AN F^7 13212, Jan. 22, 1927; AN F^7 13212, Mar. 10, 1927; GV, *L'Homme contre*, 291–301.

11. "Congrès," *NS*, Feb. 9, 1927; GV, "Le Premier," *NS*, Jan. 30, 1927; "Le Faisceau," *NS*, Jan. 30, 1927; "L'Action," *NS*, Feb. 6, 1927; GV, "Notre," *NS*, Mar. 20, 1927; GV, *L'Homme contre*, 300–304; AN F^7 13210, Dec. 30, 1926; AN F^7 13212, (n.d. [Jan. 1927?]); AN F^7 13212, Jan. 18, 1927.

12. GV, *L'Homme contre*, 301–2; "Le Premier," *NS*, Jan. 30, 1927; "Une Démission," *NS*, Mar. 20, 1927; AN F^7 13210, Dec. 14, 1926. In AN F^7 13212: Feb. 22, 1927; Mar. 25, 1927; no. 5534, CS, Lille, Oct. 17, 1927. For a nuanced critique of Valois's harsh judgment of Bucard, see Alain Deniel, *Bucard et le Francisme* (Editions Jean Picollec, 1979), 16–17, 274ff.

13. Rueff, "Préface" to Emile Moreau, *Souvenirs*, v–xv.

14. Moreau, *Souvenirs*, 108, 118–26, 133, 138–39, 146, 160–93.

15. AN F^7 13210, Dec. 17, 1926. In AN F^7 13212: Jan. 8, 1927; Jan. 18, 1927; Jan. 29, 1927. GV, *L'Homme contre*, 265–67, 269; Moreau, *Souvenirs*, 148–49, 162; GV, "Le Prestige," *NS*, Dec. 4, 1926; Dumas, "L'Etendue," *NS*, Feb. 6, 1927; "Cinq," *NS*, Feb. 6, 1927; GV, "L'Attitude," *NS*, Feb. 13, 1927.

16. GV, "L'Attitude," *NS*, Feb. 13, 1927; "Pour," *NS*, Feb. 6, 1927.

17. AN F^7 13212, Jan. 22, 1927; AN F^7 13212, Feb. 22, 1927; GV, "L'Attitude," *NS*, Feb. 13, 1927; GV, "Vers la," *NS*, Feb. 27, 1927; PP 344, 2.649, "Au Prés.," "Le Nouveau Siècle," and "La Ligue du franc-or," Feb. 18, 1927. This is the only summary report on Valois's life and activities in either AN or PP.

18. GV, "Vers la," *NS*, Feb. 27, 1927; "Octave Homberg," *NS*, Feb. 6, 1927.

19. René de la Porte, "Préface," in id., ed., *L'Avenir de la république* (LV, 1927), 24; "IIe Semaine de la monnaie," brochure in AN F^7 13212.

20. "Aux Chefs," *NS*, Feb. 27, 1927; "La Réunion," *NS*, Feb. 27, 1927; "Franc," and "Les Trois," *NS*, March 20, 1927. In AN F^7 13212: Feb. 22, 1927; Mar. 18, 1927; Mar. 19, 1927; Mar. 26, 1927; no. 520, CC, Bordeaux, Mar. 16, 1927; no. 566, CC, Bordeaux, Mar, 22, 1927; no. 614, CC, Bordeaux, Mar. 30, 1927: no. 578, CS, Toulouse, May 11, 1927.

21. In AN F^7 13212: Mar. 18, 1927; Mar. 19, 1927; Mar. 30, 1927; Apr. 4, 1927; Apr. 6, 1927.

22. GV, *L'Homme contre*, 318; cf. Rueff, "Préface" to Moreau, *Souvenirs*.

23. See chapter 3.

24. Moreau, *Souvenirs*, esp. 66–67, 181.

25. GV, *L'Homme contre*, 305–8; GV, "Moscou," *NS*, Mar. 27, 1927; GV, "A Propos," *NS*, Apr. 17, 1927; GV, "Ni Londres," *NS*, May 1, 1927; GV, "De Domrémy" and "Le Problème," *NS*, May 8, 1927; GV, "La France," *NS*, May 15, 1927.

26. In AN F^7 13212: May 8, 1927; copy of Faisceau circular, May 13, 1927; May 18, 1927; CS, no. 514, Epinal, May 23, 1927. *NS*, May 8, 1927; GV, *L'Homme contre*, 308–9; GV, *Basile*, 653.

27. In AN F^7 13212: Mar. 10, 1927; no. 882, CS, Toulouse, July 25, 1927; no. 58, CS, Bordeaux, Jan. 5, 1927; no. 3411, CS, Bordeaux, Mar. 30, 1927; no. 5561, CS, Bordeaux, June 20, 1927; Apr. 12, 1927; CS, Lille, June 15, 1927; no. 220, CS, Strasbourg, Feb. 1, 1927.

28. GV, *Basile*, xliii–xlvi, 567–68, 597–98.

29. GV, *L'Homme contre*, 312–14.

30. GV, *Basile*, entire.

31. Though the pilgrimage seems to have been in fulfillment of a vow, Philippe Valois, who joined his father, insists he never knew the reason. Personal interview, Philippe Gressent-Valois, July 24, 1987.

32. GV, *L'Homme contre*, 320–35; GV, *Basile*, 599; GV, "Sur la route," *NS*, July 24, 1927. Personal interview, Philippe Gressent-Valois, July 24, 1987.

33. GV, *L'Homme contre*, 320–27; AN F^7 13212, Apr. 25, 1927; AN F^7 1.3212, Aug. 13, 1927.

34. "Après la bataille," *La Volonté*, Nov. 16, 1926.

35. GV, *L'Homme contre*, 328–32; GV, "A la recherche," *NS*, June 19, 1927; GV, "La Situation," *NS*, July 17, 1927; Serge Berstein, *Histoire du parti radical*, vol. 2, *Crise du radicalisme* (Presses de la Fondation nationale des sciences politiques, 1982), 94–102.

36. L. [de la Porte], "Charles-Albert," *NS*, June 19, 1927; GV, *Le Fascisme*, 13; Pierre Dominique, *La Révolution créatrice* (LV, 1928); id., "Equipes nouvelles," *Le Rappel*, May 31, 1927.

37. Pierre Dominique, "A Reims? Non, à Versailles," *Paris-Phare*, June 24–30, 1926, 1; id., "Valois et Nous," *Le Rappel*, June 7, 1927.

38. Albert Dubarry, "Pour un nouveau parti," *La Volonté*, May 6, 1927; Charles-Albert, "Et pourquoi pas un fascisme de gauche?" *La Volonté*, May 13, 1927, 1–2; "Les Idées," *NS*, no. 28, July 10, 1927, 3; "Les Conclusions," *NS*, no. 29, July 17, 1927, 3; "Le Parti," *NS*, no. 26, June 26, 1927, 3.

39. "L'Organisation," *NS*, no. 26, June 26, 1927, 1, and notice at bottom of page; "Les Derniers," *NS*, no. 46, Nov. 13, 1927, 2, 6; AN F⁷ 13208, Nov. 9, 1927.

40. In AN F⁷ 13212: Nov. 28, 1927; Dec. 8, 1927; Dec. 13, 1927; Dec. 20, 1927.

41. "Une Révolution," *NS*, no. 48, Nov. 27, 1927, 2; "Le Million," *NS*, no. 30, July 24, 1927, 3.

42. "Le Faisceau," *NS*, no. 40, Oct. 2, 1927, 5; GV, "La Crise," *NS*, no. 32, Aug. 7, 1927, 5; GV, *L'Homme contre*, 264–69.

43. GV, "Les Nouvelles," *NS*, no. 29, July 17, 1927, 3–4; GV, "La Victoire," *NS*, no. 37, Sept. 11, 1927, 1; AN F⁷ 13212, "Réunion des cadres et des militants du Faisceau," Nov. 24, 1927.

44. AN F⁷ 13212, no. 351, CS, Toulouse, Feb. 13, 1928; GV, "Redressement," *NS*, no. 28, Dec. 28, 1927, 1.

45. GV, *L'Homme contre*, 336–40; In AN F⁷ 13212: Feb. 25, 26, 1928; "Le 2ᵉ Congrès national des Faisceaux," Feb. 26, 1928. "Le 2ᵉ Congrès," *NS*, Mar. 4, 1928.

46. GV, "Il y a fascisme," *NS*, Feb. 25, 1928; "La Vie," *NS*, Feb. 29, 1928; "Conseil," *NS*, Mar. 20, 1928; GV, *L'Homme contre*, 340, 342, 345; PP 344, 2.649a, "Au sujet de la Fédération . . . ," July 1928.

47. GV, *L'Homme contre*, 340–45; PP 344, 2.649a, "Au sujet," July 1928; AN F⁷ 13212, no. 1135, CC, Bordeaux, June 9, 1928.

7. THE YEARS OF RESPECTABILITY

1. See, e.g., Jean Touchard, *La Gauche en France depuis 1900* (Editions du Seuil, 1981), 14; GV, "Jacques Doriot," *NA*, Oct. 24, 1935.

2. See, e.g., the "Echos," in *CB*: no. 11 (Apr. 20, 1929), 22–24; no. 19 (June 15, 1929), 27; no. 27 (Aug. 17, 1929), 26–27; GV, "Résolutions," *NA*, July 12, 1939.

3. "Dans l'édition," *CB*, no. 31 (Oct. 12, 1929), 28–30; GV, "Commentaires," *CB*, no. 56 (Apr. 5, 1930), 19; GV, "La Politique," *CB*, no. 112 (July 11–18, 1931), 7–9; "Passé," *CB*, no. 117 (Dec. 25, 1931), 12–26; GV, "Episodes," *La Coopération culturelle* (= *NA*), July 1938.

4. Pietro Nenni, "La Faillite," *CB*, no. 25 (July 27, 1929); Francesco Nitti, "Nos prisons," 4–16, and GV, "Commentaires," 17, in *CB*, no. 46 (Jan. 25, 1930); Puglionisi, "La Presse," *CB*, no. 64 (June 7, 1930); Nitti, "Un Emprunt," *CB*, no. 79 (Nov. 8, 1930); Weber, *Action française*, 401; GV, *Finances italiennes* (LV, 1930).

5. The only work that sold better during the same period was Pierre Dominique's *Oui, mais Moscou*; "Passé," *CB*, no. 117 (Dec. 25, 1931).

6. GV, "Préface," *CB*, no. 82 (Nov. 29, 1930), 3–6, 12–14; GV, "Commentaires," *CB*, no. 103 (Apr. 25, 1931), 23; GV, "Observations," *CB*, no. 115 (Sept. 12, 1931), 8–16; "Echos," *CB*, no. 94 (Feb. 21, 1931), 27; Bach, "Bakou," *CB*, no. 106 (May 16, 1931), 3–12; "Echos," *CB*, no. 93 (Feb. 14, 1931), 27; Sauvebois, "Du syndicalisme," *CB*, no. 52 (Mar. 8, 1930), 13; Marion, "Mirage," *CB*, no. 68 (July 5, 1930), 3–17; Arturo Labriola, "Le Plan," *CB*, no. 89 (Jan. 17, 1931), 3–18.

7. GV, "La 'Trahison,' " NS, Mar. 23, 1928, 1; GV, "A longueur," CB, no. 6 (Dec. 1, 1928), 14, 20–21; GV and René de la Porte, "De Narbonne," CB, no. 17 (June 1, 1929), 4–5; "Echos," CB, no. 32 (Oct. 19, 1929), 26; GV, "Commentaires," CB, no. 50 (Feb. 22, 1930), 28; GV, "Commentaires," CB, no. 51 (Mar. 1, 1930), 23–28; GV, "Observations," CB, no. 115 (Sept. 12, 1931), 5–9.

8. Basil Dmytryshyn, USSR: A Concise History (New York: Charles Scribner's Sons, 1984), 180–81.

9. GV, "Commentaires," CB, no. 83 (Dec. 6, 1930), 27; Bernard Savigny, "Explication," with "Avant-Propos" by GV, CB, no. 90 (Jan. 24, 1931), 3–25; GV, "Observations," CB, no. 115 (Sept. 12, 1931), 3–18. See chapter 6.

10. "Passé," CB, no. 117 (Dec. 25, 1931), 12–13.

11. "La Politique," CB, no. 110 (June 20, 1931), 29–31; GV, "La Politique," CB, no. 112 (July 11–18, 1931), 3–7, 13–30; GV, "Commentaires," CB, no. 114 (Aug. 22, 1931), 24–29; "Passé," CB, 6–7, 12–15.

12. See, e.g., Berstein, Histoire du parti radical, vol. 2, Crise du radicalisme, 80–93, 103.

13. GV, "Chantiers," CB, no. 1 (Aug. 15 [?], 1928), 9; GV, "A longueur," CB, no. 6 (Dec. 1, 1928), 14–17, 21–26; GV and de la Porte, "De Narbonne," 12–13; GV, "La Révolution," CB, no. 34 (Nov. 2, 1929), 8–13.

14. GV, "La Révolution," CB, no. 34 (Nov. 2, 1929), 2–26; GV, "Le Néo-Fascisme," NA, Nov. 3, 1938; GV, Technique, 26; Berstein, Crise du radicalisme, 94–125.

15. Pierre Dominique, La Révolution créatrice (LV, 1928); GV, "Chantiers," CB, no. 1 (Aug. 15 [?], 1928), 1–10; Jean Luchaire, "Vers les," CB, no. 28 (Aug. 31, 1929); "La Querelle," CB, no. 12 (Apr. 27, 1929), 3–26; "Commentaires," CB, no. 57 (Apr. 12, 1930), 3–23; "Les Leçons," CB, no. 71 (July 26, 1930). Bertrand de Jouvenel, L'Economie dirigée: Le Programme de la nouvelle génération (LV, 1928); id., Vers les états-unis d'Europe (LV, 1930); id., Vie de Zola (LV, 1931); id., "Un Plan," CB, no. 99 (Mar. 28, 1931); and Un Voyageur dans le siècle, written with Jeannie Malige (Robert Laffont, 1979), 80–81. Berstein, Crise du radicalisme, 95.

16. De Jouvenel, Voyageur, entire and 82; Wohl, Generation of 1914, 33–35; Burrin, Dérive fasciste, 194, 407; GV, "Echos," Ch, Mar. 20, 1934; GV, "Guerre," NA, June 30, 1936.

17. Gaston Riou, Europe, ma patrie (LV, 1928); Riou, "Sur les Cahiers," CB, no. 37 (Nov. 23, 1929), 2; GV, Gaston Riou et al., "Chantiers," CB, no. 81 (Nov. 22, 1930), 3–8; GV, "Lever," CB, no. 26 (Aug. 3, 1929), 23–24; GV, "Commentaires," CB, no. 80 (Nov. 15, 1930), 21; Pierre Mendès-France, "La Banque," CB, no. 37 (Nov. 23, 1929), 3–20; "Esquisse," CB, no. 116 (Sept. 17–24, 1931).

18. GV, "Commentaires," CB, no. 107 (May 23, 1931), 28; Berstein, Crise du radicalisme, 164–67. Berstein states that in 1929 Valois subsidized La Volonté and sought to enter the Radical party (p. 119). These claims, which are supported by a single "note" in AN (F^7 13193; see Crise du radicalisme, 614), are subject to caution. That Valois flirted with joining the Radicals is possible. Any more serious gesture (and its putative rejection) would have provoked some trace in his many accounts of these years. Valois did collaborate with the editor of La Volonté in 1927 and 1928, but at this time, and in 1929, when he was desperately trying to gather funds for a new daily and successfully transform the Librairie, it is difficult to

imagine where he would have gotten the 300,000 francs mentioned in the note cited by Berstein.

19. GV, "Chantiers," *CB*, no. 1 (Aug. [15?], 1928), 10–14; GV and de la Porte, "De Narbonne," 13; GV, "La Révolution," *CB*, no. 34 (Nov. 2, 1929), 10–12; GV, "Echos," *CB*, no. 38 (Nov. 30, 1929), 25–26. GV, "Commentaires," *CB*: no. 40 (Dec. 14, 1929), 27; no. 45 (Jan. 18, 1930), 29–31; no. 48 (Feb. 8, 1930), 18–20.

20. "Echos," *CB*, no. 35 (Nov. 9, 1929), 22–23; GV, "Echos," *CB*, no. 38 (Nov. 30, 1929), 25; GV, "Commentaires," *CB*, no. 48 (Feb. 8, 1930), 18–21; GV, "Commentaires," *CB*, no. 49 (Feb. 15, 1930), 31; "Echos," *CB*, no. 53 (Mar. 15, 1930), 31; "Echos," *CB*, no. 82 (Nov. 29, 1930), 24; "Esquisse," *CB*, no. 116 (Sept. 17–24, 1931), 3, 22; *Ch*, May 1932; GV, "Revue," *NA*, Oct. 27, 1937; Marcel Déat, *Perspectives socialistes* (LV, 1930); id., *Mémoires politiques* (Denoël, 1989), 207, 234–36.

21. See Burrin, *Dérive*; Berstein, *Crise du radicalisme*, 94–95, 119–22.

22. Georges Lefranc et al., *Révolution constructive* (LV, 1932); Georges Lefranc, *Le Mouvement socialiste sous la Troisième République* (Payot, 1963).

23. Personal communication, Henry Poulaille, Mar. 25, 1975.

24. Personal communications, Henry Poulaille, Mar. 25 and Apr. 8, 1975; PP/ HP, correspondence, Valois to Poulaille; Dec. 30, 1929, Jan. 2, 1933; Poulaille, "Charles-Louis Philippe," *CB*, no. 55 (Mar. 29, 1930); Henry Poulaille, *Un Nouvel Age littéraire* (LV, 1930).

25. Poulaille, *Nouvel Age*; Poulaille, "Charles-Louis Philippe"; "Echos," *CB*, no. 106 (May 16, 1931,) 25–26; Lucien Jean, *Parmi les hommes* (Mercure de France, 1910); Charles-Louis Philippe, *Bubu de Montparnasse* (Garnier-Flammarion, 1978). See Allen Douglas, "Literature, Proletarian," in Patrick H. Hutton, ed., *Historical Dictionary of the Third French Republic* (New York: Greenwood Press, 1986), 1:573–75; Poulaille, *Nouvel Age*; Michel Ragon, *Histoire de la littérature prolétarienne* (1974); J.-P. A. Bernard, *Le Parti communiste français et la question littéraire* (Grenoble: Presses universitaires de Grenoble, 1972).

26. Personal communication, Henry Poulaille, Mar. 25, 1975. PP/HP, personal correspondence: Valois to Poulaille, Dec. 30, 1929; Valois to Floch, Dec. 8, 1930. GV, "Images," *CB*, no. 88 (Jan. 10, 1931); GV, *Journée d'Europe* (LV, 1932).

27. Personal communication, Henry Poulaille, Mar. 25, 1975; PP/HP, personal correspondence, Valois to Poulaille, Jan. 2, 1933; GV, "Episodes," *La Coopération culturelle*, Mar. 10, 1929, 15–16.

28. Personal communications, Henry Poulaille, Mar. 25, 1975, and Apr. 8, 1975; PP/HP Valois to Poulaille, Jan. 2, 1933; GV, "Le 'Cas Valois,' " *NA*, Sept. 20–27, 1936.

29. "Activité," *CB*, no. 1 (Aug. 15 [?], 1928), 25–26; "Dans l'édition," *CB*, no. 31 (Oct. 12, 1929), 31; "Note," *CB*, no. 34 (Nov. 2, 1929), 31; "Echos," *CB*, no. 37 (Nov. 23, 1929), 23–24; GV, "Commentaires," *CB*, no. 75 (Oct. 11, 1930); GV, "Considérations," *CB*, no. 113 (July 25–Aug. 1, 1931), 22–25; Andreu, *Le Rouge et le blanc*, 90–92.

30. "Activité," *CB*, no. 1 (Aug. [15?], 1928), 27; "Le P.R.S.," *CB*, no. 3 (Oct. 15, 1928), 27–28; C. E. Duguet, "Une Campagne," *CB*, no. 4 (Nov. 1, 1928), 23–25; "Echos," *CB*, no. 20 (June 22, 1929), 28; GV, "A longueur," *CB*, no. 6 (Dec.

1, 1928), 26; Paul Aubery, "Enquête," *CB*, no. 7 (Dec. [1928?]); Regley, "Les Clubs," *CB*, no. 8 (Jan. 15, 1929), 18; Dominique, "La Querelle," *CB*, no. 12 (Apr. 27, 1929), 3–26; GV, "Coeur," *CB*, no. 29 (Sept. 28, 1929), 18–21; "Les 'Nouvelles,' " *CB*, no. 37 (Nov. 23, 1929), 21–22.

31. "Le P.R.S.," *CB*, no. 3 (Oct. 15, 1928), 28–29; "L'Activité," *CB*, no. 6 (Dec. 1, 1928), 29.

32. GV et al., "Une Grande," *CB*, no. 3 (Oct. 15, 1928); GV, *Technique*, 239–42.

33. "Société de valorisation," and "Société immobilière," *CB*, no. 72 (Aug. 2, 1930), 27–29; GV, "Une Méthode," *CB*, no. 73 (Aug. 9, 1930).

34. "Société immobilière," 28–29; GV, "Episodes," *La Coopération culturelle*, July 1938, 6–17; Burrin, *Dérive*, 406.

35. GV, "Commentaires," *CB*, no. 74 (Oct. 4, 1930), 25; "Echos," *CB*, no. 84 (Dec. 13, 1930), 22; Sammy Beracha, "Etudes," *CB*, no. 86 (Dec. 27, 1930).

36. GV et al., "Une Grande," *CB*, no. 3 (Oct. 15, 1928); Beracha, "Etudes," 15–17.

37. "Saint-Gaudens," *CB*, no. 108 (May 30–June 6, 1931), 26.

38. GV, "Commentaires," in *CB*: no. 74 (Oct. 4, 1930), 22–24, and no. 75 (Oct. 11, 1930), 20–22; "Passé," *CB*, no. 117 (Dec. 25, 1931), 11.

39. GV, "Commentaires," in *CB*: no. 91 (Jan. 31, 1931), 18–19; no. 100 (Apr. 5, 1931), 25–28; and no. 104 (May 2, 1931), 28–30. GV, "Voyages," *CB*, no. 108 (May 30–June 6, 1931), 3–22; GV, "Episodes," *La Coopération culturelle*, July 1938, 15–16; PP/GV, Carton No. 2, Dossier "Affaire Banque des coopératives," note of July 28, 1933, and Dossier "Valois—Verguin," note "Affaires Verguin—Valois."

40. "Passé," *CB*, no. 117 (Dec. 25, 1931), 11–13; GV, "Episodes," *La Coopération culturelle*, July 1938, 16–21; PP/GV, Carton No. 2, Dossier "Valois—Verguin," which includes a balance sheet for the Real Estate and Tourist Society dated Dec. 31, 1932.

41. "Echos," *CB*, no. 71 (July 26, 1930), 30; GV, "Commentaires," *CB*, no. 77 (Oct. 25, 1930), 25. On the responsibility of the plutocrats, see, e.g., "Passé," *CB*, no. 117 (Dec. 25, 1931); Beracha, "Etude," *CB*, no. 86 (Dec. 27, 1930), 25.

42. GV, *Technique*, 24–26, 112–13; GV, "Le 'Cas Valois,' " *NA* Sept. 20–27, 1936, 3–4, 7–10; GV, *L'Homme contre*.

43. GV, *Un Nouvel Age de l'humanité* (LV, 1931); GV, "Commentaires," *CB*, no. 91 (Jan. 31, 1931), 18–19; GV, *Guerre ou révolution*, 216; GV, *Economique* (LV, 1931), 170.

44. GV, *Nouvel Age*, 20.

45. Ibid., 15–16, 27–29; GV, *Guerre ou révolution*, 33.

46. Ibid., 19–24, 56–57.

47. Ibid., 36–38, 45–49.

48. Ibid., 47–53, 65, 70–71, 87–97.

49. Ibid., 101, 106–8, 118–19.

50. Ibid., 69, 73–78, 119–20, 133–41; GV, "Commentaires," *CB*, no. 41 (Dec. 21, 1929), 13–15; GV, *Journée*.

51. GV, *Nouvel Age*, 53–54; GV, "Echos," *CB*, no. 39 (Dec. 7, 1929), 25–26; GV, "Revue," *NA*, Feb. 16, 1938, 2; Kuisel, *Capitalism and the State*, 84–92, 105–7; Kuisel, *Mercier*.

52. GV, *Nouvel Age*, 79, 150–65.

53. Ibid., 170; Kuisel, *Capitalism and State*, 82–83; E. H. Goodman, "The Socialism of Marcel Déat" (Ph.D. thesis, Stanford University, 1973), 272–73.

54. GV, *Nouvel Age*, 65–66.

55. GV, *Guerre ou révolution*, 43–46.

56. Ibid., 17–19; GV, "Commentaires," *CB*, no. 64 (June 7, 1930), 19–20; GV, "Commentaires," *CB*, no. 77 (Oct. 25, 1930), 20; René Quinton, *Maximes sur la guerre* (Grasset, 1930).

57. GV, *Guerre ou révolution*, 47–49, 52–55, 71–73, 89–102, 119–21, 131, 133, 145.

58. Ibid., 75–87.

59. Ibid., 10–14, 23, 56–59, 60–63; GV, "Commentaires," *CB*, no. 64 (June 7, 1930), 21.

60. GV, *Guerre ou révolution*, 28–29, 37, 115–19, 138–60, 208–9.

61. Ibid., 138–40, 158–59; "Documents," *CB*, no. 65 (June 14, 1930); GV, "Commentaires," *CB*, no. 68 (July 5, 1930), 21–22; GV, "Commentaires," *CB*, no. 114 (Aug. 22, 1931), 27–29. Cf. the discussions in "Documents," *CB*, no. 65 (June 14, 1930).

62. GV, "Images," *CB*, no. 88 (Jan. 10, 1931), 28; GV, *Guerre ou révolution*, 63–64, 161–69, 214–15.

63. GV, *Guerre ou révolution*, 16, 65–71, 176–89.

64. GV, *Economique*, 24–27, 48–49, 93–95.

65. GV, *L'Homme qui vient*, 35–36; GV and François Renié, *Les Manuels scolaires*; GV, *Economique*, 25–26; Bergson, *L'Evolution créatrice*.

66. GV, *Economique*, 23–25, 115, 124–25. The argument was closer to Kropotkin in both its biologism and its optimism than to Sorel, Kropotkine, *Oeuvres*, 50; Clark, *Social Darwinism*, 88.

67. GV, *Economique*, 42–44, 115–23.

68. Ibid., 117, 120–24.

69. Ibid., 29, 39.

70. Ibid., 48–49, 115, 125–26, 135–43.

71. Ibid., 152–57.

72. Ibid., 127–34.

73. See, e.g., ibid., 163.

8. EVERYTHING IS POSSIBLE

1. GV, "Commentaires," *CB*, no. 61 (May 10–17, 1930), 24.

2. *NA*, July 15–16, 1936; Antoine Prost, "Les Grèves de Juin 1936," in Pierre Renouvin and René Rémond, eds., *Léon Blum, chef de gouvernement* (Presses de la Fondation nationale des sciences politiques, 1981), 75, and 178–80 for Pivert's famous article of this title; Jacques Delpierrie de Bayac, *Histoire du Front populaire* (Fayard, 1972), 229ff.

3. See, e.g., Jacques Kergoat, *Le Parti socialiste de la Commune à nos jours* (Le Sycamore, 1983), 117–46.

4. "Esquisse," *CB*, no. 116 (Sept. 17–24, 1931); *Ch*, May 1932; GV, "Chantiers," *Ch*, July 1932; *Ch*, Jan. 7–14, 1933.

5. GV, "La Nouvelle," *Ch*, June 1932, and July 1932; GV, "Chantiers," *Ch*, July 1932; GV, "Plan," *Ch*, Jan. 7–14, 1933, 1; GV, "La Coopération," *Ch*, Jan. 15, 1934.

6. "Déclaration," *Ch*, numéro spécial (n.d. [1932?]); GV, "Episodes," *La Coopération culturelle* (= *NA*), July 1938.

7. "Organisation," *Ch*, May 1932; "Nouvelles," *Ch*, June 1932; GV, "Chantiers," *Ch*, July 1932; "F.N.C.C.O.," *NA*, July 19, 1934; "Un Episode," *NA*, July 26–Aug. 2, 1934; GV, "Le Plan," and Diamant-Berger, "La Nouvelle," *Ch*, Jan. 7–14, 1933; *Ch*, Mar. 8, 1933; "F.N.C.C.O.," *NA*, July 19, 1934; "Un Episode," *NA*, July 26–Aug. 2, 1934; "Documents," *NA*, July 26–Aug. 2, 1934; GV, "Episodes," *La Coopération culturelle* (= *NA*), July 1938; GV, *Basile*, 234–43.

8. "F.N.C.C.O.," *NA*, July 19, 1934; "Un Episode," *NA*, July 26–Aug. 2, 1934; "Batailles," *NA*, Sept. 27, 1934; "Manoeuvres," *NA*, Apr. 13–20, 1935; GV, "Le 'Cas Valois,' " *NA*, Sept. 1936; "Episodes," *La Coopération culturelle* (= *NA*), July 1938.

9. "Les Collaborateurs" and "Situation," *Ch*, May 1932; *Ch*, Jan. 21–28, 1933, GV, "Ce que" and "Chantiers," *Ch*, July 1932; Kuisel, *Capitalism and the State*, 105–7. Rodrigues's passionate teaching failed to impress one of his more famous students, Claude Lévi-Strauss (*Tristes tropiques* [Plon, 1984], 52).

10. GV, *Guerre ou révolution*, 144–45, 216; GV, *Economique*, 152–55; GV, Nouvel Age, 179–87; GV, "Pour," *Ch*, May 15, 1933. See chapters 6 and 7.

11. GV, "Plan," *Ch*, Jan. 7–14, 1933; GV, "Pour," *Ch*, May 15, 1933; GV, "Les Deux"; GV, "Sur notre," *Ch*, June 15, 1933. See also chapter 6.

12. *Ch*, May 9, 1934; *NA*, June 1, 1934; "César Chambrun," *NA*, Nov. 15, 1934; "La Liberté," *NA*, June 7, 1934; "Création," *NA*, June 7, 1934; "Une Agression," *NA*, Sept. 4, 1935. Six of thirteen SCANA board members were professors, "Pour," *NA*, June 14–21, 1934.

13. GV, "Nécessité," *NA*, June 1, 1934; GV, "La Calomnie," *NA*, Dec. 8, 1936.

14. *Ch*, May 9, 1934; "Nécessité," *NA*, June 1, 1934; "*Nouvel Age*," *NA*, June 1936.

15. "Propagande," *NA*, Jan. 31–Feb. 7, 1935; GV, "Le Trust," *NA*, Nov. 1–15, 1936; GV, "Le Trust," *NA*, June 2, 1937; GV, "La Vente," *NA*, July 23, 1937; GV, "La Vente," *NA*, July 24, 1937.

16. "Nous cherchons," *NA*, June 28, 1938; "Le Dîner," *NA*, Dec. 20, 1938; personal interview, Philippe Gressent-Valois, July 18, 1987.

17. "Lettre," *NA*, July 25, 1935; "Pour," *NA*, Apr. 25, 1937; GV, "Lettre," *NA*, Oct. 2, 1937; "Nous cherchons," *NA*, June 28, 1938; "Nos journées," *NA*, Oct. 20, 1938; GV, "Notre coopération," *NA*, Nov. 24, 1938.

18. "Technique," *NA*, June 1, 1934; *NA*, Oct. 22–24, 1938.

19. César Chambrun, "3ᵉ semaine," *Ch*, May 25, 1933; "Troisième semaine," *Ch*, June 15, 1933; GV, "Les Semaines," *NA*, Sept. 4, 1935; GV, "Enfin," *NA*, May 10, 1938. On the first two semaines, see chapters 3 and 6.

20. "Troisième semaine," *NA*, June 15, 1933.

21. GV, *Technique*, 78–84; "Le Plan," *NA*, Feb. 1936; GV, "La Commune," *NA*, Feb. 28, 1937; GV, "Etatisme," *NA*, July 7, 1937; "La Nouvelle," *NA*, Sept. 10–16, 1938.

22. GV, *Technique*, 19, 47, 77–100.

23. GV, *Nouvel Age*, 70–71; GV, *Technique*, 93–100; "Le Plan," *NA*, Feb. 1936; GV, "La Commune," *NA*, Feb. 28, 1937.

24. GV, "L'Avenir," *NA*, Apr. 27–28, 1938; GV, "Le Nouvel," in *NA*, Dec. 5 and 6, 1938; Dec. 21, 1938; *NA*, Jan. 25, 1939.

25. GV, "Problèmes," *NA*, June 28, 1938; GV, "Problèmes," *NA*, June 30, 1938; GV, "Problèmes," *NA*, July 1, 1938; GV, "Notre action," *NA*, Feb. 2, 1939, Feb. 10, 1939.

26. See, e.g., "Esquisse," *NA*, July 25–Aug. 1, 1931.

27. Gustave Rodrigues, *L'Unique Solution du problème social: Le Droit à la vie* (Editions liberté, 1934); "Le Plan," *NA*, Feb. 1936.

28. GV, "Révision," in *NA*, Dec. 9, 1937, and Dec. 10, 1937.

29. "La Coopération," *Ch*, Jan. 15, 1934; "Le Plan," *NA*, Feb. 1936; GV, "La Commune," *NA*, Feb. 28, 1937.

30. GV, *Technique*, 93–94, 119–23; GV, "Lettre," *NA*, Oct. 17, 1935; *NA*, Sept. 10–16, 1938; Paul Lafargue, *Le Droit à la paresse* (Maspéro, 1982).

31. Jacques Duboin, *Ce qu'on appelle la crise* (Les Editions nouvelles, 1934); Groupe Dynamo, *Pauvre Français . . . ! Introduction au recensement des richesses de la France* (Editions Fustier, 1936), 7–24; GV, "Revue," *NA*, Jan. 23, 1936; "Le Plan," *NA*, Feb. 1936; "A côté," *NA*, June 28–29, 1936; GV, "Revue," Dec. 12, 1936; GV, "Revue," *NA*, Dec. 18, 1936; GV, "Revue," *NA*, May 11, 1937; GV, "Revue," *NA*, May 12, 1937; GV, "L'Erreur," *NA*, May 19, 1937; GV, "Pour mettre," *NA*, May 20–22, 1939; personal interview, Roger Maria, July 22, 1987.

32. "Le Plan," *NA*, Feb. 1936; "Déclaration," *NA*, Apr. 3–10, 1936; "A côté," *NA*, June 28–29, 1936; Rozner, "Une Grande," *NA*, June 30, 1936; "La Constitution," *NA*, July 10, 1936; PP/GV, Carton No. 1, Dossier "Valois—Duboin correspondance."

33. GV, "Revue," *NA*, Dec. 12, 1936; GV, "L'Agression," *NA*, May 4, 1937; GV, "Revue," *NA*, May 5, 1937; GV, "Revue," *NA*, May 11, 1937; GV, "Note," *NA*, May 29, 1937; GV, "Le Plan," *NA*, May 25, 1939; GV, "Revue," *NA*, June 7, 1939; Rozner, "Nous demandons," *NA*, Nov. 19, 1936; GV, "Revue," *NA*, Dec. 18, 1936; GV, "La Commune," *NA*, Feb. 28, 1937; "Questions," and GV, "Il faut," *NA*, Apr. 11, 1937; "Ce qu'a," *NA*, May 1, 1937; GV, "Pour mettre," *NA*, May 20–22, 1939, May 23, 1939, May 24, 1939, May 25, 1939; "Front," and GV, "Revue," *NA*, May 27–June 5, 1939; Jacques Duboin, *En route vers l'abondance* (Editions Fustier, 1935), 127–40; PP/GV, Carton No. 1, Dossier "Valois—Duboin correspondance," and Carton No. 2, Dossier "Duboin."

34. "Echos," *Ch*, Mar. 1, 1934.

35. GV, "Nous accusons," *Ch*, Feb. 11, 1934; also in GV, *Technique*, 160–77.

36. GV, "La Révolution," *NA*, Jan. 24, 1935; "Sur les préparatifs," *NA*, March [3?], 1936; "Vers la," *NA*, Feb. 12, 1936; GV, "Le Dilemme," *NA*, May 7, 1936; Renzo de Felice, *Interpretations of Fascism*, translated by Brenda Huff Everett (Cambridge, Mass.: Harvard University Press, 1977).

37. GV, "A propos," *NA*, July 3, 1936; GV, "Revue," *NA*, July 12, 1938.

38. GV, *Technique*, 17–42, 162–63; "Conférences," *Ch*, Mar. 28, 1934; "Cinquième," *Ch*, Apr. 18, 1934; "Explications," *Ch*, May 30, 1934; "FNCCO,"

NA, July 19, 1934; GV, "Contre," *Ch*, Mar. 28, 1934, 1; GV, "Dénonciation" and "Opinions," *NA*, June 7, 1934; *La Table ronde*, Jan. 1, 1934, and Feb. 1, 1934.

39. GV, *Technique*, 38–39, 162–63, 177–91; "FNCCO," *NA*, July 19, 1934.

40. "A bas," *Ch*, Mar. 11, 1934; "Pour les Etats-Généraux," *NA*, Oct. 4, 1934; "Devant," *NA*, Oct. 11, 1934; "Décisions," *NA*, Oct. 18–25, 1934; "Nos objectifs," *NA*, Autumn 1934; "Vers les," *NA*, Nov. 1, 1934; Rodriques, "Tous pour," *NA*, Nov. 22, 1934.

41. "Les Anciens," *Ch*, March 28, 1934; "Motion," *Ch*, Apr. 18, 1934; Antoine Prost, *Les Anciens Combattants et la société française* (Presses de la Fondation nationale des sciences politiques, 1977), 1:159–76.

42. GV, *Technique*, 161, 170, 173, 177; "A bas," *Ch*, Mar. 1, 1934; GV, "Un Des," *Ch*, Mar. 20, 1934; GV, "La Nouvelle," *Ch*, Mar. 20, 1934; "Attention," *Ch*, Mar. 28, 1934; Gustave Rodrigues, "Les A.C.," André Saint-Lagué, "Que sont?" and GV, "Appel," *Ch*, Apr. 18, 1934; GV, "Opinions," *NA*, June 7, 1934; "Aux," *NA*, July 5, 1934; GV, "Explications," and "Congrès," *Ch*, May 30, 1934.

43. "Appel," and GV, "Congrès," *Ch*, May 30, 1934, "Création," *NA*, June 7, 1934; "FNCCO," *NA*, June 14–21, 1934; "Nous dénonçons," *NA*, July 5, 1934; "Dégonflage," *NA*, July 12, 1934; GV, "Revue," *NA*, Sept. 6, 1934.

44. GV, *Technique*, 239–305; GV, "Chantiers," *Ch*, July 1932; GV, "Le Plan," *Ch*, Jan. 7–14, 1933; "Le Plan," *Ch*, Mar. 1, 1934; "Le Plan," *Ch*, Mar. 20, 1934; See also, Sternhell, *Ni Droite*, 136–232.

45. "L'Echéance," *NA*, Sept. 6, 1934; GV, "Revue," *NA*, Sept. 6, 1934; "Un Nouveau," *NA*, Sept. 13, 1934; "Préparation," *NA*, Sept. 27, 1934; "A propos," *NA*, Sept. 27, 1934; "A bas," *NA*, Dec. 13, 1934; Kuisel, *Capitalism and the State*, 100–102.

46. GV, "Revue," *NA*, Nov. 29, 1934; GV, "Le Piège," *NA*, Dec. 6, 1934.

47. GV, *Technique*, 124–28; GV, "Revue," *NA*, Nov. 29, 1934; "A bas," *NA*, Dec. 13, 1934; GV, "Fin," *NA*, Dec. 13, 1934; "Objectifs," GV, "Revue" and "Fin," *NA*, Dec. 20, 1934; "Socialisme," *NA*, Jan. 10, 1934; GV, "Socialisme," *NA*, Feb. 21, 1935.

48. "Flandin," *NA*, Dec. 6, 1934; "Alerte," *NA*, Jan. 31–Feb. 7, 1934; "Devant," *NA*, Jan. 31–Feb. 7, 1934.

49. "Explications," *Ch*, May 30, 1934; Rodrigues, "L'Echec," and GV, "Revue," *NA*, Jan. 17, 1935; "Le Plan," *NA*, Jan. 31–Feb. 7, 1935; "Nos résultats," *NA*, Feb. 14, 1935; "Une Décision," *NA*, Feb. 21, 1935.

50. GV, "Réflexions," *Ch*, Apr. 25, 1934; GV, "Dans la coopération," *Ch*, May 2, 1934; GV, "Revue" *NA*, Jan. 24, 1935; PP/GV, Carton No. 2, Dossier "Affaire Banque des coopératives."

51. "Aux coopérateurs," *NA*, Nov. 15, 1934; "Tribune," *NA*, Dec. 6, 1934; GV, "La Question," *NA*, Dec. 20, 1934; "Déclaration," *NA*, Jan. 10, 1935; GV, "Revue," *NA*, Jan. 17, 1935; GV, "Sur les relations" and "Revue," *NA*, Jan. 24, 1935; GV, "Nouvelles" and "Les Mystères,"*NA*, Mar. 14, 1935; GV, "Le Scandale," *NA*, Mar. 21, 1935; *NA*, Apr. 4, 1935; "Manoeuvres," *NA*, Apr. 13–20, 1935; GV, "Epuration," *NA*, May 2, 1935; "Ernest Poisson," *NA*, May 9, 1935; "Dans la," *NA*, May 23, 1935; GV, "La Coopération," *NA*, June 6–13, 1935; GV,

"Autour," *NA*, June 6–13, 1935; PP/GV, Carton No. 2, Dossiers "Affaire Banque des coopératives" and "Avalistes de la Banque des coopératives."

52. GV, "A la mobilisation" and "Avis," *NA*, June 28, 1934; "Devant," *NA*, Sept. 6, 1934; "Pour la troisième," *NA*, Sept. 20, 1934; "Valois," *NA*, Nov. 22, 1934; "Valois," *NA*, Nov. 29, 1934; "Informations," *NA*, Jan. 10, 1935; GV, "Devant," *NA*, Mar. 28, 1935.

53. See, e.g., Nicolas Faucier, *Pacifisme et anti-militarisme dans l'entre-deux-guerres* (Spartacus, 1983), 147–48; Danielle Tartakowsky, "La SFIO et le fascisme dans les années trente," *L'internazionale operaia e socialista tra le due guerra: Annali fondazione Giangiacomo Feltrinelli*, 1983–84), 738–43.

54. GV, *Technique*, 70–74, 84–91; GV, "Chantiers," *Ch*, July 1932; GV, "Où se trouve" and "Revue," *NA*, May 16, 1935; "La Révolution," *NA*, May 23, 1935; GV, "Revue," *NA*, June 19, 1936; Rodrigues, "Une Disciple," *NA*, July 18, 1936; "Le Crime" and "L'Expérience," *NA*, Sept. 13–20, 1936; GV, "Le 'Cas Valois,' " *NA*, Sept. 20–27, 1936; GV, "Revue," *NA*, Dec. 19, 1936; Rodrigues, "U.R.S.S.," *NA*, Jan. 28, 1937.

55. GV, "De Moscou," *NA*, June 20, 1935; "Documents," *NA*, June 20, 1935; Faucier, *Pacifisme*, 109–14. See, e.g., Robert Louzon, Introduction to Georges Sorel, *Lettres à Paul Delesalle* (Grasset, 1947), 9–78; Burrin, *Dérive*, 178–85; Roth, *Cult*, 215–17.

56. "Documents," *NA*, June 20, 1935; GV, "Les Semaines," *NA*, Sept. 4, 1935; "Une Agression," *NA*, Sept. 4, 1935; "Le 'Cas Valois,' " *NA*, Sept. 26, 1935; GV, "Le Cas," *NA*, Oct. [10?], 1935; GV, "Jacques Doriot," *NA*, Oct. 24, 1935; Louis Loréal, "Un Fiasco lamentable," *La Patrie humaine*, Aug. 23, 1935; "La Conférence," *Le Libertaire*, July 1935; Maîtron, *Dictionnaire*, 22:220–31. See also Faucier, *Pacifisme*, 113–14.

57. "Une Agression," *NA*, Sept. 4, 1935; GV, "Le 'Cas Valois,' " *NA*, Sept. 26, 1935.

58. "Valois," *NA*, Oct. [10 ?], 1935; GV, "Lettre," *NA*, Oct. 17, 1935; "Sur le 'cas Valois,' " *NA*, Dec. 21, 1935.

59. "La Bureaucratie," *NA*, Nov. 16, 1937; Rodrigues, "Je suis," *NA*, Nov. 18, 1937.

60. "Le 'Front,' " *NA*, June 27, 1935; "Où ira," *NA*, July 14, 1935; "Sur la," *NA*, July 14, 1935.

61. *NA*, Nov. 7–11, 1935.

62. "Tactique," *NA*, June 6–13, 1935; GV, "De Moscou," *NA*, June 20, 1935; "Où ira" and "Sur la," *NA*, July 14, 1935; GV, "Informations," *NA*, Aug. 2, 1935; "Vous et nous," *NA*, Oct. 24, 1935; GV, "Revue" and "A qui," *NA*, Nov. 7–11, 1935; GV, "Les banques," *NA*, Nov. 21, 1935; GV, "Nous," *NA*, Dec. 5, 1935; GV, "Le Coup," *NA*, Dec. 12, 1935. Valois's early devaluation was proposed to the Blum government by both Raymond Pâtrenotre and René Belin. See Delpierrie de Bayac, *Histoire*, 207, and Pierre Miquel, *Histoire de France* (Marabout, 1976), 204, who suggests that Blum's error in not devaluing immediately was fatal.

63. GV, "Le Dilemme," *NA*, May 7, 1936; "La Révolution," GV, "Comment" and "Revue," *NA*, June 18, 1936; "Réflexions," *NA*, June 20, 1936.

64. "Lettre," *NA*, June 1–15, 1936; headline, *NA*, July 15–16, 1936.

65. "Lettre," *NA*, June 1–15, 1936; GV, "Les Finances," *NA*, June 21, 1936; GV, "Revue," *NA*, June 21, 1936.

66. GV, "Les Finances," *NA*, June 21, 1936; GV, "La Dévaluation," *NA*, Oct. 4–11, 1936.

67. GV, "La Dévaluation," *NA*, Oct. 4–11, 1936.

68. Rodrigues, "Casse-cou," *NA*, June 28–29, 1936.

69. See, e.g., Pierre Renouvin, "La Politique extérieure du premier gouvernement Léon Blum," in Renouvin and Rémond, *Blum*, 330–38.

70. "Lettre," *NA*, June 1–15, 1936; "Contre," and GV, "Revue," *NA*, August 2–16, 1936; "Pour l'Espagne," *NA*, Aug. 16–23, 1936; GV, "L'Heure," *NA*, Dec. 10, 1936; GV, "Le Salut," *NA*, Dec. 15, 1936; Faucier, *Pacifisme*, 125–27.

71. See, e.g., Delpierrie de Bayac, *Histoire*, 341–44.

72. GV, "Le Trust," and Rodrigues, "Leur presse," *NA*, Nov. 1–15, 1936; GV, "Revue," *NA*, Nov. 11, 1936.

73. Headline, *NA*, Nov. 11, 1936; "Le Premier," *NA*, Nov. 11, 1936; GV, "Revue," *NA*, Nov. 11, 1936; Maurice Barrès, *Leurs figures*, in *Oeuvre*, 4:326–40.

74. GV, "Revue," *NA*, Nov. 19, 1936; GV, "L'Organisation," *NA*, Nov. 20, 1936; GV, "Revue," *NA*, Nov. 20, 1936; Rodrigues, "Lettre," *NA*, Nov. 21, 1936; GV, "Léon Blum," *NA*, Nov. 24, 1936; "Contre," *NA*, Nov. 24, 1936; GV, "Lettre," *NA*, Nov. 24, 1936; GV, "Revue," *NA*, Nov. 27, 1936; "La Lutte," *NA*, Dec. 2, 1936; Rodrigues, "Contre," *NA*, Dec. 2, 1936.

75. "Nos numéros," *NA*, Nov. 19, 1936; GV, "Double," *NA*, Nov. 26, 1936.

76. GV, "La Dévaluation," *NA*, Oct. 4–11, 1936.

77. "Les Ententes," and GV, "Le Fascisme," *NA*, Aug. 23–30, 1936; "La Rupture," GV, "Revue," and J.R. [Jacques Rozner], "La Nouvelle," *NA*, Nov. 28, 1936; "A nos," and Escat, "Une Loi," Nov. 29–30, 1936; GV, "La trahison" and "Revue," *NA*, Dec. 3, 1936; GV, "Organisez," *NA*, Dec. 4, 1936; "En plein," and GV, "Notre quotidien," *NA*, Dec. 5, 1936; GV, "Le Néo-capitalisme," *NA*, Dec. 13–14, 1936; "Contre," *NA*, Dec. 16, 1936; GV, "Comment," *NA*, Dec. 18, 1936; GV, "L'Affaire" and "Revue," *NA*, Dec. 22, 1936.

78. GV, "Malentendus," *NA*, Nov. 29–30, 1936; GV, "Pour le mouvement," *NA*, Dec. 1, 1936; GV, "La Trahison," *NA*, Dec. 3, 1936; GV, "Organisez," *NA*, Dec. 4, 1936; GV, "Comment opérer," *NA*, Dec. 18, 1936; GV, "Bilans," *NA*, Dec. 24, 1936; GV, "Lettre," *NA*, Feb. 14, 1937; GV, "Explication," *NA*, Feb. 21, 1937.

79. GV and Rodrigues, "Le Coup," *NA*, Mar. 10, 1937; GV, "Le Sedan," *NA*, Mar. 10, 1937.

80. GV, "Explication," *NA*, Feb. 21, 1937; GV, "Le Sedan," *NA*, Mar. 10, 1937.

81. "Le Maître," *NA*, June 8, 1937; GV, "Revue," *NA*, June 8, 1937; GV, "La Chute," *NA*, June 9, 1937; GV, "Ce que," *NA*, June 9, 1937; GV, "Le Néo-fascisme," *NA*, June 10, 1937; GV, "Revue," *NA*, June 10, 1937; GV, "Le Drame," *NA*, June 11, 1937; GV, "Revue," *NA*, June 11, 1937; and headlines from the above; GV, "L'Abcès," *NA*, June 17, 1937.

82. Rodrigues, "La Révolution," *NA*, May 4, 1937; "Pour l'ordre," *NA*, May 4, 1937; "Pré-panique," *NA*, June 15, 1937; "A bas," and GV, "Revue," *NA*, June

16, 1937; "L'Accord," *NA*, June 17, 1937; headline, *NA*, June 19, 1937; "La Crise," and GV, "Fin," *NA*, June 22, 1937; editorial, *NA*, June 23, 1937.

9. WAR OR REVOLUTION

1. The term *totalitarian* was long used by Valois in a positive sense as equivalent to *integral*. GV, "Etatisme," *NA*, July 31, 1937; "La Pluie," *NA*, Mar. 3, 1938; "Un Régime," *NA*, Mar. 4, 1938; "Appel," *NA*, Sept. 10–16, 1938; GV, "Racisme," *NA*, Sept. 23–24, 1938; "Il Faut," *NA*, Oct. 27, 1938; Rodrigues, "Hitler," *NA*, Nov. 15, 1938; GV, "Le Problème," *NA*, Sept. 17, 1938 and Nov. 18, 1938.

2. GV, "Pour arrêter," *NA*, Nov. 5–6, 1937; GV, "Revue," *NA*, Nov. 9, 1937; GV, "Revue," *NA*, Nov. 16, 1937; "Grands," *NA*, May 14, 1937; "La Guerre," *NA*, July 7, 1937; GV, "La Guerre," *NA*, Sept. 4, 1937, 5–6; GV, "La Guerre," *NA*, Oct. 8, 1937; "De Versailles," *NA*, Oct. 28, 1937; GV, "Le Salut," *NA*, Dec. 15, 1936; "Faits," *NA*, Oct. 16, 1937; Roth, *Cult*, 128–38; GV, *Prométhée vainqueur, ou, Explication de la guerre* (Editions liberté, 1940), 61. See chapter 2.

3. GV, "Revue," *NA*, June 3, 1937; "Contre-révolution," *NA*, June 12, 1937; GV, "Revue," *NA*, June 15, 1937; GV, "La Guerre," *NA*, June 30, 1937; GV, "Revue," *NA*, July 8, 1937; GV, "Revue," *NA*, Oct. 14, 1937.

4. GV, "La Guerre," *NA*, June 26, 1937; GV, "Revue," *NA*, July 8, 1938.

5. GV, "Revue," *NA*, May 27, 1937; GV, "Opérations," *NA*, June 19, 1937; GV, "Revue," *NA*, June 22, 1937; "Finances," *NA*, June 30, 1937; GV, "Revue," *NA*, June 30, 1937; GV, "Faillite," *NA*, July 1, 1937; headline in *NA*, July 6, 1937; GV, "Le Plan," *NA*, July 23, 1937.

6. Headline, *NA*, July 22, 1937; GV, "La Banque," *NA*, Aug. 7, 1937; GV, "Revue," *NA*, Oct. 1–2, 1937; GV, "A propos," *NA*, Oct. 9, 1937; GV, "Le Roman," *NA*, Oct. 15, 1937; GV, "Mystères," *NA*, Oct. 16, 1937; GV, "Les Achats," *NA*, Oct. 20, 1937; GV, "Mystères," *NA*: Oct. 21, 1937, Oct. 22, 1937, Oct. 23, 1937; GV, "Défense," *NA*, Aug. 20–26, 1938; GV, "Revue," *NA*, Oct. 6, 1937; GV, "Le Contrôle," *NA*, Oct. 19, 1937; GV, "Plan," *NA*, Oct. 27, 1937; GV, "Complots," *NA*, Nov. 17, 1937; GV, "Staliniens," *NA*, Nov. 18, 1937; GV, "Le Complot," *NA*: Nov. 20, 1937, Nov. 23, 1937, Nov. 24, 1937.

7. Headline and GV, "L'Agonie," *NA*, Jan. 11, 1938; GV, "Nouvel," *NA*, Jan. 27, 1938; GV, "Bénéfices," *NA*, Feb. 3, 1938; "La Guerre," *NA*, May 6, 1938; GV, "La Vérité," *NA*, May 6, 1938; "Le Sort," *NA*, May 7–9, 1938; GV, "Revue," *NA*, June 30, 1938; "Inflation," *NA*, July 13, 1938; GV, "L'Inflation," *NA*, July 18, 1938; GV, "La Solution," *NA*, Nov. 11–14, 1938; GV, "Les Opérations," *NA*, Nov. 15, 1938; "Réflexions," *NA*, Nov. 16, 1938; GV, "Les Tonnes," *NA*, Mar. 11–13, 1939.

8. GV, "Lettre," *NA*, Dec. 13, 1938.

9. GV, "La Banque," *NA*, Aug. 7, 1937; GV, "Brève," *NA*, Sept. 15, 1937; GV, "Pour sortir," *NA*, Oct. 1–2, 1937; "Bons," *NA*, Oct. 12, 1937; GV, "Revue," *NA*, Oct. 26, 1937.

10. "Bons," *NA*, Oct. 12, 1937; GV, "Revue," *NA*, Oct. 26, 1937; "Caisse," *NA*, Jan. 12, 1938; "La Caisse," *NA*, Jan. 18, 1938; GV, "Paix," *NA*, Jan. 20, 1938; "La," *NA*, July 19, 1938.

11. GV, "L'Inflation," *NA*, July 18, 1938; GV, "Défense," *NA*, Aug. 20–26, 1938; "L'Avenir," *NA*, Oct. 1, 1938; "Caisse," *NA*: Nov. 17, 1938; Nov. 22, 1938; Dec. 7, 1938; Feb. 27, 1939.

12. Gandon, "Le Salaire-or," *NA*, May 16, 1938; "Pour le," *NA*, May 17, 1938; "Silence," *NA*, May 17, 1938; "Batailles," *NA*, May 26–27, 1938; *NA*, July 1938; "La Campagne," *NA*, July 5, 1938.

13. GV, "La Trahison," *NA*, Aug. 27–Sept. 2, 1938. See also Régis Debray, *Le Pouvoir intellectuel en France* (Editions Ramsay, 1979), 104–8; Heurgon-Desjardins, *Desjardins*, and on Valois's participation see, in this work, Rolph Nordling and Georges Lefranc, "L'Activité sociale de Paul Desjardins," 216–18.

14. GV, "Le Scandale," *NA*, June 28, 1938; GV, "La Trahison," *NA*, Aug. 27–Dec. 2, 1938.

15. GV, "Le Scandale," *NA*, June 28, 1938; GV, "Le Cas," *NA*, June 29, 1938; "Pour une," *NA*, June 30, 1938; GV, "Revue," *NA*, July 1, 1938; GV, " 'Un Fait,' " *NA*, July 5, 1938; "Nouvelles," *NA*, July 5, 1938; GV, "Revue," *NA*, July 5, 1938; GV, "Revue," *NA*, July 12, 1938; "Textes," *NA*, July 13, 1938; GV, "Le Scandale," *NA*, July 19, 1938; GV, "Objectifs," *NA*, July 20–21, 1938; GV, "La Trahison," *NA*, Aug. 27–Dec. 2, 1938; Rolph Nordling and Georges Lefranc, "La Rencontre franco-suédoise de 1938," in Heurgon-Desjardins, *Desjardins*, 223–32.

16. GV, "Sorel," *NA*, Apr. 5, 1938; GV, "L'Avenir," *NA*, Apr. 27–28, 1938; GV, "A propos," *NA*, May 13, 1938; GV, "Le Scandale," *NA*, June 28, 1938; GV, " 'Un Fait,' " *NA*, July 5, 1938; GV, "La Trahison," *NA*, Aug. 27–Dec. 2, 1938; cf. Debray, *Pouvoir*, 107; Jean-Paul Aron, "Les Décades de Pontigny et de Cerisy," in *Histoire sociale: Sensibilités collectives et mentalités. Mélanges Robert Mandrou* (Presses universitaires de France, 1985), 399–405.

17. GV, "Dossiers," *NA*, Dec. 21, 1937; GV, "Le Salaire-or," *NA*, June 23, 1938; GV, "Le Cas," *NA*, June 29, 1938; "La Trahison," *NA*, June 29, 1938; GV, "Revue," *NA*, July 5, 1938; "Echos," *NA*, July 6, 1938; "A propos," *NA*, July 6, 1938; GV, "X . . . et autres," *NA*, July 1938; "René-Basile Belin," *NA*, Nov. 4, 1938.

18. "La Trahison," *NA*, June 29, 1938; "Le Plan," *NA*, July 1, 1938; GV, "Le Syndicalisme," *NA*, July 6, 1938; "La Rocque," and GV, "Revue," *NA*, July 7, 1938; GV, "Revue," *NA*, July 19, 1938; GV, "La Trahison," *NA*, Aug. 27–Sept. 2, 1938; Nordling and Lefranc, "La Rencontre," 223–32.

19. "Sur les," *NA*, Mar. [3?], 1936; GV, "Le Dilemme," *NA*, May 7, 1936.

20. "La Trahison," *NA*, Sept. 17, 1938; GV, "Revue," *NA*, Oct. 25, 1938; GV, "Etatisme," *NA*, July 31, 1937; "Pour l'Espagne," *NA*, Aug. 16–23, 1936; GV, "La Guerre," *NA*, June 29, 1937; GV, "Revue," *NA*, Oct. 22, 1937; "La Trahison," *NA*, Oct. 23, 1937; "Au delà," *NA*, Mar. 15, 1938; GV, "Miracles," *NA*, Mar. 18, 1938; GV, "Revue," *NA*, Mar. 18, 1938.

21. GV, "Vers la," *NA*, Feb. 12, 1936; GV, "Pour arrêter," *NA*, Nov. 5–6, 1937; GV, "Réflexions," *NA*, Feb. 1, 1938; GV, "Construction," *NA*, Feb. 2, 1938; GV, "Racisme," *NA*, Sept. 23–24, 1938; GV, "Examen," *NA*, Oct. 22–24, 1938, and Oct. 25, 1938; GV, "Alerte," *NA*, May 3, 1939; Faucier, *Pacifisme*, 133–34; Tartakowsky, "La SFIO," 739.

22. GV, "Guerre," *NA*, Sept. 4, 1937; "Voulez-vous," *La Coopération culturelle*, Sept. 11, 1937; GV, "Pour arrêter," *NA*, Nov. 5–6, 1937.

23. GV, "Pour arrêter," *NA*, Nov. 5–6, 1937; "Le Français," *NA*, March 9, 1938; GV, "Revue," *NA*, Oct. 20, 1937; "Le Blé," *NA*, Jan. 22–24, 1938; GV, "Boycottage," *NA*, Jan. 28, 1938; "Clartés," *NA*, Oct. 29, 1937; GV, "Ni la guerre," *NA*, Sept. 3–9, 1938; GV, "Le Débat," *NA*, Oct. 15, 1938.

24. GV, "Pour," *NA*, Nov. 5–6, 1937; headline, *NA*, Nov. 9, 1937; GV, "La Lutte," *NA*, Dec. 21, 1937; GV, "Racisme," *NA*, Sept. 23–24, 1938.

25. *La Coopération culturelle*, Sept. 1937, and Sept. 11, 1937; "L'Action," *NA*, Oct. 21, 1937; GV, "Episodes,"*La Coopération culturelle* (= *NA*), July 1938.

26. "L'Action," *NA*, Oct. 2, 1937; "Décisions," *NA*, Oct. 2, 1937; "Episodes," *La Coopération culturelle* (= *NA*), July 1937.

27. "L'Action," *NA*, Oct. 23, 1937; GV, "Revue," *NA*, Oct. 27, 1937; "Grande" and "Informations," *NA*, Nov. 4, 1937; "La Journée," *NA*, Nov. 9, 1937; "L'Action," *NA*, Nov. 10, 1937; Rodrigues, "L'Action," *NA*, Nov. 11, 1937; "Succès," *NA*, Nov. 16, 1937; GV, "Retirer," *NA*, Dec. 2, 1937; "Décisions" and "La Journée," *NA*, Dec. 8, 1937; GV, "Revue," *NA*, Dec. 9, 1937; headline, *NA*, Dec. 11–13, 1937; GV, "La Lutte," *NA*, Dec. 14, 1937; GV, "Appel," *NA*, Dec. 24, 1937; GV "Episodes," *La Coopération culturelle* (=*NA*), July 1938.

28. "La Lutte," *NA*, Oct. 30, 1937; GV, "Episodes," *La Coopération culturelle* (= *NA*), July 1938.

29. GV, "Staliniens," *NA*, Nov. 18, 1937; GV, "La Lutte," *NA*, Dec. 22, 1937; GV, "Revue," *NA*, Jan. 19, 1938; GV, "Devant," *NA*, May 5, 1938; GV, "Comment," *NA*, May 17 and May 18, 1938; GV, "Revue," *NA*, Nov. 3, 1938; GV, "Revue," *NA*, Nov. 25, 1938; GV, "La Lutte" and "Revue," *NA*, Mar. 23, 1939; Faucier, *Pacifisme*, 129–71; Tartakowsky, "La SFIO," 739–44.

30. GV, "Canons," *NA*, Feb. 14, 1928; "Au delà," *NA*, Feb. 15, 1938; GV, "Revue," *NA*, Feb. 15, 1938; GV, "Revue," *NA*, Oct. 21, 1938; Faucier, *Pacifisme*, 126–39; Tartakowsky, "La SFIO," 739–44.

31. GV, "Racisme," *NA*, Sept. 23–24, 1938; GV, "De la capitulation," *NA*, Jan. 17–21, 1939; GV, "Alerte," *NA*, May 3, 1939; GV, "Echanges," *NA*, June 7–12, 1939.

32. Headline and "En retard," *NA*, Feb. 18, 1938; "Echec," *NA*, Mar. 13–14, 1938; "Pour," *NA*, Mar. 22, 1938; "Au delà," *NA*, Mar. 15, 1938; GV, "Problèmes," *NA*, Mar. 22, 1938; "Méthodes," *NA*, Mar. 25, 1938; GV, "Miracles" and "Revue," *NA*, Mar. 18, 1938.

33. "Au delà," *NA*, Mar. 15, 1938; "Alerte," *NA*, Mar. 17, 1938; "Reflux," *NA*, Mar. 18, 1938; GV, "Problèmes," *NA*, Mar. 22 and 25, 1938; "Catalane," *NA*, Mar. 23, 1938; GV, "Subir," *NA*, Oct. 8, 1938; GV, "Le Débat," and "Mouvement," in *NA*, Oct. 15, 1938; GV, "Lettre," *NA*, Apr. 25, 1939.

34. "Alerte," *NA*, Mar. 17, 1938; "La Guerre," *NA*, Mar. 26–28, 1938; Jean Giraudoux, *La Guerre de Troie n'aura pas lieu* (Grasset, 1935).

35. "Au delà," *NA*, Mar. 15, 1938; "Alerte," *NA*, Mar. 17, 1938; GV, "Problèmes," *NA*, Mar. 30, 1938; editorial and GV, "Revue," *NA*, May 24, 1938; GV, "Revue," *NA*, May 26–27, 1938; GV, "Revue," *NA*, July 8, 1938; "Déclarations," *NA*, July 12, 1938.

36. GV, "Ni la," *NA*, Sept. 3–9, 1938; "Feuille," *NA*, Sept. 17–22.

37. "La Trahison," *NA*, Sept. 17, 1938; GV, "Racisme," *NA*, Sept. 23–24, 1938.

38. GV, "Ni la guerre," *NA*, Sept. 3–9, 1938; "Feuille," *NA*, Sept. 17–22, 1938; "La Trahison," *NA*, Sept. 17, 1938.

39. Headline and "Tout est possible," *NA*, Sept. 27, 1938; GV, "Il faut," *NA*, Oct. 1, 1938; GV, "Lettre," *NA*, Oct. 4, 1938.

40. GV, "Revue," *NA*, Apr. 5, 1938; GV, "Pour une," *NA*, Apr. 30, 1938; GV, "Il Faut," *NA*, Oct. 1, 1938; "La Situation," *NA*, Oct. 4, 1938; GV, "Mystères," *NA*, Oct. 21, 1938; "Bilan," *NA*, Oct. 25, 1938; GV, "De la capitulation," *NA*, Jan. 17–21, 1939.

41. "La Situation," *NA*, Oct. 4, 1938; GV, "Impuissance," *NA*, Oct. 12, 1938; GV, "La Nouvelle," *NA*, Oct. 20, 1938; "Le Reich," *NA*, Oct. 21, 1938; Faucier, *Pacifisme*, 159.

42. GV, "Dossiers," *NA*, Dec. 21, 1937; GV, "Revue," *NA*, Apr. 1, 1938; GV, "Enfin," *NA*, May 10, 1938; "Silence," *NA*, May 17, 1938; "L'Agression," *NA*, May 24, 1938; GV, "Problèmes," *NA*, June 23, 1938; GV, "Revue," *NA*, July 5, 1938; GV, "A propos," *NA*, July 6, 1938; GV, "Episodes," *La Coopération culturelle* (= *NA*), July 1938; GV, "La Nouvelle," *NA*, Oct. 20, 1938; GV, "Revue," *NA*, Oct. 28, 1938; GV, "René-Basile Belin," *NA*, Nov. 4, 1938; GV, "Annexes," *NA*, Aug. 20–26, 1938; "Nos procès," *NA*, Dec. 3–5, 1938; Faucier, *Pacifisme*, 154; PP/GV, Carton No. 2, Dossier "Affaire Laurent—Tribune des fonctionnaires."

43. "La Réponse," *NA*, Dec. 6–7, 1936; GV, "La Calomnie," *NA*, Dec. 8, 1936; insertion of judgment, *NA*, May 12, 1938; GV, "La Politique," *NA*, May 12, 1938; "Où on," *NA*, Dec. 6, 1938.

44. "En marge," *NA*, May 31, 1938; GV, "Episodes," *La Coopération culturelle* (= *NA*), July 1938; "Nos procès," *NA*, Dec. 3–5, 1938. The most important internal rebel was Anne Boirard, known as Anne Darbois. On her messy break with Valois, see also, in PP/GV, Carton No. 1, Dossier "Correspondance militants-amis, Valois—Darbois," and "D., notes"; Carton No. 2, Dossier, "Boirard Correspondance."

45. GV, "Nos procès," *NA*, Feb. 3, 1939; "Nos procès," *NA*, Feb. 15, 1939; PP/GV, Carton No. 2, Dossier "Affaire Laurent—Tribune des fonctionnaires," which includes the judgment.

46. GV, "Impuissance," *NA*, Oct. 12, 1938; GV, "La Nouvelle," *NA*, Oct. 20, 1938; GV, "Mystères," *NA*, Oct. 21, 1938; GV, "Revue," *NA*, Oct. 27, 1938; GV, "Comment," *NA*, Nov. 29, 1938.

47. GV, "La Nouvelle," *NA*, Oct. 20, 1938; GV, "Mystères," *NA*, Oct. 21, 1938; GV, "Revue," *NA*, Oct. 27, 1938; GV, "Revue," *NA*, Nov. 25, 1938; GV, "Revue," *NA*, Dec. 8, 1938.

48. "Le Néo-fascisme," *NA*, Oct. 22–24, 1938; GV, "Notre action," *NA*, Nov. 26–28, 1938; "Appel," *NA*, Nov. 29, 1938; GV, "Comment," *NA*, Nov. 29, 1938; GV, "Revue," *NA*, Nov. 29, 1938; GV, "Revue," *NA*, Dec. 7, 1938. On Bergery's evolution, see Burrin, *Dérive*.

49. GV, "Subir," *NA*, Oct. 8, 1938; GV, "Impuissance," *NA*, Oct. 12, 1938; GV, "Revue," *NA*, Oct. 12, 1938; "Conséquences," *NA*, Nov. 5–7, 1938; " 'Ma Vie," *NA*, Nov. 8, 1938; "Paroles," *NA*, Nov. 17, 1938; GV, "Revue," *NA*, Nov. 25, 1938.

50. GV, "Racisme," *NA*, Sept. 23–24, 1938; GV, "Lettre," *NA*, Oct. 4, 1938.

51. GV, "Le Problème," *NA*, Nov. 16 and 17, 1938.

52. GV, "Le Problème," *NA*, Nov. 17, 1938; GV, "Revue," *NA*, Nov. 17, 1938.

53. GV, "Le Problème," *NA:* Nov. 16, 17, 18, 19–21, 1938. "Hitler," *NA*, Nov. 22, 1938.

54. "De la Méditerranée," *NA*, Oct. 6, 1937; "Hitler," *NA*, Nov. 22, 1938.

55. GV, "Revue," *NA*, Nov. 24, 1938; GV, "Devant," *NA*, Nov. 24, 1938; "Le Complot," *NA*, Dec. 6, 1938; GV, "Revue," *NA*, Dec. 7, 1938; "La Capitulation," *NA*, Dec. 8, 1938.

56. Headline and GV, "Les Etapes," *NA*, Dec. 14, 1938; "Monzie," and GV, "La Conjuration," *NA*, Dec. 15, 1938; GV, "L'Affaire," *NA*, Dec. 15 and 16, 1938; GV, "Le Procès," *NA:* Dec. 17–19, 20, 21, 1938; GV, "De la capitulation," *NA*, Jan. 17–21, 1939; headline, *NA*, Jan. 31, 1938; "Le Procès," *NA*, Feb. 15, 1939; GV, "Revue," *NA*, Feb. 21, 1939; "Le Scandale," *NA*, Feb. 23, 1939; "Aux instituteurs," *NA*, Feb. 25, 1939; GV, "Notre action," *NA*, Feb. 26–27, 1939; "Encore," *NA*, Mar. 9, 1939.

57. "Mouvement," *NA*, Oct. 15, 1938; "Nos journées," *NA*, Oct. 20, 1938; "Qui fera," *NA*, Oct. 21, 1938.

58. "Consultation," *NA*, Nov. 9, 1938; GV, "Notre action," *NA*, Nov. 25, 1938; "Consultation," *NA*, Dec. 6, 1938; GV, "La lutte," *NA*, Apr. 29–May 2, 1939.

59. GV, "De la capitulation," *NA*, Jan. 17–21, 1939; "Lettre," *NA*, Feb. 8, 1939.

60. "Patience," *NA*, Mar. 24, 1939; GV, "Une Grande," *NA*, Mar. 25–27, 1939; "Notre plan," *NA*, Mar. 28, 1939; "Pour vous," *NA*, Mar. 31, 1939; "Vous avez," *NA*, Apr. 18, 1939; GV, "Lettre," *NA*, Apr. 25, 1939; GV, "Entre," *NA*, Apr. 26, 1939.

61. GV, "Revue," *NA*, Nov. 10, 1938; GV, "Revue," *NA*, Mar. 14, 1939; "Stratégie," *NA*, Mar. 23, 1939; GV, "La lutte," *NA*, Mar. 30, 1939; GV, "La Lutte," *NA*, Mar. 31, 1939; GV, "Entre," *NA*, Apr. 26, 1939; GV, "Comment," *NA*, Apr. 27, 1939; GV, "Alerte," *NA*, May 3, 1939.

62. "L'Europe," and GV, "Revue," *NA*, Mar. 10, 1939; "Le Capitalisme," *NA*, Mar. 21, 1939; "La Faute," and GV, "Revue," *NA*, Apr. 1–3, 1939; "Y-a-t-il," *NA*, Apr. 11–18, 1939; "Vous avez," and GV, "Revue," *NA*, Apr. 18, 1939; GV, "Revue," *NA*, Apr. 29–May 2, 1939; GV, "L'Impossible," *NA*, May 12, 1939; GV, "Au service," *NA*, June 20, 1939. GV, "Au service," *NA:* June 21, 1939; June 23, 1939; June 27, 1939. GV, "Qui est," *NA*, June 27, 1939.

63. "La Faute," *NA*, Apr. 1–3, 1939; "U.R.S.S.," *NA*, Apr. 27, 1939; GV, "Revue," *NA*, May 3, 1939; GV, "Revue," *NA*, May 9, 1939; GV, "L'Impossible," *NA*, May 12, 1939.

64. "Les Mystères," *NA*, June 24–26, 1939; GV, "La Vertu," *NA*, June 24–26, 1939; "Travail," *NA*, July 11, 1939. Emphasis added. The third volume of Valois's memoirs, to have been entitled "Conquête de sa liberté contre sa majesté l'argent," which was never published, is apparently lost. We can get a glimpse of its character from the long autobiographical defenses published in *Nouvel Age*.

65. "De Dantzig," *NA*, June 15, 1939; GV, "Revue," *NA*, June 24–26, 1939; "Guerre," *NA*, June 29, 1939; "La Nouvelle," *NA*, June 30, 1939; GV, "Revue," *NA*, June 30, 1939; GV, "Devant," *NA*, July 1–3, 1939; GV, "Dantzig," *NA*, July 4, 1939; GV, "Revue," *NA*, August 4, 1939.

66. "La Grande," *NA*, July 4, 1939; GV, "Passage," *NA*, Aug. 20–26, 1939.

67. GV, "Revue," *NA*, June 28, 1939; GV, "La Presse," *NA*, July 28, 1939; GV, "Revue," *NA*, Aug. 4, 1939; GV, "Passage," *NA*, Aug. 20–26, 1939.

68. GV, "Il Faut," *NA*, Aug. 27, 1939.

69. Ibid.; GV, "Lutte," *NA*, Aug. 28–Sept. 3, 1939.

70. "Nous nous organisons," *NA*, Aug. 28–Sept. 3, 1939; GV, "Observations," *NA*, Aug. 28–Sept. 3, 1939; tracts, *NA*, Aug. 28–Sept. 3, 1939.

10. REVOLUTION OR DEFEAT

1. GV, "Il Faut," *NA*, Aug. 27, 1939; "Nous nous organisons," *NA*, Aug. 28–Sept. 3, 1939; GV, "Lutte," *NA*, Aug. 28–Sept. 3, 1939; GV, "Economie," *NA*, Sept. 4–11, 1939; GV, "La Guerre," *NA*, Sept. 4–11, 1939; GV, "La Situation," *NA*, Sept. 4–11, 1939; "La Situation," *NA*, Oct. 10–16, 1939; GV, *Prométhée*.

2. "Comment," *NA*, Sept. 4–11, 1939; GV, "Notre travail," *NA*, Nov. 6–11, 1939; *NA*, Nov. 19–25, 1939.

3. "Nous nous organisons," *NA*, Aug. 28–Sept. 3, 1939; "Mouvement," *NA*, Sept. 4–11, 1939; "Mouvement," *NA*, Sept. 26–Oct. 2, 1939; "Nos communautés," *NA*, Oct. 10–16, 1939.

4. "Pour 'Nouvel Age,' " *NA*, Sept. 19–25, 1939; "Mouvement," *NA*, Sept. 26–Oct. 2, 1939; "Nos communautés," *NA*, Oct. 10–16, 1939; "Nos communautés," *NA*, Oct. 24–28, 1939; GV, "Economique," *NA*, Nov. 26–Dec. 2, 1939.

5. "Nos communautés," *NA*, Oct. 10–16, 1939; "Notre travail," *NA*, May 11–20, 1940.

6. GV, "Economique," *NA*, Apr. 10, 1940; GV, "A tous," *NA*, Apr. 12, 1940.

7. "Notre courrier," *NA*, Oct. 10–16, 1939; GV, "Le Mal," *NA*, March 12, 1940; GV, "Revue critique," *NA*, Apr. 30, 1940.

8. "Deux mondes," *NA*, Sept. 19–25, 1939; GV, "Economique," *NA*, Sept. 19–25, 1939; GV, "Il n'y a pas," *NA*, Oct. 2–9, 1939; GV, "Revue," *NA*, Oct. 2–9, 1939; GV, "Technique," *NA*, Feb. 22, 1940; GV, "La Politique," *NA*, Feb. 27, 1940; GV, *Prométhée*, 128–39.

9. GV, "Revue," *NA*, Oct. 17–23, 1939; GV, "Abaissement," *NA*, Oct. 24–28, 1939; GV, "Le Cas," *NA*, Dec. 5–11, 1939; "Ne compliquons," *NA*, Dec. 12–18, 1939; GV, "La Politique," *NA*, Sept. 19–25, 1939; "La Maneuvre," *NA*, Oct. 17–23, 1939; GV, "La Politique," *NA*, Oct. 17–23, 1939; GV, "La Politique," *NA*, Jan. 9, 1940; "Hitler," *NA*, Jan. 26, 1940; GV, "Lutte," *NA*, Aug. 28–Sept. 3, 1939; "La Guerre," *NA*, Sept. 26–Oct. 2, 1939; GV, "Revue," *NA*, Mar. 1, 1940; GV, "Technique," *NA*, Mar. 5, 1940, Mar. 6, 1940, Mar. 7, 1940, Mar. 8, 1940, Mar. 9–11, 1940; GV, "La Politique," *NA*, Apr. 17, 1940; GV, *Prométhée*, 78–79.

10. GV, "Revue," *NA*, Oct. 17–23, 1939; GV, "Revue," *NA*, Mar. 5, 1940; GV, "Les Mystères," *NA*, Mar. 8, 1940; GV, "L'Action," *NA*, Mar. 9–11, 1940; GV, "Le Vrai," *NA*, Mar. 17–22, 1940.

11. GV, "Revue," *NA*, Sept. 12–19, 1939; GV, "La Politique," *NA*, Sept. 19–25, 1939; GV, "Abaissement," *NA*, Oct. 24–28, 1939; "Causes," *NA*, Nov. 26–Dec. 2, 1939; GV, "Ce que," *NA*, Dec. 5–11, 1939; GV, "Le Vrai," *NA*, Mar. 17–22, 1940.

12. GV, "Nos relations," *NA*, Sept. 12–19, 1939; GV, "Abaissement," *NA*, Oct. 24–28, 1939; *NA*, Nov. 6–11, 1939; GV, "La Guerre," *NA*, Nov. 12–18, 1939; notice, *NA*, Nov. 26–Dec. 2, 1939; GV, "Présentation," *NA*, Jan. 9, 1940; GV, "Questions," *NA*, Jan. 12, 1940; GV, "Le Vrai," *NA*, Mar. 17–22, 1940.

13. "Mouvement," *NA*, Sept. 26–Oct. 2, 1939; GV, "La Feuille," *NA*, Nov. 6–11, 1939; GV, "Revue," *NA*, Feb. 9, 1940; GV, "Avis," *NA*, Feb. 17–19, 1940. Personal communication, Roger Maria, July 22, 1987.

14. GV, "Revue," *NA*, Nov. 16, 1937; "Dédicace," *NA*, Jan. 24, 1940; GV, "Revue," *NA*, Jan. 31, 1940. Personal interview, Roger Maria, July 24, 1987; GV, *Prométhée*, 3.

15. GV, "Revue," *NA*, Jan. 20–22, 1940; GV, "La Sixième," *NA*, Jan. 23, 1940.

16. GV, "La Politique," *NA*, Nov. 26–Dec. 2, 1939; GV, "Economique," *NA*, Jan. 24, 1940; GV, "Revue," *NA*, Apr. 15, 1940. See also chapter 9.

17. GV, "Revue," *NA*, Jan. 27–29, 1940; GV, "Technique," *NA*, Feb. 21, 1940; see also GV, *Prométhée*, 23.

18. "Ouvrages," *NA*, Jan. 30, 1940.

19. GV, "Le Problème," *NA*, Jan. 18, 1940, Jan. 20–22, 1940; GV, "Revue," *NA*, Jan. 20–22, 1940; GV, "La Sixième," *NA*, Jan. 25, 1940; GV, "Cinq articles," *NA*, Apr. 23, 24, 25, and 26, 1940; GV, "Conclusions," *NA*, Apr. 27–29, 1940.

20. GV, "La Politique," *NA*, April 23, 1940; "Nos relations," *NA*, June 1–3, 1940.

21. GV, "Economique," *NA*, Oct. 17–23, 1939; GV, "Economique," *NA*, Jan. 26, 1940; GV, "Economique," *NA*, Jan. 30, 1940; GV, "La Lutte," *NA*, Apr. 20–22, 1940.

22. GV, "Economique," *NA*, Oct. 2–9, 1939; GV, "Economique," *NA*, Feb. 1, 1940, Feb. 2, 1940; GV, "Technique," *NA*, Mar. 13, 1940; GV, "La France," *NA*, Mar. 23–26, 1940.

23. GV, "Revue," *NA*, Sept. 26–Oct. 2, 1939; GV, "La Politique," *NA*, Dec. 12–18, 1939; GV, "Revue," *NA*, Dec. 12–18, 1939.

24. "La Situation," *NA*, Oct. 10–16, 1939; "Résumé," *NA*, Dec. 5–11, 1939; GV, "La Politique," *NA*, Jan. 16, 1940; "Hitler," *NA*, Jan. 26, 1940; "Après," *NA*, Feb. 6, 1940; GV, "Technique," *NA*, Feb. 16, 1940.

25. "La Destruction," *NA*, Feb. 22, 1940; GV, "Droit," *NA*, Feb. 23, 1940; GV, "Technique," *NA*, Feb. 27, 28, and 29, Mar. 1, and 2–4, 1940.

26. GV, "Technique," *NA*, Feb. 13, 1940; GV, "Revue," *NA*, Mar. 7, 1940; "Esquisse," *NA*, Apr. 2–8, 1940.

27. GV, "Destin," *NA*, Feb. 13, 1940; GV, "Revue," *NA*, Mar. 23–26, 1940; GV, "Notre position," *NA*, Apr. 2–8, 1940; GV, "Revue," *NA*, Apr. 2–8, 1940; GV, "La Politique," *NA*, Apr. 10, 1940.

28. GV, "Revue," *NA*, Apr. 9, 1940; headline and "La Guerre," *NA*, Apr. 10, 1940; "Un Tournant," *NA*, Apr. 11, 1940; headline and "La Guerre," *NA*, Apr. 15, 1940; headline and "Une Victoire," *NA*, Apr. 16, 1940; "Menaces," *NA*, Apr. 25, 1940; Rodrigues, "L'Etat," *NA*, Apr. 26, 1940; GV, "La Politique," *NA*, Apr. 30, 1940; "Bonnes," *NA*, May 1, 1940; GV, "Réflexions," *NA*, May 1, 1940; GV, "La Politique," *NA*, May 4–6, 1940.

29. "La Guerre," *NA*, Apr. 10, 1940; GV, "La Politique," *NA*, Apr. 16, 1940; GV, "La Politique," *NA*, May 4–6, 1940; GV, "Revue," *NA*, Apr. 17, 1940; GV, "Revue," *NA*, Apr. 23, 1940.

30. GV, "Le Vrai," *NA*, Mar. 17–22, 1940; "Un jugement," *NA*, Apr. 11, 1940; "Bilan," *NA*, Apr. 16, 1940; "Nos procès," *NA*, May 7, 1940; "Où l'on," *NA*, May 9, 1940; GV, "Revue," *NA*, May 20, 1940; "Nos procès," *NA*, May 23, 1940.

31. GV, "La Politique," *NA*, May 11–20, 1940; GV, "Revue," *NA*, May 11–20, 1940; GV, "Nouveaux," *NA*, May 21, 1940; Rodrigues, "La Folle," *NA*, May 27, 1940.

32. GV, "Nouveaux," *NA*, May 21, 1940.

33. Ibid.

34. GV, "Revue," *NA*, May 22, 1940; GV, "La Politique," *NA*, May 31, 1940.

35. GV, "Nouveaux," *NA*, May 21, 1940; Pelossier, "Debout," *NA*, May 21, 1940.

36. GV, "Nouveaux," *NA*, May 21, 1940; "Compter," *NA*, May 22, 1940; GV, "La Politique," *NA*, May 23, 1940; GV, "La Politique," *NA*, May 24, 1940; "Des hommes," *NA*, May 25–27, 1940; "Ce qui," *NA*, May 28, 1940; GV, "La Politique," *NA*, May 25–27, 1940.

37. GV, "Nouveaux," *NA*, May 21, 1940; cf. GV, *Prométhée*, 103.

38. GV, "Revue," *NA*, March 18, 1938.

39. GV, "La Politique," *NA*, May 30, 1940; GV, "La Politique," *NA*, May 31, 1940; *NA*, May 29, 1940.

40. GV, "Henri de Man," *NA*, May 31, 1940; "L'Affaire," *NA*, May 31, 1940; GV, "La Politique," *NA*, June 1–3, 1940; GV, "Comment," *NA*, June 4, 1940; "Deux lettres," *NA*, June 4, 1940.

41. "Debout," and GV, "La Politique," *NA*, May 29, 1940; GV, "La Politique," *NA*, May 31, 1940; GV, "La Politique," *NA*, June 4, 1940; "La Décision," *NA*, June 5, 1940.

11. OCCUPATION AND RESISTANCE

1. Personal communication, Philippe Gressent-Valois, July 18, 1987; personal communication, Roger Maria, July 22, 1987.

2. Personal communications, Gressent-Valois, July 18, 1987, and R. Maria, July 22, 1987; PP/GV, Carton No. 1, Dossier "Correspondance Val d'Ardières 1941–3," GV to Fèvre, Nov. 14, 1942, and GV, circular letter, April 1944.

3. Personal communications, Gressent-Valois, July 10, 1987, and R. Maria, July 22, 1987; GV, "La Vraie Révolution," *Cahiers du Nouvel âge*, nos. 23–24 (Oct. 15, 1947), inside cover; GV, *L'Homme devant*, 22; PP/GV, Carton No. 1, Dossier "Corr. Val d'Ardières," GV, circular letter, April 1944.

4. Personal communications, Gressent-Valois, July 18, 1987, and R. Maria, July 22, 1987; Pierre Mendès-France, *Liberté, liberté chérie* (New York: Didier, n.d. [1942?]), 157–58.

5. Mendès-France, *Liberté*, 156–58.

6. Personal communications, Gressent-Valois, July 18, 1987, and R. Maria, July 22 and 24, 1987; PP/GV, Carton No. 1, Dossier "Corr. Val d'Ardières," GV to A. Diruei, Dec. 10, 1942, and GV to Mazer, Dec. 10, 1942.

7. Personal communication, Philippe Gressent-Valois, July 18, 1987; GV, *L'Homme devant*, 374–75.

8. Personal communications, Roger Maria, July 22 and 24, 1987.

9. Personal communications, Gressent-Valois, July 18, 1987, and R. Maria, July 24, 1987; PP/GV, Carton No. 1, Dossier "Corr. Val d'Ardières," GV to Maison du livre français, Nov. 1942 [?].

10. Personal Communications, Gressent-Valois, July 18, 1987, and R. Maria, July 24, 1987.

11. In PP/GV, Carton No. 1, Dossier "Corr. Val d'Ardières": GV, "Société des amis du Val d'Ardières"; GV to Rozner, Nov. 1942; Cartes Interzones, Nov. 11, 1942. Personal communications, Gressent-Valois, July 18, 1987, and R. Maria, July 24, 1987; GV, *L'Homme devant*, 4; Jean Galtier-Boissière, *Mon journal dans la grande pagaïe* (La Jeune Parque, 1950), 92.

12. PP/GV, Carton No. 1, Dossier "Corr. Val d'Ardières," entire and esp. GV to Loiseau, 1943 [?]; GV to Paul Durilhous [?], Jan. 18, 1943; GV to Perrot; GV to Magontier, Jan. 27, 1943; "Société d'études immobilières et agricoles," Dec. 12, 1942.

13. In PP/GV, Carton No. 1, Dossier "Corr. Val-d'Ardières": GV to Bertrand Pibrac, Dec. [?] 1942; GV, circular letter, Nov. 11, 1942; GV to Guérin, 1942 [?]; GV, circular letter, April 1944.

14. Personal communications, Gressent-Valois, July 18, 1987, and R. Maria, July 24, 1987; *Après*, no. 1, June 1943, no. 2, July 1943; Adam [GV], "La France trahie par les trusts," *Après*, no. spécial, 1943 (Valois is listed as editor in the catalogue of the Bureau de documentation internationale et contemporaine at Nanterre); Henri Michel, *Les Courants de pensée de la Résistance* (Paris: Presses universitaires de France, 1962), 149–50, 389–94; Marie Granet and Henri Michel, *Combat: Histoire d'un mouvement de résistance de juillet 1940 à juillet 1943* (Paris: Presses universitaires de France, 1957), esp. 122–25, 318–19.

15. GV, *Fin du Bolchévisme: Conséquences européenes de l'événement* (n.p.: LV, 1941), 49; "La France trahie," 9, 21, 24; GV, "Comment finira la guerre, ou la vraie révolution" (typescript, Le Val d'Ardières, 1942); GV, "La Vraie Révolution," *Cahiers de Nouvel âge*, nos. 23–24 (Oct. 15, 1947), inside cover (this is a publication of major extracts from "Comment finira la guerre"); personal communication, Gressent-Valois, July 18, 1987.

16. In PP/GV, Carton No. 1, Dossier "Corr. Val d'Ardières": GV to Tavernier, Nov. 18, 1942; GV to Directeur de la censure des livres, Nov. 17, 1942; GV to Marc Rechain, Dec. 19, 1943. In Carton No. 2, "Formulaire–Réponse," Mar. 21, 1943.

17. GV, *Fin du Bolchévisme*, 5, 49, which work was omitted from the list of Valois's works compiled after the war (GV, *L'Homme devant*, 382–83).

18. GV, *Fin du Bolchévisme*, 5–8, 11, 18, 22–25, 32–39; PP/GV, Carton No. 1, Dossier "Corr. Val d'Ardières," GV, circular letter, Nov. 11, 1942.

19. Ibid., 15–16, 39, 41–49.

20. Ibid., 10, 13, 17–18, 24–26, 40–44.

21. Ibid., 9, 36.

22. GV, "Comment finira la guerre," 3–23.

23. PP/GV, Carton No. 1, Dossier "Corr. Val d'Ardières," GV to Canetto, Nov. 11, 1942; and GV, circular letter, Nov. 11, 1942.

24. Adam [GV], "La France trahie," 5–6.

25. Ibid., 4, 6–7, 10.

26. Ibid., 6–7. On the birth and development of the synarchy story, see Richard Kuisel, "The Legend of the Vichy Synarchy," *French Historical Studies* 6 (1970): 365–98; Michel, *Courants*, 392–93. Many radicals, like Roger Maria, still believe it (R. Maria, personal communication, July 22, 1987).

27. Adam [GV], "La France trahie," 9, 11, 19.

28. GV, *L'Homme devant*, 336. See chapters 9 and 10.

29. Adam [GV], "La France trahie," 10–15.

30. Ibid., 11–18.

31. Ibid., 7, 17–21.

32. Ibid., 21–22; GV, *L'Homme devant*, 333–39; *Après*, no. 1, June 1943; Granet and Michel, *Combat*, 105.

33. GV, "Comment finira la guerre," 35–112 (cf. GV, "La Vraie Révolution").

34. GV, *L'Homme devant l'Eternel*, 6, 11–12, 25–32, 38–41, 52, 93, 349.

35. Ibid., 55–64.

36. Ibid., 67, 73–82, 87–123, 157–60, 310–16; GV, "Comment finira la guerre," 97.

37. GV, *L'Homme devant l'Eternel*, 8, 58, 101, 143, 198–202, 213–19, 232–33, 237, 246–54, 285.

38. Ibid., 85–86, 100–109, 200–201, 216–18, 237.

39. Ibid., 20–21, 42–52, 72–80, 115, 121, 160–82, 371–72.

40. Ibid., 372–77.

41. Personal interviews, Gressent-Valois, July 18, 1987; R. Maria, July 24, 1987; Roger Maria, "Puisqu'on m'invite à dire je," *L'Humanité dimanche*, May 6, 1983; Henri Noguères, *Histoire de la Résistance en France de 1940 à 1945* (Geneva: Farmot, 1981), 8:314–20, 333.

42. Personal interview, R. Maria, July 24, 1987; Roger Maria, "Puisqu'on m'invite."

43. Louis-Martin Chauffier, "Préface," to G. L. Fréjafon, *Bergen-Belsen: Bagne sanatorium* (LV, 1947), xiii–xv.

44. Dr. Fréjafon's account, the source of the discussion that follows, was printed as "Les Derniers jours de Georges Valois," in Fréjafon, *Bergen-Belsen*, xix–xxix.

CONCLUSION

1. Douglas, "Fascist Violence," 689–712.

Bibliography of
Works Cited

PERSONAL PAPERS

PERSONAL PAPERS OF GEORGES VALOIS

Georges Valois kept extensive personal archives, which he used, among other things, in his frequent lawsuits. Most of these papers were destroyed during the 1950s in a fire at the residence of his son, Philippe Gressent-Valois. However, a few years ago, M. Etienne Jaillet discovered some of the papers in the abandoned mill in the Beaujolais that had been Valois's headquarters during most of World War II. These materials consist of correspondence from 1941 to 1943 and a number of dossiers from the late 1930s related to recent lawsuits, which Valois had had transported to the mill. Thanks to M. Jaillais, these papers have been organized and are in the custody of M. Gressent-Valois.

PERSONAL PAPERS OF HENRY POULAILLE

PERSONAL INTERVIEWS

M. le Commissaire divisionnaire Jean Druesne
Philippe Gressent-Valois
Hélène Patou
Henry Poulaille
Roger Maria

ARCHIVAL SOURCES

Archives départmentales de Seine-et-Marne. 6E 252, Commune de Jouarre, mariages

Archives municipales de Paris, no. 9558, naissances, 14e arrondissement, v. 4E
Archives nationales. In the series F^7, cartons: 12861, 12862, 12863, 12950, 12953, 12954, 13195, 13197, 13206, 13207, 13208, 13209, 13210, 13211, 13212, 13232, 13245, 13246, 13247
Archives de Paris (Hôtel Saint-Aignan), reconstitution des actes de l'état civil, 7174
Archives de la Préfecture de police de Paris. In carton 344: dossiers 2.649 and 2.649a
Mairie du 14e arrondissement

NEWSPAPERS AND JOURNALS

L'Accord social
Action française
Après
Cahiers bleus
Cahiers de Nouvel âge
Cahiers des Etats-Généraux
Cahiers du Cercle Proudhon
Le Canard enchaîné
Chantiers coopératifs
Combat
La Coopération culturelle
Faisceau Bellifontain
L'Humanité
L'Humanité nouvelle
Le Nouveau Siècle
Nouvel Age
Les Nouvelles littéraires
L'Oeuvre
Paris-Phare
La Patrie humaine
Le Rappel
Revue critique des idées et des livres
Revue de l'Action française
La Table ronde
Terre libre
La Volonté

WORKS BY GEORGES VALOIS

NOTE: Unless otherwise stated, place of publication is Paris.

Basile, ou, La politique de la calomnie: Sténographie des dépositions, débats et plaidoiries de procès en diffamation entre Georges Valois et L'Action française. NLN, 1927.
Le Cheval de Troie. NLN, 1918.
"Comment finira la guerre, ou la vraie révolution." Typescript. Le Val d'Ardières, 1942.

Contre le mensonge et la calomnie. NLN, 1926.

D'un siècle a l'autre: Chronique d'une génération. Edition définitive. NLN, 1924.

L'Economie nouvelle. NLN, 1920.

L'Economie nouvelle [Oeuvre économique, vol. 1]. NLN, 1924.

Economique. LV, 1931.

L'Etat, les finances et la monnaie [Oeuvre économique, vol. 2]. NLN, 1925.

L'Etat syndical et la représentation corporative [Oeuvre économique, vol. 3]. NLN-LV, 1927.

Le Faisceau des combattants, des producteurs, et des chefs de famille. Librairie du nouveau siècle, 1925.

Le Fascisme. NLN, 1927.

Fin du Bolchévisme: Conséquences européenes de l'événement. N.p.: LV, 1941.

Guerre ou blocus economique. Editions liberté, 1939.

Guerre ou révolution. LV, 1931.

Histoire et philosophie sociales. NLN, 1924.

L'Homme contre l'argent: Souvenirs de dix ans. LV, 1928.

L'Homme devant l'Eternel. LV, 1947.

L'Homme qui vient: Philosophie de l'autorité. Edition définitive. NLN, 1923.

Intelligence et production. Co-authored by Georges Coquelle. NLN, 1920.

Journée d'Europe. LV, 1932.

Les Manuels scolaires. Co-authored by François Renié. NLN, 1911.

La Monarchie et la classe ouvrière. NLN, 1914.

La Monarchie protectrice des intérêts ouvriers. Saumur: Ligue d'Action française, section de Saumur, n.d.

Un Nouvel Age de l'humanité. LV, 1929.

Le Père: Philosophie de la famille. Edition définitive. NLN, 1924.

La Politique de la victoire. NLN, 1925.

Prométhée vainqueur, ou, Explication de la guerre. Editions liberté, 1940.

La Réforme économique et sociale. NLN, 1918.

La Révolution nationale. NLN, 1924.

Technique de la révolution syndicale. Editions liberté, 1935.

OTHER PUBLISHED SOURCES

Andreu, Pierre. *Le Rouge et le blanc.* La Table ronde, 1977.

Arendt, Hannah. *Antisemitism.* New York: Harcourt, Brace & World, 1968.

Ariès, Nel. *L'Economie politique et la doctrine catholique.* NLN, 1923.

Aron, Jean-Paul. "Les Décades de Pontigny et de Cerisy," *Histoire sociale: Sensibilités collectives et mentalités. Mélanges Robert Mandrou.* Presses universitaires de France, 1988.

Arthuys, Jacques. *Les Combattants.* NLN, 1925.

——— . *Comment éviter la hideuse banqueroute.* NLN, 1922.

——— . *Le Problème de la monnaie.* NLN, 1921.

Barrès, Maurice. *L'Oeuvre de Maurice Barrès.* 20 vols. Club de l'honnête homme, 1965.

Barrès, Philippe. *La Guerre à vingt ans.* Plon-Nourrit, 1924.

——— . *La Victoire au dernier tournant.* Nouvelle Librairie française, 1932.

Beau de Loménie, E. *Les Responsabilités des dynasties bourgeoises.* 4 vols. Denoël, 1943–63.

Bellanger, Claude, et al. *Histoire générale de la presse francaise.* Vol. 3. Presses universitaires de France, 1972.

Bergson, Henri. *L'Evolution créatrice.* Presses universitaires de France, 1969.

Bernard, J.-P. A. *Le Parti communiste français et la question littéraire.* Grenoble: Presses universitaires de Grenoble, 1972.

Berstein, Serge. *Histoire du parti radical.* Vol. 2, *Crise du radicalisme.* Presses de la Fondation nationale des sciences politiques, 1982.

Berth, Edouard. *Les Méfaits des intellectuels.* Marcel Rivière, 1926.

Bonnefous, Edouard. *Histoire politique de la Troisième République.* Vols. 3 and 4. Presses universitaires de France, 1968–73.

Bourget, Paul. *L'Etape.* Librairie Plon, 1902.

———. *Etudes et portraits.* Vol. 3, *Sociologie et littérature.* Librairie Plon, 1906.

———. *Pages de critique et de doctrine.* 2 vols. Librairie Plon, n.d.

Bourgin, Hubert. *De Jaurès à Léon Blum.* Librairie Arthème Fayard, 1938.

———. *Le Militarisme allemand.* F. Alcan, 1915.

———. *Le Parti contre la patrie.* Plon-Nourrit, 1924.

Brière, Jean. *Le Tartuffe démasqué.* Les Etincelles, [1929?].

Burrin, Philippe. *La Dérive fasciste.* Editions du Seuil, 1986.

Clark, Linda Loeb. *Social Darwinism in France.* University: University of Alabama Press, 1984.

Claudel, Paul. *Tête d'or.* Mercure de France, 1959.

Coston, Henri. *Partis, journaux et hommes politiques.* Lectures françaises, 1960.

Déat, Marcel. *Perspectives socialistes.* LV, 1930.

———. *Mémoires politiques.* Denoël, 1989.

Debray, Régis. *Le Pouvoir intellectuel en France.* Editions Ramsay, 1979.

Delaisi, Francis. "Les Financiers et la démocratie." *Crapouillot,* November 1936.

De la Porte, René, ed. *L'Avenir de la république.* LV, 1927.

Delpierrie de Bayac, Jacques. *Histoire du Front populaire.* Fayard, 1972.

De Man, Hendrik. *L'Idée socialiste.* Translated by H. Corbin and A. Kojevnikov. Grasset, 1935.

———. *Zur Psychologie des Sozialismus.* Jena: Eugen Diederichs Verlag, 1926.

Deniel, Alain. *Bucard et le Francisme.* Editions Jean Picollec, 1979.

Descaves, Lucien. *Les Sous-offs.* Tresse et Stock, 1889.

Dimier, Louis. *Vingt ans d'Action française.* NLN, 1928.

Dmytryshyn, Basil. *USSR: A Concise History.* New York: Charles Scribner's Sons, 1984.

Dominique, Pierre. *La Révolution créatrice.* LV, 1928.

Douglas, Allen. "Fascist Violence in France: The Case of the Faisceau." *Journal of Contemporary History* 19 (1984): 689–712.

———. " 'La Nouvelle Droite': The Revival of Radical Rightist Thought in Contemporary France." *The Tocqueville Review—La Revue Tocqueville* 4 (1984): 361–87.

Dubly, Henry-Louis. *Vers un ordre économique et social: Eugène Mathon.* 1946.

Duboin, Jacques. *Ce qu'on appelle la crise.* Les Editions nouvelles, 1934.

———. *En route vers l'abondance.* Editions Fustier, 1935.

Durand, Xavier. "L'Art social au théâtre: Deux expériences." *Le Mouvement social*, no. 91, 13–33.

Duval, Jean-Maurice. *Le Faisceau de Georges Valois*. La Librairie française, 1979.

Eisler, Jerzy. "Georges Valois et une idéologie de combattants." *Acta Polaniae Historica* 48 (1983): 133–63.

Faucier, Nicolas. *Pacifisme et anti-militarisme dans l'entre-deux-guerres*. Spartacus, 1983.

Felice, Renzo de. *Interpretations of Fascism*. Translated by Brenda Huff Everett. Cambridge, Mass.: Harvard University Press, 1977.

Fréjafon, G. L. *Bergen-Belsen: Bagne sanatorium*. LV, 1947.

Galtier-Boissière, Jean. *Mon journal dans la grande pagaïe*. La Jeune Parque, 1950.

Gaucher, André. *L'Honorable Léon Daudet*. Editions de la parole française, n.d.

Giraudoux, Jean. *Bella*. Grasset, 1926.

————. *La Guerre de Troie n'aura pas lieu*. Grasset, 1935.

Goguel, François. *Géographie des élections françaises sous la Troisième et la Quatrième Républiques*. Armand Colin, 1970.

Goodman, E. H. "The Socialism of Marcel Déat." Ph.D. diss., Stanford University, 1973.

Granet, Marie, and Henri Michel. *Combat: Histoire d'un mouvement de résistance de juillet 1940 à juillet 1943*. Presses universitaires de France, 1957.

Grave, Jean. *Quarante ans de propagande anarchiste*. Flammarion, 1973.

Groupe Dynamo. *Pauvre Français . . . ! Introduction au recensement des richesses de la France*. Editions Fustier, 1936.

Guchet, Yves. *Georges Valois: L'Action française, le Faisceau, la République syndicale*. Editions de l'albatros, 1975. Erasme, 1990.

Guérin, Daniel. *Fascisme et grand capital*. François Maspéro, 1975.

Guillemin, Henri. *Charles Péguy*. Editions du Seuil, 1981.

Hamon, Augustin. *Les Maîtres de la France*. 3 vols. Editions sociales internationales, 1938.

————. *Psychologie de l'anarchiste-socialiste*. P. V. Stock, 1895.

Hamon, Augustin, and Georges Bachot. *L'Agonie d'une société*. Nouvelle Librairie parisienne, 1889.

Heurgon-Desjardins, Anne. *Paul Desjardins et les décades de Pontigny*. Presses universitaires de France, 1964.

Hoffman, Robert Louis. *Revolutionary Justice: The Social and Political Theory of P. J. Proudhon*. Urbana: University of Illinois Press, 1972.

Hutton, Patrick H., ed. *Historical Dictionary of the French Third Republic*. 2 vols. New York: Greenwood Press, 1986.

————. "Popular Boulangism and the Advent of Mass Politics in France." *Journal of Contemporary History* 11 (1976): 85–106.

Jean, Lucien. *Parmi les hommes*. Mercure de France, 1910.

Jeanneney, Jean-Noël. *L'Argent caché: Milieux d'affaires et pouvoirs politiques dans la France du XXᵉ siècle*. Editions du Seuil, 1983.

————. *François de Wendel en république*. Editions du Seuil, 1976.

Jouvenel, Bertrand de. *L'Economie dirigée: Le Programme de la nouvelle génération*. LV, 1928

————. *Vers les états-Unis d'Europe*. LV, 1930.

———. *Vie de Zola.* LV, 1931.

———. *Un Voyageur dans le siècle.* With Jeannie Malige. Robert Laffont, 1979.

Kergoat, Jacques. *Le Parti socialiste de la Commune à nos jours.* Le Sycamore, 1983.

Keynes, J. M. *Essays in Persuasion.* New York: Norton, 1963.

Kropotkine, Pierre. *Oeuvres.* Edited by Martin Zemliak. Maspéro, 1976.

Kuisel, Richard. *Capitalism and the State in Modern France.* Berkeley and Los Angeles: University of California Press, 1981.

———. *Ernest Mercier, French Technocrat.* Berkeley and Los Angeles: University of California Press, 1967.

———. "The Legend of the Vichy Synarchy." *French Historical Studies* 6 (1970): 365–98.

Kupfermann, A. "François Coty, Journaliste et Homme Politique." Thesis for "Troisième Cycle," Paris, 1965.

Lachapelle, Georges. *Elections législatives du 11 Mai 1924.* Librairie Georges Roustan, 1924.

Lafargue, Paul. *Le Droit à la paresse.* Maspéro, 1982.

Lagrange, Henri. *Vingt ans en 1914.* NLN, 1920.

Lanoizelée, Louis. *Lucien Jean.* Plaisir du bibliophile, 1952.

Laqueur, Walter, ed. *Fascism: A Reader's Guide.* Berkeley and Los Angeles: University of California Press, 1976.

La Tour du Pin Chambly de la Charce. *Vers un ordre social chrétien.* Gabriel Beauchesne, 1929.

Latzarus, Louis. *Un Ami du peuple: M. Coty.* LV, 1929.

Laurent, Jacques. *Histoire égoiste.* La Table ronde, 1976.

Ledeen, Michael. *Universal Fascism.* New York: Howard Fertig, 1972.

Lefranc, Georges. *Le Mouvement socialiste sous la Troisième République.* Payot, 1963.

———. *Révolution constructive.* LV, 1932.

Levey, Jules. "Georges Valois and the Faisceau: The Making and Breaking of a Fascist." *French Historical Studies* 8 (1973): 279–304.

———. "The Sorelian Syndicalists." Ph.D. thesis, New York, 1967.

Lévi-Strauss, Claude. *Tristes tropiques.* Plon, 1984.

Löffler, Paul A. *Chronique de la littérature prolétarienne française de 1930 à 1939.* Rodez: Editions Subervie, 1967.

Maier, Charles S. *Recasting Bourgeois Europe.* Princeton: Princeton University Press, 1975.

Maria, Roger. "Puisqu'on m'invite à dire je." *L'Humanité dimanche,* May 6, 1983.

Maurras, Charles. *L'Avenir de l'intelligence.* Flammarion, 1927.

———. *Enquête sur la monarchie.* Nouvelle Librairie nationale, 1924.

Mazgaj, Paul. *The Action française and Revolutionary Syndicalism.* Chapel Hill: University of North Carolina Press, 1979.

———. "The Young Sorelians and Decadence." *Journal of Contemporary History* 17 (1981): 179–99.

Mazières, Georges. *L'Oeuvre économique de Georges Valois.* Castelnaudary: n.p., 1937.

Mendès-France, Pierre. *Liberté, liberté chérie.* New York: Didier, n.d. [1942?].

Menevée, Roger. "M. Horace Finaly." *Les Documents politiques, diplomatiques et financiers,* 1937.

Michel, Henri. *Les Courants de pensée de la Résistance.* Presses universitaires de France, 1962.

Mistler, Jean. *La Librairie Hachette de 1826 à nos jours.* Hachette, 1964.

Moreau, Emile. *Souvenirs d'un gouverneur de la Banque de France.* M.-Th. Genin, 1954.

Nietzsche, Friedrich. *The Birth of Tragedy and the Genealogy of Morals.* Translated by Francis Golffing. Garden City, N.Y.: Doubleday, 1956.

———. *La Généalogie de la morale.* Translated by Henry Albert. Société de "Mercure de France," 1900.

Nizan, Paul. *Antoine Bloyé.* Grasset, 1933.

Noguères, Henri. *Histoire de la Résistance en France de 1940 à 1945.* 10 vols. Geneva: Famot, 1981.

Nolte, Ernst. *Three Faces of Fascism.* New York: Mentor, 1969.

Péguy, Charles. *Notre Jeunesse.* Editions Gallimard, 1957.

Philippe, Charles-Louis. *Bubu de Montparnasse.* Garnier Flammarion, 1978.

Plumyène, J., and R. Lasierra. *Les Fascismes français, 1923–1963.* Editions du Seuil, 1963.

Poulaille, Henry. *Un Nouvel Age littéraire.* LV, 1930.

———. *Le Pain quotidien.* LV, 1931.

Première assemblée nationale des combattants, des producteurs, et des chefs de famille. NLN, 1926.

Prost, Antoine. *Les Anciens Combattants et la Société française.* 3 vols. Presses de la Fondation nationale des sciences politiques, 1977.

Quinton, René. *L'Eau de mer, milieu organique.* Masson, 1904.

———. *Maximes de Guerre.* Grasset, 1930.

Racine, Nicole, and Louis Bodin. *Le P.C. français pendant l'entre-deux-guerres.* Armand Colin, 1972.

Ragon, Michel. *Histoire de la littérature prolétarienne.* 1974.

Renouvin, Pierre, and René Rémond, eds. *Léon Blum, chef de gouvernement.* Presses de la fondation nationale des sciences politiques, 1981.

Riou, Gaston. *Europe, ma patrie.* LV, 1928.

Rodrigues, Gustave. *L'Unique Solution du problème social: Le Droit à la vie.* Editions liberté, 1934.

Romein, Jan. *The Watershed of Two Eras.* Translated by Arnold Pomerans. Middletown, Conn.: Wesleyan University Press, 1978.

Roth, Jack J. *The Cult of Violence.* Berkeley and Los Angeles: University of California Press, 1980.

Schuker, Stephen. *The End of French Predominance in Europe.* Chapel Hill: University of North Carolina Press, 1976.

Schumpeter, J. A. *History of Economic Analysis.* New York: Oxford University Press, 1968.

Sorel, Georges. *Les Illusions du progrès.* Marcel Riviere, 1927.

———. *Lettres à Paul Delesalle.* Grasset, 1947.

———. *Réflexions sur la violence.* Marcel Rivière, 1972.

———— . *La Révolution dreyfusienne*. Marcel Rivière, 1909.

Soucy, Robert. *French Fascism: The First Wave*. New Haven: Yale University Press, 1986.

Sternhell, Zeev. "Anatomie d'un mouvement fasciste en France: Le Faisceau de Georges Valois." *Revue française de science politique* 26 (1976): 5–40.

———— . *La Droite révolutionnaire, 1885–1914: Les Origines françaises du fascisme*. Editions du Seuil, 1978.

———— . *Ni droite ni gauche: L'idéologie fasciste en France*. Editions du Seuil, 1983.

Taine, Hippolyte. *Histoire de la littérature anglaise*. 5 vols. Hachette, 1895.

Touchard, Jean. *La Gauche en France depuis 1900*. Editions du Seuil, 1981.

Weber, Eugen. *Action française*. Stanford: Stanford University Press, 1962.

———— . *Varieties of Fascism*. New York: Van Nostrand, 1964.

Wohl, Robert. *The Generation of 1914*. Cambridge, Mass.: Harvard University Press, 1979.

Index

Compositor: BookMasters, Inc.
Text: 10/13 Aldus
Display: Aldus
Printer: Braun-Brumfield, Inc.
Binder: Braun-Brumfield, Inc.